The Sporting News

SELECTS

BASEBALL'S
25
GREATEST
PENNANT
RACES

The Sporting News

SELECTS

BASEBALL'S 25 GREATEST PENNANT RACES

Written by
LOWELL REIDENBAUGH

Co-Editors
MIKE NAHRSTEDT
STEVE ZESCH
CRAIG CARTER

Design
BILL PERRY
MIKE BRUNER

President and Chief Executive Officer
RICHARD WATERS

Editor/The Sporting News
TOM BARNIDGE

Director of Books and Periodicals
RON SMITH

Published in the United States by THE SPORTING NEWS
Publishing Co., 1212 North Lindbergh Boulevard,
St. Louis, Missouri 63132.

Library of Congress Catalog Card Number: 87-61058

ISBN: 0-89204-256-7
10 9 8 7 6 5 4 3 2 1

First Edition

Contents

Baseball's 25 Greatest Pennant Races

No. 1   1951   Thomson's Homer Caps Giants' Incredible Comeback .... Page   9

No. 2   1908   Merkle's Boner Costs Giants the Pennant .... Page   20

No. 3   1914   The Miracle Braves Capture America's Fancy .... Page   29

No. 4   1978   Yankees Catch Red Sox, Win A.L. Playoff .... Page   40

No. 5   1948   Boudreau's Homers Help Indians Win First A.L. Playoff .... Page   51

No. 6   1904   Chesbro's Wild Pitch Helps Boston Win Pennant .... Page   59

No. 7   1964   Phillies' Collapse Hands Pennant to Cardinals .... Page   68

No. 8   1950   Sisler's Home Run Saves the Day for Phillies .... Page   77

No. 9   1962   Giants Catch Dodgers, Win Three-Game Playoff .... Page   88

No. 10   1946   Cardinals Stop Dodgers in Playoff to Win Pennant .... Page   98

No. 11   1967   Red Sox Complete Their Impossible Dream .... Page 106

No. 12   1942   Cardinals Win 106 Games, Barely Hold Off Dodgers .... Page 117

No. 13   1940   Giebell Outduels Feller as Tigers Clinch .... Page 126

No. 14   1969   Once-Lowly Mets Pull Off Major Baseball Shocker .... Page 137

No. 15   1934   Cardinals' Late Charge Is Too Much for Giants .... Page 149

No. 16   1938   Hartnett's Homer in the Gloamin' Sparks Cubs .... Page 159

No. 17   1959   Dodgers Defeat Braves in Best-of-Three Playoff .... Page 167

No. 18   1935   Cubs Win 21 Straight Games, Overhaul Cardinals .... Page 175

No. 19   1949   Yankees Beat Red Sox in Final-Weekend Showdown .... Page 185

No. 20   1980   Astros Beat Dodgers in Playoff After Blowing Lead .... Page 197

No. 21   1920   Black Sox Scandal Helps Indians Hold On .... Page 206

No. 22   1945   Greenberg's Final-Day Grand Slam Lifts Tigers .... Page 216

No. 23   1982   Harvey's Wallbangers Survive Scare From Orioles .... Page 224

No. 24   1930   Cardinals Win 39 of Final 49 Games and a Pennant .... Page 235

No. 25   1965   Dodgers Survive Injuries, Hold Off Giants .... Page 244

Introduction

For more than a century, major league baseball's pennant races have stimulated America's heartbeat, raising it to passionate levels as two or more teams pound into the home stretch, straining every fiber to gain the slightest advantage that could lead to the World Series.

A select few transcend the others in universal appeal. To many observers, these struggles set the standard by which all others are judged.

Some fans, however, fervently maintain that there never has been an insipid race. Each is arresting, they insist, though some *are* more exciting than the rest. This breed of baseball scholar appreciates the National League race of 1902, even though the Pittsburgh Pirates outdistanced their nearest pursuer by 27½ games. The runaway, they say, did not diminish the excitement over the battle for second place—Brooklyn edged Boston by 1½ games—or the struggle for fourth—Cincinnati edged Chicago by half a length. There is more to a race than the duel up front, but the fan must be perceptive enough to recognize it.

Readers of this volume will discover that renowned managers and powerful clubs do not necessarily produce tingling pennant races. The reputations of John McGraw and Connie Mack are secure for all time. But of the 19 championships their teams combined to win, none was considered worthy enough for these pages by the editors of The Sporting News. Twice, however, McGraw's New York Giants were cast in dramatic, losing scripts, including the pennant race of 1908, which had perhaps the most turbulent finish of all. Had it not been for a rookie's failure to touch second base and a strong-willed umpire's determination to buck precedent and call him out after the winning run had crossed the plate, the name of Fred Merkle probably would have passed into obscurity.

The New York Yankees, despite their 33 championships, appear as finalists only three times in this roll call. With little doubt, their superiority was too overwhelming to allow close encounters. The 1927 Bombers, popularly regarded as the most fearsome aggregation ever, triumphed by 19 lengths. When the Yanks won seven pennants in an eight-

year period (1936-1943), their slimmest lead at the finish was nine games. In all likelihood, they could have won by even more.

Unquestionably, the Dodgers—both in Brooklyn and Los Angeles—were the most proficient at nail-biting flag drives. Every time an N.L. race ended in a tie—and frequently when it did not—the Dodgers were involved.

In 1946, when the eight members of the National

League battled for more than five months only to end up with two teams in an unprecedented tie, the Dodgers were there. And so were the St. Louis Cardinals, another team with a history of squeezing the last bit of drama from each season. That race and five others that finished dead even live again on the following pages.

The Dodgers' most ardent flirtation with the muse of history flamed in 1951. Leading by 13½ games when the shadows started to lengthen, Charley Dressen's lordly Bums were drawn back to the field, not so much by their own ineptitude as by the furious pace of the Giants. For sudden, dramatic impact, the battle between the bitter interborough rivals may never be equaled.

To legions of Giants loyalists, a muscular third baseman's rising line drive was nothing less than a minor miracle that turned deep-seated despondency into instant hysteria. Those who experienced that magic moment on October 3, both in and out of the Polo Grounds, can never be convinced that the deciding contest was not the "Game of Games" in more than 110 years of major league baseball. (See "Baseball's 50 Greatest Games," The Sporting News, 1986.)

The Dodgers made a third venture into playoff

waters in 1959 with the Milwaukee Braves, and another in 1962, when they re-engaged the Giants—this time across the continent on the West Coast.

The Dodgers have specialized in late-hour theatrics, even off the playoff stages. In 1934, when they were a sixth-place club under new Manager Casey Stengel, they dealt the Giants the kind of punishing blow that would be returned so often in later years. In 1949, they were the young challengers expected to fold in the clutch as they dashed to the wire with the Cardinals. But St. Louis succumbed to the pressure and lost four games in the final week to allow Dem Bums to win the flag on the final day of the season. But the more remarkable story that year was in the American League, where the Yankees and Boston Red Sox battled down to the final out of the 154th game to decide one of the most hotly contested races ever. The next season, the Dodgers again were hotly pursuing the league leader. Philadelphia's Whiz Kids stumbled badly in the stretch. When they looked up in the season's waning moments, the Dodgers had them right where they wanted them. Or did they?

Ironically some of baseball's heroic figures have emerged second best in duels that decided pennants. The first toppled superstar of the century, Jack Chesbro, was a 41-game winner for New York. One pitch that mattered, however, sailed high over the catcher's head, taking a club's dreams with it. In 1940, another Hall of Fame pitcher, Bob Feller, was victimized by one pitch in the final series of the season despite his 27 victories and a no-hitter on opening day.

But just as sure as wide-eyed youngsters worship their home-town hero, the game's immortals have basked in the glory of the fight. In 1945, Hank Greenberg, just back from World War II, clouted a grand-slam in the fog and drizzle of St. Louis as the Detroit Tigers fought to outlast the Washington Senators. Three years later, Lou Boudreau, the Cleveland Indians' shortstop-manager, led by example with two home runs in the first A.L. playoff. And many a Chicago Cubs fan can still squint his eyes and see Hall of Fame catcher Gabby Hartnett's "homer in the gloamin'" streaking into the left-field bleachers.

The starring roles are not always assigned to the leading actors, however. The most damaging blow in the A.L. East Division playoff of 1978 was delivered by Bucky Dent, a .243 hitter. The winner over Feller in 1940 was even lesser known. He was Floyd Giebell, who never won another major league game.

The editors' selection of the 25 most gripping races involved considerable discussion, borne of conflicting opinions. What finally made it to these pages is not designed to promote agreement. The Sporting News prefers it that way.

The Shot Heard 'Round the World

The 1951 Dodgers were a happy group after their regular season-ending comeback victory over Philadelphia had forced a pennant playoff.

Chuck Dressen, a lifelong advocate of the right of free speech and one who exercised that freedom to the utmost, was particularly voluble on the night of July 5, 1951.

There was ample cause for the dandy little skipper of the Brooklyn Dodgers to feel expansive. The preceding day the Dodgers had slapped down the New York Giants in a holiday doubleheader, and righthander Don Newcombe had completed Brooklyn's sweep of the three-game series just moments before by defeating Larry Jansen and the Giants before 33,000 fans at Ebbets Field. That triumph gave

the Dodgers a 7½-game lead over their cross-river rivals in the National League pennant race.

"We knocked 'em out," Dressen chortled. "They won't bother us anymore."

At that point, few would have disagreed with Dressen, whose club boasted a 47-26 record. Enthusiasm was sky-high in Flatbush where, a year earlier, Dodger fans had mourned the loss of the 1950 pennant to the Philadelphia Phillies on the final day of the season. The borough-wide despondency had provoked Walter O'Malley into executive action. The president of the club dismissed Burt Shot-

Eager Dodger fans arrived early on the morning of October 1 in the hope of getting tickets for the first playoff game against the Giants.

ton, a gentle geriatric who had managed the team since midseason of 1948, when Leo Durocher skipped across town to become the Giants' pilot.

To replace Shotton, O'Malley chose Charles Walter Dressen, a former National League infielder, manager of the Cincinnati Reds and coach of the Dodgers and New York Yankees. Most recently he had been manager of the pennant-winning Oakland Oaks of the Pacific Coast League. He brought his winning ways with him when he assumed control of the Dodgers in 1951. Brooklyn got off to a 5-1 start under the new skipper, then lost nine of its next 15 games before reclaiming the top spot in the N.L. standings May 13. The Dodgers held first place continuously from that point through their early-July sweep of the Giants.

Brooklyn's dominance did not end with its three-game conquest of the Giants. Before they were halted by the Chicago Cubs on July 14, the Dodgers reeled off eight consecutive victories, stretching their lead to 9½ games. First baseman Gil Hodges was smacking home runs at a brisk pace, with 28 in the team's first 74 games. Second baseman Jackie Robinson, catcher Roy Campanella, shortstop Pee

Wee Reese and outfielders Duke Snider and Carl Furillo were on their way to big years. Outfielder Andy Pafko, obtained from the Cubs in a four-for-four trade June 15, was supplying additional punch. And the pitching, led by Preacher Roe and Newcombe, was extraordinary.

On July 20, Roe launched another Brooklyn winning streak that reached 10 games and once again put the Dodgers 9½ games in front of the second-place Giants. But the Brooklyn crest still lay ahead. After Ralph Branca tamed the Boston Braves, 8-1, in the first game of a doubleheader August 11, the Dodgers' lead stood at 13½ games. They lost the second game, 8-4, but so what? The Dodgers weren't worried. They had a 70-36 record and a 13-length lead with only 48 games remaining on the schedule. All was well in Flatbush.

As Dressen and the legions of Dodger loyalists reveled in the success of Dem Bums, there were indications of an awakening across the East River. The Giants had begun to stir.

The previous year New York had finished with a rush and wound up in third place, five games off the pace. That strong finish made the Giants the

An opportunistic fan was quick to take advantage of a newly created entrance into Ebbets Field, home of the Dodgers and site of the playoff opener.

preseason favorite to win the 1951 pennant. A poll of members of the Baseball Writers' Association of America showed 99 of 204 scribes favoring the Giants and 69 picking the Dodgers. But the Giants got away to a dismal start. An 11-game losing streak in April plunged them into last place, and it wasn't until May 27 that they climbed above the .500 mark with a record of 20-19. They would not fall below .500 again.

Three moves figured prominently in the rebirth of the club. The first involved Whitey Lockman and Monte Irvin. An outfielder for most of his career, Irvin opened the season at first base, where he was ill at ease. He yearned for his old position, and in late May his manager accommodated him. Durocher brought Lockman in from left field to swap positions with Irvin.

A second personnel change involved a 20-year-old outfielder who was batting .477 for the Minneapolis farm club in the American Association. Willie Mays was promoted to the parent club May 25 and installed in center field. Though he went to bat 13 times before rapping his first hit and 14 more times before collecting his second, the Say-Hey Kid

was hitting up a storm and making dazzling plays in center field before long.

Mays' arrival left another player stranded, which led to Durocher's third—and most important—move. But that move came several weeks after Mays supplanted the Giants' veteran center fielder, Bobby Thomson.

A native of Glasgow, Scotland, Thomson grew up in Staten Island, N.Y. He signed with the Giants' organization fresh out of high school in 1942 and, after a short stay at Bristol of the Appalachian League, was shipped to Rocky Mount, N.C., in the Class-D Bi-State League. Bobby made his Rocky Mount debut in a game at Danville, Va., and went hitless in four trips to the plate. Afterward, while seated in a town cafe, Bobby failed to hear the announcement that the team bus was about to depart. The homesick youth was brooding over a glass of milk when he was found by the town cop, who suspected that Bobby had been left behind. The lawman offered Thomson the rear of his motorcycle, which zoomed off in pursuit of the team bus. When Thomson finally was reunited with his teammates, he had recovered sufficiently from his initial despondency to quip, "Gee, do you forget a guy just because he goes 0-for-4 the first time out?"

Thomson batted .241 as an 18-year-old third baseman and then spent the next three years in military service. After his release, he joined Jersey City for the 1946 season. He batted .280 with 92 runs batted in and 26 home runs in the International League and was called up to New York late in 1946 in time to bat .315 in 18 games. The next season he was moved to center field.

Robert Brown Thomson possessed all the ingredients for future stardom. Tall and graceful, he ran like a greyhound, hit for distance and had a powerful arm. There was no way the Flying Scot could miss, the experts thought, yet in his first few seasons, Bobby succeeded admirably in proving them wrong.

Thomson posted some impressive numbers in his early years with the Giants, but too many times he suffered through long stretches in which he simply could not produce.

Mel Ott, who managed the Giants when Bobby arrived, offered one explanation. Ott thought Thomson lacked concentration, that he daydreamed between pitches while in the outfield and was unprepared when a ball was hit in his direction. Moreover, Thomson flatly rejected suggestions that he adjust his batting stance. He favored the straight-up style of Joe DiMaggio, who certainly was an admirable role model. But while the posture was fine for the Yankee Clipper, it just didn't work for Bobby Thomson.

An abrupt change in Thomson's stance took place in 1951 after he had ridden the bench for a time. Lockman, Thomson's roommate, tried repeatedly to get Bobby to crouch and close his stance more, but the Scot refused. Finally, seeing Thomson in the batting cage one day, Durocher decided the time had come for drastic action.

"I spotted Leo under a full head of steam, making straight for the cage," Thomson recalled. "I could tell there was something up. He was still half walk-

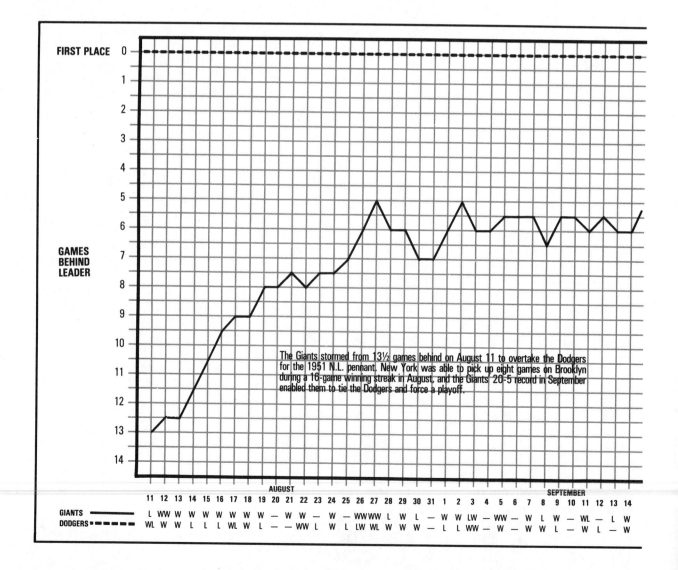

The Giants stormed from 13½ games behind on August 11 to overtake the Dodgers for the 1951 N.L. pennant. New York was able to pick up eight games on Brooklyn during a 16-game winning streak in August, and the Giants' 20-5 record in September enabled them to tie the Dodgers and force a playoff.

ing, half running, when he let me have it: 'Move closer to the plate! Shorten your stride! Crouch!' Those were the orders."

Initially, Thomson was uncomfortable in the bent-knee stance. As hits became more numerous, however, the part-time outfielder fell in love with it.

And when slump-ridden Hank Thompson suffered a spike wound in late July, Bobby was ready to take over at third base, a position he had not played in almost five years.

Durocher installed Thomson as the regular third baseman July 20. If one move can be labeled as the key to the Giants' 1951 season, that was it. Thomson, who had been hitting .237 before that date, batted a whopping .357 after being moved to third. And as Thomson's fortunes rose, so did New York's.

Despite their fixed lineup and newfound winning ways, however, the Giants still were unable to gain ground on the front-running Dodgers. They won 13 of 19 games after Thomson's move to third, but

Brooklyn still boasted a 9½-game lead. The Dodgers then swept a three-game series from the Giants, putting New York in an even deeper hole. The Giants lost their next contest to Philadelphia, so after games of August 11, 13 games separated the two clubs.

The next day, the Giants swept a doubleheader from the Phillies. That twin triumph launched a phenomenal 16-game winning streak that cut the Dodgers' lead to five games. Included in that surge were three victories over the Dodgers. It took a three-hit shutout by Pittsburgh Pirates lefthander Howie Pollet to snap the streak August 28.

While New York was losing two of three games to the Pirates, Brooklyn was sweeping a three-game set with the Reds. So, when the contenders opened a two-game series at the Polo Grounds on September 1, they were separated by seven games. That difference shrank to five after Giants righthander Sal Maglie turned in an 8-1 victory and righthander Jim Hearn followed with an 11-2 decision. New York's offensive outburst was keyed by Thomson, who hit a pair of home runs, and outfielder Don Mueller, who hit five homers in those two games.

The Dodgers bounced back to win their next five contests, including the first game of a two-game series with the Giants at Ebbets Field. In that game, Newcombe allowed only two hits in a 9-0 victory over Hearn and the Giants, who had gone 4-1 between the two series with Brooklyn. But the Giants came back to win the second game September 9 as Maglie posted his 20th victory in a 2-1 duel with Brooklyn's Ralph Branca. The race remained tight, with the Dodgers leading by 5½ games.

The last western trip of the season cost the Dodgers additional ground. By losing four of nine games while the Giants were losing only three of nine, the Dodgers saw their lead dwindle to 4½ games. But they still had the clear advantage heading into the last 10 days of the campaign. Brooklyn had a 92-52 record through September 20 with 10 games remaining, while New York had an 89-58 mark with only seven games left. Even if the Giants won all seven of those games, the Dodgers needed only to win five of their last 10 contests to clinch the pennant.

Though the odds did not favor the Giants, much of the nation did. In a matter of weeks, the Giants went from hopeless underdogs to Cinderella sweethearts. The team of John McGraw, Bill Terry, Mel Ott and Carl Hubbell had suddenly become the darling of the baseball world—excluding Brooklyn, of course.

Another two games were sliced off the Dodgers' advantage over the next four days when they dropped two of three games to the Phillies while the Giants were sweeping three from Boston. The next day, September 25, proved to be Black Tuesday for

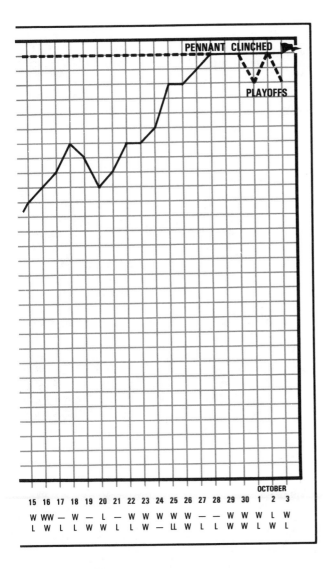

PENNANT CLINCHED

PLAYOFFS

OCTOBER

15	16	17	18	19	20	21	22	23	24	25	26	27	28	29	30	1	2	3
W	W	W	—	W	—	L	—	W	W	W	W	W	—	—	W	W	W	L	W
L	W	L	L	W	W	L	L	W	—	LL	W	L	L	W	W	L	W	L

Bobby Thomson (left), pitcher Jim Hearn (center) and Monte Irvin starred in
the Giants' 3-1 Game 1 victory over the Dodgers.

the Dodgers. While New York's Hearn beat the
Phils, 5-1, Brooklyn lost a doubleheader in Boston.
Branca dropped the opener to Warren Spahn, 6-3,
and righthander Carl Erskine lost to Jim Wilson,
14-2, in the nightcap.

One game! All that was left of the Dodgers' seemingly insurmountable 13½-game lead was a single
length in the standings!

Both teams demolished their opponents September 26. Righthander Larry Jansen was the beneficiary of New York's 10-1 triumph at Philadelphia,
while Newcombe coasted to his 19th victory in a
15-5 rout of the Braves at Boston.

But the next day, while the Giants were idle, the
Dodgers lost to the Braves, 4-3, as Chet Nichols
handed Roe only his third loss in 25 decisions.

One-half game!

That loss to the Braves will always be remembered by Brooklyn fans. The Braves' winning run
was scored in the eighth inning by Bob Addis on a
hotly disputed call by umpire Frank Dascoli. Campanella, who argued that he had tagged Addis at the
plate, and coach Cookie Lavagetto were ejected for
their violent protests, and later the Brooklyn bench
was cleared. After the game, an angry Dodger took
out his frustration on the door to the umpires'
dressing room, leaving it splintered. In the after-
math of this affair, N.L. President Ford Frick fined
Campanella and Jackie Robinson $100 each and
Roe $50.

Dascoli's questionable ruling left the Dodgers
fuming. They contended that the umpire had cost

them a crucial game, because of both his safe call on
Addis and his ejection of Campanella.

"He had no right to throw Camp out," Robinson
snapped in the stormy Dodger clubhouse. "In a
race like this, the umpires should expect tempers to
be a little frayed."

Still seething, the Dodgers moved on to Philadelphia for a three-game set to wind up the season. The
Giants, meanwhile, enjoyed a second consecutive
day of rest prior to playing their last two games of
the season in Boston.

Erskine, seeking his 17th win, was Dressen's
choice to pitch the opener in Philadelphia. The
righthander was staked to a 3-0 lead after five innings, but a single run in the sixth and Andy Seminick's two-run homer in the eighth enabled the
Phils to tie the score. The Dodgers lost the game,
4-3, when Willie Jones singled home Richie Ashburn in the ninth.

Tie!

Both teams raised their records to 95-58 by winning September 29. In the afternoon, Maglie
blanked the Braves, 3-0, on five hits for his 23rd
win, and that night Newcombe shut out the Phillies,
5-0, on seven hits for his 20th victory of the year.

Still a tie!

One decisive day remained. Both teams could win
or both could lose, thus preserving a tie atop the
standings, or one could clinch the pennant by winning while the other lost in its 154th game of the
year.

The Giants made a bid to win the flag outright by

Manager Chuck Dressen, pitcher Clem Labine, Rube Walker, Andy Pafko and
Gil Hodges had reason to smile after the Dodgers' 10-0 Game 2 victory.

shading the Braves, 3-2. Jansen limited Boston to five hits and registered his 22nd victory, while Thomson supplied the first run with his 30th home run of the year. At worst, the Giants had assured themselves of a first-place tie at the end of the regular schedule.

The Dodgers, in the meantime, were embroiled in a battle for survival at Philadelphia. The Phils knocked out sore-armed Preacher Roe in the second inning and built up an 8-5 lead after five frames. By that time the Giants' game was over. In a do-or-die situation, the Dodgers furiously battled back to knot the count, 8-8, in the eighth on four hits, including pinch-hitter Rube Walker's two-run double. The game went into overtime.

The Phils nearly pulled out a victory in the 12th inning. With the potential winning run on third base and two out, Phillies first baseman Eddie Waitkus drove a savage liner to the right side of the infield, where Robinson made a spectacular catch a few inches above the ground. As the second baseman's momentum carried him to the turf, his elbow jammed into his midsection. For a brief while, Jackie lay still, but he came to and remained in the game. Two innings later, Robinson provided a solo homer off Robin Roberts that gave the Dodgers a 9-8 victory. The winning pitcher was righthander Bud Podbielan, the last of seven pitchers whom Dressen threw into the struggle.

The regular schedule was over, but the pennant race wasn't. By winning 37 of their last 44 games (and 12 of their last 13), the Giants had caught up

with the Dodgers, who had lost 23 of their last 49 games and six of their last 10. So, both clubs were tied with identical 96-58 records. For only the second time in N.L. history, the pennant would be decided in a three-game playoff.

The sites for the playoff games were determined by a coin flip. The Dodgers won the toss, and Dressen chose to play the first game at Ebbets Field, thereby awarding the last two games to the Polo Grounds.

Jim Hearn, who had a 16-9 record but had won only two of five decisions against the Dodgers in the course of the season, was nominated to start the first playoff game for New York on October 1. His opponent was fellow righthander Ralph Branca (13-10), a two-time winner in six decisions against the Giants. Andy Pafko staked Branca and the Dodgers to a 1-0 advantage with a second-inning home run, but Thomson's two-run blast in the fourth and Monte Irvin's bases-empty clout in the eighth gave the Giants a 3-1 triumph. Dressen's decision to play the first game in Brooklyn had backfired, and the Dodgers faced the difficult task of having to beat New York twice on the Giants' home field.

The Dodgers accomplished half of that task the next day. Rookie righthander Clem Labine allowed just six hits and won, 10-0, with the help of home runs by Robinson, Hodges, Pafko and Walker. The playoffs were tied.

Once again the two teams were teetering on a high wire. Victory on Wednesday, October 3, was

Manager Leo Durocher ordered Bobby Thomson to change from an upright to a crouched stance and the move paid big dividends.

absolutely necessary if the Dodgers did not wish to be remembered as the club that squandered a 13½-game lead in August. History would be more kind to the Giants if they were to lose the deciding game, but still, the Giants did not want to be remembered as the team that overcame that large deficit and then failed to capitalize on its achievement.

Game 3 matched up a pair of 20-game-winning righthanders, Sal Maglie for New York and Don Newcombe for Brooklyn. The Dodgers assailed Maglie in the first inning as if to make an early casualty of the hard-throwing veteran. With one out, Pee Wee Reese and Duke Snider walked. Jackie Robinson's single then scored Reese and advanced Snider to second. As Larry Jansen started to warm up, Durocher conferred with his pitcher on the mound. The interlude was just what Maglie needed. He induced Pafko to dribble into a forceout at third base and retired Hodges on a pop foul to Thomson, thus keeping the Dodgers from expanding on their 1-0 lead.

The Giants threatened to tie the score in the second. Newcombe retired the first batter, Irvin, on a ground ball to Reese, but Whitey Lockman and Thomson responded with consecutive singles. Thomson, however, thought his hit was good for a double and kept on running with his head down, expecting Lockman to advance to third. Bobby ran into an easy out when he arrived at second and found Whitey still there. The next batter, Willie

Mays, flied out to end the brief uprising.

The Giants made another run at Big Newk in the fifth when Thomson whacked a one-out double. A conference with Dressen at the mound and a glimpse at the bullpen, where Carl Erskine and Branca were warming up, steadied Newcombe, who retired the side without damage. But New York finally broke through against Newcombe in the seventh inning. Irvin's double, Lockman's sacrifice and Thomson's long fly ball to center field tied the score, 1-1.

The deadlock was short-lived. Singles by Reese and Snider with one out in the eighth inning preceded a wild pitch by Maglie that gave the Dodgers a 2-1 lead. Robinson was walked intentionally, and singles by Pafko and third baseman Billy Cox drove in two more tallies. The Dodgers led, 4-1, with only six more outs to go.

Newcombe, pitching for the fourth time in eight days, retired the Giants in order in the bottom of the eighth.

Durocher had called on a pinch-hitter to bat for Maglie in that frame, so Jansen then went to the mound for the Giants in the top of the ninth. The righthander set the Dodgers down in order, but to the Giants' partisans among the 34,320 fans at the Polo Grounds, Jansen's accomplishment hardly seemed inspiring. Trailing by three runs with only three outs to go, the Giants appeared doomed.

Big Newk trudged back out to the mound to pitch the last of the ninth. Leading off was shortstop Alvin Dark, who rapped a single off Hodges' glove at first. It was the fifth hit off the big righthander that day.

Don Mueller, a lefthanded batter, followed Dark to the plate. In the press box, critics gazed at first base and wondered aloud why Hodges was holding against Dark, inasmuch as Alvin was no threat to steal with his team trailing by three runs. Sure enough, Mueller grounded a single into right field. Had Hodges been playing his normal first-base position, he likely would have fielded the ball with a good chance to start a double play. As it was, Dark was on third base, Mueller on first and the league's top RBI man at bat in Irvin, who had 24 home runs to his credit.

Dressen called time and summoned catcher Rube Walker and all the Brooklyn infielders to a conference on the mound to discuss Newcombe's pitching strategy. Irvin took the first pitch low and away for ball one and then missed the next pitch for strike one. On Newk's third delivery, Irvin fouled to Hodges outside first base. Brooklyn was two outs away from clinching its second pennant in three years.

As Dark and Mueller fidgeted off base, press box occupants heard: "Attention, press. World Series credentials for Ebbets Field can be picked up at 6

After giving Bobby Thomson a delirious victory ride
(below), appreciative Giants fans remained at the
Polo Grounds far into the night, cheering their
conquering heroes.

o'clock tonight at the Biltmore Hotel." The scribes made a mental note of that useful information and then went back to work on their stories, all of which were ready to trumpet the news that the Dodgers were going to the World Series.

Whitey Lockman, a lefthanded batter, was the next New York batter. In the playoffs, he had two hits to show for nine at-bats. As he approached the plate, Lockman sneaked a peak at the right-field wall rising 257 feet away at the foul line. "If I hit one out of here, the score is tied," the North Carolinian thought to himself.

Newcombe's first pitch to Lockman was a strike. On the second, Whitey related, "muscle memory took over." He slapped an outside pitch to left field for a double, scoring Dark and sending Mueller to third. But as Mueller slid into the bag ahead of Pafko's strong and accurate throw, he severely wrenched his ankle. He lay writhing on the ground for several minutes before being carried off on a stretcher and replaced by Clint Hartung.

During the interruption, Dressen telephoned the bullpen. He wanted another pitcher to replace Newcombe, who was pooped, and to protect the Dodgers' 4-2 lead. According to Dressen's version of the conversation, coach Clyde Sukeforth reported that Branca was throwing more impressively than Erskine. "Gimme Branca," Chuck replied.

Sukeforth later insisted that Dressen's account wasn't entirely accurate. "Erskine wasn't even working in the bullpen at that time," the coach asserted. "He had been there early, but by the ninth inning he was back on the bench. And Dressen didn't call me first. I called him early in the game when it looked as though Don Newcombe was tiring and I told him Branca was throwing great. In the ninth inning, I told him the same thing."

Even before Branca arrived at the mound, the second-guessers were busy criticizing Dressen's selection. After all, Branca had been tagged for 10 home runs by New York batters already that year, including two by Thomson, who was coming to the plate. In addition, Branca's best pitch was a fastball, but Thomson was a fastball hitter. Even though Clem Labine had pitched the day before, wouldn't the curveballer have been a better choice to face Thomson?

Furthermore, wouldn't it have been good strategy to lift Walker when Branca took over and replace him behind the plate with Roy Campanella to steer the young pitcher through the shoals? The league's best catcher was suffering from a charley horse—"the only one of my life," he said—and while he could not run, he could crouch and flash signs and put his expertise to excellent use. Dressen gave no hint of such a move.

As Thomson waited for Branca to finish his warmup tosses, Leo Durocher called him aside.

Looking toward the left-field wall only 279 feet away, the manager pleaded: "Just one little Chinese homer, Bobby! Please, just one little Chinese homer!"

The moment for the fateful confrontation arrived. It was Branca, who had been beaten in the first game of the playoffs, vs. the Flying Scot, who had already driven in three of the Giants' five runs in the playoffs.

Branca's first pitch broke over the inside of the plate. Strike one! Another pitch, high and tight. Branca put it precisely where he wanted it in order to set Thomson up for a breaking pitch low and away, just as prescribed in the pitchers' manual.

It was 3:58 p.m. when Thomson swung at what was supposed to be a waste pitch. He made solid contact. The ball took off on a low trajectory toward left field. It started sinking, and Thomson thought the ball would bounce off the wall and score both runners, tying the score. But as he rounded first base, he saw Andy Pafko gazing upward helplessly as the ball disappeared into the stands.

For a moment the spectators sat stunned, not quite sure of what they had just witnessed. Then, as if by signal, pandemonium erupted.

In the radio booth, announcer Russ Hodges screamed: "The Giants win the pennant! The Giants win the pennant! The Giants win the pennant! . . . The Giants win the pennant, and they're going crazy!"

"I heard yells . . . saw paper flying . . . saw people jumping in the air," Thomson related. "But my first thought was that we had beaten the Dodgers, not that we had won the pennant."

Hartung crossed the plate. Lockman followed, receiving a whack on his posterior from Durocher as he headed for the plate. About the same time, Leo the Lip was attacked by second baseman Eddie Stanky. The Brat leaped from the Giants' dugout when Thomson's drive disappeared and raced to third base, where he threw a bear hug around his boss.

Thomson's recollection of his triumphal tour of the bases was hazy ever after. He leaped and bounced and danced around the basepaths as dozens of tableaus blended into a wild phantasmagoria: Fans bursting the police cordon to invade the playing field . . . Jackie Robinson trailing after him to make certain Bobby tagged every base as prescribed by law . . . screams . . . howls . . . delirium . . . the world gone insane . . . and there at home plate a mob waiting to embrace the game's newest Caesar.

Thomson sank his spikes into home plate, whereupon he was hoisted to the shoulders of hysterical teammates and carried to the Giants' clubhouse in center field. But the wild-eyed celebrants on the field would not allow Thomson to enjoy an uninterrupted party with his teammates. Repeatedly, he was summoned for another curtain call by the thousands of fans crowded at the foot of the stairs. They had no intention of releasing, at least for the hour, the 27-year-old Scot who had smashed "The Shot Heard 'Round the World" and applied the finishing touches to "The Miracle of Coogan's Bluff."

Long past nightfall, legions of New Yorkers cheered and toasted the newly deified gods of the diamond. Automobile horns honked endlessly in the concrete canyons, ticker tape floated out of office windows and euphoria was abroad in the land.

Actress Tallulah Bankhead, an inveterate Giants fan, confessed to a theater audience: "I'm so happy, I don't make sense. What I've been through with this team! I wish I could care so much for my own career."

Hundreds of thousands of others, the great and the not so great, could have echoed her sentiments.

While Giants partisans celebrated with the flowing grape and grain, Brooklyn fans partook of the same libations to drown their sorrows. Nowhere was the grief more pronounced than in the sepulcher-like clubhouse of the Dodgers.

Don Newcombe, too numb to speak, showered and dressed hurriedly and departed quietly.

On a small flight of steps that bisected the dressing quarters, Ralph Branca lay sprawled with his face buried in the hand that had delivered the ill-fated pitch. He cried for a short while, but mostly he just stared at the floor in shock.

In the manager's cubicle, Chuck Dressen tried to answer questions dispassionately. One particular query evoked the greatest speculation: "Did you give any thought to walking Bobby Thomson?"

"Yes, I did," the subdued pilot answered. "Five times this year I walked the winning run and got away with it. But Thomson? The next guy (Mays) could have hit a home run, too."

Mays clouted 20 homers in 464 at-bats during the 1951 campaign, or one in every 23 official trips to the plate. When Thomson stepped to the plate to face Branca, he had hit for the circuit 31 times in 517 tries, or once every 17 at-bats.

At the Brooklyn craps table, the odds on Mays were more attractive.

Giants Owner Horace Stoneham (left) and Manager Leo Durocher (right) celebrate with the hero of the moment, Bobby Thomson.

The Pennant That Got Away

Fiery Cubs second baseman Johnny Evers opened the can of worms that put umpire Hank O'Day (right) and all of baseball in a tough spot.

When the kid from Troy, N.Y., made his debut in major league baseball in 1902, he weighed 95 pounds. Throughout his illustrious career as a second baseman for the Chicago Cubs and Boston Braves, he never weighed more than 135 pounds. Yet, weighed mentally, John Joseph Evers was a heavyweight champion.

Evers' favorite book was the baseball rule book. On the road, Johnny used to retire to his room early with a Troy newspaper, a copy of The Sporting News, a National League Guide and candy.

The sweets were intended to add pounds to his 5-foot-9 frame. But Evers was more interested in devouring his baseball literature, most of which was stored in his active cerebrum.

In an era when many colleagues idled away their spare moments in grog shops and billiard halls,

Johnny Evers studied and mastered the rule book. He became the equal of umpires in his command of the playing code, particularly Rule 59, which stated: "One run shall be scored every time a baserunner, after having legally touched the first three bases, shall legally touch the home base before three men are put out; provided, however, that if he reach home on or during a play in which the third man be forced out or be put out before reaching first base, a run shall not count. A forceout can be made only when a baserunner legally loses the right to the base he occupies and is thereby obliged to advance as the result of a fair hit ball not caught on the fly."

The rule was explicit. For years, however, when a batter hit safely to drive in the winning run with two outs in the bottom of the last inning, the baserunners customarily ran off the field without tagging the next base as soon as the deciding marker crossed the plate. This widespread practice was technically illegal, but few people ever gave the matter much thought.

Except for Evers. The precise moment when Evers discovered the inconsistency between the written word and its on-the-field execution is unrecorded. It is similarly uncertain when, if ever, he apprised his teammates of his discovery. But there can be no doubt that by September 1908, Evers was laying in wait for the next unsuspecting baserunners who flouted the rule against the Cubs.

At that point in the season, Evers was looking for anything that might give his club the edge. The Cubs were embroiled in a heated pennant race for the National League crown with the New York Giants and the Pittsburgh Pirates. After leading the pack for all but eight days of the season through July 14, the Cubs fell behind the Pirates. Pittsburgh then won 20 of its next 30 games and enjoyed a 5½-week stay atop the N.L. standings. But when the Pirates fell to second place August 24, they were replaced not by the Cubs, but by the Giants, who had been climbing steadily after struggling through the first two months of the campaign. New York swept a four-game series from Pittsburgh to go 3½ games on top August 26.

The Cubs won their last nine games in August, including three against Manager John McGraw's Giants, to draw even with New York entering September. The Giants' 69-45 record, however, gave them a slight edge over Chicago (71-47) in winning percentage. The Pirates, meanwhile, were half a game back at 70-47.

The race remained tight in early September as all three contending clubs stayed hot. New York and Pittsburgh won four games apiece on the first three days of the month, while Chicago won three of four contests. Through games of September 3, the Giants had a half-game lead on the Pirates and a full game over the Cubs.

It was on September 4, 1908, that Evers finally got his chance to put the specifications of Rule 59 to the test. The heedless baserunner was Warren Gill, a 29-year-old rookie first baseman with the Pirates.

Gill, whose future career as a dentist would prove more lucrative than his baseball endeavors, was in the starting lineup at Exposition Park in Pittsburgh when righthander Vic Willis, on his way to a 23-11 season, started for the Pirates against righthander Mordecai (Three Finger) Brown, who would finish with a 29-9 mark for Chicago. The pitchers were superb, neither allowing a run as the teams battled into the last of the 10th inning.

In the bottom of the first extra frame, however, the Pirates loaded the bases. With two out, Chief Wilson singled to center field. Fred Clarke trotted

Giants first baseman Fred Merkle became the 1908 center of controversy when he failed to touch second base.

in from third base to score the winning run and Gill, who had been on first, veered from the base line and loped into the Pirates' clubhouse. He did not touch second base.

This was the opportunity for which Evers had been waiting. He screamed at Cubs center fielder Jimmy Slagle, demanding that he throw the ball to him. When Johnny got it, he stepped on second and hollered to Hank O'Day, the only umpire working the game. Evers wanted Gill called out on a force play. O'Day refused. The arbiter reported that he had focused on Clarke tagging the plate and Wilson stepping on first base and had not witnessed Gill's infraction, if indeed there was one.

O'Day's stand did not surprise Evers. "Ol' Hank was mad at me anyway for an argument we'd had

Joe McGinnity managed to become a key figure in the 1908 Merkle controversy even though he did not play in the game.

in St. Louis a few weeks before," Johnny remembered 35 years later, "and you could tell that his whole attitude was he'd be damned if that little squirt Evers was going to get him in another jam."

When Frank Chance, the Cubs' manager/first baseman, added his voice in support of Evers, the crusty arbiter replied, "Clarke scored before the third out could have been made," and shoved his way past the two Cubs on his way to his dressing quarters.

From the ball park, Cubs Owner Charles Webb Murphy rushed to his hotel, where he dispatched a wire of protest to Harry C. Pulliam, president of the National League. The game, Murphy maintained, should be ruled a tie, not a Pittsburgh victory.

On September 9, Pulliam issued his ruling, which said in part: "The question of whether there was a force play . . . cannot be established by the evidence of players or spectators. It rests solely with the umpire. The umpire in this case, by allowing the winning run, ruled that there was no force at second, because if there had been the run could not have been scored. The protest is denied."

An editorial in The Sporting News called the Chicago protest "ill-advised, inasmuch as there was not even a remote chance that it would be sustained on the evidence submitted, and it served only to afford the carping class of patrons an opportunity to question the integrity of the game. If Pittsburgh did not fairly win the game, the Chicago club was cheated. The officials of the defeated club make no such contention, but made that issue in the attempt to profit by a technical point, which did not originate with the manager of the Cubs, who participated in the game, nor with their president, who witnessed it."

After all was said and done, the game remained a 1-0 victory for the Pirates. Because Pulliam's ruling left matters unchanged, the incident was quickly forgotten.

But not by O'Day, and certainly not by Evers. In some accounts, the umpire, upon sober reflection, agreed that Evers was entirely correct and advised him accordingly with the promise that if a similar play occurred in the future, he would rule in favor

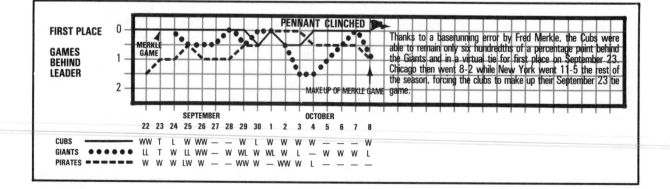

		PENNANT CLINCHED	
FIRST PLACE	0		Thanks to a baserunning error by Fred Merkle, the Cubs were able to remain only six hundredths of a percentage point behind the Giants and in a virtual tie for first place on September 23. Chicago then went 8-2 while New York went 11-5 the rest of the season, forcing the clubs to make up their September 23 tie game.
GAMES BEHIND LEADER	1	MERKLE GAME	
	2	MAKEUP OF MERKLE GAME	

	SEPTEMBER	OCTOBER
	22 23 24 25 26 27 28 29 30	1 2 3 4 5 6 7 8
CUBS	WW T L W WW — — W L	W W W W — — — W
GIANTS	LL T W LL WW — W WL W	WL W L — W W W L
PIRATES	W W W LW W — WW W —	WW W L — — — — —

Manager John McGraw (left) and pitcher Christy Mathewson held firmly to the belief that the Giants were robbed of the 1908 pennant.

of the team in the field. It is unknown whether O'Day communicated his decision to other umpires or to the league office. Though other clubs were aware of the Pittsburgh incident, they were not advised that baserunners would be in jeopardy if they mimicked Gill in the future—at least if O'Day was umpiring that game.

By coincidence, Evers, O'Day and a wayward baserunner converged on the Polo Grounds in New York on the afternoon of September 23, 1908. That day the Cubs were facing the Giants, who had been on a rampage until four days before. The Giants had won 18 of their first 19 games in September, including 11 straight through September 18, when a doubleheader sweep of the Pirates put New York 4½ games in front of the second-place Cubs and five in front of Pittsburgh. But the Pirates halted New York's streak the next day with a 6-2 triumph in 10 innings. The Giants lost to the Pirates again two days later, and the Cubs won both games of a doubleheader against New York on September 22. That sweep gave the Cubs five wins in a row and brought them even with New York. Before games of Septem-

ber 23, the top of the league standings showed:

	W.	L.	Pct.	GB.
New York	87	50	.635	---
Chicago	90	53	.629	---
Pittsburgh	88	54	.620	1½

The double defeat at the hands of the Cubs sent an estimated 28,000 Giants fans home in an ugly mood. It also brought back the next day an equal number of partisans, just as hostile and bloodthirsty. From the moment the Cubs appeared on the field, torrents of abuse engulfed them from the stands.

The pitching selections for the critical contest were lefthander Jack (The Giant Killer) Pfiester for the Cubs and righthander Christy Mathewson for the Giants. Mathewson, the pride of New York, was on a 37-victory course for the season.

Neither team scored in the first four innings, but in the fifth, shortstop Joe Tinker, a lifelong nemesis for Mathewson, faced Big Six with the bases empty and "determination writ large on his expressive features," according to W.W. Aulick, a reporter for the New York Times. The scribe continued: "Mr. Tinker drives the ball away out to right-center for what would be a two-bagger if you or I had made it, gentle reader—and this is no disparagement of the Tinker, for he is well seeming in our sight. As the ball approaches Master (Mike) Donlin, this good man attempts to field it with his foot. It's a home run, all right, when you get down to scoring, but if this Donlin boy was our boy, we'd have sent him to bed without his supper, and ye mind that, Mike."

The Giants tied the score, 1-1, in the sixth. Second baseman Buck Herzog beat out an infield single and went to second on third baseman Harry Steinfeldt's overthrow of first base, then advanced to third on catcher Roger Bresnahan's sacrifice and scored on Donlin's single to center.

The score remained deadlocked into the last of the ninth. Center fielder Cy Seymour, first up for New York, was tossed out by Evers. Third baseman Art Devlin followed with a single but was forced on left fielder Moose McCormick's grounder to Evers. Fred Merkle was the next batter to face Pfiester. The 19-year-old first baseman was making one of his infrequent appearances because veteran Fred Tenney was suffering from an injured ankle that forced him to miss his only game of the year.

Merkle rapped a long single to right field, sending McCormick to third. "The single . . . might have been a double or triple," Merkle later said, "but Jack Hayden (Chicago right fielder) made a wonderful stab and knocked down the drive. At that, I could have gone to second easily, but with one run needed to win and a man on third, I played it safe."

The correspondent for the New York Times reported that when Merkle singled, "everybody in the

Harry Steinfeldt (left) was a member of the Cubs' famous infield that also included (left to right) Joe Tinker, Johnny Evers and Frank Chance.

inclosure slaps everybody else and nobody minds. Perfect ladies are screaming like a batch of Coney (Island) barkers . . . and the elderly banker behind us is beating our hat to a pulp with his gold-handled cane. And nobody minds. Aided by these indications of the popular sentiment, Master (Al) Bridwell hits safely to center. McCormick trots home, the reporter boys prepare to make an asterisk under the box score of the game with the line—'Two out when winning run was scored'—the merry villagers flock on the field to worship the hollow where the Mathewson feet have pressed, and all of a sudden there is a doings around second base."

The doings were occasioned by Fred Merkle. Upon seeing McCormick step on the plate, Merkle turned from the base line without touching second base and started for the clubhouse in an effort to beat the legions of spectators pouring from the stands.

Until that moment, most scribes and participants were in general agreement on the details of the day's events. After that moment, however, all accounts differ.

First there is the Christy Mathewson account. "I

had started from the field," the pitcher reported, "when I heard Evers yell to (center fielder Artie) Hofman, 'Throw the ball to second.' I remembered the trick they had tried to play at Pittsburgh, and I got Merkle by the arm and told him to go to second. In the meantime, the ball had been thrown in, high over Evers' head, and fell where the shortstop ordinarily stands. Merkle touched the bag, and I was near him when he did it."

Joe Vila, perhaps the most estimable baseball writer in New York at the time, wrote in the October 1 issue of The Sporting News: ". . . Merkle, losing his head, never went near second base, but made a beeline for the clubhouse, thinking the game had been won. Evers called to Hofman to throw the ball to second base for a forceout, but (Joe) McGinnity, who wasn't in the game at all (the pitcher had been coaching at third base), rushed out on the field and intercepted the throw. Mathewson, meanwhile, hustled after Merkle and told him to run to second base. The crowd was all over the field by that time and McGinnity, in a tussle with several Chicago players, threw the ball into the crowd back of third base.

"Not knowing just what was in the wind, a wild-eyed mob surrounded umpires O'Day and (Bob) Emslie, but luckily the regular police, who had been sent to the battlefield by (police) Commissioner Bingham, kept the judges of play from being killed, perhaps.

"The ball (perhaps the one McGinnity had fired into the stands, perhaps a substitute), by this time, had been thrown to Evers while Merkle was fighting his way through another mob to the bag. Half a dozen fistfights were soon going on, and it looked as if somebody would be seriously injured. The cops took the umpires under the grandstands, where O'Day declared that the run did not count and that the game was a tie—1 to 1."

The Giants, of course, were outraged by O'Day's decision and charged that they had been robbed of a legitimate victory. Vila, however, did not share that opinion. "In spite of the yells of distress and the foolish arguments offered by scores of narrow-minded followers of the Giants," the New York newspaperman concluded, "let me say boldly that there was only one decision to render. Merkle was out for two reasons. He was forced because he did not run to second base, while McGinnity's interferrence with the attempts to get the ball to the bag was, in itself, enough to retire the New Yorkers. Baseball is played under a set of rules and this play is covered by them. The run, of course, did not count, and the game should have been continued as it was plenty light enough.

"Umpire O'Day should have called Merkle out on the field and should have ordered an extra inning. If the crowd did not leave the diamond, O'Day's duty was to forfeit the game to Chicago, 9 to 0. That is all there is to it, and I am not the only one who maintains this opinion."

O'Day's report to Pulliam differed from Vila's account in one essential detail. "I did not ask to have the field cleared," he wrote, "as it was too dark to continue play."

The version of Giants Manager John McGraw, as contained in his wife's memoir, "The Real McGraw," reported: "Evers did not get the (game) ball. It rolled through the happy, milling spectators and past third base. A substitute Chicago pitcher, Floyd Kroh, seeing Hofman making wild motions and pointing, rushed from the dugout and got the ball. Joe McGinnity ran out, too, snatched the ball from Kroh's hands and threw it into the right-field stands. That's why I have always said Evers never made the putout.

"And why was an unannounced Chicago player on the field?

"His mere touching of the ball rendered it dead. Besides, Jack Hayden, one of the Chicago outfielders, had gone to the clubhouse, thinking the game was over. The Cubs did not have nine players on the field, and no play of any kind was possible.

"But Evers appealed to Emslie (the base umpire who had dropped to the turf to avoid being struck by Bridwell's liner), now upright and brushing the dirt from his uniform, and he ignored the plea. Evers then switched his appeal to O'Day, who was walking from the plate, mask in hand, and removing spare balls from his pockets. Evers grabbed one of the balls, ran to second base, stepped on the bag and demanded that Merkle be called out. . . .

"No decision or gesture of decision was made, and we expected none. Frankly, nobody paid much attention to the squabble. . . . We even joked in the clubhouse about Evers' effort to put one over, as he had tried in vain to do in Pittsburgh."

Johnny Evers' account, undoubtedly embroidered by the passage of years, was related in 1943, four years before his death and 35 years after the event.

"Hofman's throw had gone over Tinker's head and rolled over to where Joe McGinnity, the Giants pitcher, was standing," Evers told John P. Carmichael of the Chicago Daily News. "Joe . . . knew what was in our minds as Tinker and I raced for the ball. He got it first, but before he could get rid of the thing, Joe and I had him and we wrestled around there for what seemed to be five minutes. Of course it wasn't.

"We grabbed for his hands to make sure he wouldn't heave the ball away, but he broke loose and tossed it into the crowd. I can see the fellow who caught it yet . . . a tall, stringy, middle-aged gent with a brown bowler hat on. Steinfeldt and Floyd Kroh . . . raced after him. 'Gimme the ball for just a minute,' Steinfeldt begged him. 'I'll bring it right back.' The guy wouldn't let go and suddenly Kroh solved the problem. He hit the customer right on top of that stiff hat, drove it down over his eyes, and as the gent folded up, the ball fell free and Kroh got it. I was yelling and waving my hands out by second base and Tinker relayed it over to me and I stepped on the bag and made sure O'Day saw me. He was waiting for that very play . . . he remembered the Pittsburgh game . . . and he said: 'The run does not count.' "

Did the Giants win the game, 2-1? Was it a 1-1 tie? Or was it a forfeit in favor of the Cubs because the unruly crowd made further play impossible? The issue was tossed on the desk of Harry Pulliam.

The N.L. president supported O'Day. He called the game a tie and was prepared to order the teams to play a doubleheader the following day, but action by the Chicago club prevented him from doing that. When Murphy, the Cubs' president, filed a formal claim for a forfeiture a few hours after the game, Pulliam's hands were tied. Under the league constitution, the claim for forfeiture and supporting testimony must be furnished to the other club, which is then given five days in which to formulate

Many years after retirement, former roommates Fred Merkle (right) and Larry Doyle returned to New York for Old-Timers Day festivities.

a defense. On September 24, the day after the Merkle incident, the Cubs withdrew their forfeiture claim, but by then it was too late for Pulliam to notify the Giants to have their players at the Polo Grounds in time for a twin bill.

Chicago players, however, were at the park early the next day. On instructions from Frank Chance, they arrived fully attired shortly after noon, in time to play two games should orders arrive from the league office. No umpires were present, but Chance ordered pitcher Andy Coakley to take the mound and throw several pitches to a phantom batter. This gesture, Chance believed, gave the Cubs new grounds for a claim of forfeiture against a team that did not show up. That claim was filed the next day.

Eventually, the New York players arrived and played a single game, which lefthander Hooks Wiltse and the Giants won, 5-4. Immediately thereafter, the Cubs left town, hoping, as did the Giants, that the final standings would render a replay of the tie game unnecessary.

Meanwhile, Merkle was lambasted widely for his misadventure. Though Merkle was merely following the common practice of the day, Sporting Life of Philadelphia accused him of "inexcusable stupidity." A Chicago journalist, Charles Dryden, asserted that the player had "minor league brains" and "did a bonehead baserunning stunt." Even vaudeville co-

medians made fun of the player. A line that was guaranteed to draw a roar from the audience was, "I call my cane 'Merkle,' because it has a bone head."

With the outcome of the Chicago-New York game still up in the air, the Cubs, Giants and Pirates remained in the thick of the pennant race. When the Pirates won their eighth consecutive game October 3, they stood atop the standings with a 98-55 record, half a game ahead of the Cubs, who had won seven of eight games to raise their record to 97-55. The Giants, however, won only seven of 12 games after their September 24 victory over Chicago, dropping them to 1½ games behind the Pirates, the largest margin that had separated the three teams in 12 days.

The Chicago-Pittsburgh game October 4 was pivotal in the pennant race. It was the season finale for both teams, while New York, which was idle that day, still had a three-game series with the Boston Braves on its schedule. The disputed Cubs-Giants contest still was unsettled—it was on appeal to the league's board of directors—and so any of the three contenders still had a chance to win the pennant. But Three Finger Brown and the Cubs knocked off the Pirates with a 5-2 triumph over Vic Willis. Brown's 28th victory of the season gave the Cubs a 98-55 record, while the Pirates fell to 98-56 with no games left to play. Technically, all three clubs still were in the race, but Chicago was in the driver's seat with a half-game lead, while New York had to sweep Boston in three games at the Polo Grounds to tie Chicago. Pittsburgh's only hope rested with Chicago ultimately losing the "Merkle game," which would draw the two teams even with 98-56 marks.

About that time, Pulliam convened the board of directors in Cincinnati. Pulliam had upheld O'Day and called that September 23 game a tie, but both the Cubs and Giants had appealed to the board to overturn the league president's decision. The Cubs still thought they were entitled to a forfeiture because the New York club did not appear to make up the tie game the next day; the Giants insisted they were entitled to a 2-1 victory.

After listening to testimony for two days and one night, the board announced its decision October 6.

"The game should have been won by the New York club," the directors said, "had it not been for the reckless, careless, inexcusable blunder of one of its players, namely Merkle."

Turning to the rule governing the scoring of a run, the directors noted: "This rule is plain, explicit and cannot be misconstrued by anyone. While it may not have been complied with in many other games; while other clubs may not have taken advantage of its provisions in the past under similar conditions, yet it did not deprive the Chicago club of the right to do so if it so desired, notwithstanding

CHICAGO TEAM OF 1908.

(1) Kich, (2) Trainer Simons, (3) Kling, (4) Reulbach, (5) Zimmerman, (6) Marshall, (7) Schulte, (8) Pfiester, (9) Frazer, (10) Lundgren, (11) Hofman, (12) Manager Chance, (13) Overall, (14) Hayden, (15) Coakley, (16) Steinfeldt, (17) Moran, (18) Brown, (19) Evers, (20) Sheckard, (21) Durbin, (22) Slagle, (23) Tinker, (24) Howard.

In its October 8, 1908, issue, The Sporting News (right) related the decision concerning the "Disputed Game." One week later, the Chicago Cubs were pictured as the National League champions (above).

that it might be termed as taking advantage of winning or tying a game upon a technicality."

So, the directors refused to award the Giants the victory. They also refused to give the Cubs a victory by forfeit, saying that the club's own appeal the night of September 23 precluded the possibility of playing off the tie the next day. As a result, the board upheld Pulliam's ruling and ordered "that the game be played off on the Polo Grounds on Thursday, October 8, or as soon thereafter as the weather conditions will permit, and both clubs are directed to govern themselves accordingly."

On October 5, righthander Red Ames hurled the Giants to an 8-1 victory over the Braves. New York won the second game of the series the next day when Hooks Wiltse registered a 4-1 triumph, his 23rd of the year. As the two clubs prepared to finish their regular schedules October 7, several pennant possibilities still existed. If the Giants lost to the Braves and then beat the Cubs in the playoff of the tie game, all three contenders would have 98-56 records, creating a three-way tie for the N.L. flag. If the Giants lost to both the Braves and the Cubs, Chicago would win the pennant. But if the Giants beat the Braves, the October 8 game between New York and Chicago would determine the N.L. champion for 1908.

Pirates and Cubs fans took heart when the Braves jumped out to a 2-0 lead over New York in the first inning of their last game of the year. But Ames held the Braves scoreless the rest of the way, and the Giants stormed back to win, 7-2. That series sweep knocked Pittsburgh out of the running and lifted New York into a first-place tie with Chicago as both

clubs had records of 98-55. The pennant would be decided the next day in a game that, ironically, would match Christy Mathewson of the Giants against Jack Pfiester of the Cubs—the same pitchers who were battling September 23 before Merkle's blunder made this playoff necessary.

When the Cubs' Twentieth Century Limited train arrived in New York at 9:30 the morning of the game, the players were met by an estimated 5,000 men and boys who belabored them with "vile names and language." A police cordon escorted the team away from the mob.

Upon arriving at the Polo Grounds, the Cubs found the mood just as inimical. Fans had started arriving before sunrise, and by 10:30 a.m. more than 5,000 people were waiting impatiently outside the gates. Policemen were brushed aside "like corks in a torrent" as they tried in vain to control the throng.

At 12:45 p.m., more than two hours before the scheduled starting time, an estimated 26,000 fans were jammed into every inch of the Polo Grounds. Approximately 15,000 more were on the outside, clinging to every conceivable spot that afforded a view of the playing field. The most popular vantage points outside the park were Coogan's Bluff and a rusty set of elevated railroad tracks, from which one man fell to his death. As a New York Times reporter noted, "His vacant place was quickly filled."

Several hundred fans entered the park without paying. "The great 15-foot fence back of the grandstand, topped with two strands of barbed wire, was scaled by scores of men and boys," the reporter wrote. "These showed an agility that was remarkable and a daring in jumping within the grounds that one might look for, perhaps, in life convicts endeavoring to break jail."

The attitude among the players also was hostile. As the Cubs were warming up, Frank Chance and Joe McGinnity scuffled at home plate in a dispute over the time allotted to each team for pregame practice.

Nor was Jane Mathewson shown special consideration on this turbulent afternoon. Carrying her 2-year-old son toward a box seat, the wife of the immortal Big Six ran afoul of roisterers and had to be rescued by the police.

The game finally began at 3 p.m. In the first inning, Mathewson was the consummate hurler, fanning left fielder Jimmy Sheckard, Johnny Evers and right fielder Frank (Wildfire) Schulte. As Matty strode from the mound in his peculiar knock-kneed style and the Cubs took the field, a bugler played "Taps," raising an ear-splitting roar from more than 40,000 throats.

Pfiester got away to an untidy start, hitting Fred Tenney with a pitch and issuing a walk to Buck Herzog. Pfiester stayed disaster temporarily when he struck out Roger Bresnahan and his catcher, Johnny Kling, picked Herzog off base. But Mike Donlin rifled a double inside first base to score Tenney and Pfiester followed that by walking Cy Seymour. From his position at first base, Chance waved in a reliever. Into the game came Three Finger Brown, who was well rested since winning the Cubs' last game four days earlier.

The way the righthander "contorted his bulky person and shot the ball over the plate during the subsequent innings was awful," the New York Times reporter wrote. "There was a quick subsidence of exultation. There were halfhearted toots of defiance and shrill cries from hopeful small boys, and a woman or two piped words of cheer, but the titanic yawps of the leather-lunged 40,000 faithful had ceased."

Mathewson protected the slim lead until the third, when the Cubs scored four runs. Joe Tinker launched the uprising with a triple over Seymour's head in center field and scored on a single by Kling. A sacrifice by Brown, a walk to Evers and consecutive doubles by Schulte and Chance produced three more runs. Brown wouldn't need any more.

The Giants threatened to chase Brown in the seventh when singles by Art Devlin and Moose McCormick and a pass to Al Bridwell loaded the bases with nobody out. Larry Doyle, who missed much of the season because of a leg injury, pinch hit for Mathewson and was retired on a pop foul that Kling caught amid a shower of pop bottles, seat cushions and wadded paper. Tenney's sacrifice fly scored Devlin, but Brown retired Herzog on a ground ball to Tinker to snuff out the rally. The Giants threatened no more and lost, 4-2, as the Cubs annexed their third straight pennant. The Cubs then proceeded to beat the Detroit Tigers in the World Series for the second consecutive year.

Though Fred Merkle developed into a competent first baseman and performed capably on pennant-winning New York teams of 1911, '12 and '13, he was forever branded "Bonehead" for his baserunning caper as a 19-year-old. Merkle's only outspoken supporter was his manager, who not only refused to chastise his young player, but also gave him a $500 raise.

"It is criminal to say that Merkle is stupid and to blame the loss of the pennant on him," McGraw said. "In the first place, he is one of the smartest and best players on this ball club. In the second place, he didn't cost us the pennant. We lost a dozen games we should have won. Besides, we were robbed of it (by Pulliam's ruling, in McGraw's opinion), and you can't say Merkle did that."

When Merkle returned to his home at the close of the 1908 campaign, he was quoted as saying, "It's over and must be forgotten." True, it was over, but thoughtless fans would not let him forget. Vocal abuse followed him until he retired in 1927. He settled in Daytona Beach, Fla., bitter and uncommunicative to newspapermen who wished to interview him. Merkle avoided New York, the scene of his greatest travail, until 1950, when he accepted an invitation to attend an Old-Timers Day at the Polo Grounds. He received a warm greeting and enjoyed the festivities thoroughly, particularly a reunion with Larry Doyle, his roommate for 10 years.

"When I quit baseball," Merkle told reporters, "I said I was through with it forever. I stayed away from New York for 23 years and really meant it when I said I wasn't interested in even visiting here again. But it's strange how things work out. I never had such a good time."

Forty-two years after failing to touch second base, Merkle finally felt pardoned.

The Miracle Men of 1914

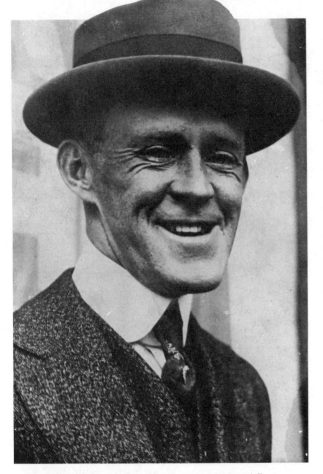

Johnny Evers arrived in Boston and helped fire up the Braves' pennant hopes.

George Stallings was the manager and architect of Boston's 1914 miracle.

Shortly after he was named manager of the Boston Braves late in the 1912 season but before he had taken active command, George Tweedy Stallings sat in the stands at the Polo Grounds watching the club that was about to become his lose yet another game to the New York Giants.

At Stallings' elbow sat James Gaffney, the Tammany politician who had changed the name of the team from Rustlers to Braves after gaining control of the franchise a short time before. Late in the game, Gaffney asked his new manager for an honest opinion of the players he was inheriting from Johnny Kling.

"This club is a baseball horror," replied Stallings, forthright as always.

Gaffney admired the candor. "Well, you're the boss," he said. "Make whatever changes you wish. We want a winner."

"I've been stuck with some terrible teams in my time," answered Stallings, "but this one beats 'em all."

The 1912 Braves finished in the National League cellar, 52 games behind the pennant-winning Giants. At that, they were an improvement over the 1911 team, which wound up 54 games back, and the 1909 aggregation, which finished 65½ games off the pace.

Stallings owned a long list of managerial credits when he accepted Gaffney's offer to lead the Braves. He directed several minor league clubs, winning a couple of pennants, in addition to major league teams in Detroit, Philadelphia and New York. His

Five of Boston's 1914 miracle workers were (left to right) Hank Gowdy, 27-game winner Dick Rudolph, George (Lefty) Tyler, Joe Connolly and Oscar Dugey.

most recent assignment in the big leagues had been from 1909-10 with the New York Highlanders, as the Big Apple's American League club was called back then. In 1910, the team was headed for a second-place finish when Stallings was dismissed late in the campaign and replaced by Hal Chase.

A native of Georgia, the swarthy Stallings had graduated from the Virginia Military Institute in 1886 and was studying medicine in Baltimore when he caught the eye of Harry Wright. "You're too good a player to be wasting your time in school," the manager of the Philadelphia Phillies told the young catcher, who abandoned Hippocrates in favor of the national pastime.

Wright's estimate of the young player's talents lacked pinpoint accuracy. Stallings spent most of his time in the minors and appeared in only seven major league games, collecting two hits in 20 at-bats before calling it a career as a player and turning his full attention to managing.

When Stallings was asked for the secret of his managerial success, he said simply, "Know the percentages." Few, if any, knew the percentages more intimately than or exercised them as flawlessly as Stallings.

The man they called "Chief" or "Big Daddy" also was a psychologist. At his plantation home, The Meadows, in Haddock, Ga., he was the epitome of Southern gentility. But in the dugout he was a dynamo, sliding endlessly up and down the bench, shouting profanities at the players, friend and foe,

as well as the umpires, whom he regarded as mortal enemies.

Stallings' favorite appellation for thoughtless players was "bonehead," a word he shrieked with fervor. Once he nodded toward catcher Hank Gowdy and shouted, "Go up there and hit, bonehead." In addition to Gowdy, five others reached for bats.

On another occasion, Stallings berated a pitcher who had walked several batters. "Go to the clubhouse," the Chief roared, "and burn your uniform." Disconsolately, the hurler slumped off the mound and disappeared into the clubhouse. Moments later, smoke was seen curling from the chimney. The pitcher had obeyed the manager's order literally, which George found hard to believe.

When Stallings was asked if he did not fear that his cruel tongue lashings would crush a player's spirit, he explained: "I go after players to find out if they're game. I've got no use for a player who isn't game. A game player fights back when bawled out, and that's what I like."

Bases on balls drove Stallings into uncontrollable fury. Perhaps the most popular anecdote associated with that abhorrence occurred when he visited a medical specialist in Georgia for a physical examination. At the conclusion of the checkup, the doctor allegedly remarked: "Mr. Stallings, you have an unusually bad heart. Is there any way you can account for this?"

Indeed, Stallings could, and did. "Bases on balls,

(profanity, obscenity, profanity) bases on balls," he seethed.

Rare was the player who took offense at Stallings' abusive manner. The athletes regarded the verbal tirades as the Chief's peculiar system for bringing out the best in them. With Stallings, purple prose "was an art," Gowdy observed years later with a reverential tone.

Herb Moran, an outfielder with the 1914 Braves, agreed with Gowdy. After Stallings left Boston and was managing Rochester several years later, he received a visit from Moran, who asked for a job with the International League club.

"We can't afford to pay you the money you'd want to play; we're not a major league club," Stallings told him.

"That's all right," Moran assured his old skipper. "Just give me a contract and I'll sign it. You fill in the figures with whatever you want to give me."

Next to his explosive temper, Stallings' most memorable trait was his superstitiousness. He turned apoplectic over scraps of paper on the field. Opposing players delighted in strolling by the Boston dugout, dropping confetti-sized bits as they passed.

If the Braves started a rally while Stallings was in a certain position, he held the stance until the inning ended. That habit often led to great physical discomfort. For instance, he was tying a shoe when Boston bats began to boom in one game. He remained in the hunched-over position until the rally ended six runs later, when some players helped him into an upright posture. On another occasion he was at the water cooler gazing toward the bullpen in the outfield when the Braves launched an outburst. Faithful to his policy, the Chief stood immobile while a coach described every pitch, every detail, for the next 15 minutes as the manager gazed intently at the distant fences.

Stallings regarded new clothes as a powerful good luck charm. Before the first game of the 1914 World Series against the Philadelphia Athletics, he purchased a new wardrobe, complete with a suit, shirt, underwear and socks. Following the Braves' victory in the opener at Philadelphia, the Chief removed his suit and handed it to his son. Then he took off his other garments, wrapped them in a tidy bundle and handed them to the younger Stallings. "Have the clothes washed and the suit pressed," he ordered. "Stay with them until they're finished and then bring 'em back here and lock 'em in the closet."

The process was repeated after each game until the Braves completed their stunning upset of the powerful A's. After the clincher, young Stallings asked if he should pay another visit to the laundry.

"No," his father answered. "Give the clothes a rest. They've done a pretty good job. But take a look at these pants."

Holding the trousers up to the light, the son could discern the pattern of the wallpaper through them. In less than a week, Stallings had slipped, slid and squirmed along the dugout bench so much that he had worn the trousers threadbare.

Stallings was as intelligent as he was superstitious. None of his peers could match him when it came to baseball strategy. As Tom Daly, a former major league catcher and coach, once said, "Stallings knew baseball as Einstein knows algebra."

For years before Stallings arrived in the majors, managers appreciated the advantages to be gained by having righthanded batters face lefthanded pitchers and vice versa. But Stallings made greater use of the principle than any previous manager. In 1914, he employed two sets of outfielders and alternated them against lefthanded and righthanded pitching. That platoon system provided maximum production from what undoubtedly was the weakest part of the Boston team.

Stallings also was the first—and probably the last—manager to flash signs with his teeth. His dark complexion provided an ideal contrast for his glistening white choppers, and baserunners knew instantly that the steal was on when they glanced into the dugout and beheld the boss with his lips parted.

Under Stallings' inspired leadership, the Braves finished fifth in the league in 1913, their highest standing in 11 years. Then, on the eve of the 1914 training season, George made a significant addition to the roster. He signed Johnny Evers, a spitfire second baseman who had been released as manager of the Chicago Cubs after one season, not because his club failed to win a pennant, but because it lost to the White Sox in the 1913 Chicago City Series. That egregious slip, according to Owner Charles Webb Murphy, cost the Cubs $60,000. It also enriched Evers by $25,000, the size of his bonus for signing a Boston contract.

Lightweight Johnny—he weighed about 130 pounds—was a top-notch player and a perfect complement for Stallings. Any player who blundered on the field was certain to receive a withering blast immediately from Evers and a second dressing-down from Stallings when he got to the bench.

"He'd make you want to punch him," shortstop Rabbit Maranville said years later, "but you knew Johnny was thinking only of the team."

The Braves spent far more time yelling at opponents than at each other. They were a noisy, profane bunch, spewing invectives in every direction. Stallings liked that attitude among his players, and he did not burden them with rules or curfews that would make their life styles off the field any different from their playing styles. The manager's only demand was that his hirelings report to the park in shape to play a couple of hours of top-flight baseball every day.

"Nobody but Stallings could have handled the 1914 Braves," Maranville said. "We had no rules except that we had to stay within the law, keep out of jail and be ready to play every day."

The Braves were always willing to back up their words with a flurry of fists. In one 1914 game with the Cubs, Evers tagged out Heinie Zimmerman on an attempted steal. Big Heinie took exception to the none-too-gentle whack on the head and came up swinging. Maranville rushed to the aid of his buddy and sent Zimmerman sprawling.

"I know who hit me," Zimmerman said as he picked himself off the ground. "It was Bert Whaling or Butch Schmidt."

Maranville draped an arm over the Cub's shoulder and walked him off the field. "I hit you," he informed Heinie.

"The hell you did," Zimmerman protested. "No

midget like you could give me a belt like that."

Next to Evers, Maranville was the most prominent regular in the Boston cast. He stood only 5-foot-5 and weighed 155 pounds. A native of Springfield, Mass., Rabbit joined the Braves in 1912, launching a major league career that spanned more than 20 years.

Behind the plate for the 1914 Braves crouched Gowdy, a native of Columbus, O. Hank seemed miscast with the rowdies on the team. His strongest epithets were "criminy sakes" and "holy cow."

By 1914, Maranville, Gowdy and pitchers George (Lefty) Tyler, Otto Hess and Hub Perdue were the only players to survive the housecleaning that Jim Gaffney advised when he handed the managerial reins to Stallings. Perdue, however, did not last long with the 1914 Braves. The righthander pitched in only nine games for Boston before being shipped to

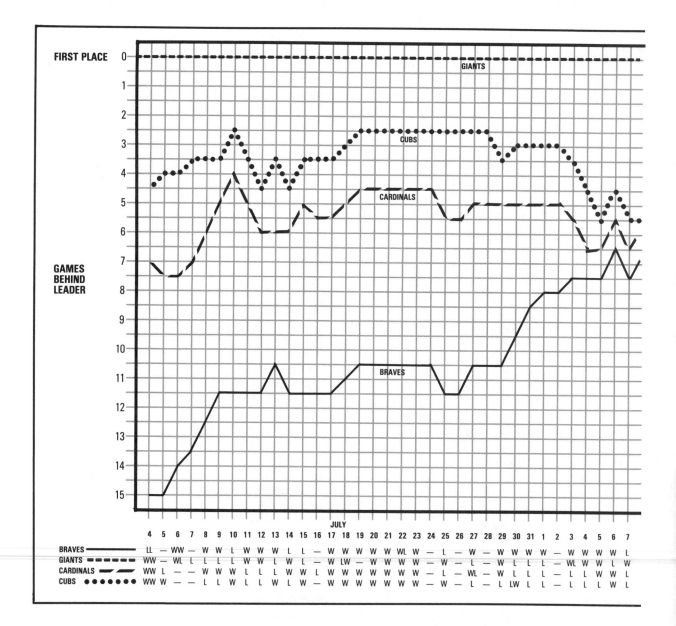

the St. Louis Cardinals. Tyler was coming off a 16-17 season in 1913, while Hess, another lefthander and a native of Switzerland, stuck with the club despite a 7-17 record in '13.

So, Evers was just one of several players added to the Boston roster after Stallings took over the Braves following the 1912 season. Other relative newcomers included outfielders Joe Connolly, Leslie Mann and Larry Gilbert, first baseman Charles (Butch) Schmidt, third baseman Charlie Deal and pitchers Bill James and Dick (Baldy) Rudolph.

James, a tall righthander from California, won only six games for the Braves as a 21-year-old rookie in 1913. But James progressed rapidly after overcoming his wildness. Rudolph, a native of New York City and a former star at Fordham, was a 5-9 righthander who had labored for six years for Toronto of the International League. He received a

couple of short tryouts with the New York Giants but was sent back to Toronto because Giants Manager John McGraw had heard reports that he was "a groove-ball pitcher." Rudolph compiled a 25-10 record for Toronto in 1912, only to discover that his contract for the next season contained a 25 percent pay cut, the result of the league directors establishing a salary limit. He threatened to quit the game and join his brother's law practice in protest, but the minor league club eliminated the need for negotiations by selling him to the Braves for $4,000. He won 14 games and lost 13 in 1913.

Stallings' initial impression of Rudolph was not favorable, but it improved quickly. Entering a game in relief, Dick walked the first batter to load the bases and ran the count to 3-and-0 on the next as the manager raged in the dugout. Then Rudolph fired three curves, striking out the batter, and Stall-

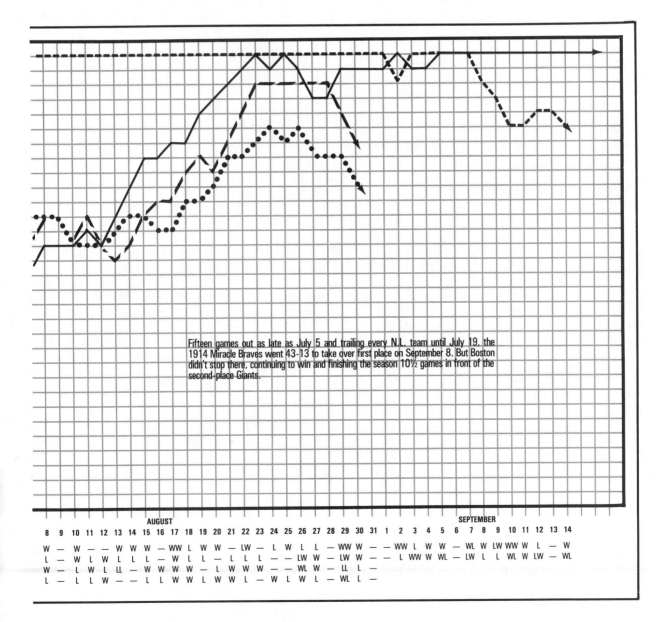

Fifteen games out as late as July 5 and trailing every N.L. team until July 19, the 1914 Miracle Braves went 43-13 to take over first place on September 8. But Boston didn't stop there, continuing to win and finishing the season 10½ games in front of the second-place Giants.

AUGUST — 8 9 10 11 12 13 14 15 16 17 18 19 20 21 22 23 24 25 26 27 28 29 30 31 **SEPTEMBER** 1 2 3 4 5 6 7 8 9 10 11 12 13 14

W — W — — W W W — WW L W W — LW — L W L L — WW W — — WW L W W — WL LW LW WW L L — W
L — W L W L L L — W L L — L L L — — LW W — LW W — — L WW W WL — LW L L WL W LW — WL
W — L W L LL — W W W W — L W W W — — WL W — LL L —
L — L L W — — LL WW L W W L — W L W L — WL L —

ings was ecstatic.

"He's got some guts," George roared. "He'll throw the curve in a pinch and get it over."

Stallings entertained no ambitions of a championship when the Braves gathered for the start of spring training at Macon, Ga., in 1914. His immediate goal, he said, was to reach the first division, a level that had eluded the club since 1902, when the team finished third. He predicted that the Giants, winners of three consecutive pennants, would furnish Boston its most formidable opposition, and in that he was correct.

The race started inauspiciously for the Braves. Lefty Tyler lost the opener at Brooklyn, 8-2, and the team dropped two more decisions before recording its first victory.

Thereafter, conditions grew steadily worse. Evers and Maranville were sick, leaving the middle of the infield severely weakened. Inclement weather contributed to other players' illnesses, and most of the pitchers were either sore-armed or excruciatingly wild.

Stallings was upset but remained relatively composed during the siege of misfortune. "The team

BRAVES' 1914 MILESTONES

Apr. 14   Braves lose, 8-2, at Brooklyn in season opener. After losing their first three games of the season, Boston finally wins its first game April 21.

July 4   Doubleheader loss to Dodgers gives Braves 26-40 record, putting them season-low 15 games behind league-leading Giants.

July 19   Boston rallies for three in ninth inning to beat Reds, 3-2, at Cincinnati. Victory gives Braves 36-43 record, moving them past Pirates into seventh place by percentage points, 10½ games behind Giants.

July 20   Tyler and James hold Pirates to four hits and Braves score game's only run in ninth inning, giving Boston 37-43 record and moving them past Dodgers into sixth place, 10½ games behind Giants.

July 21   Rudolph pitches three-hitter for Braves' second straight shutout, 6-0, at Pittsburgh. Triumph raises Boston to 38-43, moving Braves past Reds and Phillies into fourth place, 10½ games behind Giants.

Aug. 1   Braves reach .500 mark for first time in season (45-45) with 10-inning 4-3 triumph over St. Louis. Victory moves Boston to within eight games of Giants.

Aug. 6   Tenth-inning homer by Maranville beats Pittsburgh, 5-4, giving Braves ninth consecutive victory—their longest winning streak of season, putting them 6½ games behind Giants.

Aug. 10   Victory over Cincinnati moves Braves ahead of Cubs and Cardinals and into second place by percentage points. And except for August 11 when St. Louis moves ahead for one day, Braves remain in second place for next three weeks.

Aug. 23   While Braves have off-day, Giants lose to Cincinnati, putting Boston and New York into first-place tie with 59-48 records. During next two weeks Braves and Giants wrestle for lead with Braves taking first place to themselves briefly on September 2.

Sept. 8   Braves pass Giants and go into sole possession of first place for rest of season. Three-hitter by James over Giants gives Boston 69-53 record, one game ahead of New York.

Sept. 29   Braves clinch pennant with victory over Chicago while Giants lose to Pittsburgh. After day's activities, Braves have 88-56 record, nine games ahead of New York.

Oct. 6   Braves split doubleheader at Brooklyn while Giants split twin bill with Phillies to end season. Boston finishes regular season with 94-59 record, 10½ games in front of second-place Giants.

can't do anything right," he moaned. "I've never seen such bad luck. But don't think we're a tail-end club. It'll take us a month to get back in shape, but then we're going to be hard to beat."

The Braves won only four of their first 22 games and quickly settled into last place before they started to put victories back to back. Boston posted consecutive victories for the first time in 1914 on May 21 and 22 when Lefty Tyler beat the Cubs, 3-1, and Otto Hess shut them out, 2-0. A 2-1 loss to Chicago ended that short streak, but the Braves bounced back to win their next two games. Boston then resumed its hapless ways, losing nine of its next 13 contests.

The Braves started to show signs of life in mid-June. They won eight of nine games, including five in a row, to raise their record to 20-29. They finally vacated the basement when they beat the first-place Giants on June 25, but 24 hours later they were on the bottom again, where they remained for the next three weeks. About this time, Jim Gaffney revealed that the club was $40,000 in the red for the year and that if the team did not improve, he could lose $100,000 during the season.

On the Fourth of July, a portentous date for baseball oracles, the Braves lost a doubleheader to the Brooklyn Dodgers, dropping their record to 26 wins and 40 losses. As had been the case so many times already that season, both games were close. The Dodgers won the first game, 7-5, in 11 innings and captured the second contest by a 4-3 score. These games also were indicative of how hard the Braves were playing every day. In the opener, Joe Connolly was ejected for arguing over an umpire's call, and in the second game, the umpires had to step in to prevent a brawl after Tyler hit Brooklyn shortstop Ollie O'Mara on the back of the neck with a pitch. Then in the ninth inning, first baseman Jake Daubert scored the winning run for the Dodgers, but in so doing he was knocked unconscious when he collided with Hank Gowdy at the plate. It was evident that the Braves, who swept a doubleheader from the Dodgers two days later, were hanging tough.

That double triumph concluded a month-long home stand for the Braves. En route to Chicago, where they opened a lengthy western trip, Stallings' club stopped in Buffalo to play an exhibition game July 7. Evers always insisted it was against "a soap company team," although the actual opponent was the local International League club. Evers was on the right track, though, in recalling that the opponent should have been easy prey for the Braves. But on that day, Buffalo humiliated Boston, 10-2.

The embarrassing setback had a salutary effect on

Righthander Bill James, a member of Boston's crack pitching staff, won 26 games and compiled a 1.90 earned-run average.

the major leaguers. "No matter what the fans think," Gowdy later said, "no big-league club likes to lose to a minor league club, even if it is only an exhibition game. Maybe we were last, but we were still major leaguers, and the pasting we took was galling to our pride."

The Braves won seven of their first 10 games on the western swing, but on Sunday morning, July 19, they still languished in last place, 11 games behind the league-leading Giants. That date was to loom large in Braves history because that afternoon they defeated the Cincinnati Reds, 3-2, by scoring all their runs in the ninth inning. That victory, which was credited to Paul Strand in relief, pushed the Braves over the Pirates and into seventh place. Their next stop was Pittsburgh, where they ascended to fourth place by winning four of five games, all by shutouts. Tyler and Bill James collaborated on a 1-0 whitewashing in the first game at Forbes Field; Dick Rudolph won the second, 6-0, on a three-hitter; James the third, 1-0, and, after Pittsburgh won the second game of a doubleheader July 22, Tyler finished off the series by blanking the Pirates, 2-0.

The Braves returned to Boston on July 25, but their home stand got off to a worrisome start when Hess lost a 5-4 decision to Chicago. That setback dropped Boston to 40-45, 12 games behind the Giants, who had won six straight. But the Braves then reeled off nine straight victories to cut the gap to 6½ games.

On August 10, Bill James hurled the Braves to a 3-1 triumph over the Reds that lifted the club past Chicago (53-48) and St. Louis (54-49). Twenty-three days after vacating the cellar, the Braves were in second place with a 51-46 record. A 0-0, 13-inning tie and a rainout followed, so the Braves still trailed the Giants by 6½ games when they visited the Polo Grounds for a crucial three-game series starting August 13. If the Braves were to succeed in their mad dash upward, it was imperative that they win at least two of the contests against the Giants.

They did even better, sweeping the set. Rudolph beat Rube Marquard in the opener, 5-3, with the help of an 11-hit attack that included a triple by Maranville and a home run and a two-run single by Leslie Mann. Boston bats erupted for 11 hits again the next day, including a homer, double and single by Connolly, as James beat Jeff Tesreau, 7-3.

The final game evolved into a mound duel between Tyler and Christy Mathewson. The game was scoreless until the top of the 10th inning, when the Braves pushed over two runs on Gowdy's run-scoring triple and a wild pitch by Mathewson. The Giants loaded the bases with none out in the last half of the frame, but Tyler slammed the door and preserved the shutout.

The Braves were still in second place when they left New York, but the Giants' lead was trimmed to

3½ games and momentum was in Boston's favor. Even Stallings, who was not known for boasting, acknowledged that his club's prospects were good. A headline in the August 20 issue of The Sporting News reported: "Stallings Breaks Silence and Admits He Has Chance/Tells Braves It's Up to Them/He Thinks Giants Out of Race."

By that time, so did the baseball fans in Boston. A.H.C. Mitchell, a Boston baseball correspondent, reported in the August 22 issue of Sporting Life that the Braves' surge had "turned Boston daffy. There was a remarkable demonstration up at Fenway Park, the home of the Red Sox, on Saturday when the scoreboard showed that the Braves had defeated the Giants three straight games. The cheering lasted for five minutes and the battle between the Red Sox and the New Yorks, which was in progress at the time, was for the moment forgotten. . . . The way things look to the local followers at this writing is that the Braves will win the pennant."

Mitchell then gave this analysis of the team's performance to date: "The fine pitching of Rudolph, James and Tyler, who have been worked in turn almost continually since the middle of July, has been a great factor in the present position of the men under Stallings. But aside from pitching, the fielding has been airtight. In fact, the defense has been almost perfect. It is true that the team has not been hitting like a flock of Ty Cobbs, but the boys seem to have the punch in the close games."

Finally, the writer credited Stallings with the team's recent success: "He is the man who has kept the players gingered up and instilled the fighting spirit in them until they caught the fighting fever and now they are fighters from way back. . . . The present success of the Braves only goes to show what intelligent management can do."

As Stallings continued to scream from the dugout and Evers kept his teammates alert on the field, the Big Three of the mound staff—Rudolph, James and Tyler—rolled relentlessly on. Nearly every game produced an impressive pitching performance by one of the trio. On August 17, Rudolph defeated the Reds, 11-1, and James won the second game of the twin bill, 5-3. After Dick Crutcher lost a 3-1 decision to the Reds the next day, Tyler pitched a 3-2 victory over Cincinnati on August 19. Other pitchers made occasional starts, but the bulk of the work —and the winning—went to Rudolph, James and Tyler.

After Boston's sweep of New York, the Braves won five of their next seven games. Meanwhile, the Giants won one contest before losing six straight. New York's fifth defeat in that skid allowed the Braves to tie the Giants for first place August 23. New York's 3-2 loss at Cincinnati while Boston was idle gave the Giants a 59-48 record, the same as the Braves.

Rooftop seats overlooking the fence at Philadelphia's Shibe Park were going
for 25 cents when the Braves and A's locked horns in the 1914 World Series.

Ironically, the Cincinnati player who delivered the game-winning hit for the Reds was about to become a Brave. Outfielder Herb Moran, who drove home Cincinnati's third run with a ninth-inning double, was playing his last game for the Reds before being sold to Boston.

Moran was the last of several players Stallings acquired during the 1914 season. In June, Stallings had beefed up his outfield corps by sending Hub Perdue to the Cardinals for Ted Cather and Possum Whitted. Then in July, Stallings had dealt reserve infielder Jack Martin to the Philadelphia Phillies for another outfielder, Josh Devore. And earlier in August, third baseman Red Smith's contract had been purchased from Brooklyn. Stallings utilized all of the new outfielders in various platoon situations, and Smith replaced Charlie Deal, a light hitter, as the regular third baseman. These new acquisitions completed Stallings' overhaul of the club

and gave the Braves the boost they needed to rise from last place to first in five weeks.

The heady atmosphere of first place endured for only one day. A 9-5 setback at Chicago on August 24 tumbled the Braves into the second spot, and they later fell to third before stopping the plunge.

When the Braves returned to Boston at the close of a trip that netted 16 wins in 22 games, they were once more in a dead heat with the Giants (67-52) for the top berth. As luck would have it, their first opponent at the start of a lengthy home stand was New York.

To heighten the delirium that was sweeping the city, the September 7 doubleheader, consisting of morning and afternoon games, was to be played at Fenway Park, which had a seating capacity of about 32,000, or almost three times that of the Braves' South End Grounds. In a neighborly gesture, Owner Joe Lannin of the A.L. club had suggested

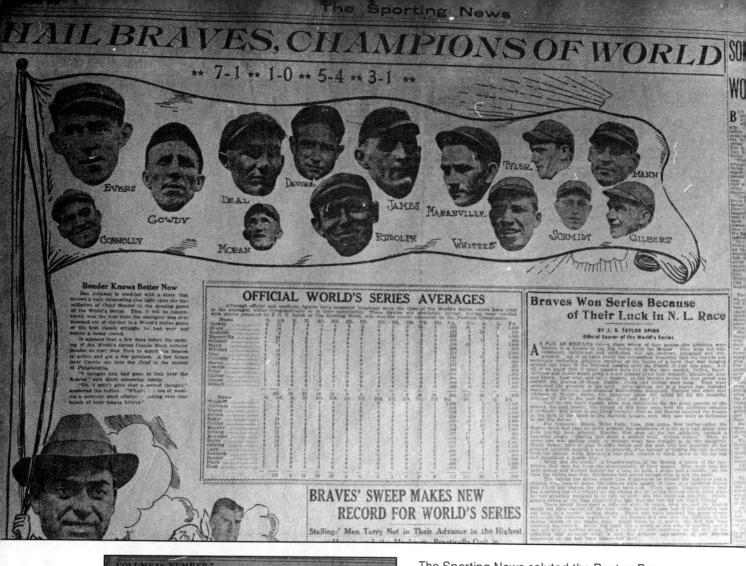

The Sporting News saluted the Boston Braves as the "Champions of the World" (above) in its October 22, 1914, issue, one week after calling Manager George Stallings the "Miracle Man of Base Ball" (left).

that the Braves play at Fenway for the remainder of the season, an offer that Jim Gaffney accepted gladly.

From a baseball spectator's standpoint, there never was a day in Boston to equal the turnout of the Labor Day twin bill in 1914. The total attendance for the two contests was announced at 74,162, with about 36,000 at the morning game.

Entering the last half of the ninth inning of the opener, the Giants held a 4-3 lead as Christy Mathewson was outpitching Dick Rudolph. Suddenly, despair turned into jubilation for Boston fans. With one out, pinch-hitter Josh Devore, a former Giant, beat out an infield single. Herb Moran then doubled into the crowd ringing the outfield.

Evers was next. When he was with the Cubs, the Trojan was a constant thorn in Matty's side. In a 1908 game against Christy's Giants, Evers had precipitated the event that forever labeled poor Fred Merkle as "Bonehead." Six years later, Big Six faced Evers again, and once more Johnny triumphed. He slapped a liner to left field on which George Burns attempted a shoestring catch. The ball fell for a hit and the tying and winning runs scampered across the plate.

Mass hysteria engulfed Fenway Park. Boston players had to battle their way to the clubhouse, and Stallings was penned in the dugout for 10 minutes by fans who wished to celebrate the home team's sole possession of first place.

The afternoon crowd was treated less handsomely. Tesreau outpitched Tyler, 10-1, in a game that involved Boston Mayor James Curley.

During a four-run sixth inning, outfielder Fred Snodgrass of the Giants narrowly avoided a bean-ball, then stuck his sleeve in the path of a pitch and was awarded first base. As he danced triumphantly down the base line, Snodgrass thumbed his nose at Tyler. The pitcher might have rushed to first base and enticed the runner to fight, but he had a better idea. Instead, Lefty pantomimed Snodgrass' igno-minious muff in the 1912 World Series. The score appeared settled.

But when Snodgrass returned to his spot in cen-ter field at the end of that half inning, the Boston crowd booed mercilessly. Snodgrass responded by making none-too-kindly gestures at the fans. That brought forth a shower of pop bottles upon Snod-grass.

Curley finally decided he had seen enough. Leap-ing from his box seat, Hizzoner demanded of a po-lice lieutenant and umpire Bob Emslie that Snod-grass be ejected from the game. The mayor, who was accustomed to winning at the polls, was outvot-ed on this issue, two to one.

While Curley was worried about Snodgrass incit-ing a riot, John McGraw was concerned that his outfielder would become a casualty of the poten-tially explosive situation. To protect his player, the manager removed Snodgrass from the game and peace was restored. Snodgrass watched from the bench as the Giants regained a tie for first place.

The deciding game of the series was played the next day. A much smaller crowd was on hand to watch Bill James hurl a three-hitter and win, 8-3, shoving the Giants back into second place.

After the Giants left town, the Phillies arrived for a doubleheader September 9. The result of the first game was not unexpected as Grover Cleveland Al-exander whipped the Braves, 10-3, for one of his 27 wins that year. The nightcap, however, produced a startling surprise. George Davis, a Harvard Law School student who had been released by the New York Highlanders two years before, allegedly be-cause he was "too independent," hurled a 7-0 no-hitter in which he allowed five walks. Two other Philadelphia batters reached base on errors. The righthander walked the first three batters in the first inning before fanning catcher Ed Burns and forcing pinch-hitter Gavvy Cravath to hit into a double play. The hitless gem was one of only three victories by Davis in 1914 and one of seven in his abbreviated major league career.

The Miracle Braves accelerated their pace in the following weeks and clinched the pennant Septem-ber 29 when righthander Tom Hughes, making his first start for Boston, defeated the Cubs, 3-2, on a five-hitter. The Braves finished with a 94-59 record, 10½ games ahead of the fading Giants. Going back to July 4, when the Giants boasted a 15-game advan-tage over the Braves, Boston thereafter gained 25½

games in just over half a season. After their 26-40 start, the Braves went 68-19 the rest of the way. To top off their remarkable climb, the Braves swept Connie Mack's A's in the World Series.

The flag formula of the Braves, who ranked fourth in the league in hitting and third in fielding, was based on extraordinary pitching and the per-centages that Stallings swore by.

Stallings' three-man rotation was superb. James, Rudolph and Tyler were credited with 69 of the Braves' 94 victories, while the rest of the Boston staff combined for a 25-28 record. James won 26 games, including 19 of his last 20 decisions, lost seven and fashioned an earned-run average of 1.90. His 30 complete games and 332 innings pitched ranked third in the league. Those numbers were bettered slightly by Rudolph, who hurled 336 in-nings and 31 complete games. Rudolph posted 12 straight victories at one stretch en route to a 27-10 record and 2.36 ERA. Among his wins were six shutouts, all registered after July 4. Tyler was 16-14 with five shutouts and a 2.69 ERA.

Offensively, Connolly (.306) and Red Smith (.314 with Boston) were the team's only .300 hitters. Butch Schmidt batted .285, Evers .279; Ted Cather hit .297 after being obtained from St. Louis.

Fittingly, a member of the Braves was named the league's Most Valuable Player. Evers edged Maran-ville and was presented a Chalmers car. Many ar-gued that Rabbit was more deserving of the honor, but Maranville demurred, insisting that "I don't care who won it as long as it was one of our boys."

If a Most Valuable Person award had been avail-able, George Stallings would have won, hands down. He was lauded far and wide for sparking a last-place team to the pennant and was known for-evermore as the "Miracle Man."

That designation endured despite Stallings' lack of success as a major league skipper after the 1914 season. He managed the Braves through the 1920 campaign but never recaptured his magic touch. The Braves finished second to the Phillies, seven games back, in 1915 and were four lengths off the pace in 1916, when they came in third. The club got progressively worse after that, never finishing higher than sixth.

But those weak seasons did nothing to detract from Stallings' revered status among the manageri-al elite. Long after Stallings' death in 1929, his play-ers recalled the real reason for the incredible success of the 1914 Miracle Braves.

"We belonged in eighth place when we were there," Tyler said, "and without Stallings, we be-longed there at the end of the season."

Gowdy agreed. "We didn't belong where we fin-ished—except for one thing," he said. "We were a great team. Not great players, except for great pitch-ers. George made us a great team."

A Yankee Star Rises

Ordinarily, tears of regret do not flow freely after a baseball team wins its fifth game in a row. But the circumstances were most unusual on July 24, 1978, when Billy Martin, sobbing and in a highly nervous state, resigned as manager of the New York Yankees.

The Yanks, who had been preseason favorites to capture their third consecutive American League East title, started sluggishly. Except for Ron Guidry, who won virtually every time he took the mound, the Yankees' pitching was inconsistent. Jim (Catfish) Hunter and Ed Figueroa, in particular, lagged behind expectations. Hunter, who had received a reported $2.85 million to sign as a free agent a few years earlier, had a 2-3 record at the All-Star break and was awaiting the recuperation of his sore right shoulder, which had put him on the disabled list twice already that year. Figueroa, whose record was 7-6 at the midway point, was streaky, and ace reliever Rich (Goose) Gossage already had been tagged with eight losses. In all, 11 pitchers had started games for the defending World Series champions in the first half of the season.

Moreover, the club was wracked with a turbulence that would not abate. The center of the storm, not too surprisingly, was Martin himself. His chief adversary was outfielder Reggie Jackson, as volatile and outspoken as his skipper. The slugger's chief gripes were being dropped from the cleanup spot in the order and being taken out of right field for use as a designated hitter, a role he detested.

The flame of their hostility was fanned during an extra-inning game in which Jackson ignored a sign from the dugout. Initially, Martin's order—flashed through third base coach Dick Howser—was to sacrifice with no outs and a runner on first. But when Martin saw the infielders creeping in, he flashed the hit-away sign. Reggie understood the sign but chose to ignore it. He continued to bunt and eventually popped out, an infraction that was followed by a five-day suspension and fine.

In itself, the Jackson episode was sufficient to fray the nerves of any manager. But on top of that, Billy had to contend with daily harassment from George Steinbrenner. As was his practice and privilege, the club owner injected himself into the daily operations of the team on the field. That practice led to frequent blasts in the New York press against vari-

Subdued Yankee Manager Billy Martin discusses the 1978 suspension handed to slugger Reggie Jackson as General Manager Cedric Tallis looks on.

ous personalities associated with the team. Martin replied to his boss in kind and an impossible situation grew infinitely worse. The solution to the problem, Billy concluded, was regular visits to bars and cocktail lounges, where he could forget Steinbrenner as well as the fact that he was in the process of losing 20 pounds.

After being swept by Kansas City at Yankee Stadium in a three-game series that ended July 17, the Yankees were in fourth place, five games over .500 but 14 games behind the Boston Red Sox, who were sweeping aside all opposition with astonishing ease. There was a strong temptation to write off the season as a Yankee flop until a pair of shutouts in Minnesota and three convincing victories in Chicago revived flickering hopes.

Despite the five-game winning streak, which brought the Yanks to within 10 games of the Red Sox, the turmoil with Jackson and Steinbrenner persisted. Martin's frame of mind improved considerably during Jackson's absence, but the return of the wayward hireling before the last game in Chicago quickly put Martin in a bad humor. The manag-

er also was annoyed by all the media attention surrounding Jackson's return as well as some of the remarks the slugger had made to reporters.

Billy was not one to sidestep an issue if he could meet it head-on. He was at the Chicago airport, preparing to board a team plane to Kansas City, when he directed a conversation with reporters to his favorite sparring partners.

"The two of them deserve each other," Billy blurted. "One's a born liar; the other's convicted."

The latter accusation referred to Steinbrenner's conviction for making illegal contributions to a political campaign a few years before.

Hours later, Billy's comment was relayed to Steinbrenner and, through the newspapers, to much of the nation. Early the next afternoon, he had two visitors at the team's headquarters in the Crown Center Hotel in Kansas City. They were Al Rosen, the club president, and Cedric Tallis, the general manager. Rosen made the trip from New York, he said, "to talk with Billy head-to-head, to find out just what he said and in what frame of mind he said it."

For two hours, Rosen, Tallis and Martin engaged in a phone conversation with Steinbrenner at his summer home in Tampa. At no time, the executives reported, was Billy pressured to resign. But later

that afternoon, Martin read a prepared statement to reporters in the hotel lobby. The manager, wearing sunglasses, expressed his sentiments between sobs.

"I owe it to my health and mental well-being to resign at this time," he said, "and I am very sorry that there were things written about George Steinbrenner. He did not deserve them, nor did I say them. George and I have had our differences, and in most cases we have been able to resolve them. I want to thank the Yankee office management, the press and the news media, the coaches and the players, and. . . ."

At that point, Martin broke down in tears. He did not complete his statement and he refused to answer questions.

Howser was on the bench as interim manager that night when the Yanks bowed to the Royals, 5-2, but the next night, when Guidry posted his 15th win in 16 decisions, Bob Lemon was on duty as the full-time pilot. Lemon, for many years a pitching mainstay of the Cleveland Indians, had been fired as manager of the Chicago White Sox less than one month before.

The Billy Martin saga of 1978 might have terminated in Kansas City. Relieved of managerial pressure, he could recover at his leisure, content in the knowledge that the club would honor his contract, which was valued at about $90,000 annually, through 1979. But one more chapter was yet to be written in that saga. The date was July 29, the place Yankee Stadium, where the Yankees held their annual Old-Timers Day. As per tradition, a goodly crowd turned out to pay homage to their idols of a bygone era.

Nostalgia was the theme of the day, but there was a tint of rancor, too. Around the stadium, fans displayed banners, the thrust of which was "Bring Back Billy," the hard-bitten kid who had risen from the sandlots of Oakland to become a key component of championship Yankee teams as a second baseman and manager.

But Billy Martin wasn't in sight. He had dropped from view five days before and, perhaps, was relaxing at this very moment, reflecting on happier days when he was a teammate of Joe DiMaggio, Mickey Mantle and Whitey Ford, all of whom were accorded thunderous applause from the assembled masses.

In the cool of the dugout, Lemon watched the unfolding drama. Years before, in this same arena, he had pitched his heart out for the Indians, trying to muffle cheers such as those that were now billowing from more than 46,000 throats.

Finally, the last old-timer, as announced by the club, was introduced and the spectators settled back in anticipation of the game between the Yankees and the Minnesota Twins. As the fans speculated on the prospects for victory on this auspicious occa-

Yankee Manager Billy Martin was sobbing and in a highly nervous state on July 24, 1978, when he resigned in Kansas City.

But Martin was back on top of the world five days later when he was introduced at Yankee Stadium as the Yanks' 1980 manager.

sion, the public address announcer broke in.

"Ladies and gentlemen, your attention, please," began Bob Sheppard, his sonorous tones reverberating through the stadium. "The Yankees announce today that Bob Lemon has agreed to a contract to continue as manager of the Yankees through the 1978 and 1979 seasons. . . ."

A chorus of boos from the Billy Martin camp interrupted the announcement.

Sheppard tried again. "Your attention to the rest of this announcement," he said. "In 1980, Bob Lemon will become the general manager of the Yankees . . . and the Yankees would like to announce at this time . . . introduce and announce at the same moment, that the manager for the 1980 season, and hopefully for many years after that, will be Number One. . . ."

Nobody heard the rest of the announcement. There was only one person who answered to the description of "Number One," and he was trotting onto the field, waving his cap to the throng of admirers who were screaming their allegiance.

Alfred Manuel (Billy) Martin would return. The fans would wait. In the meantime, two months of the season remained, 62 games in which the Yanks could try to erase the gap, which then stood at eight games, between them and the Red Sox.

To the exultation created by the Martin announcement was added the jubilation of a Yankee victory over the Twins. Ken Clay, another member of New York's crippled pitching staff, won his second game of the year, 7-3, coasting behind a 13-hit attack that included two hits apiece by Jackson, outfielder Mickey Rivers, catcher-outfielder Thurman Munson, third baseman Graig Nettles and infielder Fred Stanley.

Lemon's influence upon the mood of the Yankees was immediate. Tranquility begat proficiency. Figueroa, who had been feuding with Martin about his place in the rotation, began to win with regularity. Hunter once more resembled the pitcher who had won 20-plus games in five consecutive seasons (1971-75) with Oakland and New York.

Under Lemon's dispassionate leadership, the

Yankees moved upward. They took over third place after beating the Twins on July 30. Next, they leaped over Milwaukee into second with an August 9 victory—their fourth straight—over the Brewers. Though two more triumphs followed, progress thereafter was exasperatingly slow. The Red Sox refused to buckle, as might have been expected when pursued by a team that won 10 of 12 games in one stretch and 16 of 18 in another.

Then injuries to key players—center fielder Fred Lynn, outfielder-first baseman Carl Yastrzemski, second baseman Jerry Remy, right fielder Dwight Evans and shortstop Rick Burleson—dealt a staggering blow to the Red Sox. When the teams met in Boston for the start of a four-game series September 7, only four games separated the hunted from the hunter.

Mike Torrez was Red Sox Manager Don Zimmer's choice to halt the Yankees' charge. But the big righthander, who had won two games for the Yankees in their 1977 World Series conquest over the Los Angeles Dodgers, was no puzzle for New York. Tagged for two runs in the first inning, Torrez departed without retiring a batter in the second when the Yanks combined five singles and a walk for three more runs. To the disgust of 34,119 onlookers, the bombardment continued in the third inning with another two tallies. The Yankees added five more runs in the fourth, which featured a double by second baseman Willie Randolph, who drove in five runs during the 21-hit, 15-3 runaway. Unfortunately for Hunter, the New York starter, he was not around long enough to gain credit for the victory. A groin strain forced Catfish out of action in the fourth inning, and Clay picked up the easy victory.

With the Boston lead slimmed to three lengths, Jim Wright was asked to block the New York stampede in the second game of the series. The 27-year-old righthander fared no better than Torrez had the day before, although he was not entirely to blame. Two first-inning errors—the Red Sox committed seven in the game—helped the Yankees to two runs. Eleven Yanks paraded to the plate in the second stanza and six scored, including three on a home run by Jackson. Outfielder Lou Piniella's homer highlighted a two-run outburst in the fifth, and the Yankees widened their lead to 11-0 with a single tally in the sixth, by which time many of the 33,134 disheartened fans were filing out of the park. Righthander Jim Beattie held the Red Sox scoreless until an error opened the gates for two unearned runs in the ninth, though that hardly mattered. The 13-2 romp whittled the New York deficit to two games.

Disaster followed disaster in the third game, played before 33,611 stunned fans September 9. The home team reduced its miscues from seven to two,

Bob Lemon was Yankee Owner George Steinbrenner's choice to take over the team's sinking ship in 1978.

but the improvement failed to avert a 7-0 whipping. Dennis Eckersley, who already had posted 16 wins in his first season after being obtained from Cleveland, held off the Yankee sluggers for three innings. The righthander retired two batters in the fourth and the bases were bare when the dam broke. First baseman Chris Chambliss touched off the explosion with a double. Zimmer then ordered Eckersley to give Nettles an intentional pass, which immediately proved unwise as Piniella cracked a wind-blown double, good for one run.

Undeterred by the failure of his earlier strategy, Zimmer ordered another intentional walk, this time to outfielder Roy White. Again, it was the wrong move. Shortstop Bucky Dent and Rivers promptly laced two-run singles, and a walk, a wild pitch, a single by Munson and a passed ball produced the final two runs in the inning and the game.

The total Boston attack against Guidry consisted of first-inning singles by Burleson and outfielder Jim Rice. The shutout was the seventh in 21 wins for Guidry, who thereby completed the cycle of victories against all A.L. teams in one season and became the first lefthander to hurl a shutout at Fen-

The 1978 campaign was made special by the Cy Young efforts of lefthander Ron Guidry, who dazzled baseball with a 25-3 record.

way Park since 1974.

Bobby Sprowl, a 22-year-old lefthander lately of Bristol (Eastern) and Pawtucket (International), was given the unenviable job of halting the New York juggernaut in the series finale. The youngster lasted only two-thirds of an inning, during which time he walked four batters and gave up one hit and was charged with three runs. Two more runs in the second, one in the fourth and another in the seventh—the last driven in by Dent with his third hit of the day—were more than enough for the Yankees' 7-4 triumph, which completed the series sweep and destroyed the last reminder of Boston's once-commanding 14-game lead over New York. The victory went to Figueroa, a righthander who, before the close of the campaign, would become the first Puerto Rican pitcher to post 20 victories in a single season. Gossage notched his 23rd save.

Mercifully for the Red Sox, who had beaten New York in nine of their 11 previous contests at Fenway Park before this series, there was not a fifth game. In four contests, the Yankees mutilated Bos-

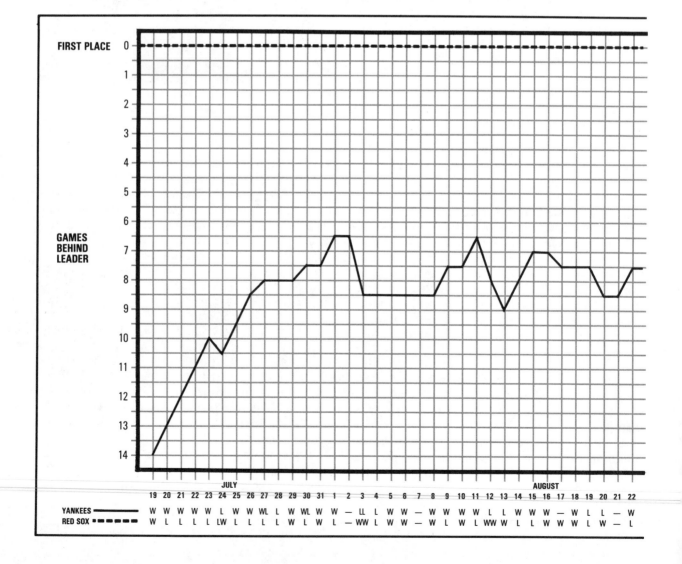

ton pitchers with 67 hits and 42 runs, while the Red Sox collected only 21 hits and nine runs. It was, undoubtedly, a modern-day Boston Massacre, circa 1978.

"They caught us at our lowest ebb," Red Sox catcher Carlton Fisk later reflected. "We were hurting, and our pitching was not consistent. But it probably didn't matter because they were playing such great ball that nobody was going to beat them."

All hope for the Red Sox did not die, however, when the last batter was retired in Boston. "It's now a 20-game season" became a popular observation after the contenders parted company with identical records of 86-56.

Four days passed, during which the Yankees moved in front by 1½ games, before the antagonists renewed their rivalry at Yankee Stadium. Guidry, who had spun a two-hitter six days earlier in Boston, repeated his effort on his home turf in the September 15 opener of the three-game series. A double by Burleson in the third inning and a single by

With the Red Sox well in front of the Blue Jays on the final day of the season, pitcher Mike Torrez suddenly became a Cleveland Indians fan.

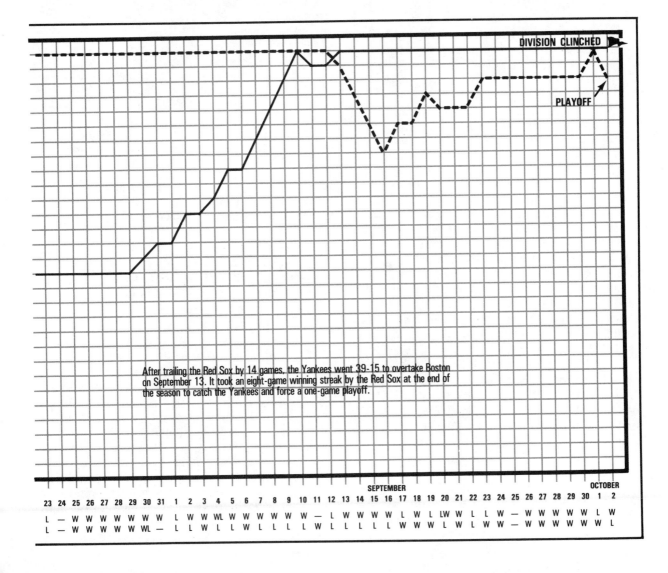

After trailing the Red Sox by 14 games, the Yankees went 39-15 to overtake Boston on September 13. It took an eight-game winning streak by the Red Sox at the end of the season to catch the Yankees and force a one-game playoff.

DIVISION CLINCHED

PLAYOFF

SEPTEMBER

OCTOBER

23	24	25	26	27	28	29	30	31	1	2	3	4	5	6	7	8	9	10	11	12	13	14	15	16	17	18	19	20	21	22	23	24	25	26	27	28	29	30	1	2
L	—	W	W	W	W	W	W	W	L	W	W	WL	W	W	W	W	W	W	W	—	L	W	W	W	W	L	W	L	LW	W	L	L	W	—	W	W	W	W	L	W
L	—	W	W	W	W	W	WL	—	L	L	W	L	L	W	L	L	L	L	L	W	L	L	L	L	L	L	W	W	W	L	W	L	W	W	—	W	W	W	W	W	L

Boston slugger Carl Yastrzemski was optimistic
after touching Ron Guidry for a second-inning
playoff home run.

Yankee slugger Reggie Jackson was ecstatic
after delivering a home run that helped his team
to a pennant-winning 5-4 victory.

Lynn in the seventh constituted the entire Boston
attack.

The Yankees tagged Luis Tiant and Andy Hassler
for seven hits, but they concentrated four of them
in the fourth inning, when they scored all their
runs in a 4-0 victory. Rivers and Randolph ignited
the uprising with singles. When Piniella grounded
into a double play, Yastrzemski, seeing Rivers make
a wide turn at third base, fired across the diamond
in an effort to complete a triple play. The throw
was wild, however, and Rivers sprinted home with
the first run of the game. A walk to Jackson and
consecutive homers by Chambliss and Nettles followed, much to the delight of 54,901 patrons.

A crowd of 55,091 was on hand the next afternoon when Hunter hooked up with Torrez. Boston
jumped out to a 2-0 lead in the first inning when
Remy singled and Rice clouted a home run, but
Jackson singled home a run in the bottom of the
first and slugged a solo homer in the fifth to tie the
score. The Yanks then pulled out a 3-2 triumph in
the ninth. Rivers led off with a triple and, one out
later, Munson stroked a sacrifice fly to right field.
The victory, which inflated the Yanks' lead to 3½

games, was their 20th in 23 tries; the loss was Boston's 11th in 13 games.

Attendance exceeded 55,000 again September 17
for the series finale, matching Eckersley and Beattie.
After six consecutive losses to New York, the Red
Sox finally emerged victorious. Eckersley and reliever Bob Stanley allowed only four hits and the
Red Sox rapped 11 in a 7-3 triumph. The Boston
attack featured a home run and a run-scoring single
by Yastrzemski and a run-scoring double by first
baseman George Scott, who had been in a 0-for-36
slump. With 14 games remaining for New York and
13 for Boston, the Yankee edge was 2½ lengths.

In the six days that followed the series in Gotham, the Yankees, finally cooling down, lost four of
seven decisions, while the Red Sox won four of six
to whittle the gap to one game. On September 24,
both clubs played their last road game of the season. Guidry hurled his ninth shutout of the year to
lead the Yanks to a 4-0 victory, but the Red Sox
stayed one game behind by beating Toronto, 7-6.
An open date the next day gave players on both
teams a chance to catch their breath before making
their last charge for the division title. New York

Boston Manager Don Zimmer sat dejectedly after the Red Sox's playoff loss, contemplating what might have been.

faced three-game series with Toronto and Cleveland, while Boston would host Detroit and Toronto for three games each.

Neither team was willing to give an inch. The Red Sox swept the Tigers and then closed out the month of September by taking the first two games from the Blue Jays. The Yankees, meanwhile, swept the Blue Jays and won their first two games against the Indians. As a result, New York still had a one-game lead heading into the decisive season finale for both clubs. With all the marbles perched on the 162nd game of the year, the Red Sox had only one hope to stay alive: They had to beat Toronto on October 1 while the Yanks had to lose to Cleveland. Such an occurrence would give both clubs identical 99-63 records, thus requiring a one-game playoff to determine the divisional champion.

And that's exactly what happened. Allowing only two hits, Tiant blanked the Blue Jays, 5-0, while Rick Waits yielded only five Yankee hits in a 9-2 Cleveland victory. By winning eight consecutive games and 12 of their last 14, the Red Sox caught the Yankees at the wire, forcing the league's first title playoff since 1948. The one-game showdown

was played October 2 at Fenway Park where, 30 years before, player-Manager Lou Boudreau had led the Indians to triumph, spoiling Boston's pennant dreams. Another shortstop, but hardly of Boudreau's hitting stature, played the same role in 1978.

Russell Earl (Bucky) Dent was a 26-year-old Georgian who had batted above .300 only once in his professional career, and then in only 22 games as a rookie in the Gulf Coast League. In 1978, when he spent three weeks on the disabled list, the shortstop batted .243 in 123 games. With only four home runs to his credit so far that year (and 22 in a six-year major league career), Dent was not a long-ball threat. The names Jackson, Munson, Nettles, Chambliss and Piniella—not to mention Guidry, who would be dueling with Torrez in the playoff game—were of more concern to the 32,925 fans at Fenway than the name of a light-hitting shortstop who occupied the ninth spot in the lineup.

The Red Sox appeared to be headed for another ugly home-field encounter with the Yankees when Torrez, a 16-game winner that season, opened the contest by walking Rivers on four pitches. The center fielder promptly stole second on the first pitch to Munson. He advanced no farther, however, as Torrez fanned the Yankee catcher and retired Piniella on a bouncer to third and Jackson on a fly to left field.

Guidry, shutout master of the Red Sox in his last two opportunities, finally was touched for a run when Yastrzemski cleared the right-field wall for a homer that gave the Red Sox a 1-0 lead in the second inning. A leadoff double by Scott in the third hinted at further scoring, but after the runner was sacrificed to third, Guidry retired Burleson on an infield grounder and Remy on an outfield fly.

The Yankees, who registered their first hit—a two-out double by Rivers—in the third inning, threatened again in the fourth when Piniella led off with an infield single. Torrez quashed that threat, however, by disposing of Jackson, Nettles and Chambliss in order.

The Red Sox increased their advantage in the sixth. Burleson opened with a double and was sacrificed to third. That brought up Rice, the league leader in hits, triples, home runs and runs batted in, face to face with Guidry, the circuit's most formidable hurler at 24-3. This time Rice was the victor. He laced a single to center for his 139th RBI of the year, giving the Red Sox a 2-0 lead.

Torrez, meanwhile, was keeping the Yanks at bay, allowing only two hits in the first six innings. The righthander was at his compelling best in the sixth, when he fanned Munson for the third time, got Piniella on a fly to center field and retired Jackson on a grounder to second.

Just when Torrez appeared at his strongest, how-

Bucky Dent is greeted by Yankee teammates Roy White (6) and Chris Chambliss after shocking the Red Sox with a three-run playoff homer.

ever, his mastery deserted him. One was out in the seventh when Chambliss and White singled. Jim Spencer accounted for the second out when, as a pinch-hitter for second baseman Brian Doyle, he hit an outfield fly.

Under ordinary circumstances, Lemon would have called on another substitute batter for the ninth man in the order. But with his supply of middle infielders running low (Randolph was injured), the manager let Dent bat against the hard-throwing Torrez. It wasn't an ideal situation for the Yankees, but Lemon decided to let Dent cut loose and hope

for the best.

In a box alongside the Yankee dugout, a couple of Yankee executives surveyed the situation with perhaps a little less doubt than Lemon. One was Steinbrenner, who had given Bucky a pep talk just the night before. The other was Rosen. "He's gonna hit one out," the club president said to the Yanks' owner.

As the executives looked on, Dent fouled Torrez's second pitch off his foot. In pain, he hobbled toward the dugout. An injured shortstop was all that Lemon needed to complete his day. But Bucky's

Slugger Reggie Jackson exchanges a hand slap with Yankee Owner George
Steinbrenner after hitting his eighth-inning playoff home run.

pain was not disabling; some pain-killing spray was administered, and a new bat was produced to replace the one he had cracked on the previous pitch.

Back in the batter's box, Dent swung at Torrez's third pitch and made contact. The ball arched toward left field. At worst, thought Torrez, it was a double off the wall. In most other parks it would be a routine fly ball.

But this was Boston, and the Green Monster once again spewed its venom on its longtime tenants. Lifted by a wind that had reversed its direction several innings before, the ball nestled in the screen atop the barrier and, just like that, the Yankees led, 3-2.

"I was so shocked . . ." Torrez said. "I thought maybe it was going to be off the wall. I never thought it would go out."

Torrez's shock quickly became evident. He walked the next batter, Rivers, and was replaced by Stanley, who surrendered a run-scoring double to Munson before retiring the side.

Jackson's 27th homer of the year, a solo shot, increased the New York lead to 5-2 in the eighth inning. But the Red Sox struck back in the bottom half against Gossage, who had taken over for Guidry with one out in the seventh. A double by Remy and singles by Yastrzemski, Fisk and Lynn manufactured two runs and cut the deficit to 5-4 with one inning to go.

Hassler and Dick Drago prevented any further Yankee scoring in the top of the ninth. The Red Sox were left with three outs in which to score one run and force extra innings or score twice and capture the A.L. East crown. Gossage retired pinch-hitter Evans for the first out, but Burleson drew a walk and Remy singled him to second. Coming up were Boston's most reliable hitters, Rice and Yaz.

But the Goose was golden in the clutch. Burleson tagged up and ran to third when Rice flied out to Piniella in right field, but that was as far as he got. Yaz popped weakly to third baseman Nettles in foul territory for the final out.

"I knew the season would be over as soon as Yastrzemski's pop-up came down," Fisk recalled. "It seemed like the ball stayed up forever, like everything was cranked down into slow motion. I was trying to will the ball to stay up there and never come down . . . what a dumb thing to have run through your mind. Even the crowd roar sounded like a movie projector at the wrong speed when everything gets gravelly and warped.

"After the last out, I looked around and the crowd was stunned. Nobody moved. They looked at each other like, 'You mean it's over now. . . . It can't

With the A.L. East title securely tucked away, Graig Nettles jumps into Goose Gossage's arms as other Yankees rush to join the celebration.

be over yet . . . oh, nuts. . . .' It had only been going on for half a year, but it seemed like a crime for it to end."

The Yankees' incredible climb from 14 games back on July 19 to the division title was over. Lemon, who had directed the Yanks to 48 victories in 68 decisions, became the first A.L. manager to win a title after beginning the season with another club, and Guidry, with a record of 25-3, established a major league mark for winning percentage and earned the A.L. Cy Young Award.

Many observers were calling the Yankee comeback a miracle, but the Yankees dispensed with that idea.

"We won because we're a very good baseball team," Piniella said. "There weren't any miracles."

Said Hunter, who went 10-3 after returning from his second stint on the disabled list: "It just adds to the pinstriped tradition."

While disappointed that they did not advance to the A.L. Championship Series against Kansas City, the Red Sox were, for the most part, pleased with their gritty comeback in the last two weeks.

"It's almost a shame that one of these teams had to lose," Yastrzemski said. "Both deserved to win.

The Yankees played like champions. But we played some of our best baseball in the last two weeks and caught them. I'm proud of this Red Sox team."

Zimmer echoed Yaz's comments.

"Had we not been able to come back," the manager said, "it might have been a long winter for us. . . . But the fact that we were able to get back into a playoff, winning our last eight games under unbelievable pressure of having to win every single day, is a credit to our ball club and our organization."

Dent, by the way, was not through with his heroics. After batting .200 in the A.L. playoffs against the Royals, Bucky rapped 10 hits in 24 at-bats (.417 average) and drove in seven runs to win Most Valuable Player honors as the Yankees beat the Dodgers in a six-game World Series.

But more memorable than his postseason accomplishments was the unlikely home run he smacked to decide one of baseball's most breathtaking pennant races ever.

"I've been dreaming of this," a jubilant Dent said while the Yankees were celebrating their A.L. East triumph. "You know, you dream about things like that when you're a kid. Well, my dream came true."

Boudreau Puts Indians Over Top

The 1948 Indians were molded into contenders by (left to right) Hank Greenberg,
Owner Bill Veeck, coach Bill McKechnie and player-Manager Lou Boudreau.

The start of the playoff game to determine the American League champion for 1948 was only 30 minutes away. The stands at Fenway Park were filling fast and pregame activities among members of the Boston Red Sox and the Cleveland Indians were proceeding in earnest. Yet despite all this activity in the moments before the national anthem, the identity of the Cleveland pitcher who would try to clinch the pennant for the Indians was, for the most part, a mystery.

Boston Manager Joe McCarthy was relatively certain that his counterpart in Cleveland, Lou Bou-

dreau, would not select Bob Feller for the crucial starting assignment. The Tribe's legendary right-hander had pitched and lost to Detroit in the previous day's game, which dropped the Indians into a tie with the Red Sox. Surely he would not be ready to pitch again without any rest.

A more likely candidate was converted outfielder-third baseman Bob Lemon, who had lost to the Tigers three days before. But Lem, who had 20 victories to his credit, was still lounging in the clubhouse shortly before game time. Most certainly it was not Lemon.

Two major contributors to the Indians' 1948 cause were Satchel Paige (left), a 42-year-old rookie pitcher, and budding star Larry Doby.

Another possible choice was Gene Bearden. The rookie lefthander had blanked the Tigers, 8-0, two days earlier for his second consecutive shutout and sixth straight victory. But while Lemon was relaxing in the clubhouse, Bearden was leaning against the concrete wall next to the visiting club's dugout, surveying the scene with a regal detachment that indicated he was out of consideration.

If none of these three was Boudreau's choice, who then? Sam Zoldak, a $100,000 acquisition from St. Louis in June? He finished with an 11-10 record. Perhaps Steve Gromek? He accounted for one of the Indians' 11 victories over the Red Sox. Or what about Satchel Paige? After being given his first chance to play in the major leagues when Indians President Bill Veeck signed him that year, Paige went 6-1 as a 42-year-old rookie.

At the last possible moment, Bearden grabbed his glove and ambled to the bullpen to warm up. Boudreau's secret was out, at last. It would be the 28-year-old Arkansan with the Hollywood profile who would carry the hopes of the Cleveland organization, which had been without a championship since Tris Speaker's 1920 club edged out the Chicago White Sox and followed with a World Series conquest of the Brooklyn Dodgers.

The decision to send Bearden to the mound with only one day of rest was made the previous afternoon when the Indians were in the process of losing to the Tigers. Boudreau, who played shortstop in addition to managing the Indians, and second base-

man Joe Gordon chatted as they trotted to their infield positions in the seventh inning.

"It looks like we'll have to go to Boston tomorrow for a playoff," said the manager, whose team already had lost the home-field advantage in a coin-flipping ceremony a few days before.

Gordon nodded in assent.

"What's your idea about a pitcher?" asked Lou, who respected the opinion of his veteran second baseman.

Gordon dodged the direct question. "Who's your man?" he replied.

"I was thinking of Bearden," Boudreau said.

"You took the words right out of my mouth," Gordon answered.

At that moment, Bearden was in the bullpen tossing lightly, just in case the Indians needed a relief hurler. "Tell him to go to the bench," Boudreau instructed an emissary.

After the game, as the players were packing for the train ride to Boston, Boudreau rapped for attention in the clubhouse.

"I've been talking with our coaches over our pitching selection for tomorrow," he said. "We've decided on Bearden. That's our opinion, but it's not definite. We're all in this together. It's your money as well as mine. If you have any ideas, speak up."

Nobody uttered a word until Gordon finally said: "We've gone along with you all season. That's been good enough for me. We'd be crazy not to go along with you for the big one."

There were no dissenters. "Then it'll be Bearden," Boudreau said. "But let's not talk about it. Let's not tell anyone who our pitcher will be. I don't want him bothered by people, and it's better this way for a number of reasons."

Overall, Boudreau's pitching choice was a well-guarded secret. One writer, however, revealed in his newspaper that Bearden would pitch in the American League's first playoff game. Whether the scribe made a calculated judgment or was privy to some inside information never was determined.

Regardless of the outcome of the most important assignment of his brief major league career, the fact that Henry Eugene Bearden was even in that position said a great deal about this remarkable individual's strength and determination. The native of Lexa, Ark., was a veteran of four minor league seasons when he enlisted in the Navy in 1942. He was a machinist's mate aboard the U.S.S. Helena in July 1943 when a Japanese destroyer in the South Pacific fired a torpedo into the cruiser. The order to abandon ship was issued almost immediately and Gene started to climb a ladder from the engine room to the deck. Midway up the ladder, he was hurled to the floor by the impact of a second torpedo. He lay unconscious, his knee twisted and crushed and a gaping hole in his skull inflicted by flying fragments.

Bearden, not yet 23, may have perished with the sinking ship except that an officer, searching the darkness with his flashlight, discovered the crumpled form. The officer, who never was identified, carried the unconscious sailor to the deck and lowered him into a waiting life raft.

Two days later, a Navy ship patrolling the waters near the Solomon Islands rescued Gene and his wounded buddies. The former pitcher was transferred to a naval hospital near Jacksonville, Fla., where a team of doctors examined him. Somberly, they concluded that Bearden might as well forget about returning to the diamond. His mangled knee, they said, was beyond repair.

Bearden refused to accept that verdict. He was familiar with stories of surgical miracles. All he wanted was a doctor with some imagination and the willingness to put it to work.

Eventually, such a surgeon appeared. He inserted an aluminum cap and screw into Bearden's knee and covered the hole in his head with an aluminum plate. The rest, Bearden was informed, was up to him. Recovery was directly related to his determination to regain health and mobility through therapy.

Gene spent a month in bed, then another two months in a cast as he hobbled about the hospital, first with the aid of crutches and then a cane. A series of leg exercises followed until he regained full use of the limb.

In 1945, Bearden was discharged from the hospital and went directly to Binghamton, N.Y., where he joined the New York Yankees' farm club in the Eastern League.

The lefty won 15 games for the Triplets in his first season back and matched that total with Oakland of the Pacific Coast League in 1946. But the Yankees were not sufficiently impressed to retain the pitcher and, in December 1946, traded him to the Indians in a multiplayer deal. Perhaps, Gene theorized later, the New York club had learned of his war wounds and considered him a risky chattel.

With Oakland again in 1947, Bearden posted a 16-7 record to earn a full-scale tryout with the A.L. club in '48. Under the tutelage of coaches Bill McKechnie and Mel Harder, Gene progressed rapidly. He entered the starting rotation early in the campaign and won his first three decisions and six of his first seven. By August 17, following an 8-0 shutout of the St. Louis Browns, the rookie's record stood at 12-3. He was commanding attention throughout the league for his hurling as well as for a rumpled old fishing hat he wore frequently when not on the diamond.

The headpiece was a gift from teammate Ken Keltner. During a golf outing, Bearden caddied for

Righthander Bob Feller (left) and lefthander Sam Zoldak were contributing members of Cleveland's 1948 pitching staff.

the third baseman. The sun sizzled the fairways and Bearden wished aloud for a cap. Keltner had a ready solution. Exploring the depths of his golf bag, Ken extracted the seedy fishing hat.

"It looked," Bearden recalled, "as if Ken had trampled on it for half an hour before stuffing it into the bag. But I wore it toting the clubs around the course and still had it on walking into the ball park the following night. I pitched and won, and ever since then the hat hasn't been out of my sight. . . . It's my lucky hat. I couldn't win without it."

The lefthander's knuckleball also figured prominently in his success. Darting malevolently as it approached the plate, the pitch sent batters shuffling back to the bench muttering imprecations against the hurler and his wares.

If Bearden was a popular topic in the daily press around the league, he was scarcely more newsworthy than his manager. In his seventh season as skipper, the 31-year-old Boudreau led his charges by example as well as by the spoken word. A typical example of his superb leadership occurred during the first game of a Sunday doubleheader August 8 at Municipal Stadium. The Indians, playing before a home crowd of 73,484, trailed the Yankees, 6-4, in the seventh inning. With the bases loaded and a light-hitting outfielder due to bat, Boudreau, limping on a tender ankle and favoring an injured finger that prevented him from gripping the bat tightly, inserted himself as a pinch-hitter.

Joe Page, the Yanks' premier reliever, was on the mound, and for one of the few times that season, he was overmatched. Boudreau singled to center field, tying the score, and the Tribe went on to win, 8-6. Paige earned the victory in relief, while Gromek went seven innings to win the second game, 2-1, completing Cleveland's sweep.

At that stage of the race, the top four teams in the league were separated by only 2½ games. The Indians, with a 60-39 record, and the Philadelphia A's (63-42) were tied for first. The Yankees (59-42) were two games back, while the Red Sox, who had opened with a 14-23 record before starting to win consistently under their new pilot, Joe McCarthy, were in fourth place, 2½ games back, with a 60-44 mark.

The A's contended strongly for the lead until late August. An eight-game losing streak, however, dropped them out of the race, and they finished fourth, 12½ lengths behind.

The Indians, Red Sox and Yankees, meanwhile, waged a spirited struggle into the final days of the campaign. Cleveland, never more than 4½ games off the pace, was in third after Labor Day doubleheaders September 6. But the Red Sox then started playing .500 ball at a time when the Indians were winning 13 of 15 games. The Indians drew even September 22, when Feller defeated Boston, 5-2, before 76,772 screaming loyalists in Municipal Stadium.

Two days later, Manager Bucky Harris' Yankees forged a three-way tie for the top spot by beating the Red Sox, 9-6, while Cleveland was losing to Detroit, 4-3. With nine days left in the season, the three contenders were 35 games over .500, each with 91 victories and 56 defeats.

As the three contenders thundered toward the wire, A.L. President Will Harridge flipped a coin in his Chicago office to determine the matchups should playoffs become necessary. The results were as follows: If the Yankees were involved in a two-team deadlock, the one game needed to decide the championship would be played in New York. If the Indians and Red Sox tied for the pennant, the deciding contest would be played in Boston. If a three-way deadlock developed, the Indians and Red Sox would meet in Boston on October 4, the day after the last game of the regular schedule, with the winner hosting the Yankees the next afternoon. Considering the three-way tie that developed

When credits were being handed out after Cleveland's 1948 playoff victory over Boston, (left to right) Gene Bearden, Lou Boudreau and Ken Keltner ranked high on everybody's list.

shortly after the coins were tossed, any of those scenarios certainly seemed possible.

"Any one of three teams can win the flag," Boudreau had told reporters the day before. "The Indians, Red Sox and Yankees have equal chances. I don't believe this race will be decided until a week from Saturday, next to the last day of the season."

Indeed, the race pounded into the last weekend with the Indians holding a one-game lead over their rivals. Cleveland had won four straight games, with Bearden and Feller each picking up a pair of victories, to go two games on top with three games left on each team's schedule. But a Boston triumph over Washington, a New York victory over Philadelphia and a Cleveland loss to Detroit left all three teams, on the final Saturday of the season, with a chance to win the pennant.

But with the Red Sox hosting the Yankees on October 2, there was no way for any team to clinch the pennant until the next day's season finale. Even if Cleveland won its home game against the Tigers, only one of the contenders—the loser of the Boston-New York game—would be eliminated from the race.

Righthander Jack Kramer kept Boston's flickering hopes alive. Kramer, who had been obtained from the Browns the previous winter, scattered five hits in winning his 18th game, 5-1. Outfielder Ted Williams' first-inning home run with third baseman Johnny Pesky on base was all Kramer needed to whip the Yanks for the fifth time that year and to relegate the defending World Series champions to no better than second place in the league.

The Indians, meanwhile, maintained their slight edge as Bearden, still sporting his lucky, if disreputable, fishing hat at every opportunity, blanked the Tigers to improve his record to 19-6. That triumph put the Indians in control of their own destiny. If they could beat Detroit lefthander Hal Newhouser on the final day, the race would end without the necessity of a playoff and the Indians would be pennant-winners for the first time since 1920. Even if they lost, the Indians could clinch the pennant if the Red Sox were to bow to rookie Bob Porterfield and the Yanks.

But Porterfield proved no puzzle to the Red Sox. After being staked to a 2-0 lead, Porterfield was knocked out during a five-run explosion in the third inning. The Yanks narrowed the gap to 5-4 in the fifth, knocking out Boston starter Joe Dobson, but Porterfield's successor, Vic Raschi, surrendered sixth-inning home runs to outfielder Dom DiMaggio and shortstop Vern Stephens that keyed a four-run Boston uprising. Earl Johnson, who relieved Dobson in the fifth, gained credit for Boston's eventual 10-5 victory, the club's fourth straight triumph.

The help the Red Sox needed to forge a pennant tie was forthcoming in the person of Newhouser. The slender lefthander was nigh invincible at Cleveland, scattering five hits as he hurled the Tigers to a 7-1 victory. The Tigers lashed into Feller and five relievers for 15 hits, including three doubles by outfielder Vic Wertz, as they smoothed Newhouser's path to his 21st victory. From a Cleveland stand-

But all of the Indians had reason to whoop it up in Cleveland's victorious clubhouse.

point, the only felicitous feature of the day was the gesture of Bill Veeck. The team president donated the club's share of the gate receipts produced by the throng of 74,191 to the city's Community Chest.

Veeck and Boudreau, acknowledging Newhouser's masterful pitching, accepted the outcome philosophically.

"Bob would have had to pitch a shutout to win," the manager said, "and you can't demand that of any pitcher."

Said Veeck: "We'll beat the Red Sox in the playoff tomorrow. There's no use talking about today's game. We never had the slightest chance to win."

Like Veeck, Boudreau was confident that his team would bounce back in the junior circuit's first playoff game.

"The spirit of my boys has not been broken," he said. "We feel that no matter who pitches tomorrow for Boston, he'll not be a Newhouser—certainly not the Newhouser we faced today."

En route to Boston for the October 4 game, the Cleveland contingent speculated on who that opposing pitcher would be. Ellis Kinder was a possibility. The righthander, who had beaten the Washington Senators five days before, was well rested, but he had lost his only decision to Cleveland two months earlier, lasting less than two innings. On the other hand, Kinder was riding a personal five-game winning streak.

Mel Parnell was a likely choice. En route to his 15-8 record, the 26-year-old lefthander had defeated the Indians three times and lost twice. Parnell had last pitched September 30, when he beat the Senators, so he was suitably rested.

McCarthy, however, bypassed both Kinder and Parnell. Instead, he entrusted the weighty responsibility of the all-or-nothing playoff contest to Denny Galehouse, a 36-year-old righthander whose 13-year A.L. career had begun in Cleveland and then moved

to Boston, St. Louis and back to Boston. The Ohio native had not pitched since September 26, when he allowed seven hits in three innings of relief against the Yankees. Of his eight wins, one had been achieved at the expense of the Indians. The date was July 30, when Denny held the Tribe to two hits in 8⅔ innings of relief at Cleveland. But Cleveland also had tagged Galehouse with one of his seven losses, an August 25 debacle in which he was knocked out after surrendering seven hits and four runs in less than two innings.

To take maximum advantage of the short left-field wall at Fenway Park, Boudreau made a significant lineup change. He benched Eddie Robinson, a lefthanded-hitting first baseman who had clouted 16 home runs and driven in 83 runs that year, and substituted Allie Clark, a righthanded-hitting outfielder who had not played first base since his Piedmont League days six years earlier. Clark, who had contributed 38 runs batted in while batting .310 in 80 games, was replaced in right field by Bob Kennedy, another righthanded hitter. There was no opportunity to second-guess Boudreau's strategy as neither Clark—who was replaced by Robinson in the fourth inning—nor Kennedy was a factor in the game.

But the second-guessers quickly took McCarthy to task when the Red Sox fell behind, 1-0, in the first inning. Galehouse retired the first two Cleveland hitters, outfielder Dale Mitchell and Clark, and worked the count on Boudreau to two balls and one strike. On the fourth pitch, Boudreau drove the ball to the screen atop the left-field wall. It was his 17th home run of the year.

The Red Sox knotted the score against Bearden in the bottom of the first. Pesky doubled to right-center field and Stephens singled to left to produce a 1-1 tie.

Both teams put the leadoff batter aboard in the

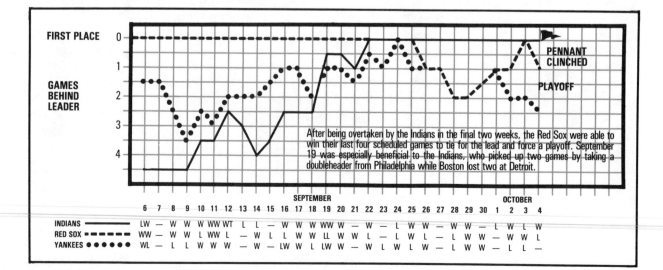

After the Indians went on to capture the 1948 World Series, Cleveland fans
gave their conquering heroes a major league welcome home.

second inning without scoring, and the third was uneventful as well. In the fourth, however, the Indians drove Galehouse to cover. Singles by Boudreau and Gordon and Keltner's 31st homer gave the visitors a 4-1 lead and brought Kinder to the mound. The reliever was not the immediate solution. A double by outfielder Larry Doby, Kennedy's sacrifice and catcher Jim Hegan's infield out produced the fourth run of the frame.

Boudreau's second home run and third hit of the game raised the Indians' lead to 6-1 in the fifth before the Red Sox tagged Bearden for two unearned runs in the sixth. Bearden, who had been effectively mixing his knuckleball, slider and an occasional curve, had retired Pesky for the first out when Gordon muffed Williams' high pop fly in short right field. That error was followed one out later by a home run off the bat of second baseman Bobby Doerr to bring the home team to within three runs of the Tribe.

"Doerr hit the one and only fastball I threw all afternoon for that homer," Bearden said later.

Bearden was virtually untouchable after the sixth. Williams accounted for the only other Boston hit, a two-out single in the eighth. In the top of that inning, Williams had dropped Bearden's long fly ball, allowing Cleveland's seventh run of the game. The final tally of the 8-3 victory crossed the plate in the ninth on a pair of singles, a wild pitch, a walk and a double play. One of the singles was supplied by Boudreau, who was accorded a standing ovation in recognition of his superlative 4-for-4 performance in a pressure-packed situation. The 33,957 spectators at Fenway Park hadn't had much else to cheer about that chilly afternoon.

But the Indians and all of Cleveland went nuts when Bearden retired catcher Birdie Tebbetts on a slow grounder to Keltner for the last out of the game. The Indians were on their way to the World Series for the first time in 28 years.

The two most sought-after players in the jubilant Indian clubhouse after the game were Bearden, who had allowed just five hits in winning his 20th game, and Boudreau, the hitting star. But neither player wanted to take credit for the victory.

"What a spot to come through," Bearden said. "What a gang of fellows to have behind you with their bats."

Boudreau deflected most of the attention to Bearden, who walked five batters but worked out of each jam.

"I never was worried about Bearden's pitching," the manager said. "He gets into holes, but I know that he almost always gets out of them himself. Imagine him going out there today with only one day's rest. He's a great pitcher."

After the celebration, the Indians moved into Braves Field in Boston for the start of the World Series. The teams split two games in the National League park, then went to Cleveland, where Bearden won the third game, 2-0. Bearden also saw action in the sixth and deciding game of the Series. Replacing Lemon, who had been staked to a 4-1 lead, with the bases loaded and one out in the eighth inning, the lefthander allowed a sacrifice fly and a run-scoring double, but that was all. Bearden shut down the Braves the rest of the way to preserve the Indians' 4-3 triumph and world championship.

By the spring of 1949, the storybook tale of Gene Bearden was coming to an end. After an off-season in which he appeared in a movie and basked in the limelight, Bearden never regained his 1948 form. His knuckleball, once so devastating, was no longer floating through the strike zone. He was forced to rely on his curve and fastball, neither of which was of major league caliber. Coaches McKechnie and Harder worked tirelessly in an attempt to find a cure for Gene's ineffectiveness.

"They had me lengthen my stride, then shorten it," Bearden recalled. "They had me move it this way, then that way. They suggested I shorten my windup, then lengthen it. But I couldn't control the knuckler like before."

Bearden won half of his 16 decisions in 1949. Short stints followed with Washington, Detroit, the St. Louis Browns and the Chicago White Sox before his major league career ended in 1953 with 45 victories and 38 losses.

It is not known whether Bearden's lucky hat stuck with him on his trek around the American League. But there is no question that he was rarely seen without the rumpled headpiece as his whirlwind rookie season reached its peak.

Getting ready to leave the clubhouse after his shutout performance in Game 3 of the World Series, Gene got a scare when he was unable to find his hat. He searched his own locker, then several of his teammates' lockers, and finally the numerous boxes and trunks scattered on the floor. Nowhere could he locate his hat.

"Somebody must think it's funny," he bellowed, fuming.

Watching the drama from a nearby locker was Feller. The pitcher let Bearden's frenzy build for a while longer before revealing his prank.

"Hey Gene, here," he yelled, reaching into his locker and pulling the hat out of the pocket of his coat. An obviously relieved Bearden grabbed the hat, put it on his head and left the clubhouse.

Feller was just having fun, but bearing in mind Bearden's incredible string of clutch performances, the future Hall of Famer thought that maybe, just maybe, there was something to this lucky hat business.

"I really ought to swipe this thing," Feller said. "I could use a little luck myself."

A Wild Pitch
Ruins Highlanders

Shortly after the close of the American League season of 1904, the manager and star pitcher of the New York club went on a hunting expedition. As they trudged through the woods, the hurler displayed little enthusiasm. He seemed preoccupied with matters other than wild game and the discharge of his firearm.

"Why don't you look for something to shoot?" asked the skipper, himself a pitcher of considerable repute in his prime.

"I was thinking," came the reply.

"About that wild pitch?"

"Yes."

"Now look here," the manager snapped. "If you ever mention that wild pitch again, I'll shoot you as I would a muskrat. Now shut up and hunt."

The pitcher was John Dwight Chesbro. Years before, while working at a mental hospital in Middletown, N.Y., he had been nicknamed "Happy Jack" in tribute to his warm personality.

Chesbro's hunting companion was Clark Calvin Griffith, who also carried a nickname. In his heyday as a righthanded pitcher with Chicago of the National League, Griffith had been tagged "Old Fox" in recognition of the sly fashion in which he pursued his profession.

The paths of Griffith and Chesbro converged in 1903 when Byron Bancroft (Ban) Johnson, president of the young American League, established a franchise in New York City that would compete with the Giants of the National League. The young circuit already had eight teams, but the majority stockholders of the Baltimore franchise sold their shares to other interests in 1902, allowing Johnson to put a franchise in the larger New York market for the 1903 season.

Johnson lined up Frank Farrell and William (Big Bill) Devery as backers of the New York A.L. club. Farrell, a onetime bartender and saloon keeper, was the proprietor of a gambling casino. Devery, a former police chief, had graduated into real estate and accumulated a substantial bankroll. To serve as a front man for the operation, the owners appointed Joseph W. Gordon, a coal merchant, as club president. Gordon was mild of manner, unlike his rough-hewn bosses.

After his first meeting with Farrell, Johnson was convinced that the high roller was sincere in his promise to field a strong team in New York. Farrell laid before him a certified check for $25,000 with the assurance that "if I don't put this ball club across, keep it." With the financing of the club guaranteed, Johnson next inveigled Clark Griffith to abandon his post as manager of the Chicago White Sox and accept the reins of the New York team.

Several players recruited for the new team were disgruntled National Leaguers who defected in favor of higher salaries offered in New York. At the forefront of the jumpers was Chesbro, whose 28 victories in 1902 had helped the Pittsburgh Pirates win their second of three consecutive pennants.

Though the financial support for and roster of the new team were starting to come together, the site of the club's home games still was a mystery less than three months before the start of the 1903 season. That was scarcely enough time to select a site and construct a ball park of sufficient dimensions to accommodate the crowds that were anticipated. But Farrell, Devery and Gordon accomplished the task. They chose a site on Broadway between 165th and 168th streets, where they erected a wooden structure capable of handling about 15,000 spectators. Because the park was located on one of the highest points in Manhattan, it was named Hilltop Park.

What about a nickname for the new club? The name "Highlanders" was chosen, partly because of the geographical elevation of the park and partly because the club president's name reminded somebody of the Gordon Highlanders, a crack regiment in the British Army of that day. The team continued to be called the Highlanders for about 10 years, by which time newspapermen, weary of trying to squeeze the name into headlines, adopted the popular designation of Yankees.

Hilltop Park was dedicated April 30, 1903, when a capacity crowd, unmindful of the roofless grandstand and the small ravine in right field, turned out to see the Highlanders play the Washington Senators. The patrons' first glimpse of the new team revealed players smartly attired in white uniforms, black stockings and cardinal jackets decorated with pearl buttons.

Among the celebrities on hand for the opening ceremonies, none was more conspicuous than Ban

Clark Griffith, alias the Old Fox, assembled a scrappy group of players for the Highlanders, New York's new American League entry.

Clark Griffith sent shock waves through Boston in 1904 when he negotiated a trade for outfielder Pat Dougherty, a favorite of Pilgrim fans.

Johnson. With the 69th Regiment Band leading the way, Johnson joined in the parade to the flagpole, clutching a miniature Stars and Stripes, as did each player. Later he tossed out the first ball, then relaxed in a box seat as the Highlanders humbled the Senators, 6-2. Right fielder Wee Willie Keeler, who had been enticed to jump leagues from the Brooklyn club, was the game's offensive star with two doubles, a pair of walks and three runs scored. The starting and winning pitcher was Chesbro, who went on to win 21 games in 1903 and help the Highlanders finish fourth in the league with a 72-62 record.

When the 1904 campaign got under way, there were several notable changes in personnel from the previous April. Norman Elberfeld, nicknamed the Tabasco Kid because of his spicy nature, was at shortstop. He had been acquired from the Detroit Tigers in June 1903 to replace the aging Herman Long. Also from Detroit came veteran catcher Deacon McGuire, whose contract was purchased in January 1904. He shared the duties behind the plate that season with Jack Kleinow, a rookie. Two players were obtained from the St. Louis Browns, pitcher Jack Powell and outfielder-first baseman John

Anderson. Also new on the pitching staff was Long Tom Hughes, who had been acquired from Boston's A.L. club the previous December and was traded away again midway through the 1904 season.

As he had done the preceding year, Chesbro pitched the opening game in 1904. Again it was an auspicious occasion. Backed by a 10-hit attack that included a double and home run off his own bat, Happy Jack defeated Cy Young and the Boston Pilgrims, 8-2, at Hilltop Park.

Boston retaliated the next day as Norwood Gibson defeated Jack Powell, 4-1, and the visitors won the third game of the series behind the pitching of Bill Dinneen, who beat Hughes, 12-6. For Dinneen, that game marked the first of 37 starts he made in 1904 without requiring relief.

After that 1-2 start, the Highlanders reached .500 (4-4) a week later. They never slipped below that level the rest of the season.

Griffith had assembled a scrappy band of players, not the least of whom was the Old Fox himself. An item in the April 30 issue of The Sporting News included this report: "Just before the game (date unspecified) Manager Griffith hit a photographer among the eye teeth, cutting the lip of the art man and spraining his own wrist. The photographer secured a warrant, which was served on the scrappy New Yorker in the fourth inning. Griffith, the constable and the photographer held a caucus under the grandstand and the injured artist settled the case out of court for $4.50, marked down from $5. Griffith said that was all he asked for, this sum being the cost of the warrant and service. However that may be, Griffith is too old a campaigner (he was 34) to indulge in such roughhouse tactics on the ball field. Strictly speaking, the fight took place under cover. The photographer approached Griffith at the New York bench a few minutes before play time and asked him to line up the team for a group picture. 'I told him we didn't have the time,' said the captain-manager. 'Some of my men were on the gate (checking receipts) and the pitchers and catchers were warming up for the game. I asked him to wait until we came on the next trip (to Philadelphia) as he represented no urgent publication, but he became abusive. Then I hit him.' Heretofore, Griffith has been extremely courteous to reporters and artists, and an athlete as good-looking as he is wouldn't dodge the camera without good reason."

Under the inspired leadership of the Old Fox and behind the spectacular pitching of Chesbro, the Highlanders gave their patrons many pleasant afternoons as they shoved into the thick of the flag race. Though the Boston Pilgrims secured an early hold on first place by jumping out to a 14-3 start, the Highlanders stayed close behind. The Pilgrims, managed by their incomparable third baseman, Jimmy Collins, were confident that the young New

Jack Chesbro, a 41-game winner for the New York Highlanders in 1904, threw a wild pitch that ruined an otherwise brilliant season.

York club was a genuine threat. In early May, W.M. Rankin, the Gotham correspondent for The Sporting News, declared that Griffith's team "is getting over the scare that Jimmy Collins' team threw into it and is now playing pennant-winning ball."

The Highlanders were in second place with a 27-20 record, 4½ games behind Boston, when Griffith negotiated a player trade that sent shock waves through the Boston camp. In the June 18 deal, New York acquired Pat Dougherty, a popular Boston outfielder who had batted .331 for the pennant-winners of 1903, in exchange for Bob Unglaub, an unproven utility infielder. Though Dougherty was in a slight batting slump at the time, Boston fans were incredulous when they learned of the swap.

In his weekly newsletter to The Sporting News, Boston correspondent Johnny Hallahan wrote in the June 25 issue: "There is not the least doubt in my mind and the vast majority of people who are interested in the world's champions that we got the worst of the exchange and all deplore the trade.

"That President (John I.) Taylor has made a great mistake is the way I dope it out, and with my present knowledge of the facts I can see no other way of summing it up. . . . If we admit that Pat Dougherty is not a crack outfielder, that he has fallen off with the stick considerably, that he has shown some sign of indifference, that, it seems to us, covers all that can possibly be said against him. . . . Inability to bat is a common disease this season, and Patsy suffered as many others who still continue to be considered notable figures in the national game. Dougherty's weakness in the field never did the team any harm, and if his batting was a good cause for considering a deal, it seems to me to be a very poor excuse. If such

was the cause, there are a number of other players on the team that might more properly figure in a deal to the possible betterment of the club."

Dougherty made his first Boston appearance in enemy uniform June 25 and collected three singles and a stolen base as Chesbro beat Cy Young, 5-3. In the second game of the series, Dougherty rapped a double and two singles as Powell registered an 8-4 triumph over Boston's Jesse Tannehill. The newcomer then went 1-for-4 in the third contest, a 5-2 Boston victory credited to Norwood Gibson.

Dougherty's splendid showing in Boston evoked the following commentary from Hallahan in the July 2 issue of The Sporting News: ". . . Dougherty was the cause of our going down to defeat. His stick work for the New Yorks was brilliant and his reception a grand one, over 16,000 persons being present to witness his debut as an Invader. While his reception was a grand one, there was no lack of praise and commendation for Captain Jimmy Collins, who was instrumental in having Patsy transferred to New York."

Though Dougherty helped the Highlanders creep to within 1½ games of the Pilgrims, the outfielder's departure had virtually no effect on the fortune of the Boston club. After taking hold of first place April 19, the Pilgrims did not relinquish that spot until August 4, when the Chicago White Sox won their 14th game in their last 16 tries and occupied first place for one day. On August 5, New York defeated Cleveland to tally its eighth victory in its last nine outings and move into the top spot for the first time since opening day. The order of the standings was unchanged four days later as New York, Chicago and Boston each lost two of their next

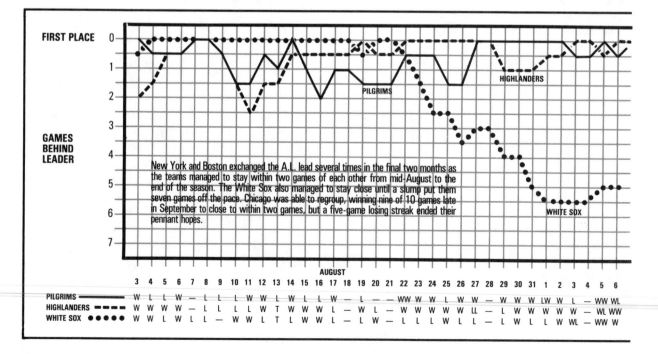

three games. But on August 10, the White Sox downed the Highlanders, 5-1, to regain the lead. Chicago managed only two hits off Chesbro in six innings, but poorly timed walks and errors made possible all five Chicago runs before Chesbro was replaced by rookie Walter Clarkson, a former Harvard great.

That victory and the schedule for the next 2½ weeks gave the White Sox an excellent opportunity to surge ahead. Including the August 10 game, Chicago had 16 consecutive contests against New York and Boston, the other front-runners for the pennant. The White Sox got off to a 4-2 start in those games, but on August 17, they ended a long home stand by suffering a 6-0 loss to the Pilgrims in which Tannehill hurled a no-hitter. Chicago had trouble recovering from that indignity. Of the 16 games they played against the Highlanders and Pilgrims, the White Sox won only six, lost nine and had another end in a tie.

Meanwhile, New York and Boston each won 10 of 16 games in that stretch. On August 27, New York (65-42) and Boston (66-43) were virtually tied for first place, while Chicago (64-47) was lagging three games back. Close behind were Philadelphia (60-44) and Cleveland (60-46).

One by one the bottom three teams dropped out of contention. Boston and New York, the remaining contenders, took turns leading the procession through the last few weeks of the season.

The only opportunity for the Highlanders and Pilgrims to engage in head-to-head competition in September was when New York traveled to Boston to start a five-game series September 14. Boston had a half-game lead when the series opened, but New York reversed that edge by winning the first game, 3-1. Dinneen outpitched Chesbro, limiting the Highlanders to only two hits, but a weak Boston defense that committed seven errors allowed the visitors to win. The lead changed hands again the next day when Boston scored a 3-2 triumph. New York loaded the bases in the top of the ninth inning, but Tannehill struck out Wid Conroy to end the game. The clubs tried to play a second game, but as had happened the day before, the game was stopped because of darkness with the score tied.

They were able to complete a doubleheader in the series finale September 16. Chesbro beat Dinneen again in the opener, 6-4, but Cy Young left his sick bed to pitch Boston to a 4-2 victory in the nightcap.

In the days that followed, New York went ahead by two games, only to fall two games behind Boston when the Pilgrims won six straight contests. The Highlanders drew even once more, however, by winning two of four games while Boston slipped into a four-game skid. With neither team able to open a commanding lead, it became apparent that the A.L. pennant would be decided in the final days of the season when the clubs were scheduled to play five games, including one makeup contest.

The entire series was to have been played at Hilltop Park, but a change was made necessary by the shortsightedness of Frank Farrell. Months earlier, before the Highlanders were considered a serious threat for the pennant, the co-owner had arranged to rent the field to Columbia University for a football game Saturday, October 8. As a result, the doubleheader slated for that afternoon was shifted to the Huntington Avenue grounds in Boston.

The Pilgrims (92-57) were nursing a half-game

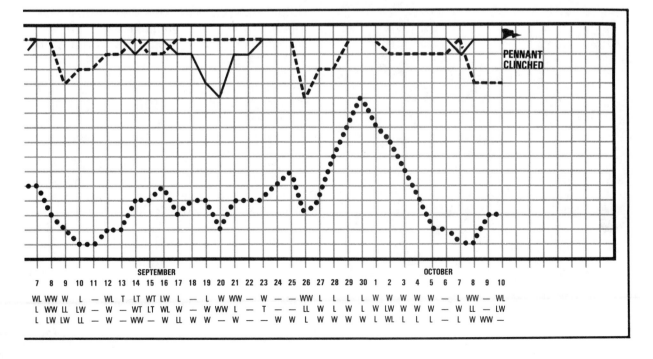

Jimmy Collins, Boston third baseman and manager, provided the steadying influence that helped his club win the 1904 A.L. pennant.

lead over the Highlanders (90-56) when the crucial series opened in New York on October 7. With five games left to play, the pennant would go to whichever club could win at least three games.

Boston's half-game margin swung quickly to the Highlanders' advantage when Chesbro beat the visitors, 3-2, on a four-hitter. Dougherty contributed a double and single to the Highlanders' five-hit attack against Norwood Gibson. The victory was Chesbro's 41st of the season, a figure that no 20th Century pitcher has matched.

After the game, Griffith instructed the pitcher to remain at home while his teammates boarded the train that would take them to Boston for the Saturday twin bill. The manager wanted Chesbro rested for the concluding two games on Monday. Unless New York swept the doubleheader in Boston—in which case it would win the pennant outright—at least one of the Monday games would decide the A.L. championship race.

Chesbro disregarded the instructions. When the Old Fox arrived at Grand Central Station, the righthander was already at the gate and waiting impatiently to board the train. Reluctantly, Griffith purchased an extra ticket.

Once aboard the train, Chesbro turned to his skipper. "Who you gonna pitch in Boston?" he asked.

"I figured Al Orth for the first game and Jack Powell for the second," Griffith replied.

"What the hell's the matter with me?" Chesbro wondered. "Don't I work for this club anymore?"

"But you worked yesterday," the Old Fox countered. "You can't pitch 'em all."

"You want to win the pennant, don't you?" the hurler persisted. On the strength of that argument, Griffith let his premier pitcher start the first game.

Chesbro's mound opponent was Dinneen, a righthander who, like Happy Jack, was a former National Leaguer. Big Bill, a native of Syracuse, N.Y., won 14 games for Boston's N.L. club in 1901 before switching his allegiance to the Pilgrims. He captured 21 decisions in 1902 and matched that total in 1903, when he gained added distinction by defeating the Pittsburgh Pirates three times in the first modern World Series.

Chesbro started out impressively. He was staked to a 1-0 lead in the first inning and blanked the Pilgrims through three frames. But excessive toil took its toll in the fourth when the Pilgrims scored six runs en route to a 13-2 laugher. Jimmy Collins, shortstop Freddy Parent and second baseman Hobe Ferris each contributed three hits for the Pilgrims.

In the next issue of The Sporting News, Johnny Hallahan wrote: "The 'Champs' not only outplayed the New Yorks, but sent to the stable, after giving him the most severe drubbing he has received this season, that greatest of all spitball artists, Jack Ches-

Boston righthander Bill Dinneen outdueled Highlanders ace Jack Chesbro in two key games late in the 1904 A.L. pennant chase.

Cy Young was an aging righthander by 1904, but still good enough to win 26 games for the Boston Pilgrims.

bro. He had nothing that could puzzle the Champs, for they took kindly to all his curves after they got ahead in the fourth inning. Then Clarkson, the ex-Harvard twirler, was given a chance to display his ability as a professional to the local fans, but like his predecessor had nothing that could fool the Champs, as eight hits were made off him and seven runs in the remaining innings of the first game."

In an effort to salvage a split in the twin bill and return home with his half-game lead intact, Griffith asked righthander Powell, his 23-game winner, to pitch the nightcap. His opponent was 37-year-old righthander Cy Young, who already had captured 25 decisions.

Before the game was halted by darkness after seven innings, Powell allowed four hits, Young seven. But Powell's impressive performance was not enough. One of three errors by Wid Conroy enabled the Pilgrims to score the only run of the game in the fifth inning, and Boston's first-place lead expanded to 1½ games.

"We were lucky to get away with the second game," Hallahan wrote, "but such is the fortune of baseball. We profited by the Invaders' mistakes, one of which proved fatal. . . . Powell had slightly the better of old Cyrus Young, but the support

given the latter was far ahead of that tendered to big Jack. These two victories have given the boys and fans much courage, for it was thought after Gibson had lost the first game (of the series) in New York that the Griffith bunch would break even in this city and the same in New York. But they didn't and Boston is again ascendant."

With Sunday baseball illegal in Boston and New York, the teams rode the rails back to Gotham on October 9. Compared to their adversaries, the Pilgrims found the journey quite pleasant. They were in the enviable position of needing only one victory to clinch the flag. The Highlanders, on the other hand, had to sweep the doubleheader to achieve the identical goal.

About 200 Boston fans made the trip to New York to root for the visitors in the deciding games October 10. Somehow, a reported 28,450 baseball enthusiasts elbowed their way into Hilltop Park, with its 15,000 capacity. The grandstand overflow stood about a dozen deep in the outfield, while thousands more were turned away.

The pitching pairings for the opening game matched the rivals of the Saturday before: Dinneen, seeking his 23rd win, and Chesbro, again in search of his 42nd. Since opening day in April, Chesbro had hurled 445 innings, including six shutouts, and had established himself as the top pitcher in the league that year. The righthander was starting his third game in as many consecutive playing days. Chesbro began brilliantly, shutting out the Pilgrims for six innings. In the meantime, the Highlanders scored twice in the fifth off Dinneen. With two out, Jack Kleinow rapped a single and Chesbro, who also whacked a triple in the game, bounced a single off Dinneen's hand. Dougherty, the Boston hero of a few months before, belted a third straight single to plate the first run. Bases on balls to Willie Keeler and Kid Elberfeld forced in the second run before Dinneen retired Jimmy Williams on an infield grounder to close out the inning.

The Pilgrims tagged Chesbro for two runs in the seventh with the aid of a throwing error. First baseman Candy LaChance ignited the outburst with an infield single, and Hobe Ferris was safe on a hard-hit ball that second baseman Williams was unable to handle. Catcher Lou Criger's sacrifice placed runners on second and third, bringing Dinneen to the plate. Big Bill was a .212 hitter in 118 at-bats for the season, and New York partisans envisioned no trouble when the batter rolled meekly toward second base. But Williams, trying to nail LaChance at the plate instead of throwing to first base for the second out, heaved the ball into the dirt. Both runners scored in the time it took Kleinow to recover the ball.

The teams remained tied, 2-2, when the Pilgrims came to bat in the top of the ninth. Criger, a .217 hitter and slow-footed in the bargain, led off the frame and outlegged a slow roller to Kid Elberfeld at shortstop. Dinneen sacrificed successfully, and left fielder Kip Selbach's infield out moved Criger to third base.

Freddy Parent then stepped into the batter's box. Chesbro's first pitch to the .296 batter was a called strike, the second a foul for strike two. Parent watched a waste pitch sail outside the strike zone and dug in for what he was sure would be Chesbro's

devastating spitball, which some observers insisted dropped as much as a foot.

This time, however, the ball did not drop. Happy Jack had either over- or undersaturated the baseball because it took off, sailing over Kleinow's head as Criger lumbered home with the tie-breaking run. Parent subsequently singled, but it is a matter of conjecture whether the batter could have delivered a key hit were the runner still on third.

Still the Highlanders had another turn at bat. If the home team could strike back and score at least one run, Chesbro's costly wild pitch might yet be erased from memory. With two out in the bottom of the ninth, that potential run was on second base, the go-ahead marker on first and Dougherty at the plate. The scenario was tailor-made for 11th-hour heroics as the outfielder faced his former teammate. Dinneen got two quick strikes on the batter, then ran the count to 3-and-2. He threw once more. Dougherty unloosed his most vicious cut—and missed. Criger tossed his cap in the air and danced off the field clutching the pennant-winning baseball in his catcher's mitt.

Though the second game was meaningless, both pilots played most of their regular players. George Winter started for Boston and Ambrose Puttmann for New York, which won the game, 1-0, in 10 innings.

To win the championship, the Pilgrims played 157 games, including three ties. From start to finish, they were remarkably fortunate in avoiding crippling injuries. For example, LaChance and outfielders Chick Stahl and Buck Freeman appeared in every game. Collins and Ferris missed only one game apiece, Parent two.

Having clinched a second consecutive pennant, the Pilgrims issued a challenge to the New York Giants to engage in a World Series, similar to the one of 1903. They were soundly rebuffed. Giants Owner John T. Brush and Manager John McGraw, still bristling over the way the American League had invaded their territory, rejected the suggestion that the N.L. champions appear on the same field with the poachers.

Credit for the league championship, of course, was due to the superb talents of the players and their skipper. But others were partly responsible for the flag, as Hallahan noted in the October 22 issue of The Sporting News: "The Boston rooters figured in the winning of the championship in no small measure by their incessant shouting and singing of 'Tessie' (a popular tune of the day), which proved to be the hoodoo of the Pittsburgh bunch last year. Over 500 strong were the followers of Collins and his boys, and with seats behind the Boston bench they howled with glee when Big Bill Dinneen fanned their once great favorite, Patsy Dougherty. Just as the players, the fans were all in at the end of the first game, so much so that over half a dozen innings were played in the second game before the majority of them knew there was a game being played."

On their arrival back in Boston, the new champions were feted at the Boston Theatre. Contributions from the fans netted each player about $100 apiece, while Owner John I. Taylor tossed in an order for a suit of clothes for each member of the club. Manager Collins already had been honored with the presentation of a silver cup valued at close to $500. The players had donated $75 toward the trophy, Taylor had contributed $50 and the balance had come from "every notable fan in the city." A group of Boston fans also gave the team a trophy, which Collins accepted with becoming modesty.

"The players did it all," he said. "I had a great team of ball players to manage. They did everything I asked of them."

In New York, the baseball public mingled its pride over the Highlanders' accomplishments with regrets over the manner in which the pennant was permitted to slip away. Correspondent W.M. Rankin assigned a large share of the blame to the "poor throw home by Williams and dumb work on the part of Kleinow in his tardy recovery of the ball (that) helped the Bostons to score twice (in the sev-

enth inning) and put them on an even basis with the home team."

All of that criticism was valid. But the world undoubtedly would remember that it was Chesbro's errant heave that enabled Boston to score the run that won the 1904 pennant.

In the years that followed, some apologists for Happy Jack endeavored to have the wild pitch converted to a passed ball. The sentiment was that a blemish on the record of a rookie catcher would be far less damaging to his reputation than the wild pitch was to the reputation of Chesbro, this century's only 41-game winner.

The issue remained unresolved as late as 1941, when a New York newspaper reopened the issue. The following winter, veteran baseball historian Fred Lieb encountered Kid Elberfeld in Florida. Lieb asked the old shortstop whether the play could have been ruled a passed ball.

"Hell no," Elberfeld fairly shouted. "That ball rode so far over Kleinow's head that he couldn't have caught it standing on a stepladder."

Let the record show it was a wild pitch.

Giants Owner John T. Brush and Manager John McGraw, obviously upset about the A.L.'s invasion of New York, refused to meet the new league in a 1904 World Series.

1964: The Philadelphia Story

By universal agreement, one of the sharpest managerial intellects in baseball—probably the keenest of all—in 1964 was the exclusive property of Gene William Mauch, youthful skipper of the Philadelphia Phillies.

There was an abundance of evidence to support such an opinion, dating to the time he joined the Brooklyn Dodgers as an 18-year-old infielder during World War II. Gene was with the Dodgers only a short time when Branch Rickey, the club president and acknowledged master of character analysis, asserted: "You look at him and he looks like he's 16. You talk to him and you think he's 26. You talk baseball to him and you think he's 36."

That was Gene Mauch, baseball-wise beyond his years. He habitually sat next to his manager on the bench, studying strategy, analyzing decisions, inquiring endlessly and forming his own conclusions, pro and con.

Once he walked into the office of Leo Durocher, his manager, and asked: "Why did you hit-and-run in the third inning with a man on first and Pee Wee Reese up? It looked to me like a bunt situation."

"Kid," the manager replied, "people talk about percentages. I have my own percentages."

That encounter was one of many that went far toward shaping the managerial philosophy of Mauch, who implemented that philosophy for the first time in 1953, when he was only 27. He accepted an offer from the Braves, then in transit from Boston to Milwaukee, to be a player-manager for their Atlanta farm club. He led the Crackers to a third-place finish in the Southern Association race and, by most evaluations, had done a competent job. Gene disagreed. He insisted he was too young to manage and cited his impatience with players as his major weakness.

Mauch returned to the ranks from whence he had come. He spent three seasons with the Los Angeles Angels of the Pacific Coast League and then played briefly with the Boston Red Sox before he was offered the job of field boss with the Minneapolis Millers of the American Association. This time he felt he was ready. Again as a player-manager, Mauch led the team to second- and third-place finishes in his two years at the helm.

Mauch was at Pompano Beach, Fla., in April 1960, preparing for a third season with Minneapo-

lis, when he received a telephone call from John Quinn, general manager of the Phillies and a longtime friend. Quinn had some startling news. Shortly after the Phils had lost their season opener, Eddie Sawyer had resigned as manager, offering the succinct explanation that "I'm 49 and would like to see 50."

Was Gene interested in the job? "You're our first choice," Quinn assured him. The answer was an unqualified affirmative. Gene, who had long dreamed of managing in the majors, was on his way to join the club.

It required little time for Mauch to recognize the inadequacies that had prompted Sawyer to quit after an opening-day defeat by the Cincinnati Reds. Talent was in short supply; prospects were grim. The Phils, who had finished last in the National League in each of the previous two years under Sawyer, fell from 64-90 in 1959 to 59-95 in 1960, 36 games out of first place.

As depressing as that season was for a manager of Mauch's competitive nature, even drearier days lay ahead. In 1961, the Phillies lost their first two games, quickly plunged into the basement and never emerged. Gene lived in perpetual frustration, a condition that was reflected in his relations with umpires and players. Encounters with arbiters and subsequent suspensions were not unusual.

One of the skipper's chief adversaries among the players was Robin Roberts, for many years the club's pitching stalwart and a future Hall of Famer. Age had deprived the righthander of his once-devastating fastball, but he resisted Mauch's suggestions that he develop an assortment of curves and slow pitches to retain his effectiveness.

"He throws like Betsy Ross," Mauch sneered. Roberts, a favorite of Phils Owner Bob Carpenter, resented Mauch's criticism and asked to be traded, a request that was granted after the season.

By July 28, 1961, when John Buzhardt won the second game of a doubleheader to halt a five-game losing streak, the Phillies lagged 29 games behind the leaders with a record of 30-64. But starting the next day, the Phils embarked on another skid. By the time Buzhardt earned an August 20 victory at Milwaukee, the Phils had set a modern major league record with 23 consecutive losses.

With a mark of 31-87 and buried out of sight in

the N.L. cellar, there was little cause for levity when the team boarded a flight to Philadelphia. A somber atmosphere pervaded the cabin until the plane taxied to a stop at the Philadelphia airport. Then a player, gazing out a window, spotted a large crowd waiting at the gate to hail their harassed heroes.

"Look at those people," he exclaimed. "Must be 200 of 'em. Why are they waiting for us?"

The remark afforded a perfect opportunity for Frank Sullivan to deliver a solemn announcement. "Go out in twos and threes, men," the pitcher said. "They're selling rocks at a dollar a pail, and that way they won't get us in one burst."

Whether Gene Mauch grinned at the wisecrack is unrecorded. But the manager did find something beneficial in the losing streak. "It made us a team," he declared. "It brought us closer together."

As a more tightly knit unit, the Phils still lost 107 games while winning 47 and finished 46 games behind the pennant-winning Reds.

By 1964, the rebuilding efforts of Mauch, Quinn and Carpenter were mirrored in the standings of the team the previous two years. The Phils became a winning club, going 81-80 (seventh place) in 1962 and 87-75 (fourth) in 1963.

The 1964 team featured more talented players, of course, than the 1961 version of the Phils. Lefthander Chris Short was developing into one of the league's best pitchers and Jim Bunning, an established American League hurler, had been acquired with catcher Gus Triandos from Detroit to give the Phils a potent 1-2 pitching punch. Dennis Bennett and Art Mahaffey, with help from Ray Culp, rounded out the starting rotation.

The club's offense had improved with the emergence of Johnny Callison and Richie Allen. Callison, who had been obtained in a 1959 trade with the Chicago White Sox, was a bona fide star by 1964. He swung a productive bat and exhibited a powerful arm. Twice he had led N.L. outfielders in assists, and he would make it three in a row in '64.

Allen, a 22-year-old rookie in '64, filled a hole for Philadelphia at third base. He went on to bat .318 with 29 home runs and 91 runs batted in, statistics that earned him N.L. Rookie of the Year honors.

In addition to Callison, the outfield was patrolled by Wes Covington and Tony Gonzalez. Roy Sievers opened the campaign at first base, with Tony Taylor at second, Bobby Wine and Ruben Amaro at shortstop and Allen at third. Clay Dalrymple and Triandos shared the catching chores.

A preseason poll of major league baseball writers made the Phils definite underdogs in the 1964 pennant race. They were the fifth choice of the scribes, trailing the Dodgers, Giants, Cardinals and Reds. Despite this lack of initial respect, the Phils won 10 of their first 12 games and gained a foothold on first place.

If the club had one glaring weakness, it was at

Gene Mauch, a bright, young managerial talent, had his Phillies primed for a pennant run when the fateful 1964 season opened.

The aces of the Phillies' 1964 staff, Chris Short (right) and Jim Bunning, faltered down the stretch when asked to pitch on short rest.

first base. Sievers played the position for 33 games but batted under .200 and was sold to the Washington Senators in July. Amaro was given a shot at the job, and though he was an improvement at the plate (.264), he was not the answer.

The search for a competent first baseman and a proven righthanded hitter ended August 7, the day the New York Mets arrived in Philadelphia for a three-game series. Weeks of dickering with the Mets ended with the acquisition of Frank Thomas, a 35-year-old Pittsburgh native who had played with the Pirates, Reds, Cubs and Braves before joining the Mets in 1962.

The slugging outfielder-first baseman saw limited service with the Mets early in 1964, partly because of a glandular infection that sidelined him for six weeks. He had started only once in the Mets' last nine games when he boarded the team bus to ride to Connie Mack Stadium on August 7. Arriving at the ball park, he learned that he no longer was a member of the 10th-place Mets; he had been obtained by the league leaders.

"Happy? Sure, I'm happy," he said in the clubhouse after his first game as a Phillie. "It's tough to leave New York . . . but it's also nice to go to a pennant contender. Seventeen years I've played now, and I've been in last place many of those years. The highest I ever got was second with Pittsburgh in '58 and fourth with Milwaukee in '61."

Thomas celebrated his good fortune by rapping a double and a single and driving in two runs as the Phils defeated the Mets, 9-4. In the Phils' sweep of his ex-teammates, Thomas collected two singles, a double, a homer and five RBIs.

When Thomas joined Philadelphia, his new team led the second-place San Francisco Giants by 1½ games. In the succeeding month they built their advantage to 6½ games over St. Louis, followed by San Francisco and Cincinnati. A large share of credit for the improvement was attributed to Thomas, who batted .302 with seven homers and 26 RBIs in 33 games.

When all forces seemed to be working together in favor of the Phils, injury suddenly struck down Thomas. Diving headfirst into second base September 8, he jammed his right hand into the bag and broke his thumb. A few weeks later, Thomas attempted to come back, but the cast on his hand was too big a handicap and, for all practical purposes, he was through for the season. To replace Thomas on the roster, the Phils acquired Vic Power from the Los Angeles Angels. He, too, was of little help, the result of dulled reflexes from too many days on the bench.

Initially, the loss of Thomas failed to slow down the Phils. After Bennett and reliever Jack Baldschun shut out the Houston Colts on September 15, the Phils still boasted a six-game margin over their closest pursuers. The next night, however, Mauch implemented a curious bit of strategy. It was Mahaffey's turn to start, but Mauch announced that Bunning, who had pitched a perfect game June 21 against the Mets, would be an excellent choice to face a team he already had beaten four times that year. Excellent except for one notable fact: The staff ace had pitched against the Giants only three days earlier.

"Why bring him back with only two days' rest?" the manager was asked repeatedly.

"Bunning wants to pitch and I want him to pitch," was the answer.

Bunning had won eight games in a row, improving his record to 17-4, when he was rushed back to the mound. He quickly demonstrated that his 32-year-old right arm was not adaptable to the accelerated schedule. The league's weakest-hitting club drove him to cover during a four-run explosion in the fifth inning and he was tagged with a 6-5 loss.

As sportswriters continued to grope for a satisfactory explanation for Mauch's irregular move, the Phillies flew to Los Angeles for a four-game series. The Phils earned a split in the set with the Dodgers when Bunning, pitching this time with normal rest, won the finale, 3-2, on a five-hitter.

With a 90-60 record, a comfortable lead of 6½ games and only 12 contests still to be played, the team returned to Philadelphia to open a seven-game home stand. Confidence in the ranks was high, and for good reason. With any luck at all, the Phils could clinch their first N.L. pennant in 14 years at home. And with that pennant all but guaranteed, applications for World Series tickets would be accepted within a few days.

Amaro, a Mexican-born infielder-outfielder, was so certain of the Phils' impending triumph that he called his father in Mexico and asked him to come watch him play in the World Series.

"I remember my father saying, 'I don't like to sound pessimistic or anything,'" Amaro recalled, "'but I wouldn't really be sure of playing (in the World Series) until I know you have clinched the pennant.'"

As the Phils prepared to launch their final stand at Connie Mack Stadium, the Cardinals took on the Mets in New York. In their own way, the Cards were having a remarkable season, too. As late as mid-June they had languished in eighth place, but as the trading deadline approached, General Manager Bing Devine had engineered a multiplayer trade with the Cubs that transformed the year from potential disaster into stunning success.

The principal players in the June 15 swap were Ernie Broglio and Lou Brock. Broglio, a righthanded pitcher, had won 18 games in 1963, when the Cardinals made a late-season bid for the pennant that fell short. In 1964, however, Broglio, nearly 29, won only three of his first eight decisions and was considered expendable. Brock, three days short of his 25th birthday, was in his fourth year as a professional. He was widely recognized for his speed, but while many observers believed he had potential as a hitter, he had been given little chance to blossom as

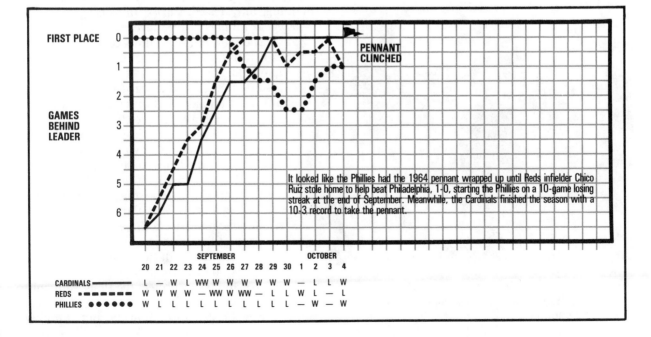

It looked like the Phillies had the 1964 pennant wrapped up until Reds infielder Chico Ruiz stole home to help beat Philadelphia, 1-0, starting the Phillies on a 10-game losing streak at the end of September. Meanwhile, the Cardinals finished the season with a 10-3 record to take the pennant.

		SEPTEMBER										OCTOBER			
	20	21	22	23	24	25	26	27	28	29	30	1	2	3	4
CARDINALS	L	—	W	L	WW	W	W	W	W	W	W	—	L	L	W
REDS	W	W	W	W	—	WW	W	WW	—	L	L	W	L	—	L
PHILLIES	W	L	L	L	L	L	L	L	L	L	L	—	W	—	W

Young, talented third baseman Richie Allen emerged in 1964 as one of Philadelphia's top offensive weapons.

a part-time outfielder with the Cubs, for whom he was batting .251.

Nobody in St. Louis turned cartwheels over the trade of an established pitcher for a relative unknown, nor was unbounded joy displayed in late July when the club acquired Barney Schultz from Jacksonville of the International League. The 37-year-old righthander had gone 8-5 at Jacksonville, a record that was none too encouraging to a team that entertained ambitions of becoming a contender. But Manager Johnny Keane, who had managed Schultz in the minor leagues, was familiar with his talents, which became evident when Schultz saved 11 games for the Cards, allowing nary a run in his last eight appearances and finishing with a 1.65 earned-run average in 30 games.

Brock was even more spectacular. The left fielder batted .348 and stole 33 bases as a Cardinal, establishing himself as one of the majors' brightest young stars.

While Schultz and Brock were positive factors in the Cardinals' climb, there was a third development, negative in nature, that was regarded by some as a spur to the team's resurgence. In mid-August, when the team was in fifth place, Cards President August A. Busch Jr. asked Devine to resign. Whether the dismissal of the popular executive prodded the players into better performances, as was alleged, or whether the improvement was coincidental, the fact remained that St. Louis had moved into a contending position when the season entered its final fortnight.

While the Cardinals were splitting two games with the Mets, the Phils were dropping three straight to the Reds, who closed to within 3½ games. The Braves followed the Reds into Philadelphia, bringing added grief for Mauch and his minions. Bunning, fully rested, started the first game and lasted six innings in a 5-3 defeat.

The Phils' jovial confidence was starting to waver by this time, and Mauch revived his hurry-up pitching program. On two days' rest, Short started the second game against Milwaukee. Short kept Philadelphia in the game until leaving in the eighth, but the club still suffered a heartbreaking 7-5 loss in 12 innings, despite Callison's game-tying, two-run homer in the eighth and Allen's game-tying, inside-the-park, two-run homer in the 10th. Mahaffey started the next game, which the Phils lost, 6-4, when Rico Carty tagged reliever Bobby Shantz for a three-run triple in the top of the ninth inning.

Again with two days' rest, Bunning returned to the mound September 27 to face Milwaukee and try to protect the Phils' slim half-game lead in their last home appearance of the season. Callison blasted three homers, but Bunning

and four successors were bombed for 22 hits in a
14-8 Milwaukee romp. With the loss and a doubleheader sweep of New York by Cincinnati, the last
remnant of the Phils' once-substantial lead disappeared. They were in second place, one length behind the Reds, who had just won their ninth consecutive game, and half a game ahead of the Cardinals,
who were in the midst of an eight-game victory
streak. In addition, the Giants, despite dropping a
doubleheader to Chicago, were only 4½ games off
the pace. All four teams were included in an elabo-
rate playoff schedule devised by N. L. President
Warren Giles involving two, three and four teams.
The Giants were not eliminated mathematically
until October 3, the next-to-last day of the season.

Meanwhile, the Phils flew to St. Louis for
three games. Here they had an opportunity to recover lost ground and atone
for recent transgressions. They did
neither, losing the series by scores of
5-1, 4-2 and 8-5. Cards lefthander
Ray Sadecki defeated Bennett in the
second game to become a 20-game
winner, while overworked Short
and Bunning dropped the first and
third games to Bob Gibson and Curt Simmons, respectively. The unprecedented late-season skid by a
front-runner rose to 10 games.

In the two weeks after Mauch first employed the
accelerated schedule for his two aces, Bunning had
worked on short rations three times, Short twice—
and the Phils lost each time. Over and over Mauch
was asked to explain his extraordinary strategy.
What was the need for the hurry? Why the urgency
to speed up the rotation when his top hurlers, given
proper rest, would likely have performed more
creditably?

"I couldn't live with myself," the manager later
explained, "if there was anything I could do that I'd
left undone. That's what a manager kicks himself
for—something he didn't try.

"Using Frank Thomas with a broken hand,
pitching Bunning with short rest; you have to give
those things a chance. If they don't work, OK, it's
my skin."

Trailing by 2½ lengths with only two games to
play following their triple loss in St. Louis, the Phillies (90-70) still retained a glimmer of hope in the
face of prohibitive odds. If the 10th-place Mets
could defeat the Cardinals (92-67) three times in St.
Louis while the Phils won a pair in Cincinnati (92-
68), the race would end in a three-way tie. A San
Francisco (89-70) sweep of the Cubs would forge a
four-way deadlock.

The first act in the pulsating drama was played
Friday night, October 2. In Cincinnati, Short, Ed
Roebuck and Baldschun combined on a four-hitter
and the Phils won, 4-3, finally bringing their horrid

A 1964 midseason trade with the Chicago Cubs
brought young Lou Brock to St. Louis and started
the Cardinals on the road to a pennant.

A subdued St. Louis crowd watches the New York Mets delay the Cardinals' 1964 pennant express on the second-to-last day of the season.

losing streak to an end. The Phils' third triple play of the season and a four-run rally in the eighth backed up the strong pitching.

From St. Louis came the heartening word that Al Jackson had hurled the Mets to a 1-0 win over Gibson and the Cards. A single by Ed Kranepool drove in ex-Cardinal George Altman, who had singled and stolen second, with the only run. And in San Francisco, Bobby Bolin's 9-0 shutout of Chicago kept the Giants in the race.

While the Phils and Reds enjoyed a day of idle-

ness October 3, the Mets staggered the Cards again. Uncorking a 17-hit attack that included five homers, New York smashed St. Louis, 15-5, and forced the losers into a first-place tie with the Reds, one game ahead of the Phils. The Cubs knocked the fourth-place Giants out of the race with a 10-7 triumph at San Francisco.

With a three-way tie still possible on the last day of the season, Mauch called on Bunning—this time with three days' rest—to keep the Phils' hopes alive. The righthander came through handsomely, beat-

St. Louis players swarm around Barney Schultz after the ace reliever had recorded the last out of the Cardinals' 1964 pennant-clinching victory.

ing John Tsitouris and the Reds, 10-0, and snapping his personal three-game losing streak.

"I was perfectly calm," Bunning recalled. "I knew I could beat Cincinnati. I knew the club was in a much better frame of mind than it had been."

After the game, the Phils and Reds could only sit in the visitors' clubhouse at Crosley Field, hopeful that Galen Cisco, with a 6-18 record, could pitch the Mets to victory over the Cards' Simmons, who had a mark of 18-9.

At first the reports from Busch Stadium were encouraging. Two runs in the fifth inning chased Simmons and gave the Mets a 3-2 lead. Almost immediately, however, came depressing news. A three-run outburst in the bottom of the fifth, featuring the second RBI of the game by infielder Dal Maxvill, a replacement at second base for the injured Julian Javier, vaulted St. Louis into a 5-3 advantage.

More agonizing moments passed for the Phils in Cincinnati. The Mets were mounting a rally against Gibson, who was called on to relieve Simmons with

little more than 36 hours of rest. Runners were on second and third with two out when Keane ordered an intentional walk to catcher Jesse Gonder, a .270 hitter, to load the bases and get to second baseman Bobby Klaus, who was batting .225. The strategy misfired when Gibson walked Klaus to force in the fourth New York run, but the Cards escaped additional damage by retiring shortstop Roy McMillan.

The Mets got no closer than that 5-4 margin. A three-run uprising in the bottom of the sixth, including first baseman Bill White's home run and doubles by Brock and catcher Tim McCarver, put the game out of the Mets' reach. The Cardinals completed their scoring in the eighth with another three runs, including outfielder Curt Flood's homer. Schultz took over for Gibson to record the last two outs in the ninth, thus preserving St. Louis' 11-5 victory. In nailing down their first pennant since 1946, the Cards sprang the trap door on the Philadelphia and Cincinnati gallows.

"Nobody said anything to anybody," Bunning

Reserve catcher Bob Uecker gets a champagne shower from pitcher Roger
Craig during the Cardinals' pennant-clinching celebration.

said, reflecting on the gloom that pervaded the Phillies' clubhouse when the Cards' pennant-clinching victory became final. "It was a total blah. We were out of it. We were let down. We were completely gone. We had it; it was ours, and we let it go."

Also contributing to the Phils' lost pennant was a strong second-half performance by St. Louis. The Cardinals were 39-40 at the All-Star break, but they bounced back to post a 54-29 mark after the midsummer classic.

"This team played hard," Cards shortstop Dick Groat said. "It wasn't that we were dedicated or a team of destiny or anything like that. But in all the years I've been in baseball, I've never seen a team play such hard-nosed ball over a sustained period of time. For the last two months of the season, everybody was bearing down all the way, going all out."

Keane, who managed the Cardinals to a World Series triumph over the New York Yankees before resigning to take Yogi Berra's place as Yankee manager, was quick to answer when asked what marked the turning point in the season for St. Louis.

"It has to be the addition of Lou Brock," said Keane, who submitted his resignation the same day the Yankees fired Berra. "He picked the club up. The other players suddenly realized how good a ball player he was. Of course, none of us expected to see him come so fast."

Brock's outstanding performance was a vindication of sorts for Devine, the ousted general manager who had acquired the little-known outfielder.

"Brock could be the best deal I ever made," Devine said.

For the Phils, the nightmare was over. But Mauch had one final chore to perform. He had to face the media.

"I wish I had done as good a job as the players," he told reporters. "That's all I have to say."

One of the scribes wrote that Mauch appeared "as though he would give the national debt for the privilege of punching somebody in the nose. Anybody."

On the lugubrious flight back to Philadelphia, Mauch was asked which of the defeats in the horrendous 10-game slump hurt the most.

"I guess the one I remember first," he replied, "is when we had Milwaukee down, 4-0, September 26. They came back to beat us. I'm not blaming my guys. Put it all on me."

Beyond that game, Gene Mauch would remember the abuse he received from self-appointed critics. And he was ready for them.

"To hell with 'em," he barked. "I'm not going to defend myself to anybody. Inside, I know I did everything I could to win it."

The Survival
Of the Whiz Kids

Hall of Famer George Sisler (center), a scout for the Brooklyn Dodgers, posed with his sons Dick (left) and Dave midway through the 1950 season.

It was bad enough having to overcome the burden of playing in his father's shadow, but then to lose his job to a guy who had spent most of the previous summer recovering from a gunshot wound was enough to make a guy mad.

And Richard Allan Sisler was mad. After taking over as the Philadelphia Phillies' starting first baseman when teammate Eddie Waitkus was shot by a deranged woman in a Chicago hotel in June 1949, Sisler had performed admirably, finishing with a .274 average, 11 home runs and 56 runs batted in. He had come to spring training in 1950 with the understanding that he would retain his job unless Waitkus proved he was the better man.

After the first few intrasquad games, Sisler was confident that he had outplayed Waitkus. But when the lineup card was posted for the Phillies' first exhibition game in Clearwater, Fla., the starting first baseman was Waitkus, not Sisler.

Dick took the startling news hard. It was yet another disappointment for the 29-year-old St. Louis native, whose exploits to date had not come close to matching those of his father, Hall of Fame first baseman George Sisler. He already could hear the fans in Philadelphia muttering, "Just goes to show that he'll never measure up to his old man."

Sisler was sorely tempted to stomp into the office of Eddie Sawyer and tell off his manager in no uncertain terms. After all, Sawyer had told reporters that Waitkus would have to win the first-base job back, and as far as Dick was concerned, Eddie hadn't done it.

Upon further reflection, however, Sisler decided on a different course.

"I can play the outfield better than some of the fellows you have," a calmer Sisler said to his manager the next day. "How about a try?"

Sawyer, beginning his second full season as Phillies manager, was skeptical, but he liked the player's initiative. "OK," he said, "report to (trainer) Frank Wiechec tomorrow morning."

That was all the encouragement Sisler needed. He

Phillies Manager Eddie Sawyer (left) poses with his Whiz Kid staff of (left to right) Bubba Church, Robin Roberts, Bob Miller and Curt Simmons.

quickly went to work to prove his ability as an outfielder, a position that was not entirely new to him. He had played the outfield exclusively in four minor league seasons in the St. Louis Cardinals' organization, and he had played both first base and the outfield after his promotion to the major league club in 1946. Sisler remained with the Cardinals for two years before being traded to the Phillies in April 1948. The Phils left him at first base until Dick, out of desperation, suggested that Sawyer give him a chance in the outfield.

When Sisler reported to the Phillies' trainer the day after his chat with Sawyer, he began a grueling four-week regimen. Each morning he was put through strenuous paces by Wiechec, who turned him over to coach Benny Bengough in the afternoon. The training was extremely harsh, but it paid dividends. When the season started, Dick was running faster, releasing his throws quicker and judging fly balls better. He won the starting left-field job.

Moreover, Sisler made important contributions to the Phils' attack after the season began. In a May 4 game at St. Louis, he rapped five hits in a row, then returned the next day and collected three more hits, all in succession, before the streak was snapped. He played in 141 games but would have appeared in even more had he not injured his wrist

while sliding late in the season. He finished with a .296 average, 13 homers and 83 RBIs.

At 29, Sisler was among the older members of the club in 1950. By the end of the season, the Phillies' regular lineup had an average age of 26½, while the club's top seven pitchers averaged a shade over 27 years. The Phils' youth, combined with their zeal and combativeness, earned them the nickname "Whiz Kids," a moniker borrowed from the University of Illinois basketball team of a few years before.

Sisler's outfield partners were a pair of fuzzy-cheeked youngsters, 25-year-old Del Ennis in right and 23-year-old Richie Ashburn in center.

Ennis signed with the Phillies right out of Olney High School in Philadelphia. After a year in the minor leagues and two years in military service, Del made his major league debut in 1946, batting .313 with 17 homers and 73 RBIs. He led the Phils with 31 homers and 126 RBIs in 1950.

Ashburn, a stout defensive player, first attracted the attention of a major league club when he was 16. The young Nebraskan attended a tryout camp conducted by the Cardinals, who were prevented from signing him because of his age. The Cleveland Indians later offered Richie a contract when he still was too young and had to pay a fine. The Nashville Vols (Southern Association) actually got his signature on paper, but that pact was voided by an irregularity. The Phillies finally got him on their payroll in 1945, when Ashburn made his professional debut with Utica (Eastern). He joined the Phils in 1948 and immediately showed his talent. Though he missed the last month of the campaign because of a broken finger, Ashburn's .333 average and National League-leading 32 stolen bases in 117 games were sufficient to earn him Rookie of the Year honors. He was a .303 batter in '50.

The oldest member of the Phils' regular infield was the 30-year-old Waitkus. Eddie had been obtained from the Chicago Cubs before the 1949 campaign, but his first season in Philadelphia was cut short when a female baseball fan summoned him to her room and fired a bullet into his chest. He was sufficiently recovered in 1950, however, to push Sisler off first base and play in all but three games, batting .284.

The rest of the Philadelphia infield consisted of second baseman Mike Goliat, 24, a product of the Pennsylvania coal country who was in his sophomore season with the Whiz Kids; shortstop Gran Hamner, 23, a Virginia native who had joined the Phils as a 17-year-old and then apprenticed in the minors before coming up to stay in 1948, and third baseman Willie (Puddin' Head) Jones, a 25-year-old South Carolinian who walloped 25 homers in 1950, his second full year with the Phils. Handling the bulk of the catching chores was 30-year-old Andy Seminick, a no-nonsense former coal miner from West Virginia who smacked 24 homers in '50.

The pitching rotation was headed by Robin Roberts, a 24-year-old righthander, and Curt Simmons, a 21-year-old lefthander.

Roberts, a Michigan State alumnus, was enriched by $25,000 when he signed with the Phillies in 1948. He went 7-9 and 15-15 in his first two years in Philadelphia before posting the first of several 20-victory seasons in 1950.

Simmons was the showpiece of the Phillies' family. As a teen-ager in the town of Egypt, Pa., Curt had compiled astonishing records with his high school and American Legion teams. When he was graduated from high school in 1947, scouts from numerous major league clubs sought his signature.

The prize went to the Phillies who, through their own benevolence, inadvertently escalated the bidding. As a good-will gesture, the club management agreed to play an exhibition in Egypt against the local team, which featured Simmons on the mound. The game officially was to mark the dedication of the community's war memorial baseball field, but the Phils gambled that a sound thumping by the major league club would help hold down Curt's bonus demands.

The Phils gambled and lost. Simmons fanned 11 major leaguers and would have won the game if not for two outfielders, each eager to catch a fly ball that would have ended the game, colliding and dropping the ball. That mishap permitted the Phils to score the run that produced a 4-4 tie.

Instead of driving down the price tag, the exhibition game had pushed it upward. One by one, the bidders dropped by the wayside until only the Phils remained. Simmons' father notified the Phils that their offer of $65,000 was tops. Though a subsequent Boston Red Sox offer, reportedly for

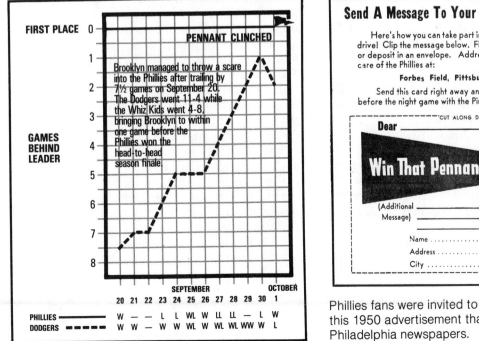

Phillies fans were invited to catch pennant fever by this 1950 advertisement that appeared in Philadelphia newspapers.

Catcher Andy Seminick (21) went on an August home run tear as the
Whiz Kids proved to fans and foes that they were a legitimate pennant threat.

$125,000, was submitted, the elder Simmons stuck
to his word and awarded the prize to the Phils.

A few months of seasoning prepared Curt for the
majors. He joined the Phils late in 1947 and put in
two mediocre years before bursting out in stardom
in 1950, when he won 17 of 25 decisions.

Another former schoolboy sensation on Philadelphia's pitching staff was Bob Miller. The 24-year-
old righthander from Detroit won his first eight
decisions in 1950 and was called "the biggest surprise" of the year by his manager before a pulled
shoulder muscle limited his late-season effectiveness. Miller finished with 11 victories.

Other substantial pitching contributions were
made by righthander Emory (Bubba) Church, a 25-
year-old rookie from Birmingham, Ala.; Russ
Meyer, a 25-year-old righthander; Ken Johnson, a
27-year-old lefthander who was obtained from the
Cardinals in an April 1950 trade, and righthander
Jim Konstanty.

Konstanty didn't fit the image of the 1950 Phillies
—he was 33—but he was the biggest star on the
Whiz Kids' pitching staff. His professional career
had begun nine years earlier, after his graduation
from Syracuse University, where he was a four-
sport star. But the scouts weren't drooling over the
bespectacled pitcher. Konstanty drifted from Syra-

cuse (International) to the Cincinnati Reds in the
war years and then was traded to the Boston Braves
after a year of military duty. Before long he was
back in the International League, this time pitching
for Toronto, where Eddie Sawyer finally came to
his rescue in 1948. Sawyer was managing the Toronto club when the Phillies summoned him to take
over as skipper in July 1948. Sawyer asked the Phils
to acquire Konstanty shortly thereafter, and by
1950 Jim was one of the league's top relievers.

Jim was available for both long and short relief.
For instance, he made a single pitch to save an August victory at St. Louis. But he also worked nine
innings in a 15-inning victory at Pittsburgh, and he
pitched 10 frames in a 19-inning Philadelphia triumph over Cincinnati. By season's end, Konstanty
had set major league records by pitching in 74
games and finishing 62 of them. He also protected
countless leads, produced 16 victories and posted a
2.66 earned-run average—all of which earned him
N.L. Most Valuable Player honors.

Adding to the Konstanty mystique was his rela-
tionship with Andy Skinner, a mortician in
Worcester, N.Y. Skinner, Konstanty's catcher in
winter workouts, could determine at a glance any
defect in Jim's pitching form and was constantly on
call when his friend needed help. When Konstanty

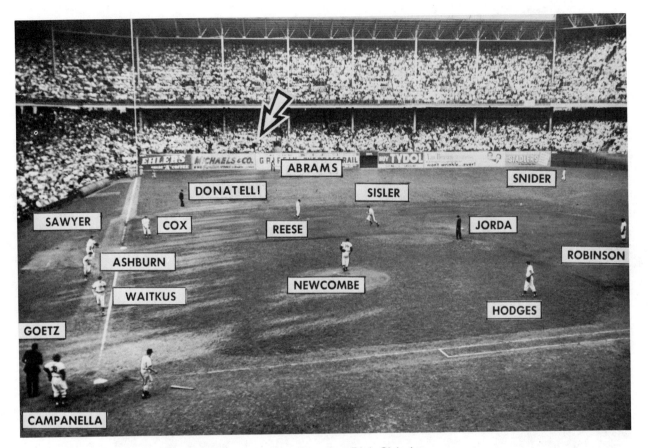

Three Phillies circle the bases amid Dodger dejection after Dick Sisler's pennant-winning homer landed in the left-field stands at Brooklyn's Ebbets Field.

was experiencing difficulty with his slider midway through the 1950 season, the undertaker made a hurried trip to Philadelphia and discovered the malfunction within minutes.

In retrospect, it's fairly simple to pick out Konstanty, Roberts, Simmons, Ennis, Ashburn, Sisler and the other talented players who made the Phillies a pennant contender in 1950. But before the campaign opened, few people gave the Phils much hope of doing anything besides finishing in the middle of the pack. Manager Burt Shotton's Brooklyn Dodgers, who had won the pennant two of the previous three years, were an overwhelming choice to repeat as N.L. champions, according to baseball writers who were polled by The Sporting News before the season opened. The Cardinals and Braves finished second and third in the poll, respectively, followed by Philadelphia.

There was good reason for the sportswriters to expect little from the Phillies. The club had not flown an N.L. pennant in 35 years, and as recently as 1948 it had finished in sixth place, 25½ games out of first. But in 1949 the Phils climbed to third with an 81-73 record, their first above-.500 mark since 1932.

All four of the clubs expected to finish in the first division remained closely bunched at the top of the standings through the first half of the season. Brooklyn, St. Louis, Boston and Philadelphia all played steady ball, never suffering a long losing streak or falling more than six games behind the leader. Each club had held first place at some point through July 17, when only one game separated the top four teams. The next day, St. Louis and Boston forged a three-way tie with Philadelphia.

A week later, the Phillies (51-38) trailed the Cardinals (50-37) by just two percentage points in the standings when they hosted a twi-night doubleheader with the Cubs on July 25. The Shibe Park crowd of 32,726 was treated to a pair of shutout victories that moved the Phils into first place. Bubba Church won the opener, 7-0, as Sisler contributed two doubles and two RBIs and Ennis knocked in three runs with a single and a home run. Roberts earned the victory in the nightcap, 1-0. Roberts himself launched the winning rally in the ninth inning with a single, then gave way to pinch-runner Ralph (Putsy) Caballero, who scored on Ashburn's two-out single.

The doubleheader sweep opened a 16-game home stand in which the Whiz Kids won 12 games. By the time they left for Brooklyn for a two-game series with the Dodgers, the Phils had a four-game lead over the second-place Braves.

Jackie Robinson (center) and Carl Furillo (right) lead a dejected group of
Dodgers back to the clubhouse after the Phillies had clinched the pennant.

Philadelphia won both games at Brooklyn to drop the Dodgers to fourth place, 6½ games back. The Phils then returned home to play four games with the New York Giants and two games with Boston. After splitting the first two contests with New York, Roberts faced Sheldon Jones on August 12 in one of the most memorable games of the year. It was Kids' Day at Shibe Park, and players on both clubs did their part by acting like juveniles.

The stage had been set for childish antics the day before. In that game, Giants second baseman Eddie Stanky employed a tactic that infuriated the Phillies. Whenever Seminick came up to bat, Stanky moved behind second base and waved his arms to distract the Phillies' catcher. An infuriated Sawyer protested to the umpires, who reported that the rule book did not specifically prohibit arm-waving

by fielders. Nevertheless, Giants Manager Leo Durocher instructed Stanky after the game to desist until N.L. President Ford Frick could make a ruling on the matter.

The next day, Stanky made a big show by remaining frozen when Seminick appeared for his first at-bat in the second inning. That "good-boy" display didn't last long, however. Seminick walked, and when Goliat followed with a single to left, the catcher charged around to third at full speed and crashed into Hank Thompson, who was trying to make the tag. Thompson was knocked unconscious and had to leave the game.

The Giants were furious. "If that's the way the Phillies want to play, it's all right with me," Durocher told reporters after the game. "After all, this is not Chinese checkers we're playing. As far as I'm concerned, no holds are barred on the ball field after 1:30, but it should be the same for everyone. So, I told Stanky to go ahead and wave if he wanted to."

Stanky did. On the second pitch to Seminick in the fourth inning, Eddie resumed his wild gyrating behind second base. He was promptly ejected from the game. When Seminick reached base on an error, nerves on both clubs were on razor's edge.

The next batter, Goliat, hit a slow roller to shortstop Alvin Dark, who threw to Bill Rigney, Stanky's replacement, for the forceout on Seminick. But Andy barreled into Rigney, and both players came up swinging. A five-star free-for-all ensued, and peace could not be restored until a few policemen rushed on the premises.

Seminick and Rigney were ejected and the Phillies eventually won the game, 5-4, in 11 innings, with Konstanty earning the victory. Jim Hearn earned a series split for the Giants the next day by shutting out the Phils, 2-0, but the rhubarb with the Giants seemed to ignite the Phils for the rest of the month. They swept both home games against Boston and then embarked on a productive trip in which they won 11 of 14 games, raising their advantage to seven games over second-place Brooklyn.

The Phillies opened that trip August 18 in New York, where Giants fans showered Seminick with a vicious torrent of abuse. Andy responded in his first at-bat by walloping a home run. It was the first of six homers Seminick contributed during the Phils' swing through New York, Cincinnati, Pittsburgh, Chicago, St. Louis and Boston.

Until this time, Philadelphia fans were reluctant to warm up to the Phillies. Since the heyday of Connie Mack's Athletics in 1929-31, Quaker City fans had suffered through years of high expectations and low finishes from both clubs, and they insisted that the Whiz Kids be genuine contenders before they would display undue enthusiasm.

By September 3, they had the evidence they demanded. The Phils had come through that long trip, which was seen as a testing ground for the club's mettle, with flying colors. To demonstrate their allegiance, an estimated 30,000 fans waited through intermittent showers to howl their welcome to their conquering heroes at the Philadelphia airport.

The Philadelphians' newfound confidence in their team was put to the test right away. The Phils lost their first five home contests, being shut out in the first three (a doubleheader loss to New York and the first game of a twin bill against Brooklyn). Before Russ Meyer broke the skid by pitching a 4-3 victory over the Dodgers on September 8, their lead had been trimmed to 4½ games.

The Phils went on an 8-3 tear to raise their advantage to 7½ games over both Boston and Brook-

lyn, which were tied with 79-61 records through games of September 20. It seemed highly unlikely that Philadelphia would squander such a lead with just 11 days left in the season, but the team was laboring under a serious handicap: Simmons was gone. Ten days earlier, he had departed for military service, three victories shy of what was shaping up to be a 20-win season. The Phils still had Roberts, but injuries to a couple of other key pitchers (Church and Miller) were exacting their toll. Philadelphia had one of the league's lightest batting attacks, so any problems with the pitching staff were dangerous.

That weakness soon became evident. The Phillies lost two games to the Dodgers to wrap up their last home stand of the year. Don Newcombe outdueled Roberts, 3-2, on September 23, and Erv Palica cruised to an 11-0 shellacking of Church and three Phillie relievers the next day. With nine games to go—all on the road—Philadelphia's lead over Brooklyn stood at five games.

The tour opened in Boston, where the Phillies won two games out of three. That knocked the Braves out of the pennant race, leaving only the Dodgers to challenge the Phils.

Doubleheaders on consecutive days in New York were next. A split in the series would guarantee the Phils at least a tie for the flag, regardless of how Brooklyn fared, but the Whiz Kids were unable to muster even one victory. In the opener September 27, the Phils tied the score by tallying five runs in the eighth inning, only to lose, 8-7, in the 10th. First baseman Monte Irvin scored the winning run for New York on Alvin Dark's single and exacted a measure of revenge for the Giants by knocking Seminick dizzy with a hard slide at the plate. Seminick spent the last few days of the season hobbling on a tender ankle.

The Giants also took the nightcap, 5-0, as Jim Hearn blanked the Phils for the third time that season. An inside-the-park grand slam by center fielder Bobby Thomson in the first inning provided Hearn with more then enough runs. That same day, the Dodgers split a doubleheader with the Braves, meaning that any combination of two Philadelphia wins or Brooklyn defeats would clinch the flag for the Phillies.

The Phils got halfway there September 28, but not through their own efforts. The Dodgers again split a twin bill with the Braves while the Phils lost a pair at the Polo Grounds. Sal Maglie handed Philadelphia a 3-1 setback in the first game, and Sheldon Jones outpitched Roberts by the same score in the second. The last defeat was particularly painful for the Phils. The game was decided when Giants left fielder Whitey Lockman, pulling away from an inside pitch, made accidental contact with the ball and looped a freak two-run single to left.

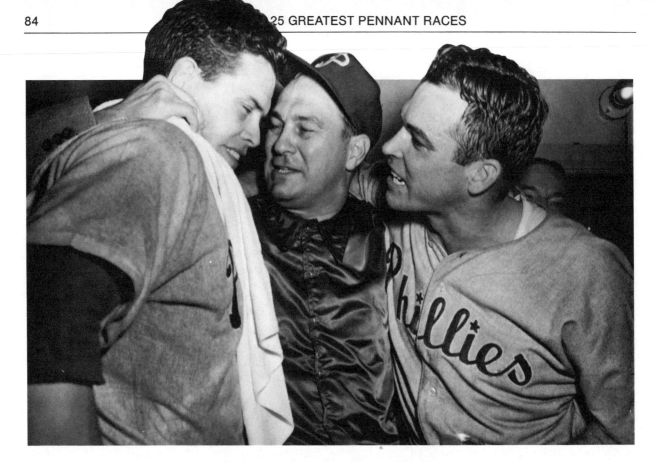

Phillies Manager Eddie Sawyer (center) celebrates with conquering heroes
Robin Roberts (left) and Dick Sisler after his team's title-clinching victory.

September 29 was a day of rest for the Phils, but the Dodgers were slated to host their third double-header with the Braves in as many days. A Dodger loss in either game would eliminate Brooklyn and clinch the pennant for Philadelphia.

The Whiz Kids weren't that lucky. The Dodgers came from behind to win both contests, sending many of the 5,843 fans in attendance scurrying to the Ebbets Field advance sale ticket windows. Boston carried a 5-2 lead into the bottom of the eighth inning of the opener, but Brooklyn tallied five un-earned runs to win, 7-5. In the second game, the Braves blew a 6-3 lead as the Dodgers rallied in the sixth to knot the count. Second baseman Jackie Robinson then led off the Dodger seventh by rock-eting a long shot into the stands in left-center field, and Carl Erskine pitched three innings of scoreless relief to ice the 7-6 victory.

The Dodgers were still alive, trailing the Phils by two lengths with two games left to play. But their fate rested in their own hands because their last opponent of the season was none other than Phila-delphia. By winning both games at Ebbets Field, Brooklyn would create a tie for first place, thus ne-cessitating a three-game playoff. Anything less would give the Phillies their first pennant since 1915.

Burt Shotton nominated Erv Palica to start for the Dodgers. Palica, a 22-year-old righthander, was seeking his 13th victory of the season. His oppo-nent, Miller, was looking for win No. 12.

Miller absorbed his sixth loss instead. The right-hander lasted only 4⅔ innings. With one out in the fifth, Miller gave up a single to third baseman Billy Cox, who advanced to second on Palica's infield out and scored on left fielder Cal Abrams' scorching single to center. Shortstop Pee Wee Reese then tri-pled home Abrams, sending Miller to the showers. Konstanty came in but was of little help. The sec-ond pitch from the league's foremost reliever was knocked over the right-field fence by center fielder Duke Snider to give the Dodgers a 4-0 lead.

The Phillies raked Palica for three runs in the sixth inning, two of which scored on Sisler's triple, but the Dodgers pushed across three insurance tal-lies in the eighth when catcher Roy Campanella blasted his 31st homer of the season. The 7-3 deci-sion marked Brooklyn's 13th victory in its last 16 games, while Philadelphia suffered its eighth loss in its last 10 tries (as well as its fifth consecutive set-back). With a 90-63 record, the Phils led the Dodgers (89-64) by only one game. The Whiz Kids' magic appeared to be waning in the wake of Brook-lyn's strong charge.

For the second year in a row, the pennant race narrowed to one game. In 1949, the Dodgers and Phillies also had met in the season finale to deter-mine the league champion, but the Phils were not in the pennant race that time. Their 9-7 loss in 10 innings merely preserved Brooklyn's one-game lead

The triumphant Phillies, with Manager Eddie Sawyer (seated, center) leading, posed for a group cheer after their crucial victory over the Dodgers.

over St. Louis and prevented the Dodgers from having to play a three-game playoff with the Cardinals.

Each manager called upon his best pitcher for the
crucial October 1 encounter that would determine
success or failure for both clubs in 1950. The selections were a pair of 19-game winners, Roberts for
Philadelphia and Newcombe for Brooklyn. The
better rested of the two hurlers was Big Newk, who
had made only one other start since earning his
19th victory September 23. Roberts, on the other
hand, was making his third start in the last five days
and was trying for the sixth time to earn victory
No. 20. Roberts had lost 11 times in 1950, Newcombe 10.

An over-capacity crowd of 35,073 looked on as
the two righthanders battled on even terms through
the first five innings, preventing either team from
scoring. The Phillies finally touched Newcombe for
a run in the top of the sixth inning on consecutive
singles by Sisler, Ennis and Puddin' Head Jones.

Philadelphia's 1-0 advantage lasted only until the
Dodgers batted in the bottom of the sixth. The
Ebbets Field crowd cheered wildly when Reese
drove a ball to right field that lodged between the
screen and the top of the fence for a bizarre home
run.

The 1-1 stalemate lasted into the home half of the
ninth, which Roberts opened by walking Abrams.
Reese followed with his third hit of the game, a line
single to left field. Abrams had to stop at second
base, setting the stage for the most controversial
play of the year.

Snider was the next batter. The 24-year-old outfielder had 31 homers and 107 RBIs to his credit
that season; he had sacrificed only six times. But
with sluggers Jackie Robinson, Carl Furillo and Gil
Hodges following Snider in the order, it seemed
likely that Snider would try to move the lead runner to third base with a bunt.

But Snider did not sacrifice. He rapped a single to
center that Ashburn fielded cleanly. Abrams raced
to third and turned to home at the frantic urging of
coach Milt Stock. But Ashburn's strong throw to
catcher Stan Lopata was perfect, and Abrams was
tagged out a good five feet from the plate.

Though the Dodgers had failed to score the run
that would have thrown the pennant race into a tie,
their situation still was far from hopeless. Reese and
Snider both had advanced while Abrams was being
tagged out, so runners were on second and third
base with one out and the heart of the lineup coming up. A hit, a fly ball, an error—almost anything

—still could produce the winning run and erase Abrams' baserunning faux pas.

But no one came through. Roberts walked Robinson intentionally to load the bases and then retired Furillo on a pop foul to Waitkus and Hodges on a fly ball to Ennis in right field. The decisive game of the season went into extra innings, just as it had done in 1949.

Though the Philadelphia pitcher was scheduled to lead off the top of the 10th inning, Sawyer allowed Roberts to stay in the game. Robin, who had allowed just five hits and walked three batters through the first nine innings, responded by singling to center field against the tiring Newcombe. Waitkus then looped a single to the same sector. The next batter was Ashburn, an adept bunter. This time, however, he failed. Newcombe pounced on Richie's bunt and forced Roberts at third base.

That brought up Sisler, the fourth straight left-handed batter. In his first four appearances against Newcombe, Sisler had fanned once and stroked three successive singles.

As Sisler stepped into the batter's box, a slender gentleman of 57 summers squirmed in his seat near the Brooklyn dugout. He watched as Big Newk made his first pitch. It was strike one in the judgment of umpire Larry Goetz.

Sisler swung at the second pitch and missed. Strike two. The third delivery was wide. Ball one.

Again Newcombe fired. Sisler swung and fouled the ball into the stands. The crowd roared, interpreting the foul as an indication that Newcombe still had his blazing fastball.

For the fifth time Newcombe threw. The ball was speeding across the outside of the plate when its path was diverted by the sudden intervention of Sisler's bat. The ball changed course abruptly and described a high arc toward left field. As Sisler ran to first base, he saw Abrams retreat several steps and then watch the ball sail overhead and disappear into the bleachers. At that point his pace slowed noticeably. Seven months after suffering the disappointment of losing his starting first-base job, Sisler trotted slowly around the bases, savoring the moment. He knew he could play every day, and now everyone else knew it, too—thanks to his timely three-run homer.

As Sisler toured the bases, the gentleman who had been squirming in his box seat tossed his hat into the air and emitted some whoops and a holler. In the midst of general bereavement, he cheered to the echo.

The man was George Sisler, the Hall of Fame first baseman who, in this one paradoxical moment, permitted parental pride to overshadow company loyalty.

"I felt awful and terrific at the same time," explained Sisler, an assistant to Branch Rickey, majordomo of the Dodgers.

While Sisler's three-run homer gave Philadelphia a 4-1 lead and dealt a smashing blow to Brooklyn's pennant dreams, it did not necessarily sound the death knell. Miracle finishes had a way of happening at Ebbets Field, and perhaps this was the day for just one more.

Campanella was the first batter to greet Roberts in the Brooklyn half of the 10th inning. Campy had one of the five hits yielded by Roberts, but he was not to get a second. He socked a liner to left field that was hauled in by speedy Jack Mayo, a defensive replacement for Sisler.

Cox, hitless in three attempts, was next, but Shotton sent up Jim Russell to pinch-hit. It was the veteran outfielder's 32nd birthday, but he marked it in a highly inauspicious manner. He struck out.

Tommy (Buckshot) Brown, a 22-year-old Brooklyn native who was hitting .294 as a part-time outfielder, was the Dodgers' last hope. Batting for Newcombe, Brown fouled out to Waitkus.

With that out, the Phillies had avoided the most colossal collapse in major league history and secured their first pennant in 35 years. The big heroes for Philadelphia that day were Roberts, who became the club's first 20-game winner since 1917, when Grover Cleveland Alexander posted 30 victories; Ashburn, whose strong heave nailed Abrams at the plate in the ninth inning, and, of course, Sisler.

Sisler's game-winning homer placed fresh emphasis on Abrams' ill-advised attempt to score on Snider's ninth-inning hit. After the game, many participants and observers were focusing their 20-20 hindsight on that play, including Abrams himself, who said, "I think they should have held me at third." In his own defense, however, Milt Stock said, "I'd make the play the same way if I had it to do over again."

Ashburn was surprised by Abrams' foolhardy dash. "I was playing close—not unusually close, because you can't play Snider shallow—and the ball was hit sharp," he said. "It came to me perfectly, and I was all set for a throw."

Sawyer said he thought the Dodgers failed to appreciate Richie's improved throwing ability. "Ashburn's arm was weak early in the year and people got in the habit of running on him," the skipper said. "But it's improved recently."

Shotton, the mild-mannered Brooklyn manager, blamed only himself. The Dodgers' downfall, he maintained, lay not with Stock's decision to send Abrams home, but with his own decision to let Snider swing away.

"I should have bunted," Shotton said. "If you don't believe me, look in the newspapers."

It was there that the omnipresent second-guessers were practicing their freedom of speech.

The 1950 season was a dream come true for Phillies star Dick Sisler, who is shown waving to appreciative fans from the balcony of his well-decorated house in Norristown, Pa., after hitting his pennant-clinching home run.

9

A Giant
Step Forward

Despite a mid-September stint in the hospital, Willie Mays was the major
force behind the San Francisco Giants' 1962 pennant drive.

An air of expectancy surrounded the San Francisco Giants when they embarked on their last trip of the season in mid-September 1962. A seven-game winning streak had elevated their spirits and lifted the team to within half a game of the pace-setting Los Angeles Dodgers. The prospects of the club winning its first National League pennant since forsaking New York five years before were quite good.

Headed by righthanders Juan Marichal and Jack Sanford and lefthanders Billy O'Dell and Billy Pierce, the pitching staff was functioning smoothly. And the offense, which was dominated by outfielders Willie Mays, Felipe Alou and Harvey Kuenn and first baseman Orlando Cepeda—all of whom were hitting .298 or better—made enemy hurlers pay dearly for their mistakes.

The team's first stop on its 11-game trip was Cincinnati. The Giants already had won four of seven games in Crosley Field and 11 of 16 overall against the Reds. But the defending N.L. champions had a definite stake in the race, resting only 5½ games behind the leaders. Righthanders Bob Purkey and Joey Jay already had won 21 games each for the Reds, while lefthander Jim O'Toole had contributed 15 victories to date.

Oppressive heat and humidity greeted the Giants when they deplaned in Cincinnati. It was typical summer climate in the Ohio River Valley, but to a major league baseball player accustomed to the bracing atmosphere of San Francisco it represented sheer misery.

Nobody viewed the conditions with greater trepidation than Mays. As he relaxed in the dugout and watched Jay complete his warmup tosses for the night game of September 12, the Say-Hey Kid was reminded of a promise made by Alvin Dark the previous year when he took over as manager of the club. The former Giants shortstop had announced that he planned to give Mays occasional rests throughout the summer in order to conserve his energy. For one reason or another, Mays had appeared in every game of the 1961 season and had played in every contest so far in 1962 as well. Even for a 31-year-old athlete in the pink of condition, such an unbroken workload could be devastating. The Cincinnati climate didn't help matters, either.

Furthermore, Willie reflected, there was a game in 1954 at the Polo Grounds in New York played under conditions that were strikingly similar to those prevailing in Cincinnati. On that day eight years before, Mays had swatted an inside-the-park homer. Returning to his center-field position, he was stricken by a sudden attack of dizziness. The vast horseshoe was swirling and twisting before his eyes, and he felt faint. Nothing came of it, however, because Willie bent over and placed his hands on his knees. The dizziness passed, but the experience lingered in Willie's memory.

In September 1962, Willie was in the thick of another pennant race, making this game against the Reds an important one. The Giants failed to score in the first inning. In the home half, however, the Reds roughed up Pierce, a former American Leaguer in his first campaign with the Giants. A two-run homer by Frank Robinson and a solo blast by the next batter, Wally Post, provided a sizable cushion for an artist such as Jay.

The score remained unchanged after two innings. The Giants still were trying to solve the deliveries of the Cincinnati righthander in the third when a flurry of activity directed attention to the visitors' dugout. Players were milling around a prostrate figure on the floor. The team trainer was working feverishly to revive the victim.

Mays had passed out. A stretcher was procured and Mays, who was out cold for 20 minutes, was rushed to a hospital. For the next two days, doctors probed for causes of the collapse. Finding nothing physically wrong, they concluded that Mays had suffered from extreme exhaustion.

The Giants, meanwhile, lost both games to the Reds and moved on to Pittsburgh. Mays was back in the dugout the night of September 14 for the start of the series, but Dark insisted on resting his worn-out slugger.

"Nobody, just nobody, wants to win a pennant more than I," Dark told reporters. "But I'm not going to do it at the risk of shattering somebody's nerves, perhaps permanently."

After missing three games, Mays returned to the lineup September 16. He celebrated the occasion with his 44th home run of the season, a three-run shot that tied the score, 4-4, in the eighth inning. But the Giants succumbed to the Pirates eventually on Smoky Burgess' two-run homer in the 10th inning.

Until his incapacitation, it had been an excellent season for Mays and the Giants. Underdogs to the Dodgers as preseason pennant picks, the Giants broke smartly from the starting gate and won their first five games, all at home, as Mays clouted three home runs. Marichal shut out Milwaukee in the opener and O'Dell allowed one run the next day. Sanford captured the decision, with help from reliever Stu Miller, to complete the three-game sweep of the Braves. Pierce made it four in a row, again with the assistance of Miller, as the Giants beat the Reds. Righthander Don Larsen, who had been acquired with Pierce from the Chicago White Sox the previous winter, won the fifth game in relief of rookie Gaylord Perry and with the additional help of four home runs, two each by Cepeda and Alou. The season-opening streak was snapped by the Reds when Purkey edged Marichal, 4-3.

San Francisco was not the only N.L. team to get off to a good start. St. Louis won its first seven

San Francisco's 1962 pitching staff was anchored by (left to right) Don Larsen, Stu Miller, Billy O'Dell, Billy Pierce, Jack Sanford and Juan Marichal.

games, while Pittsburgh did even better, winning 10 contests before suffering its first setback of the young season. But after that hot start, the Pirates lost 14 of their next 18 games. Though they later enjoyed three separate seven-game winning streaks, the Pirates never got closer than 2½ games behind the league leaders the rest of the campaign. Before long, the Cardinals also slipped from contention.

From April 25 to May 4, the Giants reeled off 10 straight victories as their cast of sluggers erupted in an almost daily bombardment of home runs. Mays whacked four homers, including one grand slam, and Cepeda blasted five homers in that stretch. For more than a month, the Giants held undisputed possession of first place.

Then Los Angeles surged into the race. The Dodgers forged a tie for the lead June 1 by winning their 13th consecutive game. A Los Angeles loss to Philadelphia and a doubleheader sweep of the fledgling New York Mets by San Francisco the next day, however, pushed the Dodgers back into second place. But that status was short-lived. Pierce, who had won his first eight starts, finally was tagged with a loss June 7 when the Chicago Cubs beat him and the Giants, 4-3, cutting San Francisco's lead to half a game. Despite homers by Mays and outfielder-first baseman Willie McCovey, who spent much of the season battling charley horses, the Giants slipped to second the next day when Bob Gibson and the Cardinals beat Marichal and the Giants, 8-4.

A four-game Dodgers-Giants series at Candlestick

Park preceded the first of two All-Star Games in July. The Dodgers gained a split in the series when Sandy Koufax and Don Drysdale combined to blank the Giants, 2-0, in the last game before the intermission. The Dodgers and Giants had swapped the lead six times by then, but when the break commenced, the Dodgers were in first place by half a game with a 58-31 record.

The Dodgers had won four of their first five games after the All-Star break when tragedy befell them July 17. Their gifted lefthander, Koufax, already had a no-hitter to his credit and was fanning batters at a record pace en route to a 14-4 record when Manager Walter Alston had to take him out after the first inning of a game at Cincinnati. Koufax had developed a numbness in the index finger and palm of his left hand and was sidelined for two months with what was diagnosed as a circulatory ailment.

Drysdale, however, hurled brilliantly and helped keep Los Angeles in front of the pack during his teammate's absence. The big righthander earned his 19th victory against only four defeats when the Dodgers completed a three-game sweep of the Giants at Dodger Stadium on July 29, boosting their lead to four games. That advantage had risen to 5½ games and Drysdale boasted a 21-4 record when the Dodgers invaded Candlestick Park for three games August 10-12.

The sojourn proved a total loss for the visitors. More than 40,000 fans turned out for each contest

Heading Manager Alvin Dark's (center) large Latin American cast were (left to right) Matty and Felipe Alou, Jose Pagan, Manny Mota, Orlando Cepeda and Juan Marichal.

and cheered wildly as O'Dell coasted to an 11-2 win over Johnny Podres in the opener, Pierce outdueled Drysdale in the second contest, 5-4, and Marichal vanquished Stan Williams, 5-1, in the finale. The triple setback dug deeply into the Dodgers' lead, but they recovered, and even after losing three of four games to the Giants at home in early September, they remained 1½ games in front. As late as September 22, with only seven games remaining on the newly expanded 162-game schedule, the Dodgers still enjoyed a seemingly impregnable lead of four lengths. Contributing to that advantage was a six-game San Francisco losing streak that began the night Mays collapsed in the dugout.

But in the last week of the season, the Dodgers, who had lost four of their six previous games, turned even more feeble. On September 23, the Cardinals knocked out Drysdale in the fourth inning and romped to a 12-2 triumph over Los Angeles. Meanwhile, O'Dell defeated Houston, 10-3, at Colt Stadium to reduce the Giants' deficit to three games.

After an open date, the front-runners returned to action September 25. Both clubs were blessed with the opportunity to play their six remaining games at home, and they even faced three-game sets with the same opponents—the sixth-place Cardinals and eighth-place Colt .45s. The Dodgers, hosting Houston first, dropped a 10-inning, 3-2 verdict to Dick Farrell, who handed Ed Roebuck, a 10-game winner, his first loss of the campaign. In San Francisco, Sanford defeated the Cardinals, 4-2, and the Los

Angeles lead was shaved to two games. The Dodgers maintained that advantage the next day as both contenders won, Podres defeating Houston, 13-1, and Pierce beating the Cards, 6-3.

The Dodgers missed a chance to clinch a tie for the flag September 27 when Koufax, making his second start since returning to action, lasted only five innings and reliever Ron Perranoski was tagged with an 8-6 loss to Houston. Earlier that day, the Giants had been battered by the Cards, 7-4, as Stan Musial went 5-for-5 and Gene Oliver belted a decisive three-run homer.

While the Giants' first game with Houston was being rained out September 28, Larry Jackson was hurling the Cardinals to a 3-2 victory over the Dodgers. Perranoski again took the loss in relief as the Dodgers' lead shrank to 1½ games.

San Francisco had a chance to gain some precious ground on Los Angeles the next day when it entered its doubleheader with Houston. Home runs by Cepeda, McCovey and catcher Tom Haller propelled the Giants to an 11-5 triumph in the opener as Sanford collected his 24th victory. But Marichal's 4-2 loss to Bob Bruce in the nightcap left the Giants with a 100-61 record with one game to go. If Drysdale and the Dodgers (101-59) could beat St. Louis later that night, Los Angeles would have its second N.L. flag in four years and the season finales would be meaningless.

But that's not what happened. Ernie Broglio yielded only two hits and hurled the Cards to a 2-0 win over the Dodgers, whose lead dwindled to one game.

The Giants, who had been looking up at Los Angeles in the standings since July 8, still had a chance to tie the Dodgers on the last day of the season. If Johnny Keane's Cardinals could complete the sweep of their series in Dodger Stadium, San Francisco could force the race into a dead heat by defeating Houston at Candlestick Park.

O'Dell, a 19-game winner for the Giants that year, was Dark's choice to pitch the crucial contest. With 41,327 fans watching in the stands, O'Dell hurled effectively but was denied his 20th victory. Miller picked up the 2-1 decision when Mays broke a 1-1 tie in the eighth inning with his 47th homer of the season. The Giants still had a chance as they hurried into the clubhouse to await the results of the Dodgers-Cardinals game.

They didn't have to wait long. Podres and St. Louis' Curt Simmons kept the game moving along by allowing no runs through seven innings. Then in the eighth, Oliver slugged a home run to give the Cardinals a 1-0 victory. Miraculously, the Giants had caught the Dodgers just in time to force a three-game playoff, the fourth in N.L. history.

The Giants' feat was all the more miraculous considering their mediocre performance down the stretch. They won five of their last seven games but only seven of their last 17. If not for the Dodgers' collapse—they lost six of their last seven and 10 of their last 13 contests—the Giants already would have been making plans to watch their West Coast rivals play the New York Yankees in the World Series.

"The last 10 days of the race we could see the Dodgers slipping and knew we had a chance," said Pierce, a 15-game winner entering the playoffs. "It keyed us up."

Mays, who had homered in his first and last at-bats of the season's regular schedule, was shocked that the Giants had managed to close the gap.

"So much had to happen," he said. "No matter how hard we played or how much we won, it was hard to believe the Dodgers would lose all those games the final week in their own park. We had to have help. And we got it from the Cardinals, who beat them three in a row."

Only two victories were required in the next three games to determine a new N.L. champion. Both clubs were familiar with the format, the Dodgers having participated in all three previous N.L. playoffs, including one against the Giants in 1951. The Dodgers, then based in Brooklyn, lost that battle as well as one of their other sudden-death series. Their only playoff victory had come three years before when they swept the Milwaukee Braves in two games to bring the West Coast its first pennant.

N.L. President Warren Giles flipped a coin to determine the playoff sites. The Dodgers won the toss and opted to open the series in their rivals' park and play the remaining game, or games, at home.

Controversy wreathed the playing field even before the playoffs got under way at Candlestick Park on the afternoon of October 1. Through their publicity director, Red Patterson, the Dodgers squawked bitterly about the condition of the basepaths, contending that the Giants' groundkeeper, Matty Schwab, had dumped "tons of sand" on the skinned area as a means of handicapping shortstop Maury Wills, who had stolen 100 bases already that season to set a modern major league record.

Unable to locate Giles, Patterson lodged a complaint with Jocko Conlan, umpire-in-chief for the game.

"Now they've got sand on it," Patterson told the umpire, "and after infield practice they'll turn on the sprinklers and wet it down like it was for a water follies."

The arbiter stuck his toe into the sand around first base and announced, "They've got to put this field in regulation condition."

Conlan and Dark exchanged sharp words when the San Francisco skipper refused to summon Schwab. But the groundkeeper eventually was located and under Conlan's watchful eye, several wheelbarrows of sand were carted away. Schwab also was instructed not to wet down the field.

"All we did was run the harrows over it a little," said Schwab, who denied that extra sand had been dumped on the infield. "As for wetting down the field before the game, we always do that."

With that matter settled, both teams got back to the business at hand. The Giants had to contend with Koufax, Alston's selection to start on the mound for the Dodgers. The lefthander was trying for his 15th win of the year for the third time after recuperating from his hand ailment, which still bothered him a little.

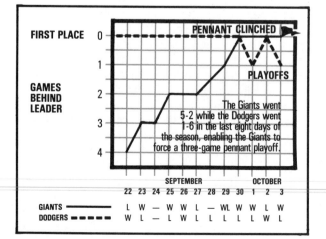

FIRST PLACE   0   PENNANT CLINCHED

GAMES
BEHIND   1
LEADER   PLAYOFFS

              2
                        The Giants went
              3   5-2 while the Dodgers went
                    1-6 in the last eight days of
                    the season, enabling the Giants to
              4   force a three-game pennant playoff.

                        SEPTEMBER   OCTOBER
                22 23 24 25 26 27 28 29 30 1 2 3
GIANTS   L W — W W L — WL W W L W
DODGERS   W L — L W L L L L L W L

The Dodgers were ecstatic after coming from behind in the second playoff
game to defeat the Giants, 8-7.

Opposing Koufax was Pierce, a 35-year-old left-hander who had spent 14 years in the American League before his trade to the Giants the previous winter. Eleven of Pierce's victories in 1962 had come at windswept Candlestick Park, where he had a fairly simple secret of success. "Pitch mainly fastballs," he preached, "and make the batters hit to left field, where the wind blows in and holds up the ball."

Pierce had only six losses, all on the road. There was little doubt that Billy would have been a 20-game winner if not for a spike wound that forced him to miss several starts.

The veteran lefthander was at his best in the playoff opener. He scattered three hits, including a double by pinch-hitter Doug Camilli, and coasted behind a 10-hit attack. A two-out double by Alou and Mays' home run gave the Giants a 2-0 lead in the first inning, and third baseman Jim Davenport's leadoff homer in the second added a third marker.

When catcher Ed Bailey followed with a single, Koufax gave way to Roebuck. The Dodger right-hander blanked the Giants for four innings, but in the sixth, consecutive homers by Mays (No. 49) and Cepeda (No. 35) off Larry Sherry provided the home team with a 5-0 margin.

In the eighth, three walks, a double by shortstop Jose Pagan and a throwing error by outfielder Frank Howard produced the last three runs in the Giants' 8-0 victory. The shutout was the third in a row suffered by the Dodgers, while the defeat represented their fifth in succession.

"That was the most satisfying game I ever pitched," Pierce said afterward.

The second game was played October 2 before a disappointing crowd of 25,321 at Dodger Stadium. The short notice that the game would even be played was blamed for the turnout, but more than 7,000 more fans had shown up at Candlestick the day before on even shorter notice. "This town has

given up on the Dodgers," explained a taxi driver who was unaccustomed to the light traffic at the stadium. "We're disgusted. It's a boycott."

Even a pitching matchup of the league's top two winners, Drysdale (25-9) and Sanford (24-7), was insufficient to fill the stands. The 26-year-old Drysdale was leading the league in innings pitched and strikeouts as well as victories en route to the Cy Young Award. Sanford, meanwhile, was enjoying his best season since 1957, when he went 19-8 for the Phillies and was named N.L. Rookie Pitcher of the Year. When his record slipped to 10-13 the next season, however, the righthander was traded to the Giants. In his first three seasons with San Francisco, Jack won 40 games but at no time hurled in a manner to portend the exceptional season he enjoyed in 1962.

Two months into the campaign, Sanford was only a break-even pitcher with six wins and as many losses. But when he defeated the Cardinals June 17, he launched a winning streak that endured for three months. He tied together 16 straight wins before having his streak snapped September 15 by Bob Friend and the Pirates.

"It's ridiculous," Sanford said after recording what would be the last of his 16 consecutive victories. "I don't care how good a guy is. If he's real good, maybe he'll win five or six in a row, then bad luck will catch up with him. But 16! The whole thing is ridiculous."

Sanford won his last two decisions after the streak-ending defeat. His last victory had come only three days before his Game 2 playoff start when he pitched the first game of the doubleheader against Houston. In addition to working on just two days' rest (as was Drysdale), he was suffering from a heavy cold. Dark could only hope for the best as his ace pitcher returned to the mound.

The Giants staked Sanford to a 1-0 lead in the second inning when Cepeda singled and scored on Alou's double. That lead grew to 5-0 in the sixth. After Haller walked with one out, Pagan doubled the catcher to third. The next batter, Sanford, surprised the Dodgers by bunting on a 2-2 count. Drysdale was unable to field the ball cleanly, allowing Haller to score and Sanford to reach first base. Run-scoring singles by second baseman Chuck Hiller and Davenport brought on Roebuck in relief of Drysdale, who was charged with the final run

Maury Wills gave the Giants a demonstration of his disruptive baserunning abilities in Games 2 and 3 of the 1962 N.L. playoffs. Wills (above) scored the winning run in the ninth inning of Game 2 after tagging up at third on a short fly to the outfield. He scored the Dodgers' fourth run of Game 3 (below) when he stole third and continued home on catcher Ed Bailey's errant throw.

(albeit unearned) of the inning when McCovey produced a clutch single.

That inning gave Sanford a substantial cushion, but it also took its toll on the pitcher, who ran the bases in a windbreaker and scored a run with a heavy slide across the plate. When Sanford walked infielder Jim Gilliam to open the home half of the sixth inning, Dark could tell that his starter was worn out. Though he had allowed only two hits in five innings, he was replaced by Miller, a righthander who was making his 59th appearance of the year.

Outfielder Duke Snider greeted the slender reliever with a double and outfielder-third baseman Tommy Davis hit a sacrifice fly that snapped the Dodgers' runless drought at 35 innings. When first baseman Wally Moon walked and Howard singled across the Dodgers' second run, Miller departed and O'Dell was rushed from the bullpen.

The lefthander was little improvement. Alston called on three successive righthanded pinch-hitters, none of whom was retired. Camilli singled to load the bases, and Andy Carey was hit by a pitch that forced home a run, reducing the Giants' advantage to 5-3. Lee Walls then was called on to bat for Roebuck, and when the reserve outfielder blasted a double, three runners scampered across the plate to give the Dodgers a 6-5 lead.

Larsen replaced O'Dell and the Dodgers scored their seventh run of the inning when Wills grounded to first to score Walls, who kicked the ball out of

Haller's glove on a close play at the plate.

The Giants knotted the score at 7-7 with two runs in the eighth inning. Consecutive singles by Davenport and Mays leading off the inning prompted Alston to bring in Jack Smith in relief of Perranoski. The righthander promptly surrendered a run-scoring single to pinch-hitter Bailey, but a big inning was averted when Mays was called out at third by Conlan, who ignored Mays' vehement objections that he had beaten the throw. The star center fielder would have scored on the next play because Howard dropped Cepeda's low line drive for his second error in as many days. But the tying run later scored when Williams relieved Smith, walked Alou and gave up a sacrifice fly to backup catcher John Orsino.

When the game went into the bottom of the ninth with the score still tied, Dark employed four pitchers in a futile effort to force the game into extra innings. He started with Bob Bolin, who had pitched a hitless eighth. When the righthander issued a leadoff walk to Wills, he was replaced by Dick LeMay, a lefthander who walked Gilliam. That was all for LeMay. Daryl Spencer was an-

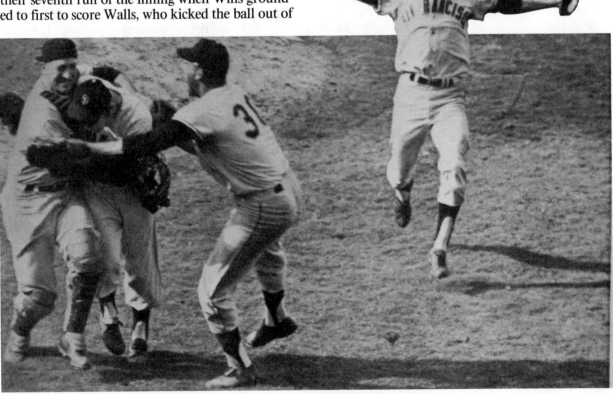

Pitcher Billy Pierce is mobbed by catcher Ed Bailey and Orlando Cepeda (30) as Jose Pagan dances into the picture after San Francisco's pennant-clinching playoff victory.

nounced as a pinch-hitter for Snider, whereupon Dark beckoned Perry, a 24-year-old rookie who had won three of four decisions.

With a sacrifice in order, Pagan raced from his shortstop position to third base, hoping for a force-out on Wills, the lead runner. The strategy failed when Perry, after fielding Spencer's bunt, ignored Pagan and threw to first to retire the batter.

Once more Dark went to his bullpen. He signaled for Mike McCormick, the eighth San Francisco pitcher of the day. After an intentional walk to Davis, the league's leading hitter, loaded the bases, Ron Fairly lifted a short fly to Mays, who made a strong throw to the plate, but not powerful enough to head off the speedy Wills, who tagged up and scored to give Los Angeles an 8-7 triumph. With all the managerial maneuvers—Dark used 23 players, Alston 19—the game consumed four hours and 18 minutes, setting a record for a nine-inning game.

The maneuver that spawned the most second-guessing was Dark's removal of Sanford when the Giants had a 5-0 lead in the sixth. Though the move backfired, Dark nevertheless defended his initial decision.

"Jack was exhausted," the manager explained. "He had pitched Saturday and he had a bad cold, and he didn't have anything left. I thought we could hold it (the lead) for him, but we didn't."

Sanford agreed that he was pooped. "Alvin made the right move," he said.

Williams, who earned the victory in relief (Bolin took the loss), said he was especially pleased that the Dodgers had managed to win without going to extra innings.

"Willie Mays would have been the first batter for the Giants in the 10th inning," he said, "and I wasn't really anxious to pitch to him."

Williams didn't have to pitch to Mays the next day, either. But he did play a crucial role in the outcome of the decisive third playoff game October 3 at Dodger Stadium.

Marichal, an 18-game winner, drew the starting assignment for the Giants. He was opposed by Podres, a 15-game winner who, for the first time in his career, was pitching with only two days' rest. The lefthander had 20,000 more fans on hand to cheer him on than Drysdale had had the day before.

Both teams matched zeroes in the first two innings before Los Angeles charity helped the Giants to a pair of runs in the third. The madcap merry-go-round started after Pagan opened the frame with a single. On Marichal's sacrifice, Podres threw the ball into center field, permitting Pagan to reach third. A single by Kuenn drove home Pagan and advanced Marichal to second. When Hiller missed on a sacrifice attempt, Marichal was hung up between bases, but he reached third safely when catch-er John Roseboro's throw sailed into center field. Hiller then flied out to Snider in left field, and while Marichal held third on the return throw to the infield, Kuenn was trapped between first and second. But second baseman Gilliam muffed the relay, and that error allowed Marichal to score the second run while Kuenn returned safely to first. The Giants later loaded the bases with only one out, but Cepeda grounded into an inning-ending double play. Snider, playing his last game in a Dodger uniform, doubled to lead off the bottom of the fourth inning. He took third when Davis singled and scored the team's first run when Howard grounded into a forceout.

The Giants drove Podres to cover in the top of the sixth on singles by Cepeda, Bailey and Davenport that loaded the bases with none out. The left-hander was succeeded by Roebuck, who had developed into the club's ace fireman. Despite the fact that he was appearing in his sixth game in seven days, the righthander stopped the Giants cold by getting the next two batters to hit balls to Wills. Pagan's grounder was turned into a forceout at the plate, and Marichal's grounder was converted into a double play.

Snider ignited a second Dodger outburst in the bottom half of the inning with a single to left field. He loped home ahead of Davis when the third baseman smacked a 400-foot homer into the left-field seats to give the Dodgers a 3-2 advantage. It was Tommy's 27th homer and league-leading 152nd and 153rd runs batted in of the year.

Wills single-handedly added a fourth run to the Dodger total in the seventh inning. With one out, mercurial Maury singled to center field for his fourth hit of the day off Marichal. On the first pitch to Gilliam, Wills stole second. After Gilliam flied out to left field, Maury swiped third (No. 104 of the season) and continued across the plate when Bailey's poor throw skipped past Davenport.

After extricating the Dodgers from the sixth-inning predicament, Roebuck stopped the Giants the next two innings on a pair of hits, a double by Hiller and a single by Bailey. With only three outs to go, the game appeared all but clinched, the pennant all but locked up. The Dodgers led, 4-2, and 45,693 hysterical partisans were already celebrating.

But the strain of working so many games down the stretch exacted a stiff price on the 31-year-old righthander. A single by pinch-hitter Matty Alou started Roebuck's downfall, and one-out walks to McCovey and Felipe Alou loaded the bases. The passes were the second and third issued by Roebuck in eight innings of toil during the playoffs.

So, it was the top of the ninth, the visitors were trailing by two, the bases were loaded . . . and up to the plate strode none other than Willie Howard Mays Jr.

"I couldn't have asked for more," Dark later reflected on the unfolding scenario.

Hopeful that another disaster could be averted as it had been three innings earlier, Alston let his overworked reliever pitch to Mays, who was hitless in two official at-bats with two walks. The result was a wicked smash to the mound that struck the pitcher's bare hand for a run-scoring single, Willie's 141st RBI of the year. With the bases still full, the Giants trailed by a slim 4-3 margin.

Exit Roebuck. Williams was next. The previous day's hero and 14-game winner was tagged for a sacrifice fly by Cepeda, tying the score with two out. When Williams uncorked a wild pitch that allowed Felipe Alou to go to third and Mays to take second, Alston ordered an intentional walk to Bailey to load the bases again. But Williams then surrendered an unintentional base on balls to Davenport to force in the go-ahead run. Perranoski was summoned to record the final out, but that was delayed when second baseman Larry Burright, a late-inning defensive replacement, fumbled Pagan's grounder. Mays crossed the plate with San Francisco's fourth run of the inning, giving the Giants a 6-4 lead.

Dodger Stadium was hushed as Pierce set the Dodgers down in order in the last half of the ninth. Pierce, who had humbled the Dodgers in the play-off opener, thus saved the victory for Larsen, who had hurled one hitless inning in relief.

After a season in which they had played only .506 ball on the road and still managed to win 103 games, the Giants were champions. Champagne flowed freely in the San Francisco clubhouse, although most of it dripped down shoulders rather than thirsty gullets.

"If we drank all this stuff, we'd be sick for a week," said Bailey, realizing that he and his teammates had to face the Yankees in San Francisco the next day. "And if we had blown that game today, we'd have been sick for a year."

Drinking was going on in the Dodger clubhouse, too, but it was more of the hard-liquor variety, intended to induce mind-numbing forgetfulness. Reporters were locked out of the locker room for nearly an hour, at which point Moon, the team's player representative, spoke briefly on behalf of his teammates.

"It's rough," said Wally, his voice cracking. "How would you feel if you had just blown $12,000 (each winning player's share)?"

For veteran Dodgers such as Snider who remembered the club's Brooklyn heritage, the Giants' four-run explosion in the ninth inning that day evoked terrifying memories. Precisely 11 years before, on October 3, 1951, Bobby Thomson's "Shot Heard 'Round the World" had sparked the Giants to another four-run, ninth-inning explosion that deprived the Dodgers of another flag.

"For impact, you'll never beat 1951," said Giants coach Wes Westrum, who had been a catcher for the New York Giants in '51. "But I'll tell you this: This is a better Giant team. These guys are real tigers."

Teammates Chuck Hiller (left) and Orlando Cepeda share a locker-room hug after the Giants' Game 3 playoff win over the Dodgers.

10

Cardinals Meet Great Expectations

Eddie Dyer stared moodily at the walls of his drawing room as the train carrying the St. Louis Cardinals rolled out of Cincinnati on its way to Chicago on a late May evening in 1946.

The normally chipper manager of the Cardinals was the soul of dejection, not so much because of the two defeats his club had suffered in three meetings with the Reds, but primarily because of what had occurred three days earlier in New York. On May 23, Dyer had learned that three key Cardinals —pitchers Max Lanier and Fred Martin and infielder Lou Klein—had succumbed to the blandishments of the Pasquel brothers and jumped to the Mexican League, which was controlled by the fabulously wealthy siblings.

The loss of Lanier was the most damaging blow. Unquestionably, with a record of 6-0 in six starts, the chunky North Carolinian was the best lefthander in the National League, if not the league's best pitcher, period. Martin, a minor league standout before spending four years in the Army, was regarded as the Cards' foremost righthander. Klein had been a mainstay on the pennant-winning St. Louis club of 1943, and Dyer thought highly enough of him in 1946 that he often started Klein at

second base ahead of Red Schoendienst, a superior hitter.

The defections imposed an additional handicap on Dyer, who already was laboring under a heavy burden of expectations. The '46 season was his first as a major league pilot. When Billy Southworth, whose St. Louis clubs had won three pennants in the last four years, resigned his position with the Cardinals to accept a similar post with the Boston Braves, Dyer was appointed his successor.

Unlike most first-year skippers, Dyer was expected to win. The St. Louis roster was crammed with returning servicemen, most of them established major league stars before marching off to war. Outfielder-first baseman Stan Musial and right fielder Enos Slaughter were foremost among that group.

In a preseason poll by the Associated Press, the Cards came up four votes shy of being a unanimous selection to win the N.L. flag. Even Branch Rickey, the former Cards general manager who had moved to the top spot in the Brooklyn Dodgers' organization before the 1943 season, had expressed fears

With the defection of some key Cardinal pitchers to the Mexican League in 1946, Howie Pollet offered Manager Eddie Dyer his durable left arm for extra duty.

publicly that St. Louis would make a runaway of the race. But on the evening of May 26, when the Cardinals were en route to Chicago, Brooklyn was atop the N.L. standings with a 23-10 record, 2½ games ahead of St. Louis (20-12). And the recent jumps to the Mexican League by three important players made the outlook a bit more grim for the Cardinals.

As Dyer brooded on the plight of his team, his reverie was interrupted by a knock on the door.

The visitor was no stranger to the skipper. They had met initially eight years earlier, when Dyer was a scout for the Houston Buffaloes of the Texas League as well as the supervisor of the Cardinals' farm clubs in the South and Southwest. Acting on a tip from a Texas oil man who was a friend of the club president's, Dyer had gone to New Orleans to check on a 17-year-old pitcher who, he was told, possessed poise and guile far beyond his tender years.

Dyer, a former hurler himself at Rice Institute and in the St. Louis organization, met the prospect and watched him pitch for an American Legion team.

By December of that year, Dyer had in his hands a signed contract bearing the name of Howard Joseph Pollet and a provision for a signing bonus of $3,500. The signature on the contract, however, belonged to Howie's mother, who endorsed the deal on behalf of her son, a minor.

When the 1939 season opened, Dyer was the Houston manager and Howie Pollet was one of his pitchers. In July, Pollet was sent down to New Iberia of the Class-D Evangeline League, where he posted a 14-5 record. He was returned to Houston in 1940, once again teaming up with Dyer.

At 19, Pollet was the class of the league. The stylish lefthander's record of 20-7 included 12 consecutive victories. The Buffs won 105 games and the Texas League championship.

The next year Pollet improved his record to 20-3. He pitched a no-hitter and led the league in winning percentage and earned-run average (1.16). Again the Buffs won the pennant.

Before the Buffs clinched that championship, the Cardinals purchased Pollet's contract from Houston in August 1941. Howie won five games for St. Louis in '41 and then went 7-5 in 27 appearances in 1942. He had an 8-4 record in 1943 before he was summoned to military service. As was the case for many former major leaguers, the 1946 season marked Pollet's return to professional baseball.

It also marked Pollet's reunion with Dyer. Their friendship had grown close through the years—so close that Howie had given Eddie his power of attorney while he was away at war. In the off-season, Pollet worked for Dyer's insurance company in Houston.

So, it was more than just a player who entered his skipper's drawing room on a train in May 1946. It was a trusted friend. They discussed matters of the moment, such as the defection of the three teammates.

"I know I can't make up for those three fellows," Pollet told Dyer, "but I'll tell you what I can do. You let me start one day and give me one day of rest, and I can go in and relieve for you the next day. One more day off and I can start again the day after that."

Pollet was not given to idle promises. His major league credentials were convincing. Before entering the service in July 1943, he had hurled three consecutive shutouts and led the league in ERA. Dyer knew Pollet was serious, and he decided to give his friend a chance to prove it.

For the remainder of the 1946 season, Howie was on call on alternate days. He started 32 games, 22 of which he completed, and relieved in eight more. He led the circuit in innings pitched (266), victories (21) and ERA (2.10). Without his workhorse efforts, the Cardinals probably would not have contended for the N.L. pennant.

They did, although Rickey's fears of a St. Louis runaway were not realized. The flag chase developed early into a two-team struggle between the Cardinals and Dodgers—and Brooklyn had the upper hand for most of the first half of the season. The lead switched back and forth several times in April and May, but right after St. Louis suffered its Mexican League losses, the Cards lost three of their next four games. The Dodgers pounced on that opportunity and assumed a lead they held almost continuously until late August.

The Dodgers were managed masterfully by Leo Durocher, who had directed the club to finishes of third place or better in six of his seven seasons at the helm. Like Dyer, Durocher had his share of problems—the loss of catcher Mickey Owen to the Mexican League for one—but he managed to get the most out of his odd array of seasoned veterans (right fielder Dixie Walker and pitcher Kirby Higbe, among others) and such unknowns as center fielder Carl Furillo and pitcher Joe Hatten.

The Dodgers enjoyed their biggest lead of 7½ games on July 2, when they won their seventh straight game and the Cards lost their fourth in a row. St. Louis then won six of its next seven contests to cut that deficit to five games at the All-Star break. And when the Dodgers arrived in St. Louis for the start of a four-game series July 14, their margin was down to 4½ games.

It was a battered Brooklyn team that left St. Louis with just a half-game lead three days later. The Cardinals won all four games. Musial's game-winning home run in the 12th inning of the nightcap highlighted a doubleheader sweep July 14, but

St. Louis Manager Eddie Dyer (center) was grateful for the return of Enos Slaughter (right) and pitcher Johnny Beazley from military duty in 1946.

the victory in the final game was the most dramatic. Trailing 4-2 entering the last of the ninth, the Cardinals shocked the Dodgers with a three-run explosion on a hit batsman, a single and a pinch homer by Erv Dusak, who had failed in attempts to sacrifice. Pollet earned the victory, his 10th.

Two days later, the Dodgers lost their sixth straight game. Meanwhile, righthander Murry Dickson came on in relief to pitch the Cardinals out of a jam and get the win in a 5-4 triumph over the Philadelphia Phillies. That victory gave St. Louis undisputed possession of first place for the first time since May 20.

But the Cards' reign atop the standings was brief. The next day, the Dodgers beat the Cincinnati Reds while St. Louis and Philadelphia were rained out, lifting Brooklyn into a first-place tie that lasted for five days. The Dodgers then regained the lead July 24 and didn't let go for a month. The Cards, who took two out of three games from Brooklyn during that span, remained within striking distance, however, largely because of the effective hurling of Pollet.

The lefthander registered his 15th victory August 20 when he held the Boston Braves to three hits. Two days later, he responded to an eighth-inning emergency in the first game of a twin bill and

stopped a Phillies rally. He then received credit for his 16th victory when Musial blasted a home run in the 12th. That triumph gave Pollet 12 wins in his last 15 decisions and a 16-6 record overall. When lefthander Harry Brecheen beat the Phillies in the nightcap of that August 22 doubleheader, the Cardinals tied the Dodgers for the lead in the pennant race.

By this time, Dyer had come to expect such workhorse efforts from Pollet. The indefatigable craftsman had evoked high praise from his boss almost daily, especially after his strong performance July 12 against the New York Giants.

"He worked the first game of a doubleheader and won it," Dyer recalled years later. "You know what most fellows do after that. They go in and have a shower and change clothes and maybe watch the second game from the stands.

"Pollet stayed in uniform for the second game, and when things began to get tight he went out to the bullpen without even saying anything to me. When I needed a relief pitcher, Howie was already warmed up."

And Dyer needed a relief pitcher that afternoon. After checking the Giants, 2-1, on five hits in the opener, Pollet came out of the bullpen in the ninth inning of the second game. St. Louis had a 5-4 lead,

The 1946 Cardinals boasted a strong infield of (left to right) Whitey Kurow-ski, Marty Marion, Red Schoendienst and Stan Musial.

but New York had runners on first and third with none out. Pollet promptly retired first baseman Johnny Mize on a short fly ball that failed to bring in the runner from third. He then got catcher Ernie Lombardi to hit into a double play, ending the game and saving the victory for righthander Red Barrett.

Pollet's willingness to assume a workhorse role came at a time when Dyer was suffering from mound deficiencies other than those caused by the loss of Max Lanier and Fred Martin.

Red Barrett, a 23-game winner in 1945, fell on troubled times. His July 12 victory over New York was one of only three in '46, and his ERA rose from 3.00 to 4.03.

Johnny Beazley, the rookie hero of the Cardinals' 1942 world championship club with 21 victories, returned from military service in poor physical condition. The righthander contributed only seven wins.

Still a third hurler, righthander George Munger, who was an 11-3 performer before joining the Army midway through the 1944 campaign, did not return from the service until August. Munger then went 2-2 in 10 games late in the '46 season.

St. Louis and Brooklyn had identical 73-45 records when the Dodgers visited St. Louis on August 25 for the start of a four-game series at Sportsman's Park. The teams split a doubleheader the first day. In the opener, Pollet suffered a 3-2 defeat, his first

setback in three weeks. The Cardinals bounced back to win the second game, 14-8. Dickson then pitched St. Louis to a 2-1 victory August 26, giving the Cards a one-game lead. But the Dodgers forged another tie and earned a split in the series when Higbe posted a 7-3 victory over the Cards in the August 27 finale.

The next day, the Dodgers played at Chicago while the Cards hosted two games with the Giants. It was on that day that St. Louis finally moved into the lead for an extended period. While the Dodgers were losing to the Cubs, 4-3, the Cards were sweeping the Giants. The nightcap was highlighted by another remarkable St. Louis comeback as pinch-hitter Walter Sessi slugged a two-run, game-winning homer with two out in the bottom of the ninth inning. When Pollet blanked New York, 4-0, a day later and Chicago again edged Brooklyn, 3-2, St. Louis had a 2½-game advantage.

Two weeks later, the Cardinals visited Brooklyn for the last scheduled series of the year between the two rivals. Despite winning nine of their last 10 contests, the Dodgers still trailed St. Louis by 1½ games.

Pollet enlarged the Cardinals' lead September 12 with a 10-2 victory in the first game. The southpaw allowed only five hits and was given all the batting support he needed in the first inning when the Cards exploded for five runs, two riding home on outfielder Dick Sisler's two-out single and three on catcher Joe Garagiola's two-out homer.

A four-run uprising against Munger in the first inning enabled the Dodgers to win the second game, 4-3. That triumph paved the way for a singular bit of strategy by Durocher in the critical third contest.

In selecting a starting pitcher for the game of September 14, the Brooklyn skipper bypassed his regulars and chose Ralph Branca, a 20-year-old right-hander who had languished in the bullpen for much of the season. Handicapped by a sore arm and poor control, he had made just seven starts in 19 appearances, and his only victory had come in relief.

Why Durocher would make such an unlikely choice mystified most observers, but there was a method in his apparent madness. By sending the righthander to the hill, the skipper reasoned, Dyer would pack the Cardinal lineup with lefthanded batters. After the youngster pitched to one batter, the crafty Leo then would bring in a lefthander, Vic Lombardi, who would be more likely to shackle the southpaw swingers.

"It is a percentage move that may work," Durocher explained.

Such a tactic was not new to baseball annals. In the seventh game of the 1924 World Series, Bucky Harris had used it successfully in counteracting hot-hitting New York Giants first baseman Bill Terry, who had devastated Washington's righthanded hurlers. The Senators won after Harris' ploy effectively eliminated Terry from the lineup.

Branca, however, made Durocher's strategy backfire in a most pleasant way by pitching his best game of the year. The product of New York University disposed of Schoendienst, the leadoff batter, and Durocher allowed Branca to try his stuff against the No. 2 batter, center fielder Harry Walker. He, too, was retired, as was the third hitter, Musial. Meanwhile, Lombardi waited impatiently in the bullpen.

St. Louis batters came and went in routine fashion. Innings slid by easily and after nine, Branca, the sacrificial lamb, owned a three-hit, 5-0 victory. The only run that Branca needed to register his sec-

ond win of the year was provided by third baseman Cookie Lavagetto on a second-inning homer off Brecheen. The game was witnessed by 32,960 fans, who swelled the Ebbets Field attendance for the year to a league record 1,509,755, surpassing the old mark of 1,485,166 set by the Chicago Cubs in 1929.

Leading their closest pursuers by only half a game, the Cardinals moved on to the Polo Grounds for a three-game series against the last-place Giants. In the opener of a doubleheader September 15, Dickson scattered three hits and won, 3-0.

As the second game got under way, Pollet took a seat in the bullpen and watched his teammates build a 5-1 lead behind lefthander Al Brazle. Pollet still was lounging in the bullpen when the somnolent Giants erupted in the eighth inning. One run was in, runners were at second and third, and left fielder Sid Gordon, a righthanded hitter, was due to bat.

Dyer signaled to the bullpen for Munger, but the righthander proved ineffective. Gordon singled to make the score 5-3, bringing first baseman Babe Young, a lefthanded hitter, to the plate.

Dyer glanced toward the bullpen. His gaze fell on Pollet, his reliable friend. Under the mistaken impression that the southpaw already had warmed up, the manager summoned Pollet to face Young.

Dutifully, Pollet trudged to the mound and threw his allotted warmup pitches to his catcher. The game resumed.

"I put everything I had in the first pitch, much to my regret," Pollet recalled years later. "I felt a stab of pain below the shoulder blade."

Young eventually scratched out an infield single that drove home another run. The Giants had narrowed the gap to 5-4, but Pollet stopped the rally by retiring the next two batters to end the inning.

Musial slugged a two-run homer in the top of the ninth to give the Cards more of a cushion. Despite pitching in discomfort, Pollet finished the game, setting the Giants down in order, and the Cardinals won, 7-4. St. Louis was idle the next day, but on September 17 Pollet took his regular turn and defeated the Giants, 10-2, despite allowing 11 hits. The

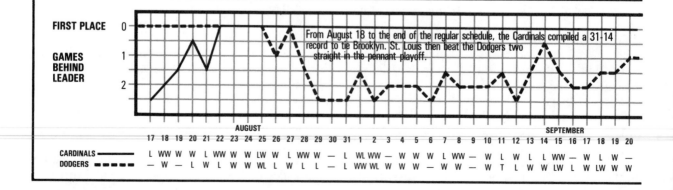

victory was his 20th of the year, making him the first N.L. lefthander to win 20 games in a season since 1937.

The effort was costly, though. He was favoring his left arm, as he continued to do the rest of the season.

"I did not follow through properly," he explained, "in order to avoid recurrence of pain."

He did continue to pitch, however, as the torrid pennant chase thundered into the final days of the campaign. On September 26, the Dodgers inched to within half a game of the lead by whipping the Phillies, 8-2, while the Cardinals were idle.

The victory carried a high price tag for the Dodgers. Left fielder Pete Reiser suffered a leg fracture while sliding back into first base in the first inning. When his season came to an abrupt end, Pistol Pete was batting .277 with 73 runs batted in.

After holding first place alone continuously since August 28, the Cardinals fell back into a tie with the idle Dodgers on September 27 when they bowed to the Cubs, 7-2. The sore-armed Pollet, who had been blasted by Chicago five days before, again was ineffective. He was removed during the Cubs' three-run rally in the fourth inning.

Both contenders won September 28, the next to last day of the season. In Brooklyn, the Dodgers shelled Boston ace Johnny Sain in the first inning and Joe Hatten held the Braves to five hits en route to a 7-4 victory. That night in St. Louis, the Cardinals whipped the Cubs, 4-1, behind the four-hit pitching of Brecheen. The only run off the little lefthander was a home run by center fielder Phil Cavarretta, who fanned on three other trips to the plate.

The final day of the season, September 29, found Brooklyn and St. Louis still tied. To win the pennant, one team would have to win while the other lost, but neither club was up to the task. Righthander Mort Cooper, a former Cardinal, helped his ex-teammates by blanking the Dodgers, 4-0, in Brooklyn. And in St. Louis, lefthander Johnny Schmitz hurled the Cubs to an 8-3 win over the Cards.

The 154-game schedule was over, but there was

no pennant winner. With records of 96-58, the Cardinals and Dodgers still were deadlocked. For the first time in major league history, a playoff was necessary to determine the champion. Under N.L. rules, a three-game series was required.

The sites were determined by a flip of the coin by N.L. President Ford Frick in New York. While Durocher listened on an extension, Cardinals President Sam Breadon called the toss—incorrectly. Durocher chose to open the playoffs in St. Louis, thereby giving Brooklyn the home-field advantage for the second and, if necessary, third games.

The ticket sale for the 25,000 available seats at Sportsman's Park commenced at 9 a.m. September 30. Initially, each patron was permitted to purchase 20 tickets, but as the supply diminished the number of tickets sold to each fan also decreased. As the last purchasers stepped to the windows, they could buy no more than four tickets each.

Many of the prized pasteboards found their way into the hands of scalpers. These speculators told fans interested in purchasing a $1.75 reserved seat that they could do so—for $10. A box seat could be had for $20. But ticket sales on the black market were slow, and as game time neared on October 1, the scalpers were offering a reserved seat ticket for $1. There was scant interest outside the park, perhaps because those fans who might have bought a ticket already had resigned themselves to the fact that the game was a sellout. Moving inside, the speculators sought to recover some of their investment and offered tickets to fans with general admission stubs for as little as a quarter. There still were few takers, and so the official attendance of 26,012 fell 8,000 fans short of the record attendance for the St. Louis-Chicago game two days before.

Pollet was eager to start the first playoff game despite his painful shoulder. As long as Pollet was willing, Dyer was happy to give him the ball, so the matter was settled. Already that season, Howie had defeated the Dodgers four times while losing twice.

Durocher, recalling his successful gamble of a few weeks before, entrusted the important first game to Branca. After humbling the Cardinals on September 14, Branca had blanked the Pittsburgh Pirates, 3-0, in his next start September 18.

But Branca's second appearance against the Cardinals was a poor imitation of his first. From the moment he left Brooklyn there were indications that the youngster was unprepared for the assignment. Upon arriving in St. Louis, he learned that he had left his glove at home. When he reported to the park, he discovered that his wallet, containing about $200, had been left under a pillow in his hotel room. He eventually recovered the wallet, money and all.

The Cards added to Branca's embarrassment by collecting three first-inning hits, matching their

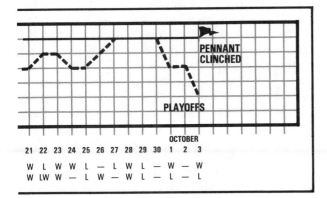

PENNANT CLINCHED

PLAYOFFS

OCTOBER

21 22 23 24 25 26 27 28 29 30 1 2 3

W L W W L — L W L — W — W
W L W W — L W — W L — L — L

Fiery Dodgers Manager Leo Durocher fought umpires and helped his veteran team scratch and claw its way into the 1946 pennant race.

Cardinals Manager Eddie Dyer sits dejectedly after watching his team lose its regular-season finale and chance to clinch the N.L. pennant.

total for the entire game in their last tangle with Branca, and scoring one run, driven in by Garagiola. A home run into the left-field bleachers by Dodgers first baseman Howie Schultz tied the score in the top of the third before St. Louis went ahead to stay in the home half. A base on balls to Musial, a single by Slaughter, a fielder's-choice grounder by third baseman Whitey Kurowski and singles by Garagiola and Harry Walker scored two runs and brought Higbe to the relief of Branca.

The Dodgers tagged Pollet for their second run in the seventh inning on singles by shortstop Pee Wee Reese, catcher Bruce Edwards and Schultz. Slaughter's throw after fielding Schultz's hit nailed Edwards at third base and averted further damage.

The Cardinals scored the final run of their 4-2 victory in the bottom of the seventh when Musial tripled off the right-center field wall and Garagiola looped a single just beyond Reese's reach.

The Dodgers mounted their last threat in the eighth inning. Second baseman Eddie Stanky drew a leadoff walk and, with one out, left fielder Joe Medwick singled for the last of the losers' eight hits. The uprising died when Dixie Walker grounded into a forceout and Furillo lined out to Marty Marion at shortstop. Pollet retired the Dodgers in order in the ninth to record his 21st victory.

After a day off for travel, the playoffs resumed October 3 at Ebbets Field. The starting pitchers were Dickson for St. Louis and Hatten for Brooklyn.

The crowd of 31,437 was provoked into early ec-

stasy when the Dodgers took a 1-0 lead in the first inning. Third baseman Augie Galan's infield single with two out, a walk to Dixie Walker and first baseman Ed Stevens' single through the middle of the diamond sent roars rolling through Flatbush, but that was the last opportunity the loyalists had to cheer their heroes for nearly two hours.

Through the next seven innings, Dickson was outstanding. He permitted only one ball to be hit to the outfield, a fly off the bat of Stevens. He allowed no hits, though he did issue three walks. Fifteen putouts were accounted for by grounders, three batters popped out and two struck out as Dickson stormed into the bottom of the ninth inning with an 8-1 lead.

The Cardinals had given Dickson that edge by cuffing Hatten and five successors for 13 hits, including two by Dickson. The Cards' first tally came in the second inning when Dusak tripled and Marion hit a sacrifice fly. Catcher Clyde Kluttz followed with a single and scored on Dickson's triple.

The Cardinals drove Hatten to cover in the fifth with three more runs. Two were out when Musial doubled and Kurowski drew an intentional base on balls. Slaughter's triple to right-center made the score 4-1, and Dusak's single added the fifth run.

A pair of walks, a sacrifice and Marion's squeeze bunt produced a single run for St. Louis in the seventh. The Cards scored their final pair in the eighth when Schoendienst singled, Terry Moore smacked a ground-rule double into the left-field seats, Musial drew an intentional walk and Kurowski singled to

Brooklyn fans braved rain and early-morning chill for a chance to buy Cardi-
nals-Dodgers playoff tickets.

right field, scoring Schoendienst and Moore.

Trailing 8-1, the Dodgers burst their hitting bonds with a vengeance in the ninth inning as Dickson finally weakened. Galan ignited the bombardment with a double. After Dixie Walker was retired, Stevens tripled home Galan to tally the second Brooklyn run. A run-scoring single by Furillo, a wild pitch and a walk to Reese excused Dickson for the day and brought on Brecheen. The lefty, who had gone 15-15 that season, started shakily, yielding a run-scoring single to Edwards and a walk to pinch-hitter Lavagetto. The bases were loaded with one out, but it was there that the rally, and the season, died for the Dodgers. Stanky was called out on strikes and Schultz also struck out, giving St. Louis an 8-4 victory and its fourth N.L. pennant in the last five years.

"We gave the folks a thrill at the last, anyway," a dejected Reese said after the game.

It was a thrill that Breadon could have done without. "It's a good thing I have a good heart," the Cardinals' president said. "Otherwise, I never would have lived through it. I almost died during that Dodger rally in the ninth inning."

Breadon said he was most pleased for Dyer, the rookie manager who had lived up to the exorbitant expectations for him and his club. "Many persons didn't appreciate the job he did for us and the things he had to overcome," Breadon said.

It took Pollet some time to recover from the damage his shoulder incurred when he entered that September 15 game without warming up. He suffered a 3-2, 10-inning loss to the Boston Red Sox in the first game of the World Series and was unable to make it through the first inning of his Game 5 start. Though Pollet was the pitching star for the Cardinals in the regular season, the Series heroes

for St. Louis were Brecheen, who won three games, and Slaughter, who made his famous dash from first base on Harry Walker's short double to score the Series-winning run in the eighth inning of Game 7.

The 1947 season was a difficult one for Pollet. He slumped to 9-11 with a 4.35 ERA as he tried to regain his former proficiency with an aching arm.

"Every pitch hurt," he said. "I couldn't follow through. I began to pitch with a half-motion, using my elbow instead of my back. I stopped midway. My control was terrible and I began to feel a lump in my elbow. It frightened me. I was afraid I was through."

X-rays revealed a calcium deposit on his elbow and Pollet underwent surgery that winter. His record improved to 13-8 in 1948, and by 1949 he was sufficiently recovered to enjoy one last season of glory. He posted a 20-9 record with a 2.77 ERA and hurled five shutouts, tying for the league high.

Pollet's record dropped to 14-13 in 1950, his last season with double-digit victories. After stints with the Pirates, Cubs and Chicago White Sox, he retired at the close of the 1956 season.

Pollet and Dyer maintained their close friendship through the years. After abandoning his playing career, Pollet returned to Houston to work full-time in Dyer's insurance business.

Dyer always had the highest regard for the determined pitcher. "I used to sit in St. Louis and hear the fans get on Pollet," he told a reporter near the end of Pollet's pitching days. " 'Dyer's Pet,' they'd call him, because we both live in Houston and in the winter he works with me as a partner in my businesses there. 'Dyer's Pet,' they'd holler at him.

"The fans were right. He was Dyer's pet. He still is."

11

Impossible Dream Comes True

Dick Williams, a 38-year-old manager, and young slugger Carl Yastrzemski
(right) were the architects of Boston's 1967 Impossible Dream.

Gales of laughter swirled through the clubhouse, mingled with the sound of popping corks and shrieks of delight from athletes who were riding an emotional crest.

At the center of the bedlam, locked in earnest embrace, stood the aging proprietor of the Boston Red Sox and his 38-year-old rookie manager.

"Thank you for everything; this is the happiest day of my life," Thomas Austin Yawkey yelled above the ear-splitting babble.

"Thank you for giving me the chance to manage," Richard Hirshfeld Williams responded in a strained voice.

The date was October 1, 1967, and "The Great Race" had just come to a thunderous climax in the consummation of "The Impossible Dream."

Thirty-four years before the magic moment of 1967, Tom Yawkey had purchased the woebegone Red Sox, determined to restore the club to the glories it had known before World War I. In the intervening years, Yawkey had paid fancy salaries and huge bonuses in pursuit of his goal. His lavishness, however, had produced only one pennant and countless heartbreaks.

In 1964, Dick Williams completed a major league career that had begun in 1951 in Brooklyn and later wound through Baltimore, Cleveland, Kansas City and Boston, where he had spent the last two years as a utilityman for the Red Sox. Told that he could have the managerial job with Boston's Internation-

Fans of the 1967 Red Sox took great pride in the hard-hitting young outfield of (left to right) Carl Yastrzemski, Reggie Smith and Tony Conigliaro.

al League club at Toronto, Williams replied that the offer appealed to him, but he wanted to consult Paul Richards before giving a definite answer.

At that time, Richards was the general manager of the Houston Colts. Why did Williams want to speak with him?

"Because the guy picked me up four different times," Williams explained, "three at Baltimore and once at Houston (although he was traded before ever playing for the Colts). There must have been something about me he liked, and I want to be available if he has a job in mind for me."

Richards, a former field manager and general manager with the Baltimore Orioles, could not match the Boston offer. Williams took the Toronto job and won the league playoffs in 1965 and '66.

While Williams was reaping success in the Triple-A circuit, the Red Sox were harvesting failure in the American League. They finished ninth both years, and in 1966 they lost 90 games, 10 fewer than in '65 but one more than the last-place New York Yankees. Even before that disastrous campaign came to a close, Red Sox executives launched a search for a successor to their deposed pilot, Billy Herman.

The quest turned toward Williams, whose cause was championed most ardently by Neil Mahoney, the club's farm director. Years before, while scout-

ing for the Red Sox, Mahoney had spotted Williams as a young outfielder with Fort Worth of the Texas League. He was impressed with the teen-ager's hustle and mature approach to the game, and he explored the possibility of obtaining him from the parent Brooklyn Dodgers. The Dodgers were not interested in a trade at that time, and the Red Sox did not acquire Williams until 1963.

But Mahoney never forgot the dedicated kid. After Dick was acquired from Baltimore, he and Neil spent hours together talking baseball.

Williams' managerial formula, he told interviewers, was compiled from the doctrines of three masters: Richards, Bobby Bragan at Fort Worth and Chuck Dressen at Brooklyn.

"All were disciplinarians without being martinets," he said. "They all had the respect, but not necessarily the affection, of their ball players. They all paid close attention to little details. And they were all a couple of jumps ahead of everyone else because they were always thinking ahead. Bragan was a master of sarcasm, Dressen an egotist and Richards a thinker."

Such was the personality of Dick Williams—particularly on the matter of discipline. His tough style earned the players' respect, but rarely their affection.

With two games left in the 1967 season, Minnesota's Harmon Killebrew (left)
and Carl Yastrzemski were tied for the A.L. home run lead with 43. . . .

Williams didn't mind. "I don't expect to make friends," he said. "I'm not running a popularity contest."

In Williams' first tour of duty with the Red Sox, a country club atmosphere permeated the ranks. Discipline was loose, and those who were so inclined could obey regulations with impaired vision. Williams observed the derelictions in mild horror, but lacking any authority, kept his lips sealed.

When he returned as manager, however, the situation changed abruptly. Anyone caught breaking curfew, he announced, would be subject to a $500 fine.

Wasn't that amount excessive, he was asked? Wouldn't a $50 penalty be more in keeping with the crime?

Williams said no. "A guy will pay $50 for a night on the town," he said. "For $500, he'll think twice."

One of Dick's first directives as a major league skipper dealt with housing regulations during spring training at Winter Haven, Fla. Married players, he said, could live with their families, away from the team hotel. Unmarried players would live at the team headquarters.

The order found disfavor with Tony Conigliaro, the young and free-spirited right fielder who announced casually upon arriving at camp that he would arrange his own housing accommodations.

"You'll live in the same place as everyone else," the manager declared, and Tony C moved into the hotel that afternoon.

Another "loser" in the Williams scheme of things was left fielder Carl Yastrzemski, who was stripped of his team captaincy. "I'm the boss," Williams asserted, "and we don't need a captain."

Instead of a bitter reaction, as many expected, Yastrzemski reported that he was pleased with the move because it relieved him of a worrisome responsibility.

From the start of spring training, observers were impressed with the young manager's well-organized program. Idleness was forbidden. Of particular interest to veteran camp visitors was the sight of pitchers, who were not engaged otherwise, playing volleyball. When scoffers ridiculed the revolutionary plan, Dick scoffed right back. "I'm the manager," he said, "and the pitchers will continue to play volleyball."

He also scoffed at preseason polls that picked the Red Sox for another ninth-place finish and the Las Vegas line that established 100-to-1 odds against his club winning the pennant. "We'll win more games than we lose," he said time and again. Then he went back to his tongue lashings. Nobody escaped his wrath—players, umpires or executives.

The season was not far gone before he became

. . . But home run No. 44 (above), a three-run shot, lifted the Red Sox and Yaz to victory that afternoon, even though Killebrew also hit his 44th homer.

engaged in a heated dispute with an umpire. Rather than unleash a profane string of epithets, as was common among players and managers, Williams got his point across with a witty remark. "You could wear that suit, those shoes, that chest protector, that mask and carry that indicator in your hand and appear on 'What's My Line?'" he told the arbiter, "and no one could guess your occupation."

After one occasion when Williams was embroiled in a dispute with an umpire, he was told that his performance had been witnessed by A.L. President Joe Cronin and Cal Hubbard, the league's supervisor of umpires.

"What does Cronin know?" Williams snapped. "He left before the game was over. And what does Hubbard know? He wore earmuffs on account of the cold and went to sleep in the ball park."

Players who exceeded the weight limitations prescribed by Williams and trainer Buddy LeRoux also were certain to feel the sting of a managerial rebuke. Sometimes it could be a silent censure, as in the case of George Scott.

Once when the slugging first baseman was found to be overweight, he was benched for a three-game series at California. The games were important to the Red Sox, and Scott's big bludgeon might have reversed the outcome of the games, all of which the Angels won by one run. But Williams stood firm. Scott made three pinch-hitting appearances, but he did not don a glove during the series.

The Angels found the whole situation rather comical. "Nine teams in this league have managers," they cracked, "but Boston has a dietitian."

Williams filed away the comments for future reference.

Few fans were ecstatic when they obtained their first glimpse of the 1967 Red Sox, but there were signs that Williams had wrought worthwhile changes. No longer a "country club," the Red Sox reflected determination and dedication. They clearly were more interested in winning than sinning after hours.

Righthander Jim Lonborg won the April 12 season opener, beating the Chicago White Sox, 5-4, at Fenway Park with the help of a three-run home run by Rico Petrocelli. Rico's daily appearance at shortstop was a happy omen. In 1966, his general unhappiness regarding the manner in which he was treated was an almost-daily news item.

After losing to the White Sox the next day, the Red Sox traveled to New York. On April 14, Bill Rohr, a 21-year-old lefthander, made his major league debut. He held the Yankees hitless for 8⅔ innings. The rookie had a 3-2 count on Elston Howard when the Yankee catcher spoiled the no-hitter with a single. But Rohr retired the next batter and won the game, 3-0.

A week later, Rohr faced the Yanks in Boston and turned in a 6-1 victory. He failed to win another game in six additional starts, however, and was back in the minors by midsummer.

Yastrzemski, on the other hand, started rapidly and never faltered. It was apparent that Yaz was intent on having the type of season that had been predicted for him since his rookie year of 1961. His every move mirrored his early declaration to Williams that "I'm here to play ball the best way I know how. Nothing else matters. I'll do anything you tell me to. All I want is for this club to have a good year."

While not a spectacular start, the Red Sox enjoyed a good April, winning eight games and losing six. After the team won 14 games and lost 14 in May, Williams sent a message to the front office. It

was imperative, he said, that he obtain infield reinforcements. His request was answered June 2 with the acquisition of Jerry Adair from Chicago in exchange for reliever Don McMahon and a minor league pitcher.

Some viewed the swap as the second stroke of misfortune for Adair in as many seasons. The previous year he had been traded to the White Sox by Baltimore and missed out on the Orioles' world championship. Then he was forced to leave Chicago at a time when the White Sox were one game out of first place. The Red Sox were only 4½ games out, but no one was taking Boston seriously then, while Chicago was considered a serious pennant contender.

Adair fit perfectly into Williams' scheme. He played second base, third base and shortstop and was a solid replacement for Petrocelli when Rico missed a month with a severely bruised wrist. After batting .204 for Chicago, Jerry hit .291 for the Red Sox.

On June 3, lefthander Dennis Bennett won a 6-2 decision over Cleveland. The Indians' losing pitcher, Gary Bell, didn't know it yet, but the club that had just handed him his fifth defeat in six decisions was about to acquire him. The next day, the Red Sox sent first baseman Tony Horton and outfielder Don Demeter to Cleveland for Bell, a 30-year-old righthander who had won 14 games in 1966.

Williams immediately inserted Bell into the starting rotation, and the newcomer responded wonderfully. In 29 games (24 starts), Bell went 12-8 for Boston.

Though the Red Sox did not yet know how well Adair and Bell would perform for them, they were elated with their newest acquisitions.

"We improved our pitching considerably. . . . We gave up two players who were not playing for us to get an established pitcher who made the All-Star team twice," Williams said about Bell.

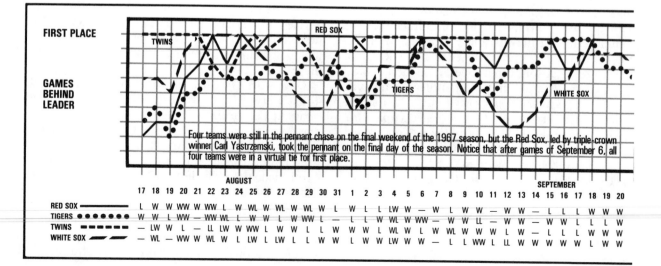

Four teams were still in the pennant chase on the final weekend of the 1967 season, but the Red Sox, led by triple-crown winner Carl Yastrzemski, took the pennant on the final day of the season. Notice that after games of September 6, all four teams were in a virtual tie for first place.

"We now feel we can remain in pennant contention for the entire season," General Manager Dick O'Connell said boldly. "This is a wide-open race, and we believe we can be in it."

White Sox Manager Eddie Stanky unintentionally helped Boston's cause a couple of nights later when he made a careless remark that was published widely. Stanky called Yastrzemski a moody player and said, "He may be an All-Star, I suppose, but only from the neck down."

The Chicago skipper had occasion to regret that comment when the Red Sox were at Comiskey Park for a June 8 doubleheader. In the two games, which the teams split, Yaz rapped six hits, including a double and his 12th home run of the year. On his tour of the bases on his homer, Yaz gallantly tipped his cap to Stanky while the Boston bench went wild. The beneficiary of Yastrzemski's output was Bell, who won his Red Sox debut, 7-3.

The motivation provided by Stanky's remark continued to spark Yaz when the Red Sox returned to Fenway Park the next day. He hit a pair of homers and made two tremendous catches in left field to lead Boston to an 8-7 victory over the Washington Senators. The crowd of 25,326 showed its appreciation by giving Yaz four standing ovations.

"This is the best streak I have ever had," Yastrzemski said. "I'm pulling the ball better than I ever did before."

The next week, the White Sox, who had moved back into first place, visited Boston for three games. Stanky was ejected from two of them and was subjected to a barrage of missiles from howling Boston fans. Eddie feared for his safety in future games at Boston and instructed his wife to sue Tom Yawkey and other officials in the event he were ever injured there.

Boston won two of those three games to pull within four lengths of Chicago. The Red Sox played only .500 ball over the next four weeks, however,

and were in fifth place at the All-Star break, six games behind the White Sox. With a 47-33 record, Chicago had a two-game lead over the Detroit Tigers, 2½ games over the Minnesota Twins and 4½ games over the Angels. Detroit and California stormed into the break, both clubs winning seven of their last eight games. The Red Sox, however, had lost five straight before Lonborg posted his 11th triumph with a 3-0 whitewash of the Tigers in the last game before the intermission.

The Red Sox were the hottest club in the league immediately after the All-Star break. They won 11 of their first 12 contests, including 10 in a row, to rise to second place, half a game behind the White Sox. Lonborg and righthander Lee Stange each won three games during that stretch, while Yastrzemski blasted five homers, Conigliaro four.

A doubleheader sweep of the Indians on July 23 gave Boston its ninth and 10th wins in succession and wrapped up a perfect trip to Baltimore and Cleveland. When the Red Sox returned to Boston that night, about 10,000 fans were on hand at Logan Airport to give them a jubilant welcome.

"I have never seen anything like this in my life," Williams said. "This is fantastic. They told us on the plane that there would be some fans at the airport, but I never dreamed it would be like this."

The Red Sox won half of their 12 games on that home stand. Then, on August 3, they reinforced their shaky catching department with the acquisition of Elston Howard from the Yankees for cash and two players. Though the veteran backstop batted only .147 in a Boston uniform, he provided a steadying influence for the young pitching staff. Howard was the final addition the Red Sox needed to remain in contention for the A.L. flag.

By that time, other teams had come to regard Boston as a genuine pennant threat. The Red Sox had folded down the stretch many times before, but the presence of Williams on the Boston bench made the club a more legitimate contender than in past years. Sometimes snarling, other times charming, he drove his players to the limits of their talents and frequently to the edge of their endurance. But his system paid off. The Red Sox were in the thick of the chase.

Boston's success did not make Williams any more tolerant of his players' transgressions. It was in mid-August that the manager benched Scott for being overweight. The fact that the Red Sox were only two games out of first place did not deter Dick.

"George must get his weight down," he said. "He is not going to be allowed to get away with things that other players do not get away with."

Scott disagreed. "I think I should be playing even if I weigh 500 pounds," he said. But after dropping eight pounds to get back under his maximum weight, he hit three homers in his first two games

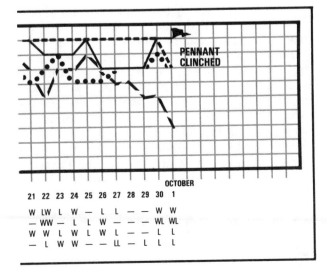

PENNANT CLINCHED									
OCTOBER									
21	22	23	24	25	26	27	28	29	30	1
W	LW	L	W	—	L	L	—	—	W	W
—	WW	—	L	L	W	—	—	—	WL	WL
W	W	L	W	L	W	L	—	—	L	L
—	L	W	W	—	—	LL	—	L	L	L

Excited fans gave pitcher Jim Lonborg the victory ride of his life after he pitched the Red Sox to a season-closing 5-3 victory over the Twins.

back in the starting lineup. The Red Sox won both contests over the Tigers.

"Maybe the man was right," Scott said. "I never felt better in my life than I do at this weight."

The Red Sox were 3½ games back when they welcomed the Angels to Fenway Park on August 18 for the first of four games. They won all four but suffered a great loss. In the opener, Conigliaro was struck below the left eye by a pitch from Jack Hamilton. The slugging young outfielder suffered a fractured cheekbone and was hindered by faulty vision. He was finished for the season.

The roster vacancy created by Tony C's injury was filled a few days later. The Red Sox signed Ken (Hawk) Harrelson, an outfielder-first baseman who had been released by Kansas City after calling A's Owner Charles O. Finley a detriment to the game. Harrelson, who was platooned in right field with Jose Tartabull, hit only .200 for the Red Sox in 23 games, but he had some clutch hits to knock in 14 runs.

On August 25, Boston moved into first place for the first time since April 29. Scott and center fielder Reggie Smith each had three hits to lift the Red Sox over the White Sox, 6-2, and to move half a game in front of Minnesota. A doubleheader split with Chi-

cago the next day left the Red Sox one percentage point below the Twins in the standings, but they were back on top by half a game at the end of the month.

The four-team flag scramble pushed into September as Boston, Minnesota, Detroit and Chicago remained bunched atop the standings. With two weeks to go, there still was no indication of any contender breaking stride.

After being swept by the Orioles in a three-game series at Fenway Park, the Red Sox traveled to Detroit, where they dealt the Tigers a staggering blow.

Boston staged ninth-inning rallies on consecutive nights to pull out a pair of victories September 18 and 19. In the first game, Yastrzemski's solo homer in the top of the ninth tied the score, 5-5. Boston won it in the 10th on a solo homer by third baseman Dalton Jones, who contributed four hits. The victory created a three-way tie for the lead among Boston, Detroit and Minnesota, but the Tigers fell to fourth place the next night when Earl Wilson uncorked a wild pitch that contributed to a three-run Boston rally in the ninth. The Red Sox won, 4-2, to remain tied with the Twins. The winning pitcher both nights was righthander Jose Santiago, who raised his record to 10-4.

Red Sox Owner Tom Yawkey (left) enjoyed a pennant-winning embrace with General Manager Dick O'Connell (center) and Manager Dick Williams.

The Red Sox swept two games from the Indians in Cleveland, but the Twins kept the pace by beating Kansas City for the fourth consecutive time. From that pinnacle, Williams' club tumbled to a pair of losses in four games at Baltimore, then returned home and dropped two decisions to Cleveland.

Fortunately for the Red Sox, none of the other contenders could sustain the winning habit, either. After Boston's first loss to Cleveland on September 26, only 1½ games separated the top four teams. Minnesota was in front with a 91-68 record, followed by Chicago (89-68) and Boston (90-69), both one game back, and Detroit (89-69), 1½ games back.

The favorites at this point were Minnesota and Chicago. The Twins were in first place and had won seven of their last nine games, but they also had to finish their season with two games in Boston. Meanwhile, the White Sox would close out their schedule with two games on the road against last-place Kansas City and three at home against Washington, the seventh-place occupant.

For Chicago's September 27 doubleheader in Kansas City, Stanky nominated righthander Joe Horlen and lefthander Gary Peters, the league's earned-run average leaders, as his starting pitchers.

Neither scintillated, however, Peters losing the opener, 5-2, and Horlen the nightcap, 4-0.

The White Sox fell to fourth place and were left only with hopes of a first-place tie. But they expired as contenders two nights later when 24-year-old lefthander Tommy John lost a heartbreaker to the Senators, 1-0. Completing their fadeout, the White Sox lost their last two games as well and finished the season with five straight setbacks.

The race was compressed into the final weekend of the season as three clubs were still alive. Rain prevented Detroit and California from playing each other September 28 and 29, so games on the last Saturday and Sunday of the campaign would determine the A.L. flag winner.

Because of the rainouts, the Tigers (89-69) and Angels had to finish with a pair of doubleheaders in Detroit. At the same time, the first-place Twins (91-69) and second-place Red Sox (90-70) would play single games each day in Fenway Park.

Lefthander Jim Kaat, a 16-game winner, started the September 30 game for the Twins. He was opposed by Santiago, who was seeking his 12th victory.

Kaat was given a 1-0 lead in the first inning when right fielder Tony Oliva singled home shortstop

The Red Sox's clubhouse exploded into champagne-pouring jubilation when word reached Boston that the Tigers had lost their 1967 season finale.

Zoilo Versalles, who had singled and moved up on a walk to first baseman Harmon Killebrew. The Red Sox, meanwhile, made little noise in the first two innings.

Kaat was pitching effortlessly, as smoothly as he had done in winning all seven of his decisions in September.

In the third inning, however, Jim "heard something pop" while pitching to Santiago. A muscle in his left forearm had torn. Kaat managed to strike out Santiago, but after a couple of pitches to the next batter, second baseman Mike Andrews, he had to give way to righthander Jim Perry.

"He was throwing as well as I've seen him this year," lamented Cal Ermer, who had replaced Sam Mele as Minnesota manager June 9, when the team was in sixth place.

Boston scored two runs in the fifth with the help of a mental blunder by Perry. A leadoff double by Reggie Smith and singles by Dalton Jones and Adair produced the tying run and brought Yastrzemski to the plate. Yaz grounded the ball between first baseman Killebrew and second baseman Rod Carew, who made a fine play. But Perry neglected to cover first base, Yaz was safe with a single and Jones scored to give Boston a 2-1 lead.

Minnesota tied the score in the sixth on pinch-hitter Rich Reese's run-scoring single. Ermer then turned the Twins' mound chores over to righthander Ron Kline in the bottom of the sixth. On the

classy fireman's first pitch, Scott deposited the ball in the center-field bleachers to put the Red Sox back on top, 3-2.

Another fundamental error helped Boston deliver the crushing blow an inning later. After Andrews scratched out an infield hit with one out, Adair hit a grounder to Kline, who threw to Versalles at second base to start an inning-ending double play. But Versalles dropped the ball. Both runners were safe with Yastrzemski coming up.

Ermer removed Kline and brought in lefthander Jim Merritt to face Yaz. Merritt proceeded cautiously, but on a 3-1 pitch, Yaz hammered his 44th homer of the year, a club record for lefthanded batters. The three-run blast gave Boston a more comfortable 6-2 lead.

Santiago, who had worked out of a couple of jams earlier in the game, tired in the eighth. After walking the leadoff man, left fielder Bob Allison, Williams brought in Bell to relieve. Bell held the Twins at bay until two were out in the ninth, when third baseman Cesar Tovar doubled.

On the Boston bench, Williams contemplated his options. The batter was Killebrew, who had 43 homers to his credit. If the manager ordered Bell to pitch to Harmon and he homered, Yastrzemski would be forced to share the league home run lead. It also could tarnish the Triple Crown he had all but won.

On the other hand, if Bell were instructed to

pitch carefully to Killebrew, there was the possibility of a base on balls, in which case a home run by the next batter (Oliva) would cut the Boston lead to a single tally.

Williams decided to challenge Killebrew. Though Harmon clouted a fastball over the left-field wall, the Twins failed to score additional runs and Boston won, 6-4.

Afterward, Williams explained his thinking to Yastrzemski, who agreed it was the proper course. He was willing to exchange a blemish on his Triple Crown for a team victory.

Meanwhile, the games in Detroit appeared to be going the Tigers' way. Lefthander Mickey Lolich scattered three hits and won the first game, 5-0, with left fielder Willie Horton providing all the runs he needed on a first-inning homer. The Tigers jumped out to a 6-2 lead in the second game and coasted into the late innings. But as the Tiger Stadium crowd watched in horror, the Angels erupted for six runs in the eighth. Singles by shortstop Jim Fregosi, who had homered in the fourth, started and ended the rally, and the Angels won, 8-6.

With a single day's activity remaining on the 162-game schedule, the Twins and Red Sox were tied (91-70) for the lead. The Tigers (90-70) trailed by half a game. For Detroit fans, only a twin-bill sweep on the closing day would do. If the Tigers could beat California twice, they would finish in a dead heat with the Boston-Minnesota winner and force a one-game playoff for the league championship.

Fenway Park's largest crowd of the season, 35,770, greeted the Red Sox on October 1. Appropriately, each team's top winner was on the mound for the critical engagement, Jim Lonborg for the home team, Dean Chance for the visitors.

Lonborg, a biology major at Stanford University, already had won 21 games, including two while on one-day passes from Army Reserve duty in Georgia. He also had lost nine games, including three to the Twins without a victory.

Chance, like Lonborg a righthander, had 20 victories to his credit and had beaten the Red Sox four times in five decisions.

As Lonborg took the mound, the huge scoreboard in left field announced that the Tigers were leading the Angels in the first game of their doubleheader. They eventually won, 6-4, as Horton hit his 19th homer of the season and Joe Sparma earned his 16th victory.

Lonborg retired the first two batters in the opening inning in Boston and then walked Killebrew on four pitches. He fired two strikes past Oliva before the lefthanded batter sliced a drive to left field. Yaz retreated as if to make the catch, but the ball caromed off the wall. The Red Sox still had a chance to get Killebrew, who was trying to score, but Scott's relay throw to the plate was wild. Kille-

brew scored easily.

The Twins struck again in the third inning. Tovar worked Lonborg for a base on balls and Killebrew singled to left, where Yastrzemski misplayed the ball for an error, allowing Tovar to score the Twins' second run.

"I thought it might be a long day when they got those unearned runs off me," Lonborg said.

Chance, who blanked the Red Sox through five innings, faced Lonborg leading off the sixth. Lonborg's bat represented little danger to the opposing hurler. Jim had 13 hits for the season, was batting .135 and had sacrificed six times in barely 100 plate appearances.

But Jim had singled off Chance his first time up—and he was observant, too. He noted that Tovar was playing deep at third base. In a surprise bit of strategy, Lonborg laid a perfect bunt down toward third base. No one could make a play, and Lonborg was safe at first. Singles by Adair and Jones loaded the bases before Yastrzemski tied the score, 2-2, with a single to center field.

Harrelson followed with a grounder to Versalles. The shortstop threw home too late to retire Jones, who scored the third run—still with nobody out.

Chance was finished. He was replaced by Al Worthington, whose initial task was to retire Scott. But the righthander uncorked two wild pitches that permitted Yaz to score and Harrelson to move to third. The last Boston marker in a five-run outburst scored when Killebrew mishandled a grounder and Harrelson crossed the plate.

The Twins made their final run at Lonborg in the eighth. Singles by Killebrew, Oliva and Allison pushed across one tally, but that was all. The Red Sox won, 5-3.

When Petrocelli caught the game-ending pop fly, a mob converged on Lonborg. A sea of joyous spectators carried the pitcher off the field, clawing at his uniform in a bid for a souvenir of the wondrous occasion. One fan removed one of Lonborg's shoelaces but left the shoe behind.

"I was scared before the game," the pitcher said. "I was terrified afterward."

The pandemonium shifted outside Fenway Park, where fans packed streets and sidewalks so tightly that a player, even if he had wished, could not have walked to his car without enormous risk of personal harm.

All the hysteria could have been premature because, in Detroit, the Tigers and Angels still were doing battle. A Detroit victory would force the season into a 163rd game the next day.

And for a while, the Tigers were winning. They took a 3-1 lead in the second on center fielder Jim Northrup's two-run homer and shortstop Dick McAuliffe's run-scoring triple. But the anxious players in the Boston clubhouse, listening to the game on radio, cheered when Denny McLain, a 17-game winner, was shelled in the third inning. The Angels scored three runs, two on a home run by first baseman Don Mincher, to take a 4-3 lead.

Manager Mayo Smith sent eight Detroit pitchers to the mound in an attempt to silence the California bats, all to no avail. The Angels won the game, 8-5, shattering the Tigers' dream of a miracle finish and dropping them into a second-place tie with the Twins, one game behind the champion Red Sox.

Throughout New England, songs of praise rang loud for the miracle Red Sox, who had won their first pennant since 1946. Three men in particular were accorded special reverence. The pitching hero was Lonborg. Jim captured the A.L. Cy Young Award with his 22 victories and 246 strikeouts, tops in the circuit.

Without question, Boston's big producer and the league's Most Valuable Player was Yastrzemski, who rapped seven hits in eight at-bats in the final, pressure-packed days of the race. He also won the Triple Crown with 44 homers, a .326 batting average and 121 runs batted in. In addition, his 189 hits, 112 runs, 360 total bases and .622 slugging percentage were tops in the league. As few players before or since, the outfielder enjoyed a truly remarkable campaign in what came to be known as The Year of Yaz.

And then, of course, there was Williams. Partisans rhapsodized endlessly over the crew-cut skipper who had converted a group of country-club cutups into a championship unit and won Manager of the Year honors in his first season.

In his moment of triumph, the rookie pilot recalled the Angels' reference to him as a "dietitian" several weeks earlier. "Maybe there were nine managers and one dietitian," Williams cracked. "But the dietitian won the pennant."

Triple Crown winner Carl Yastrzemski received a victory cigar light from Massachusetts Governor John Volpe.

St. Louis' Swifties Catch the Dodgers

The Brooklyn Dodgers had just completed a successful home stand by sweeping a doubleheader from their cross-borough rivals, the New York Giants, before about 34,000 scalp hunters at Ebbets Field.

Any victory over the hated adversaries was cause for a civic celebration in Flatbush, but the manner in which the twin triumph was achieved on August 23, 1942, was even more stimulating to those who worshiped at the shrine of Leo Durocher and his league-leading Bums.

In the first game, a two-run homer by first baseman Johnny Mize in the top of the 10th inning gave the Giants a 4-2 lead. It proved insufficient. Singles by shortstop Pee Wee Reese and third baseman Lew Riggs and a walk to center fielder Pete Reiser loaded the bases in the last half of the frame. That ended Hal Schumacher's tour of duty on the New York mound. In came Harry Feldman, who made one pitch. Last seen, the ball was screaming over the right-field wall, dispatched there by first baseman Dolph Camilli and producing a 6-4 victory.

The second game was just a shade less dramatic but equally as fulfilling. After the Giants scored four runs in the top of the fifth inning to tie the game, 5-5, the Dodgers countered in their turn with a pair, both driven in by second baseman Billy Herman's single. Darkness ended the day's activity at that point with the Dodgers victorious, 7-5.

With only five weeks of the season remaining and the Flatbush Flock leading the second-place St. Louis Cardinals by 7½ games, who in New York's largest borough would not have been exultant? Certainly not the Brooklyn players as they boarded a train later that evening for their last western trip of the year. First stop, St. Louis.

Spirits knew no limits when the players bounded onto the cars. Exhilaration was everywhere on what somebody called "The Victory Special." Male voices were raised in song. Wisecracks flourished, and a high-stakes poker game attracted older players. Above the din, Durocher's voice could be heard with each turn of a card.

A National League official who was aboard the westbound train was invited to sit in the game. An hour later he walked away with $400 of new capital.

But why worry about financial losses when the Dodgers were winning? Any deficits sustained on

The 1942 Brooklyn Dodgers were a fiery bunch, led by such volatile personalities as (left to right) coach Chuck Dressen, team President Larry MacPhail and Manager Leo Durocher.

A collision with the center-field wall proved costly for Pete Reiser (above left with Manager Leo Durocher) and the Dodgers' pennant hopes.

this joyride undoubtedly would be wiped out by a World Series check, with plenty to spare.

Forgotten in the midst of the euphoria was a warning issued by Larry MacPhail a few days before. The Dodgers had just completed a series against the last-place Philadelphia Phillies when they were invited to meet with the club's chief executive officer in the press room at Ebbets Field.

Speculation over the purpose of the conclave

raced through the clubhouse. Perhaps MacPhail, free spender that he was, planned to reward them for their sparkling performances, which had all but locked up a second consecutive pennant.

Larry had no such thing in mind. Instead, he told the athletes that he was deeply concerned that the Dodgers were not leading their nearest pursuers by 20 games or more. The players had grown fat, smug and self-satisfied, he declared, and unless there was an abrupt reversal in attitude, they were in danger of blowing their seemingly foolproof cushion.

MacPhail was about to take another sip from his drink when a dissenting voice was heard. It belonged to Dixie Walker, the veteran outfielder whose popularity had earned him the nickname "People's Cherce."

"I'll bet you $200," Dixie drawled, "that we win the pennant by eight games."

Larry chose to ignore the remark. His silence, however, served to reinforce the players' belief that they were a lock to win the flag.

Between that day of stinging rebuke and this night of revelry, the Dodgers had made a conscientious effort to prove their boss wrong. The Giants, riding a six-game winning streak, had invaded Flatbush and departed with four straight losses on their record.

MacPhail had to be impressed by the conquest of the Giants and the crowd reaction to Camilli's game-winning grand slam. In the opinion of Tommy Holmes, the Brooklyn correspondent for The Sporting News, "no noise since creation has ever been louder than the spontaneous roar that came from 34,000 throats."

By all reckoning, it had been an eventful season so far for Dem Bums, an affectionate nickname hung on the team by sports cartoonist Willard Mullin and adopted by the masses. On opening day they had visited the Polo Grounds and whipped the Giants, 7-5, before more than 42,000 fans as Pee Wee Reese, with a home run and double, led the barrage against Carl Hubbell.

A few days later, the Dodgers gained sole possession of first place and held it continuously ever since. Their slimmest lead after April 19 was on May 4, when they were only half a game in front of the Pittsburgh Pirates. The Dodgers then won 11 of their next 12 games to give themselves a more comfortable buffer. By July 6, they day of the All-Star Game, Brooklyn had an 8½-game lead over second-place St. Louis. The Dodgers reached their zenith August 5, when 10 games separated the Cardinals from the league leaders.

Brooklyn clung to its lead despite some cruel blows along the way. A four-game series in St. Louis in July, for example, produced a double whammy. Dropping three decisions to the Cardinals was bad

The St. Louis Cardinals, managed by gentlemanly Billy Southworth (above), kept constant pressure on the league-leading Dodgers.

enough, but even worse for the Dodgers was the loss of two key players.

First, premier reliever Hugh Casey suffered a finger fracture when struck by a line smash off the bat of left fielder Stan Musial in the first game of a July 18 doubleheader. The righthander went on the shelf for almost three weeks.

The next day, when the clubs again battled twice, a painful fate befell Reiser, the league's leading hitter. The Dodgers and Cardinals were deadlocked, 6-6, in the last of the 11th inning of the second game when right fielder Enos Slaughter drove a Johnny Allen pitch to deep center field. Reiser gave chase. He gloved the ball while going full tilt and crashed into the concrete wall.

As the ball trickled free, Reiser lay stunned for a few moments, then picked himself off the turf, staggered after the ball and started a relay toward the plate. Slaughter beat the second throw and St. Louis won the game, 7-6, to complete the twin-bill sweep.

Doctors determined that Reiser had suffered a concussion. Though he was expected to be idle for 10 to 14 days, Pete returned to action after only six days of rest and whacked a pair of singles. Severe headaches eventually took their toll, however, and Reiser's batting average dropped steadily.

In some ways, the incident characterized the Dodger fiber. They were a truculent bunch, led by

Durocher and his first lieutenant, equally pugnacious Chuck Dressen. Each was a master at provoking intense hatred by other teams. Several times during the heat of combat, Brooklyn pitchers, acting on orders from their skipper, precipitated brawls by firing beanballs at opposing batters. The Chicago Cubs and Boston Braves, in particular, felt the sting of horsehide on flesh. The practice grew to epidemic proportions until N.L. President Ford Frick fined the culprits and warned that stiffer penalties—including some to the managers—would follow if the headhunters did not cease and desist.

MacPhail also possessed a well-developed talent for churning the baseball waters. In five years as majordomo of the Brooklyn franchise he had aroused hostility with his explosive temper and abrasive pronouncements. But nobody, not even his detractors, could deny that Leland Stanford MacPhail knew how to promote baseball, whether it was at Columbus (American Association), where he launched his career, or at Cincinnati, where he revived a moribund franchise, or at Brooklyn, where he performed similar therapy.

As the train carrying the Brooklyn club rolled westward on the night of August 23, no one could overlook the dissimilarities between the Dodgers and their closest pursuers, the Cardinals. MacPhail had assembled the Dodgers in the marketplace. Branch Rickey, father of the farm system, had produced the Cards on the fertile acres of the far-flung minor league empire.

Of the Dodger regulars, catcher Mickey Owen and outfielders Joe Medwick and Reiser were former St. Louis properties. Camilli was acquired from the Phillies, Herman from the Cubs, Reese from the Boston Red Sox organization, third baseman Arky Vaughan from the Pirates and Dixie Walker from the Detroit Tigers. Among the regular pitchers, 33-year-old righthander Whit Wyatt was obtained after spending several years in the American League, while Kirby Higbe was acquired from the Phillies, Curt Davis from the Cards, Larry French from the Cubs and Johnny Allen from the St. Louis Browns.

By contrast, the Cardinals were virtually all homegrown. Catcher Walker Cooper, first baseman Johnny Hopp, second baseman Jimmy Brown, shortstop Marty Marion, third baseman Whitey Kurowski and outfielders Musial, Terry Moore and Slaughter all came up through the St. Louis farm system.

As a group, the Cardinals, who were managed by gentlemanly Billy Southworth, resembled uncaged rabbits. "They're not baseball players," cracked Casey Stengel, the Braves' manager. "They're a

This was St. Louis Swifty, the fast-talking riverboat gambler portrayed by the pen of New York cartoonist Willard Mullin.

track team." Willard Mullin labeled them the "St. Louis Swifties."

Moreover, the Cardinals had flaming youth in their favor. Only one everyday player, Moore, had observed his 30th birthday—and he was just three months past that milestone. Brown also was 30, but he shared second base with 24-year-old Creepy Crespi.

The St. Louis pitching staff was constructed around Mort Cooper, 28, Walker's older brother; Johnny Beazley, a 23-year-old rookie, and lefthander Max Lanier, 27. Howie Krist, 26, excelled as the Cardinals' fireman and contributed 13 victories in 1942, chiefly in relief roles.

Perhaps most important to the Cardinals' pennant drive was the handling of the team by Southworth. The 49-year-old Nebraskan maintained a positive outlook that infected his players with the belief that the Dodgers were not invincible.

"They haven't had their slump yet," Billy said while the Dodgers were storming along at a .700 clip. "We have had ours; so have all the other clubs in the league. I've been around a long time and never saw even the best team fail to hit some kind of a slump sooner or later."

When the Dodgers arrived in St. Louis on August 24, they found baseball enthusiasm at a fever pitch. The city had been without a pennant since 1934, and the rapidly improving Cardinals held the populace firmly in their grip. The St. Louis fans were anxious to see their team hack away at the Dodgers' 7½-game lead.

More than 25,000 people paid their way into Sportsman's Park for the first of the four games between the two contenders. French, whose only loss in 14 decisions had been inflicted by the Cards,

started for Brooklyn, while Lanier started for St. Louis.

Almost from the beginning, it was no contest. As Lanier scattered four hits, the Cards assaulted French and two successors for 12 hits. Moore had two singles and a double, a stolen base, four runs scored and two runs batted in to pace St. Louis to a 7-1 victory.

The largest night crowd in St. Louis history, 33,527, was on hand the next night for a pitching duel between Mort Cooper and Wyatt. As had been his custom for the last few starts, Cooper changed his uniform number to agree with the victory he was seeking. On this occasion he wore number 16, belonging to reserve catcher Ken O'Dea.

For 12 innings the two righthanders were superb, each holding the opposition scoreless. Cooper was the first to weaken. The Dodgers broke the deadlock with a run in the 13th inning on a single by Owen, a sacrifice by Wyatt and a single by Lew Riggs.

A one-out walk to Slaughter and consecutive singles by Musial and Walker Cooper enabled the Cards to tie the score in the last half of the inning. Cooper's blow also knocked out Wyatt and brought in French, the loser of the previous night. When pinch-hitter Coaker Triplett ripped one of the lefthander's pitches up the middle, it appeared that the Cardinals were about to win. But Herman made a scintillating stop behind second base and started an inning-ending double play.

Mort Cooper blanked the Dodgers in the top of the 14th before Kurowski beat out a bunt to open the bottom half of the inning. Exit French. Enter Les Webber, a 27-year-old rookie righthander. Marion reached base safely when Camilli fielded his bunt but threw belatedly to second. A bunt by Mort Cooper was turned into a forceout at third base before a walk to Jimmy Brown loaded the bases.

With the infielders playing in, Moore whistled a hot grounder to Riggs. The ball knocked the third baseman down, and by the time he regained his feet and fired to the plate, Marion was safely across with the winning run.

Durocher furnished an extra surge of excitement for the record throng in the 12th inning when he persisted in complaints over umpire George Barr's ball-and-strike decisions. The Lip was banished, as was Dressen when the coach renewed the rhubarb later in the same frame.

The Dodgers were clearly slumping. Their lead over St. Louis was down to 5½ games. Maybe Larry MacPhail hadn't been kidding after all.

For the third contest, Durocher chose Max Macon, a 26-year-old lefthander who had shared a room with Lanier when both were Redbird farmhands at Columbus, O., some years before. Macon, who had been recalled from Montreal (International) in July, won only five games for Brooklyn in 1942 but had a nifty 1.93 earned-run average. Southworth's choice to slice another game off the Brooklyn lead was 15-game winner Beazley.

The Cardinals scored one run in the second inning on Johnny Hopp's run-scoring single and threatened to break the game wide open with none out and the bases loaded. But the uprising expired there. Macon fanned Beazley and forced Brown to ground into a double play.

The Dodgers tied the score on their next opportunity. Vaughan singled, went to second on an infield out and scored on Camilli's single. The teams then swapped zeroes until the last of the 10th inning. The concluding chapter in the tense struggle bore a striking resemblance to the climax of 24 hours earlier.

With one out, Brown coaxed a base on balls and moved up on Moore's single. When Slaughter hit a bouncer to the mound, Macon could only retire the batter. Triplett then hit a slow dribbler to the left side, where it was fielded by Macon. Like Riggs the previous night, Macon skidded and fell. His hasty throw to the plate was too late to nail Brown. The Cardinals had their second consecutive 2-1, extra-inning victory, and the Brooklyn lead shrank to 4½ lengths.

The Dodgers had one more opportunity to avoid total disaster at the first stop on their western swing. For the series finale, Durocher picked Curt Davis to start. St. Louis fans were acquainted with Davis. The rawboned righthander had won 22 games for the Cardinals in 1939, his last full season in St. Louis before being shipped to the Dodgers. Irreverent Brooklyn players called him Daniel Boone; others referred to him as Coonskin. In this twilight encounter of August 27, the grizzled 35-year-old veteran was loaded for "bear"—or Cardinals.

For St. Louis, Lanier tried to come back with only two days' rest. Max was furnished a one-run lead in the third inning with the help of a miscue by Herman on a potential inning-ending forceout. Slaughter took advantage of that opportunity, doubling home a run.

Lanier blanked the Dodgers until the fifth, when Owen and Vaughan, who had singled, scored on a single by Davis. Curt had given himself all the runs he needed to win, but his teammates added two more markers later in the inning. Brooklyn won, 4-1.

The Dodgers left St. Louis with a lead of 5½ games. Though the Cards had failed to sweep the league leaders, Southworth was encouraged by the results of the series.

"We'll keep after them," the manager said, "and if we keep hustling on every play, we can pass them.

The ace of the Cardinal pitching staff was Mort Cooper, whose number usually corresponded to the victory total he was seeking that day.

And once we do, they'll never catch us."

The Dodgers were not overly concerned about the three setbacks to St. Louis. They were confident in their ability to waltz through the rest of their schedule, which included only two more games against the Cardinals. With a month of the season remaining, there still was ample time for the leaders to regain their footing, resume the brand of baseball they had displayed in earlier weeks and toss MacPhail's accusations back into his florid countenance.

In addition, the Cardinals might even slacken off from their furious pace, thereby creating a more congenial atmosphere for the Bums. But the Birds refused to let up. Their pressure was constant, and the Brooklyn advantage eroded daily.

"Don't worry about us," Durocher said in late August. "We'll win the pennant again, though it may be a little harder job than we anticipated. Sure, the Cardinals are hotter than blazes right now. They have a good team and a great manager in Billy Southworth. But if they keep going on that way, we'll simply have to get hotter."

On the afternoon of September 10, when the Dodgers entertained the Cubs and the Cardinals visited the Giants, the Brooklyn lead stood at three games. For Dodger aficionados, the day's results presented the same old hackneyed tale. Lon Warneke, who had been sold to Chicago by St. Louis two months before, subdued the Dodgers, 10-2.

Across the river, the Cards' Howie Pollet, a 21-year-old lefthander, humbled the Giants, 5-1. Carl Hubbell had been scheduled to start for the Giants, but an errant throw by Musial in pregame drills struck the veteran lefthander on the head. While Hub was taken to the hospital for X-rays, Hal Schumacher was rushed to the mound. Prince Hal warmed up hurriedly and yielded three first-inning runs that decided the outcome.

The Brooklyn lead was down to two games, the team's slimmest margin since May 9. In their last 32 games, the St. Louis Swifties (92-46) had won 27 times and lost only five. The Dodgers, meanwhile, had gone 10-9 over their last 19 games as their record fell to 94-44.

The Cards' next stop was Ebbets Field for the last two meetings of the year between the contenders. For the critical series, Southworth primed his aces, Mort Cooper and Lanier, and he could not have planned more wisely.

A sullen throng of 29,774 was on hand for the September 11 encounter. Most of them undoubtedly wished they had sought entertainment elsewhere.

Cooper, wearing Coaker Triplett's uniform number 20 to match his immediate victory objective, was overpowering. He scattered three singles and permitted no runner to reach second base. The 3-0 victory, making Mort the first major leaguer to post 20 wins in 1942, was his eighth shutout of the cam-

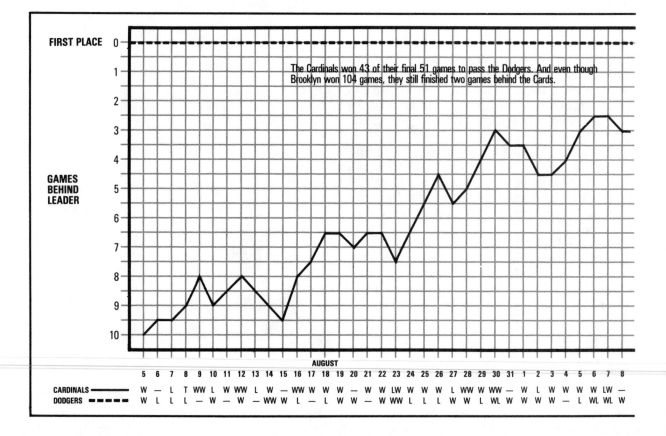

The Cardinals won 43 of their final 51 games to pass the Dodgers. And even though Brooklyn won 104 games, they still finished two games behind the Cards.

paign and his third over Brooklyn. It also was his fifth consecutive victory, raising his record to 20-7.

Adding to the Dodgers' embarrassment, Mort collected two hits and scored as many runs. He led off the sixth inning with a single against Wyatt, was sacrificed to second and scored on Slaughter's single.

Cooper also opened the eighth with an infield hit. He took third on Brown's double and crossed the plate ahead of Brown on Moore's single over shortstop.

The September 12 contest matched the two former minor league buddies, Lanier and Macon. The result of the engagement was described by Roscoe McGowen in the next day's editions of the New York Times:

"Flatbush fandom's worst fears today are a woeful reality. Those irrepressible St. Louis Cardinals are tied with Brooklyn's Dodgers for the National League lead.

"To achieve that end, Billy Southworth's Redbirds turned back the Brooks at Ebbets Field yesterday, 2-1 . . . and sent 27,511 fans home muttering to themselves about lost opportunities."

The issue was resolved in the second inning. Walker Cooper's single and Kurowski's ninth homer of the year, a wallop into the left-field seats, gave Lanier a 2-0 lead. Brooklyn recovered one of the runs in the home half. Camilli singled but was forced at second by Owen, who scored on Reese's double.

That ended the scoring for the day, but not the excitement. In the seventh inning, umpire Al Barlick called Owen out on a close play at first base, transforming Durocher into a loud, quivering mass of protoplasm. The dandy little skipper trailed the arbiter nearly to the right-field fence, protesting the decision every step of the way. For his efforts, Leo got Barlick's deaf ear and imperious thumb. He was ushered off the premises, along with Dressen, the first-base coach.

Each club's reaction to the Cards' two-game sweep was interesting. The Cardinals were convinced that they were on their way to the N.L. championship.

"I think we're in," said Cards President Sam Breadon, who approved the printing of World Series tickets immediately after his club tied the Dodgers. "We've won 29 out of 34 and those fellows have lost six of their last nine."

The Dodgers also were confident, but the brash cockiness they had displayed a few weeks before was no longer evident.

"All right, they caught up," Durocher barked in the Brooklyn clubhouse after the Cardinals left town. "It took them five months to do it. Let's snap out of it and get after them now."

MacPhail, who had warned his players of this possibility weeks earlier, was surprisingly upbeat about the Dodgers' status.

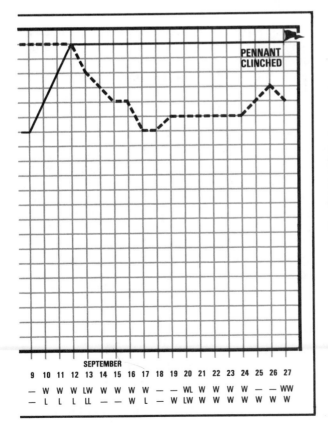

	SEPTEMBER																		
9	10	11	12	13	14	15	16	17	18	19	20	21	22	23	24	25	26	27
—	W	W	W	LW	W	W	W	W	—	—	WL	W	W	W	W	—	—	WW
—	L	L	L	LL	—	—	W	L	—	W	LW	W	W	W	W	W	W	W

No matter how hard Manager Leo Durocher scratched and clawed, the Dodgers could not hold their once-comfortable lead.

Dodger players, with veteran Dolph Camilli (right) serving as spokesman,
said goodby to team President Larry MacPhail with a $500 watch.

"I feel better now than I've felt in a couple of days," he said. "They're even with us, and I know you can win. Something's going to happen soon—a break that will start our rally. Something like the bases full, two out and a dropped pop fly. And then an explosion—six straight hits."

The Dodgers got just such a break the next day. In Philadelphia, the Cardinals blew a 1-0 lead in the bottom of the ninth inning of the first game of a doubleheader. Brown, Hopp and Slaughter failed to communicate on a pop fly that fell for a double, Walker Cooper dropped a perfect throw to the plate by Moore and the surehanded Marion bobbled a grounder, paving the way for the last-place Phillies to win, 2-1. The Dodgers had their chance to regain the lead.

And they blew it. They lost both ends of a doubleheader to the Cincinnati Reds. When Moore's solo home run in the fifth inning gave the Cardinals a 3-2 victory over Philadelphia in the nightcap of their twin bill, the Dodgers tumbled to second place. The last time Brooklyn had been out of the top spot was April 18, when the season was only five days old.

After the double defeat, MacPhail dashed off a blistering wire to Bill McKechnie, accusing the Cin-cinnati skipper of saving his best pitchers for games against the Bums. Deacon Bill, one of the game's most gentlemanly personalities, fired back a telegram that was equally sulphurous. There the matter dropped.

There still were two weeks to go—plenty of time for a Dodger reversal. Though the Cardinals won nine of their next 10 outings to raise their record to 104-48, their advantage over Brooklyn stood at only 1½ games going into the final day. If the Dodgers (103-50), who had won seven games in a row, could defeat the Phillies on September 27 while the Cards lost a doubleheader to the Cubs, the race would end in a dead heat.

Higbe scattered 10 hits in 7⅓ innings in hurling the Dodgers to a 4-3 triumph at Shibe Park. But as early as the fifth inning, the scoreboard announced that the Brooklyn cause was nigh hopeless. The Cards were leading the Cubs, 4-1, and they went on to a 9-2, pennant-clinching victory behind the five-hit hurling of lefthander Ernie White. With the exception of Musial, Southworth benched all his regulars in the second game. It mattered little. The Cards won that game as well, 4-1, to give Beazley his 21st win of the year.

The sweep raised the Cardinals' record to 106-48,

Twenty years after their 1942 heroics, Terry Moore (left), Stan Musial (center) and Enos Slaughter, one of the best outfields in history, were reunited.

the most victories by an N.L. team since the 1909 Pirates won 110. The Brooklyn total of 104 victories was the most for a runner-up club since the 1909 Cubs won as many.

St. Louis' furious pace in the last two months produced 43 victories in 51 decisions. That .843 winning percentage exceeded that of the legendary 1914 Braves, who played at a .787 gait in climbing from last place to first.

"We won this one the hard way," a jubilant Southworth told reporters after the Cards clinched the flag. "No one won it for us. We went out and won it ourselves."

In the gloom of the visitors' clubhouse at Philadelphia, one Dodger spoke for all the members of the defeated club. "I declare," Dixie Walker said, "I didn't think it was possible."

On the train ride back to New York, reported one newsman, the conversation "could have been written on the back of a postage stamp."

The season was over not only for the Dodgers. It also marked the end of the line for MacPhail. Some time before the chief executive had taken a physical examination for duty in World War II.

But four days before the curtain fell, MacPhail revealed that while he had been declared physically

fit for military service, he was denied, at age 52, the active duty he sought. The field artillery captain of World War I had to be content with a lieutenant colonel's commission in the War Department's Service of Supply. He then walked away from a lucrative five-year contract with the Dodgers in order to enter the service.

Just before the end of the campaign, MacPhail was summoned to the Brooklyn clubhouse, where Camilli presented him with a $500 watch on behalf of the players. These athletes, who had failed to heed their boss' warning about complacency many weeks before, wanted to acknowledge his ability as a baseball executive and his commitment to the country's war effort.

An obviously touched MacPhail had to leave the room before he could regain his composure.

"They said you collapsed," he told the Dodgers. "Nothing of the sort. You have won more games than any other team in the history of Brooklyn baseball. You may yet win the pennant. If you don't, you will have done your best, and the blame for the Brooklyn failure will rest with the Cardinals."

MacPhail may have been a prophet, but he wasn't the type to say "I told you so."

Tigers Overcome 'Crybaby' Indians

Cleveland Indians Owner Alva Bradley (left) was asked by discontented players in 1940 to fire Manager Oscar Vitt (right).

The telephone rang in the office of Alva Bradley on the morning of June 13, 1940. On the line was Mel Harder, veteran pitcher of the Cleveland Indians, requesting an audience with the club owner.

Harder did not reveal the purpose of his visit, nor did Bradley inquire. The owner willingly granted the request, expecting that Harder alone would arrive at the assigned hour.

That same morning the Indians had returned from an eastern trip on which they lost eight of 13 games, a statistic that Bradley recognized all too well. What he was not aware of was the players' growing discontent with their manager, Oscar Vitt.

Almost to a man, the players felt that Vitt held them in low esteem, that he regarded them with contempt. Though they had contended for first place since the start of the American League season, the outspoken pilot belittled the players to the press and derogated them individually to teammates

when out of earshot. He compared them unfavorably with the Newark Bears, the New York Yankees' farm club that Ossie had led to a runaway International League pennant in 1937.

On June 12, Vitt removed Harder from a game against first-place Boston when the pitcher failed to stop a rally that gave the Red Sox a 9-5 victory. "It's about time you won one, (considering) the money you're getting," the disgusted manager said to Harder.

The day before, when Bob Feller was experiencing a rare bad day and the Red Sox won, 9-2, Vitt had griped: "Look at him. He's supposed to be my ace. I'm supposed to win a pennant with that kind of pitching." Vitt uttered that insult while storming around the dugout and pounding the bat rack.

Disharmony had been on the rise almost from the time Vitt took charge of the club after the 1937 season, but it came to a boil during the team's east-

The young second base-shortstop combination of Ray Mack (left) and Lou Boudreau (right) was not asked to join in the players' crusade against Cleveland Manager Oscar Vitt (center).

ern junket. At a meeting of the players in Boston, it was agreed that deteriorating morale required drastic action. The time had come to present their grievances to Bradley.

"I could have gotten along with Vitt," Harder recalled in later years. "And (pitcher) Johnny Allen could get along with him. The same was true with Bob Feller, the star of the team. But we agreed to go along with the others to show a unified front.

"Allen and I offered to visit Mr. Bradley in his home and discuss the matter, but the others insisted that all of us go to his office and air our complaints."

On that Thursday morning, the players arrived separately at the Marion Building in downtown Cleveland. But as the group began to assemble, observers guessed that a grave issue was at stake. The nature of the matter, however, was a mystery to them, just as it was to Bradley when the contingent entered his office a few minutes later.

Missing from the delegation were center fielder Roy Weatherly, who had no sympathy for the movement; right fielder Beau Bell, who only recently had been acquired from the Detroit Tigers, and star shortstop Lou Boudreau and second baseman Ray Mack, who were excluded because of their relative youthfulness.

In addition to Harder, Allen and Feller, those

willing to air their complaints included third baseman Ken Keltner, pitcher Al Milnar, catcher Rollie Hemsley, utility infielder Oscar Grimes and outfielder Jeff Heath. In all, 11 players stood before Alva Bradley.

"What can I do for you?" asked Bradley, opening the dialogue.

"We think we have a good chance to win the pennant," replied Harder, the group's appointed spokesman, "but we'll never win it with Vitt as manager. If we can get rid of him, we can win. We all feel sure of that."

About that time, Bradley's phone jangled. The caller was Hal Trosky, who had been prevented from joining the malcontents because of the death of his mother in Iowa.

"I just want to tell you," the slugging first baseman said, "that I am 100 percent in favor of the story you are now hearing. Those are my sentiments without qualification."

Bradley directed his attention to his visitors again. He asked for a bill of particulars against the manager who had led the Tribe to a pair of third-place finishes.

"He makes everybody nervous," somebody volunteered.

"He pops off too much to newspapermen," offered a second player.

Young Bob Feller (left) and veterans Ken Keltner (left center) and Hal Trosky (right center) were among the 1940 insurgents against Manager Oscar Vitt (right).

"He showboats too much," added a third.

"He flies into rages in the dugout," responded a fourth.

"He tears us down to other teams," commented a fifth.

Bradley listened patiently to all the grievances. Then he told the players: "This is a serious business. . . . We're not going to arrive at any hasty decisions. I want to see that justice is done, but there must be a complete investigation."

Bradley dismissed the players with this injunction: "I want you to go out there and play your best as though this hadn't come up. We're only two games behind Boston in first place. Worse tangles than this have been straightened out. The main thing is secrecy. Don't breathe a word of this meeting."

But somebody did tattle. Shortly after the conference adjourned, Gordon Cobbledick, a baseball writer for the Cleveland Plain Dealer, was on the phone with Bradley, asking the club owner to confirm the details of the meeting as they had been related to him. The final edition of the Plain Dealer the next morning screamed the story of the Tribe rebellion on page one, featuring it above the major international development of the day, the fall of Paris to the Germans.

The source of Cobbledick's scoop never was iden-

tified positively. "For a long time," Harder said, "people thought that I was the guilty party because Cobby and I were the best of friends and socialized frequently. On those occasions, however, we never talked about the Indians, only the other teams."

Pursuing his probe of the player rebellion, Bradley invited Vitt to tell his side of the story to the club's board of directors. Bradley apparently was satisfied with Vitt's explanation because a short while later, Ossie reported to the athletes without apparent emotion or rancor that "Mr. Bradley informed me that I'm still the manager of the team."

The following Sunday, June 16, Vitt was cheered and the players were hooted as the Indians swept a doubleheader from the Philadelphia A's. After the second game, Bradley visited the clubhouse and told the players: "No matter how you feel, we must go on. There can be no action now."

He asked the players to sign a paper withdrawing charges against their skipper. "This will not mean the matter is completely closed," he said, "but it will be the best for all concerned."

The declaration of amity read: "We, the undersigned, publicly desire to withdraw all statements referring to the resignation of Oscar Vitt. We feel this action is for the betterment of the Cleveland baseball club."

Vitt conceded that he was not entirely blameless

in the uprising. The front page of the June 20 issue of The Sporting News trumpeted the headline: " 'I'll Be Nice as I Can,' Says Vitt of Tribe Truce / Leader Under Fire, Adds He'll Criticize Mistakes, If Made."

The beleaguered pilot was surprised by the players' uprising. "I knew there was a couple of fellows on the team who don't have much use for me," he said, "but I never dreamed of anything like this."

Vitt admitted he had made some offensive remarks to players. "But isn't anyone liable to speak unthinkingly," he asked, "when he's fighting for first place and sees his club losing a close game?"

Public sentiment favored Vitt in the wake of the rebellion. Bradley had warned the players after their conference that "if this story ever gets out, you'll be ridiculed the rest of your life." It quickly appeared as if the owner was right. Rather than gaining sympathy for their plight, the players were perceived, both in Cleveland and abroad, as whiners. It wasn't long before a fresh batch of new nicknames—"Crybabies," "Bawl Team," "Half Vitts" and so on—were tagged on the Indians. Fans across the A.L. map took great pleasure in jeering the Tribe.

In the face of public scorn, however, the Indians started to play winning baseball. The Red Sox, who had held first place continuously since May 6,

dropped to second June 20, when the St. Louis Browns swept a twin bill from Boston and the Indians beat the Washington Senators, 12-1. That triumph was the seventh in eight tries since the disgruntled players marched into Bradley's office, and it was the fifth in what would become an eight-game winning streak.

While the Red Sox began a tumble that landed them in a fourth-place tie with the Chicago White Sox at season's end, the Indians held first place for all but one day through July 4. After splitting a doubleheader with Detroit on Independence Day, the traditional date for projecting pennant winners, the Tribe (44-28) enjoyed a one-game lead over the Tigers (41-27).

Little had been expected of the Tigers in Del Baker's second full year as manager. A fifth-place club in 1939, Detroit was picked for fourth in a 1940 poll of 266 baseball writers. The Indians were picked for third, the Red Sox for second and the Yankees, who had won four consecutive championships, for first.

One of the factors in the experts' low opinion of the Tigers was the ages of some key players. Second baseman Charlie Gehringer, 36, shortstop Dick Bartell, 32, who was obtained in an off-season deal with the Chicago Cubs, and third baseman Pinky Hig-

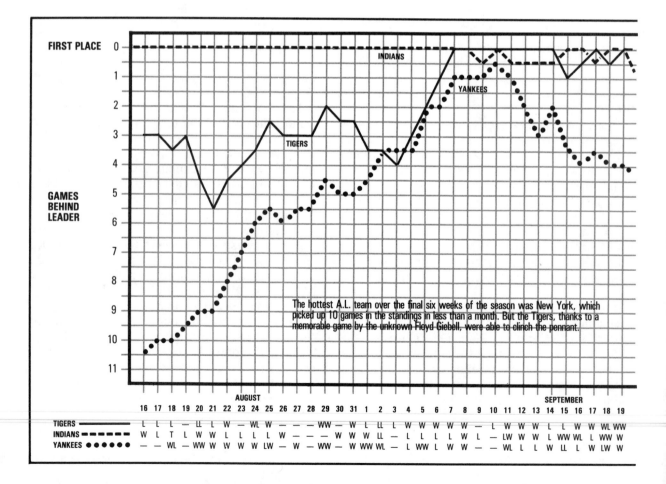

The hottest A.L. team over the final six weeks of the season was New York, which picked up 10 games in the standings in less than a month. But the Tigers, thanks to a memorable game by the unknown Floyd Giebell, were able to clinch the pennant.

gins, 30, were among the veterans on whom Baker was counting to repeat past success. The two players expected to share right field—Pete Fox, 31, and Bruce Campbell, 30, a former Indian—also were past their primes.

A major experiment also made the Tigers hard to figure. The left fielder was Hank Greenberg, who had consented—with fiscal persuasion—to switch to the outfield so that Rudy York, a failure as a catcher, third baseman and flyhawk, could play first base. Greenberg and York swung the lustiest bats for Detroit, but it remained to be seen how they would adjust to their new positions.

The starting pitchers included Louis Norman (Bobo) Newsom, a 20-game winner in 1939; 33-year-old Tommy Bridges, who was starting to taper off as a big winner; Lynwood (Schoolboy) Rowe, a mainstay of pennant-winning Detroit teams in 1934 and '35 who had been handicapped by a sore arm for several years, and several others with lesser reputations.

The experts agreed that the Tigers had no worries in center field, which was patrolled by 22-year-old Barney McCosky, a .311 hitter as a rookie in 1939. The club also was well fortified behind the plate, where Birdie Tebbetts, 25, was flirting with star-

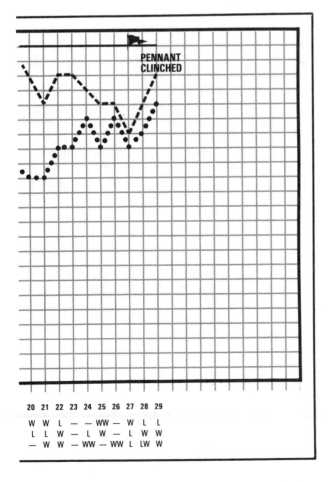

PENNANT
CLINCHED

20	21	22	23	24	25	26	27	28	29
W	W	L	—	—	W W	—	W	L	L
L	L	W	—	L	W	—	L	W	W
—	W	W	—	W W	—	W W	L	L W	W

The Detroit Tigers, under Manager Del Baker (above), were not expected to be much of a factor in the 1940 pennant race.

dom.

If veterans could forestall the ravages of time, if rookies produced as expected and if the Greenberg experiment succeeded, the Tigers could finish in the first division, according to Sam Greene, the Detroit correspondent for The Sporting News. Otherwise, he feared, "the club might sink into the depths."

The writer's worst fears were not realized. Age did not seriously hamper the veterans, the younger players measured up as expected and the Greenberg experiment came off handsomely. Though neither Greenberg nor York was outstanding defensively, both were powerful at the plate. Greenberg led the league with 41 home runs and 150 runs batted in, while York added 33 homers and 134 RBIs.

After a 15-14 start, the Tigers won 11 of their next 15 games to move into second place June 11. By winning their last three games before the July 9 All-Star Game, the Tigers ascended to first place with a 44-27 record, half a game better than the Indians (45-29). Cleveland resumed the lead immediately after the break, but by July 18, Detroit was on top for an extended stay. The Tigers held sole possession of first place for all but three days over the next 3½ weeks.

The Indians stayed close, however, never falling more than 1½ games behind the leaders. By August 12, when the Tigers visited Cleveland for a two-game series, the teams were dead even with 64-44 records.

Feller broke the deadlock in the first game. The 21-year-old righthander, who still was being referred to as the "Boy Wonder" in his fifth season with Cleveland, defeated lefthander Hal Newhouser, 8-5, to become the major leagues' first 20-game winner of 1940. Trosky, Bell and Weatherly hit home runs in support of Feller. The Tribe also won the finale, 6-5, as Harry Eisenstat beat Al Benton to put the club two games in front. The next night, a Cleveland Stadium crowd of 59,068—the largest ever to attend a night game—watched lefthander Al Smith hurl a one-hit, 4-0 shutout against Chicago. The Indians won their next two games as well to open their lead to three games, their largest of the season. That spurt rated this headline in The Sporting News: "Tepid Tepee Turns Red Hot as Indians Put on Full Steam."

Though the Tigers were slipping, they remained optimistic. "We've run into some trouble, but it doesn't figure to last," Del Baker said. "We lost Charlie Gehringer for nine games. Schoolboy Rowe (who was 11-2 at the time) had to leave because of his mother's illness. Harold Newhouser had a sore arm. Buck Newsom was hit by a summer cold about the time he recovered from his broken thumb. These things slowed down our pace, but we'll get going again."

The Tigers tumbled as far as 5½ games behind

Cleveland in August. The deficit was down to four lengths by September 4, the day Cleveland and Detroit opened a three-game series at Briggs Stadium in the Motor City.

While the Tigers were struggling to catch up with the Indians, however, the Yankees were making a belated rush for the pennant. After August 8, when New York was in fifth place with a 50-51 record, Manager Joe McCarthy's defending A.L. champions won 21 of 25 contests. When the Tigers lost their fourth straight game September 3, the Yankees moved into second place, half a game ahead of Detroit.

Having spent the last 2½ weeks on the road, a return to Detroit was just what the Tigers needed to regain their footing. In the first game against Cleveland, Greenberg, Campbell and Gehringer each homered and Rowe beat Feller, 7-2. The Detroit home run parade continued the next day as Campbell and York each socked a three-run blast to lift the Tigers to an 11-3 triumph.

The public image of the "Crybabies" took another beating after that second loss to Detroit. A group of Cleveland players met in their Detroit hotel that night to discuss ways to spark the club, which had lost its last four games. The next day, headlines in Cleveland papers shouted the news that the players had decided to institute new strategic moves on the field—without Vitt's approval. Though players and club officials alike denied the story, the Indians once again were portrayed as cunning mutineers. In any event, it was clear that dissension still racked the Indians.

In the series finale September 6, Detroit walloped Cleveland, 10-5. The Tigers then edged the Browns the next day, 5-4, while the Indians lost to the White Sox by the same score. The Indians thus saw the last chunk of their 5½-game lead vanish, although they still were in first place by two percentage points.

Over the next two weeks, Detroit and Cleveland swapped the lead back and forth seven times, with New York staying close on the leaders' heels. When the Indians paid their last visit of the season to Detroit on September 20, the teams were tied for first with identical 85-61 marks. The Yankees (80-64) were four games back.

The Indians arrived in Detroit the evening before the series opener rather than on the morning of the game, as had been their normal practice. In departing from policy, the Tribe had hoped to arrive in the city without fanfare.

As in the case of the player insurrection, however, secrecy was not the club's strong suit in 1940. Word of the revised schedule preceded the team into the Motor City and 1,000 fans lay in wait, ready to ambush the players with all sorts of produce in varying stages of decay. As the players made a dash for safety, the Tiger fans hollered "Cryba-

The New York Yankees remained in the 1940 pennant chase, thanks to the big bats of (left to right) Joe DiMaggio, Charlie Keller and Tommy Henrich.

bies, crybabies!" and tried to stuff baby bottles into their pockets.

The next afternoon, a baby buggy was rolled onto the roof of the Tribe's dugout at Briggs Stadium. Nearby, a spectator amused the crowd by sucking on an oversized nipple attached to a quart milk bottle. Throughout the three-game set, the Indians were booed mercilessly.

Vitt selected Harder and Baker chose Newsom to pitch in the first contest. For seven innings, the Cleveland veteran was superb, holding the Tigers to three hits and one run. He also drove Newsom from the mound in the sixth with a single as the Indians built a 4-1 lead.

Harder was rolling along smoothly in the last of the eighth when McCosky drew a one-out walk and Gehringer tagged the righthander for a single, sending McCosky to third. With Greenberg approaching the plate, Vitt trotted to the mound. After a brief powwow, Vitt gestured to the bullpen. Sur-

prisingly, Feller emerged, the same Rapid Robert who had pitched two complete games in the previous five days and had informed his manager that his arm was tired.

The fact that Feller's arm did need rest readily became apparent when Greenberg, York and Pinky Higgins smote consecutive singles. Before Joe Dobson retired the side, the Tigers scored five runs and were on their way to a 6-5 victory.

Criticism of Vitt was bitter. Why would a manager, the second-guessers asked, take out a pitcher who had handled Greenberg and York with comparative ease in the past and bring in a tired starter?

The harried skipper explained that "Harder was tiring a little. . . . Greenberg and York were coming up, and all I could see was one of those big apple-knockers catching hold of an inside curve and parking it in the stands.

"Feller is the best pitcher in the business. He was warmed up, and the bullpen reported he had plenty of stuff. Naturally, the way it turned out, I wish I had let Harder stay in the game. But if the same circumstances came up again, I'd do exactly the same thing."

The Tigers also won the second game, 5-0, as Rowe allowed only five hits and posted his 16th win in a remarkable comeback campaign. The big right-hander also drove in the first run and scored the second.

Feller prevented a total collapse of the Indians by winning the series windup, 10-5, for his 27th victory of the year. The Tribe routed Bridges and five Tiger relievers for 12 hits, including home runs by Feller, Trosky, Weatherly, Keltner and left fielder Ben Chapman.

With only one game separating them, the two front-runners parted company briefly, the Indians to play two games against St. Louis, the Tigers to engage Chicago in the same number of games before they clashed again in the final three games of the year at Cleveland.

On September 24, the Browns handed the Indians a 7-2 setback. A day later, Milnar hurled a 4-2 victory over St. Louis while the Tigers defeated the White Sox twice, 10-9 in 10 innings and 3-2. Newsom won both ends of the doubleheader, pitching two innings of shutout relief in the opener and a complete game in the nightcap.

As a result, Cleveland (87-64) fell two games back. To capture their first pennant since 1920, the Indians had to sweep the final three games against the Tigers (89-62). Detroit, on the other hand, was within a single victory of that franchise's third flag in seven seasons.

All of that, however, still depended partly on the Yankees, who figured in the pennant picture, too. After sweeping a twin bill at Philadelphia while Detroit and Cleveland were idle September 26, New York had an 86-64 mark, 2½ games behind the Tigers. The Yanks had won eight straight contests and 36 of their last 49 to keep their slim flag hopes alive. By winning their last four games against Philadelphia and Washington, New York could forge a first-place tie on the last day of the season as long as Cleveland won at least two of its three games with Detroit. But the A's forced the Yankees to stay home during World Series week for the first time since 1935 by posting a 6-2 victory September 27.

The Tigers' reception in Cleveland that same morning was patterned after the welcome extended to the Indians in Detroit a week earlier. Overripe fruit and vegetables pelted the players as they alighted from the train. Like football players in a broken field, they zigzagged through the hostile crowd, covering their faces with whatever means were available in their mad run for cover.

There was no question about who would pitch the first game for Cleveland. It was Feller, who pro-

nounced himself recovered from his recent arm weariness and ready to try for his 28th victory.

The identity of the Detroit starter was a closely guarded secret. While Baker refused to name his choice, the manager did nothing to discourage the notion that it would be Rowe. On that premise, most pregame stories tabbed the Schoolboy as the Tigers' starter.

But as game time approached, Rowe was nowhere to be seen. Warming up instead was a slender blond whose statistics were as unfamiliar to most folks as the correct spelling and pronunciation of his name: Floyd Giebell. Once the righthander was identified positively, the press box became a scene of feverish activity as scribes scampered to uncover the background of this unlikely pitching choice.

The mystery surrounding Giebell was understandable. He posted a 1-10 record for Toledo (American Association) in 1939 before he was recalled late that summer by Detroit, where he went 1-1. In 1940, he won 15 games and lost 17 for Buffalo of the International League, after which he joined the Tigers and won his first start September 19 against Philadelphia.

Steve O'Neill, manager of the Buffalo club, insisted that Giebell's record with the Bisons was misleading. "He pitched only two bad games for us. . . . He was beaten 17 times," O'Neill said, "but he lost 10 of those games by the margin of one run. He lost four games by 1-0 scores, and on one trip he was beaten three straight games . . . each time by the score of 2-1.

"I would call him a spot pitcher. He'll pitch a good game against an all-star team of major leaguers if you tell him what spots to pitch to. . . . He's got an easy windup and movement, and while he doesn't throw a blazing fastball, he throws a very deceptive one. It's on top of you before you realize it on account of the way he delivers it; not much motion."

En route to Cleveland, Baker convened some veteran players and disclosed his thoughts on a starting pitcher. Newsom had pitched 11 innings two days before, so he was not a candidate. Knowing that Feller would start for Cleveland, Baker wanted to hold back his hottest pitcher, Rowe, to face Harder, a more beatable opponent, in the second game. Newsom, a 21-game winner, then would be available in the finale. It made sense, Baker pointed out, to start a pitcher of lesser stature in the opener. And he liked Giebell. With only Greenberg opposing the selection, the matter was settled. Giebell it was.

"I figured that it would be to my best advantage to start (Giebell) against Feller," Baker later told reporters, "because if Feller is right, nobody beats him. So why waste a good pitcher trying it?"

When Baker handed a baseball to Giebell and

Rudy York (left), pitcher Floyd Giebell (center) and catcher Billy Sullivan Jr. were key figures in Detroit's 1940 pennant-clinching victory over Cleveland.

told him to start warming up, the 30-year-old rookie followed directions without a "blink or murmur," the skipper reflected. From all anyone could tell, Floyd was immune to the pressure that was about to be thrust upon him. He displayed no more emotion than he might have done if he were back in West Virginia pitching batting practice for his old Salem College team.

The imperturbable youngster was in the midst of his warmup routine when tomatoes and other produce landed nearby. They were calling cards from the Ladies Day crowd of 45,553. Giebell paid no attention.

In the batter's box, however, Greenberg noticed

the missiles aimed in his direction. The league's homer and RBI king waved merrily at his tormentors and awaited the next pitch.

Hank's mood changed in the bottom of the first inning, however, when he circled under a fly ball hit by Weatherly. More garden products rained upon him in left field as he made the catch. The game was interrupted for 10 minutes while groundkeepers removed the debris.

Baker was furious. He accosted Bill Summers, the umpire in chief, and threatened to pull his team off the field if the rowdies were not curbed.

"Don't worry, Baker," the umpire replied, "if one more thing goes wrong, I'll forfeit this game to you and give you the pennant."

Summers stalked to the edge of the field. Grabbing the public address microphone, he warned the spectators that, unless the disturbances ceased, any Cleveland batter who hit an outfield fly would be declared out automatically.

The progress of the game also was interrupted a short while later when a spectator in the second deck dropped a bushel basket partially filled with tomatoes and empty beer bottles on the occupants of the Detroit bullpen. The basket, many believe, was intended for Rowe, but it struck and knocked out Tebbetts, who was seated close by. When Birdie regained consciousness, he chased after the culprit, who was being escorted from the stadium by policemen, and planted a solid punch on the fellow's kisser.

The episode had a sobering effect on the spectators. Thereafter, only an occasional tomato sailed onto the field.

Though not as coldly efficient as his mound rival, Giebell succeeded in blanking the Tribe in the early innings. The Indians threatened to break through in the third when they placed runners on first and third with none out, but the "Icicle Kid" proved equal to the task by fanning Feller and Chapman and retiring Weatherly on an outfield fly.

"We were in a horrible batting slump," Harder remembered years later. "We couldn't have beaten a Class-A pitcher."

In the first three innings Feller allowed only one hit, a Greenberg double that Weatherly lost in the sun. But the complexion of the contest changed in the fourth. With two out and Gehringer on base via a walk, Rapid Robert faced York, who already had clubbed 32 homers that year.

After Feller's first three pitches, the count on York stood at 2-and-1. Bob threw again. The pitch to the righthanded batter was a bit higher than he would have wished. York swung and made contact, just solid enough to lift a fly toward left field. It looked like a routine chance for Chapman.

The former Yankee speedster retreated to the wall and leaped, but his jump was inches short. The ball barely eluded his glove and fell into the stands, 320 feet from home plate and only inches inside the foul pole.

Feller, trailing 2-0, allowed only one more hit, a fifth-inning single by reserve catcher Billy Sullivan. Meanwhile, Giebell was in trouble frequently. In the fourth, with two runners aboard, Floyd fanned Ray Mack to retire the side. The next inning, after the first two batters reached base, Giebell escaped once more, striking out two of the next three batters. In the seventh, with runners on second and third and one out, Chapman struck out for the third time and Weatherly grounded out. Giebell's performance wasn't pretty, but it was efficient. He made Detroit's 2-0 lead stand up.

On the strength of York's homer—it would have been an easy catch in Detroit—the Tigers captured the most hotly contested A.L. pennant since 1904. The victory was the Tigers' 18th in 23 games and seventh out of their last eight.

As York planted his foot on first base to account for the last putout of the flag-clinching victory, hysterical teammates rushed to the mound and carried Floyd George Giebell off the field. The unknown hurler had made Baker look like a five-star genius with his six-hit shutout.

When reporters invaded the Detroit clubhouse, they found wildly cheering players in all stages of dishabille. But where was Giebell, who had become a celebrity under the most trying circumstances?

Floyd was discovered at his locker in a corner of the room, calmly removing his uniform. Asked about the victory, he replied with a smile, "I would say that Chapman (who struck out three times, stranding six runners) was of considerable help to me."

The newly minted hero was ineligible for the World Series against the Cincinnati Reds. He also had only $500 coming to him from the upcoming Series pool because the Detroit players already had voted on shares before that game. But amid the whooping and hollering, Tigers Owner Walter Briggs, an invalid, was wheeled into the visitors' clubhouse at Cleveland Stadium. Gripping Giebell's hand, Briggs promised to make up the difference between the $500 and a full Detroit share, which amounted to $3,531.81.

Expectations were high for Giebell in 1941, but he never lived up to them. He pitched in 17 games without a decision and was sent to Buffalo in August.

Giebell spent the next few years in the service and the minors. He retired after winning 10 games and losing 11 for Dallas of the Texas League in 1948. After reaching the crest of his career on September 27, 1940, Floyd Giebell never won another major league game. But by clinching the pennant for the Tigers, he was truly king for a day.

Mets Amaze Baseball World

The 1969 Mets were amazing in more ways than one, as evidenced by their post-World Series singing engagement on the 'Ed Sullivan Show.'

They were the universal symbol of failure, born to be bullied and more to be pitied than censured.

They were children of expansion, the product of the union of the National League and the City of New York in 1962, five years after the metropolis was abandoned by its faithless tenants, the Giants and Dodgers.

They were innovators, constantly devising schemes for courting disaster. They embraced futility with unrestrained ardor and wholehearted dedication.

Casey Stengel, their first manager, called them "amazin'" because he was genuinely astonished when they wrenched an infrequent victory from the claws of certain defeat.

When they lost 80 more games then they won in their baptismal season, the New York Mets were indisputably the sorriest major league team since the turn of the century.

Still, in their ignominy, this brotherhood of bunglers stirred the collective heart of the masses. For many, watching the Mets display their singular brand of ineptitude evoked warm recollections of the many frustrations they endured while trying to master the mechanics of the game as children. Who would not be enraptured by the sight of the Mets suffering through the same growing pains?

As the guffaws from the galleries mounted in

Mets Manager Gil Hodges (left) benefited from the emergence of Tom Seaver (center) and Jerry Koosman as top-flight pitchers.

those early years, so did the annual attendance. From 922,530 in the club's initial season at the antiquated Polo Grounds, the gate soared to 1.768 million in the fourth year, by which time the team was performing at new Shea Stadium.

Artistically, the Mets did not match their ballooning gate figures. They lost at least 109 games in each of their first four years, and when the final results were tabulated, there were the lovable Mets prettily ensconced in last place and gazing upward in wide-eyed wonderment.

Twice, in 1966 and '68, the team oozed into ninth place, but even in the latter season, when the club posted its best record ever (73-89), the Mets still finished 16 games below .500 and 24 games out of first place. When the league braintrust awarded franchises to San Diego and Montreal in 1969 and restructured the circuit into two six-team divisions, some hope was entertained for advancement by the Mets, if only for the fact that they could no longer finish ninth or 10th.

At the conclusion of spring training in 1969, Gil Hodges was asked for a prediction on his club's chances in the pennant race. "We'll win at least 85

games," the second-year manager replied soberly. In the light of the club's 1968 achievements, when they finished one game out of the cellar, the forecast represented an improvement of 12 games.

It also represented a lofty goal for expansion clubs in general and the Mets in particular. On the other hand, who was to gainsay the word of Gilbert Ray Hodges, a strong, no-nonsense type who had grown accustomed to winning during his years as first baseman on the powerful Brooklyn Dodger teams of the late '40s and the 1950s?

Still, if the Mets fulfilled Hodges' prophecy, it was questionable whether 85 victories would spread fear through the ranks of the defending-champion St. Louis Cardinals or such intrepid contenders as the Chicago Cubs and Pittsburgh Pirates.

Hodges' blue-sky prediction found quick acceptance in New York, but in Las Vegas, the seat of realism, it was regarded as merely a managerial ploy to generate enthusiasm back home and accelerate the ticket market. Oddsmakers in the gambling mecca quoted the Mets as 100-to-1 choices to win the N.L. pennant. The favored team was St. Louis.

The Mets' opportunistic outfield consisted of (left to right) Cleon Jones, Tommie Agee and Ron Swoboda.

The club that Hodges shepherded north out of Florida lacked firepower. Its 1968 batting average of .228 was the weakest in the league, with individual marks among the regulars ranging from Cleon Jones' .297 downward to Tommie Agee's .217.

Elsewhere, the Mets were somewhat better. Fielding percentages of the previous year showed them with the fourth-highest figure (.979). With a staff earned-run average of 2.72, they also were fourth in pitching. The mound corps was dominated by Jerry Koosman, a 19-game winner, and Tom Seaver, who had posted 16 victories the year before.

Seaver was the Met pet, a wholesome, refreshing youngster with a mind as sharp as his right arm. He was the embodiment of the good fortune that smiled on the Mets after years of ill luck. The manner in which he was acquired by the Mets was positively extraordinary.

The native of Fresno, Calif., was a star at the University of Southern California when he was drafted by the Los Angeles Dodgers in 1965. The club failed to sign the phenom, however, and Seaver's name was tossed back into the hopper of draft eligibles. He then was selected in the January 1966 draft by

the Atlanta Braves, who obtained his signature for a bonus of $40,000.

As the Braves prepared to assign Seaver to a farm club, they were informed that the signing had taken place after Tom already had pitched for the 1966 Trojans, a clear violation of the agreement between baseball and the colleges. Southern Cal officials then ruled Seaver ineligible for collegiate competition.

After being advised of the circumstances of the matter, Commissioner William D. Eckert declared Seaver a free agent. But so as not to penalize Seaver, who had signed the contract in good faith, Eckert advised all the major league clubs (other than Atlanta) that if they were willing to match the $40,000 bonanza, they should notify his office in New York. A drawing then would be held to determine which club would gain signing rights to the prospect.

The Philadelphia Phillies, Cleveland Indians and Mets expressed their willingness to risk that amount on the untried kid. On April 4, 1966, Eckert drew the name of the Mets from a hat. The Mets then signed the 21-year-old prospect to a minor league contract calling for $50,000.

As the 1969 season wore on, Mets fans became more rabid and willing to
follow their heroes to foreign soil.

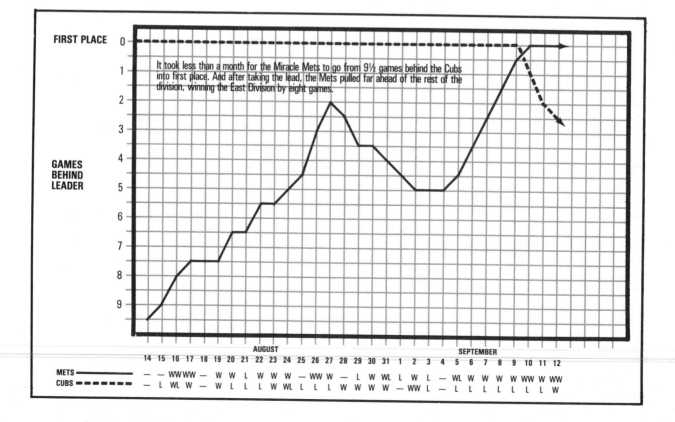

It took less than a month for the Miracle Mets to go from 9½ games behind the Cubs
into first place. And after taking the lead, the Mets pulled far ahead of the rest of the
division, winning the East Division by eight games.

FIRST PLACE

GAMES
BEHIND
LEADER

AUGUST   SEPTEMBER

14 15 16 17 18 19 20 21 22 23 24 25 26 27 28 29 30 31 1 2 3 4 5 6 7 8 9 10 11 12

METS   — — W W W W — W B W L W W W — W W W — L W W L L W L — W L W W W W W W W W
CUBS   — L W L W — W L L L W W W L L L L W W W W — W W L — L L L L L L L W

Assigned to Jacksonville, Seaver was an immediate sensation. He led International League pitchers in starts and went 12-12 with a 3.13 ERA for a seventh-place club. After just one year of minor league preparation, Tom accounted for 16 of the Mets' 61 victories in 1967 and was acclaimed N.L. Rookie of the Year.

Koosman, two years older than Seaver, was not so well endowed financially. In 1964, the lefthanded native of Appleton, Minn., was pitching for an Army team at Fort Bliss, Tex., where his batterymate was the son of an usher at the Polo Grounds. Through that connection, word reached the Mets' minor league department about the pitcher's talent. Jerry accepted a bonus of $1,200 and arrived in the majors to stay in 1968.

When the 1969 season opened, Seaver started for the Mets before 44,541 fans at Shea Stadium. On that April 8 afternoon, 10 New York runners thundered across the plate. Unfortunately for the Mets, the expansion Montreal Expos counted 11 times. The setback preserved the Met record as the only major league club never to win a season inaugural.

The Mets squared their record the next day when Tug McGraw, pitching in relief, beat the Expos, 9-5. They won again the third day as rookie righthander Gary Gentry beat the same opponent, 4-2, with the help of two home runs from the suddenly revitalized bat of Tommie Agee.

Thereafter, injuries and fundamental misplays sent the team reeling. Hodges could accept sore arms and sprained ankles as inevitable, but the mental blunders he could not. On May 15, after the Braves handed the Mets their eighth one-run loss of the year, the exasperated skipper took action. He locked the clubhouse door—an uncharacteristic move for the even-tempered manager—and took his wayward hirelings to task. No players were named, but Hodges recited the misdeeds so eloquently that there could be no doubt about the identity of each offender.

"It wasn't just this game that brought it on," Seaver told reporters afterward. "It's the repetition of mental mistakes . . . the same mistakes over and over."

The players realized that Hodges' scathing attack was brought on by his confidence in their potential to be winners.

"He's just trying to get the most out of us," second baseman Ken Boswell said.

"We could be a first-division club," Hodges told his sinning athletes, "but we can't afford these mistakes."

The message bore results quickly. The Mets won their next three games to raise their record to 18-18 on May 21. It was the latest date in club history that the Mets had had a .500 record.

Seaver, who allowed just three hits while blank-

ing the Braves, 5-0, in the game that evened New York's record, was unimpressed by the team's achievement.

"Really, it isn't that big a deal," he said. "To me, it's nothing. What is .500? It's right in the middle. It's neither here nor there. . . . That kind of ball isn't going to get us very close to a pennant."

Some of the older players found some satisfaction in their accomplishment, but they, too, expected more of themselves.

"I was here when .500 was not even in existence," said pitcher Al Jackson, a member of the original 1962 Mets. "But it doesn't seem like so much now. . . . We can't settle for .500 now. We're much better than a .500 ball club. We can be contenders."

Such a bold statement sounded quite odd coming from a Met, and true to form, New York lost its next five games. The skid was halted May 28 when a bases-loaded single in the bottom of the 11th inning by shortstop Bud Harrelson gave the Mets a 1-0 victory. But unlike previous New York teams that would have quickly fallen into another slump, the Mets went on to win 10 more games before losing again. They weren't scoring many runs, but they were getting enough to win, thanks to strong pitching performances by Seaver, Koosman, Gentry and assorted spot starters.

The resurgence catapulted the Mets from fourth place into second, seven lengths behind Chicago in the East Division. The Cubs, who got off to an 11-1 start and led the race from their opening day to date, were setting a brisk pace under the whip of Manager Leo Durocher.

If not elated over the results of his closed-door meeting, Hodges at least was satisfied that he was on the right course in building a contender. Whether the team made a concerted drive on the leaders, he maintained, depended on the front office. If those in charge could acquire a long-ball hitter, the same sort he had been during his heyday with the Dodgers, the team's chances would improve substantially.

Hodges laid the matter before Johnny Murphy, who lent an attentive ear. As a pitcher for the New York Yankees in the 1930s and '40s, the Mets' general manager had won many a game because of a potent attack. He understood Hodges' problem.

Murphy launched a search for a player with some dynamite in his bat and located his man as the trading deadline of June 15 approached. He was Donn Clendenon, who was not as productive as in his prime with the Pirates, but still packed some wallop at age 33.

The first baseman had been acquired by Montreal in the expansion draft in October 1968. Before he had a chance to play for the Expos, however, he was swapped, along with Jesus Alou, to the Houston Astros for Rusty Staub.

Here again, as in the case of Seaver three years before, the tide of fortune ran in favor of the Mets. If the eighth-year veteran had accepted the trade, he would have been a full-time employee of the Astros, and the chances of the Mets acquiring him would have been slim.

But Donn rejected the deal and announced his retirement from the game. He said he planned to devote his time to an executive position he held with a pen company and to a supper club he owned in Atlanta.

At that point, the trade should have been dead, with Staub returning to Houston, Alou to Montreal. But the situation became more muddled a few days later when Clendenon indicated that he still would be interested in talking to other clubs about possible employment. The Astros were outraged, of course, because if Clendenon was not retired, they expected him to play for them.

Commissioner Bowie Kuhn then got involved in the affair, which proceeded to become even more messy. When the trade finally was resolved in early April 1969, money and a couple of young players satisfied the Astros, who retained the services of Alou; Staub stayed in Montreal, and Clendenon was lured back to the game by a two-year contract with the Expos.

Clendenon's agreement with Montreal was announced five days before the start of the pennant race. It was insufficient time for the big fellow to get into proper condition. Donn was batting only .240 with four home runs in 38 games when he was traded to the Mets for infielder Kevin Collins and three minor league pitchers.

Clendenon welcomed the trade to New York, even if Ed Kranepool did not. Kranepool, the club's first bonus player ($85,000 in 1962) and a lefthanded batter, went on platoon duty at first base after the arrival of Clendenon, a righthanded hitter.

Platoon play was no rarity with the Mets. The second baseman could be Boswell, Al Weis or Wayne Garrett, the shortstop Harrelson or Weis, the third baseman Garrett, Ed Charles or Bobby Pfeil, the right fielder Ron Swoboda or Art Shamsky. Only catcher Jerry Grote, left fielder Cleon Jones and center fielder Agee were certain of daily work.

The Mets were riding comfortably in second place, five lengths behind the Cubs, when the league leaders visited New York for a series in early July. If New York could win two of the three contests, then repeat the performance the next week in Chicago, they would have to be regarded as bona fide challengers.

There was no love lost among the rival players. Durocher had the well-developed faculty for arousing animosity wherever he managed, and this year was no different from past seasons.

Moreover, Cubs third baseman Ron Santo had introduced a victory gesture that incensed opposing players. After each win, he would leap upward and click his heels, take a few more steps and repeat the celebration until he left the field. In Chicago, it was a popular victory salute. Elsewhere, losing players considered the display unprofessional, just another reason to loathe the Cubs.

The series opener July 8 at Shea Stadium matched Koosman against Ferguson Jenkins. For eight innings, the Chicago righthander was supreme, holding the Mets to one hit, a homer by Kranepool in the fifth. As the home team came to bat in the last of the ninth, it trailed, 3-1. It was not precisely what the throng had paid good money to see.

Boswell batted for Koosman to start the Mets' final turn. His fly ball to center field sent a groan through the stands until the ball was misplayed by rookie Don Young and fell for a double. One out later, Clendenon batted for Pfeil and lifted another fly toward center field. Another groan! But Young misplayed that ball, too, for a double. With runners on second and third, Jones doubled to tie the score. Durocher made no move to lift Jenkins, his 11-game winner, who issued an intentional walk to Shamsky. Jenkins retired Garrett on an infield out, but Kranepool slashed a single to left field and Jones sprinted home with the winning run.

The next night produced less drama but more tension. Seaver set Chicago batters down with rhythmic regularity for eight innings as not one Cub reached base. Catcher Randy Hundley led off the ninth for the Cubs and attempted to spoil Seaver's perfect game with a bunt. His unsuccessful attempt evoked an ear-piercing raspberry from the record crowd of 59,083.

Jim Qualls, the center-field replacement for Young and a switch-hitter, was up next. Playing in only his 18th major league game, Qualls had hit once to the right side of the field and once to the left side in previous trips to the plate. On his third appearance, the Mets played him straight away.

Seaver's first pitch was a fastball. Qualls arched it toward left-center field. Neither Agee nor Jones had a chance to make the catch and the ball dropped in for a single. Seaver retired the next two batters and walked off the mound with a 4-0 victory, his eighth in a row and 14th of the year (against only three losses). The Chicago lead was down to three games.

Righthander Bill Hands held the Mets to three hits in the last game of the series, a 6-2 Chicago triumph that halted a seven-game New York winning streak. Two errors contributed to a five-run Cubs rally in the fifth inning.

After the game, Durocher couldn't resist taking a stab at the Mets when someone asked him if those were the "real Cubs" playing that afternoon. "No," he snickered, "but those are the real Mets."

Pitcher Gary Gentry (center) and teammates were mobbed by ecstatic fans
after the Mets clinched the East Division title with a victory over St. Louis.

Santo, who contributed a two-run homer to the victory, also had a few choice words for the New Yorkers. "Wait till we get 'em in Wrigley Field next week," snorted the third baseman, breathing vengeance.

The contenders were separated by 4½ games when they resumed their head-to-head rivalry at Wrigley Field on July 14. The first game produced a classic pitching duel between Seaver and Hands. Though the New York ace allowed only five hits, he was charged with a 1-0 loss when outfielder Billy Williams singled to drive in shortstop Don Kessinger, who had beaten out a bunt for a single and advanced on an infield out. The victory injected extra gusto into Santo's heel-clicking celebration.

Durocher sent Dick Selma, a former Met, after a victory in the second game. The righthander came up empty-handed when he was sabotaged by the least likely member of the Mets' troupe. Weis, a slender 31-year-old infielder who had smacked only four homers in six-plus major league campaigns, was the upstart.

Weis singled and scored on Agee's triple to give the Mets a 1-0 lead in the third inning. After the Cubs tied the score in the bottom half of that frame, Al faced Selma with two runners aboard in the fourth. The .172 hitter of the year before ran the count to 1-and-2, then swung at a fastball. The result was a drive that landed outside the park.

"The wind was blowing pretty good," a humble Weis acknowledged.

A subsequent homer by Boswell, almost as unlikely a choice for such heroics, produced the deciding run in a 5-4 New York victory. The Mets concluded the series with a 9-5 triumph over Jenkins that featured homers by Agee, Shamsky and, wonder of wonders, another by Weis. "Now don't try to make me out a home run hitter," Weis said in response to his sudden long-ball binge. "In fact, I'm not even a hitter."

The Mets, who did some heel-clicking themselves in the clubhouse after the game, left Chicago trailing the leaders by 3½ games. But they lost some ground over the next two weeks. When the Astros arrived at Shea Stadium for a July 30 doubleheader, the Mets were 4½ games back.

By most calculations, the Astros should have posed no serious problem for the home team. Houston was in fifth place in the West Division and had a team batting average (.245) that was almost as bad as New York's (.243).

But statistics can be misleading. In the ninth inning of the first game, the Astros scored 11 runs, eight on grand slams by shortstop Denis Menke and center fielder Jimmy Wynn, to win, 16-3. The second game was just as distressing for the Mets. The Astros tallied 10 times in the third inning and coasted to an 11-5 triumph.

During the outburst in the second game, catcher Johnny Edwards slapped a drive to the left-field corner for a double. Jones gave a halfhearted chase and then lobbed the ball back to the infield.

As Cleon resumed his position, Hodges emerged from the dugout and commenced walking toward the pitching mound. But he didn't stop there. The manager continued instead to left field as 28,922 puzzled

spectators looked on.

Manager and player talked briefly. Hodges then turned and started back toward the dugout, Jones trailing by a few steps. Later, the press was informed that Jones left the game because he had suffered a hamstring pull on the previous play.

The version of the publicly ridiculed player differed. "It looked like what you guys thought it was," said Jones, who was leading the club in hitting (.346) but was nonetheless embarrassed by the episode.

The Astros captured the series finale, 2-0, and heaped further indignities on the struggling Mets by sweeping three games at Houston in mid-August. By that time the Mets were 9½ games behind the Cubs, raising suspicions that Durocher might have been correct in telling the world that the Mets would

Nolan Ryan, who held the Braves to three hits after replacing Gary Gentry in Game 3 of the N.L. Championship Series, gets a big greeting from catcher Jerry Grote after recording the final out in the Mets' pennant-clinching victory.

cave in when subjected to pennant pressure.

Such suspicions were quickly put to rest. In the wake of the Houston debacle, the Mets won 12 of their next 13 games. In that same stretch, the Cubs lost nine of 14 contests, allowing the Mets to draw within two games of first place. A six-game Chicago winning streak then put five games between the two teams, but the Cubs quickly resumed their losing ways. They had dropped four consecutive decisions when Durocher led his troops into New York for their final visit of the year. Only 2½ games divided the pursued and the pursuers.

Koosman and Hands were the starting pitchers in the series opener September 8. Koosman disposed of the Cubs in the first inning and Agee stepped into the batter's box to start the bottom half. He did not remain upright long.

Hands' first pitch sent Agee sprawling in the dirt, a clear signal that Durocher was up to his old trick of intimidation. Very well, thought Koosman, two could play that game. Look out, Cubbies!

Santo led off the second inning and, as a 10-year veteran, he had to know what was in store. Koosman's first pitch struck the Cub captain on the wrist.

"Sure, I did it on purpose," said Koosman, who struck out 13 Cubs that evening. "You've got to protect your teammates."

If Durocher had expected to silence Agee's bat with his knockdown tactics, he was greatly mistaken. The center fielder socked a two-run homer on his next trip to the plate, then doubled and scored the deciding run in a 3-2 victory.

Seaver's five-hit mastery, backed by homers from Clendenon and Shamsky, gave the Mets a 7-1 win the next night. As a result, the battered Cubs shuffled out of town with their once-imposing lead slashed to a tissue-thin half-game.

The Cubs hoped to make up some ground the next night when they played the fifth-place Phillies. Cubs lefthander Ken Holtzman, a 16-game winner, pitched well, but his teammates provided only three

hits and the Phils won, 6-2. At Shea Stadium, meanwhile, the Mets swept a doubleheader from the Expos by scores of 3-2 and 7-1. The winning pitcher in that September 10 nightcap was a 22-year-old righthander named Nolan Ryan, who surrendered three hits and fanned 11 Montreal batters.

As the last out was recorded in the second game, the scoreboard flashed this message: "Look Who's No. 1." Below, the N.L. East standings showed the Mets with a record of 84-57, the Cubs 84-59. For the first time ever, the Mets were in first place.

In his office beneath the stands, Hodges patted the head of a stuffed white snowshoe hare, the gift of a fan. Until that night the good luck charm was unnamed. "We'll call it 'Ichi Bon,'" said the manager, explaining to reporters that the words mean "No. 1" in Japanese.

Ample time remained in the season for a New York collapse or a Chicago resurgence, but neither happened. The Mets won four more to complete a 10-game winning streak, then lost a game and won three more. The Cubs lost one more contest to make it eight in a row, then won a game and lost three more. And so it went.

Every name Hodges scribbled on the lineup card and every button he pushed further inflated his reputation as a managerial wizard. Hodges, who once went hitless in a seven-game World Series, could do no wrong this time around.

When Steve Carlton fanned a record 19 batters September 15, Swoboda socked a pair of two-run homers to beat the St. Louis lefthander, 4-3. After Bob Moose of the Pirates hurled a no-hitter against them September 20, the Mets bounced back with nine straight victories.

By the time the Cardinals arrived in

Tom Seaver leaps onto a group of celebrating teammates after the New York Mets had captured the National League pennant with a 7-4 win over Atlanta.

Shea Stadium became a scene of New York madness October 6 when the
Mets clinched the N.L. pennant and eager fans took over the field.

New York for a late-September series, the Mets
owned a 4½-game lead. If the Mets could sweep the
set against the defending league champs, they could
lock up at least a tie for the division title.

Seaver, who had not lost since early August and
eventually would post 10 straight wins, beat Nelson
Briles in the September 22 opener, 3-1. Tom aided
his own cause with a run-scoring single.

Bob Gibson, as tough a hurler as ever toed a
pitching rubber, tried to stall the New York rush in
the second game. Though he was backed by a 12-hit
attack, the future Hall of Famer bowed, 3-2, in 11
innings when Harrelson delivered a run-scoring
single. The victory, combined with Chicago's 7-3
loss to Montreal, gave the Mets a six-game lead with
six games to play. A tie represented the worst possible scenario for the Mets, and one more triumph
would carry them past the final hurdle. The first
title of any kind in the organization's eight-year history was within reach.

The starting pitchers September 24 were Carlton,
seeking his 18th win, and Gentry, working on his
12th. Carlton had been devastating in his previous
encounter with New York, but this time he was
knocked out in one-third of an inning. A three-run
homer by Clendenon and a two-run blow by Ed
Charles produced five runs in the first inning. Clen-

denon homered again in the fifth and Gentry tossed
a four-hit shutout as the Mets posted a 6-0, title-
clinching win.

As New York infielders turned a game-ending
double play off the bat of Joe Torre, hordes of spectators poured out of the stands. Straight to their
assigned tasks raced a segment of the 54,928 fans
who had witnessed the game. An enlarged police
force and special security officers stood helpless to
prevent the onslaught. The bases disappeared in the
grasp of souvenir hunters. Home plate was pried
from its moorings. Huge chunks of sod were gouged
from the surface of the six-year-old playing field.
One ambitious—or slightly inebriated—fan tried to
climb the six-story scoreboard. Twenty-five feet up,
he plunged to the ground and broke his leg. Six
other fans suffered fractures in the wild celebration.

Pandemonium also raged unchecked in the Mets'
clubhouse. Champagne, beer, liquid soap, shaving
cream—as long as it was somewhat fluid, the Mets
sprayed it. Every player, club official, newsman and
broadcaster was saturated in one form or another.
And when the supply of ammunition was exhausted, there always was the shower. "I never saw anything this wild," Clendenon exclaimed. "This is the
greatest."

At the height of the bacchanalia, Tug McGraw

When all was said and done, Mets Tom Seaver (41) and Gary Gentry surveyed the damage at the scene of their greatest accomplishments.

rubbed a trickle of champagne from his eye. "They never told me this stuff burns," the reliever shouted. "But it's a happy burn."

In the general hilarity, nobody seemed to remember that a League Championship Series against the powerful Atlanta Braves was the Mets' next objective. Until they disposed of the West Division champs, who finished with a 93-69 record, three games in front of the San Francisco Giants, the Mets were only the best in a six-team race, not champions of a 12-club league.

After an open date gave the Mets a day to recover from their celebration, they got back to business, winning four of their last five games. Their final record of 100-62 put them eight games ahead of the second-place Cubs, but the Mets still were given little respect heading into the best-of-five playoffs. They were established as underdogs, a role they knew only too well. But they also had shown that they could beat the odds.

Seaver, the winningest pitcher in the major leagues with a 25-7 record, was trailing, 5-4, when he was lifted for a pinch-hitter in the eighth inning of the first game at Atlanta. Before the third out was recorded, the Mets had racked Phil Niekro for five runs, due chiefly to a ragged Atlanta defense and a bases-loaded single by pinch-hitter J.C. Mar-

tin. They won the game, 9-5.

The second contest offered the rare sight of Koosman failing to hold leads of 8-0 and 9-1. The left-hander, who had won five games in a row, was knocked out in the fifth inning when the Braves erupted for five runs. That was as far as they got, however, as Ron Taylor came in to gain credit for the 11-6 victory and McGraw earned the save. Agee, Boswell and Jones homered for New York.

For the third game in a row, the New York starter failed to go the distance when the series shifted to Shea Stadium on October 6. Gentry departed in the third inning with none out, runners on second and third, a 1-and-2 count on Rico Carty and the Braves leading, 2-0.

His successor was Ryan, who had hurled only 89 innings that season. The lack of work was unimportant to the fireballing righthander. Nolan struck out Carty, then walked Orlando Cepeda intentionally to load the bases, fanned Clete Boyer and retired Bob Didier on an outfield fly. The selection of Ryan was another master stroke in an endless series of inspired moves by Hodges.

Ryan held the Braves to three hits (including a two-run homer by Cepeda) the remainder of the game. In addition, he singled in the fifth inning and scored on Garrett's home run. Agee and Boswell

The Mets went on to amaze the Orioles in the World Series and a flood of tickertape on Wall Street paid fitting tribute to New York's conquering heroes.

also supplied homers to help lift New York to a 7-4 victory. The sweep of the Braves clinched the N.L. pennant for the Mets.

Only one chapter remained to be written in the saga of the "Miracle Mets," the erstwhile ragamuffins who had soared from the nether regions of the league to the top in one short season. The concluding episode was enacted in the World Series against the Baltimore Orioles, who had won 109 games and posted a team batting average of .265.

As in times past, the Mets were installed as decided underdogs. When Don Buford whacked Seaver's second pitch of the first game for a home run, visions of a pitiful mismatch danced before the eyes of 50,429 spectators in Memorial Stadium.

Baltimore's Mike Cuellar won the game, 4-1, on a six-hitter. But thereafter, the spotlight shifted to the Mets. Koosman held the Orioles to two hits in the second contest and won, 2-1. When the Series shifted to New York, the Mets performed the final rites with consecutive victories by scores of 5-0, 2-1 and 5-3. The 100-to-1 shot of the previous spring had won the world championship.

Considering the type of year it had been, it was not surprising that the leading hitter for New York in the Series was one of the least conspicuous members of the cast. He was Al Weis, who had astonished everybody with a pair of homers in Chicago a few months earlier. The soft-spoken infielder batted .455 and clouted a homer to overshadow his more prominent teammates.

They were, truly, the Miracle Mets.

Gas House Gang Slays the Giants

The story is told of a July morning in 1933 when Dizzy Dean visited a children's hospital in St. Louis. For hours, the pitcher for the St. Louis Cardinals smiled benignly upon the young patients, signed countless autographs and regaled them with anecdotes about his baseball exploits.

As he was about to leave, Dean made himself available for requests. "Is there anything you would like me to do this afternoon in our game against the New York Giants?" he asked the youngsters.

"Strike out Bill Terry," piped up one member of the audience, and instantly the ward resounded with cries of "Strike out Terry! Strike out Terry!"

Dean's smile broadened. It was a big order. The Giants' manager/first baseman was a .322 hitter that season and did not fan frequently, but big-hearted Diz abounded in confidence.

"I'll do it," he promised, "and if I get a chance, I'll do it with the bases filled. I'll pitch this game for you."

Several hours later, the big righthander led the Giants, 2-0, after eight innings. He retired the first batter in the ninth before three consecutive singles drove home one run. A base on balls to Hughie Critz then loaded the bases, bringing Terry to the plate.

As related by J. Roy Stockton in his book "The Gashouse Gang and a Couple of Other Guys," Diz

The immortal Babe Ruth was playing his final season in 1935 when he posed with young St. Louis ace Dizzy Dean (left) and Manager Frankie Frisch (right).

The strong right arms of the Dean brothers, Paul (left) and Dizzy, were the Cardinals' ticket to the 1934 National League pennant.

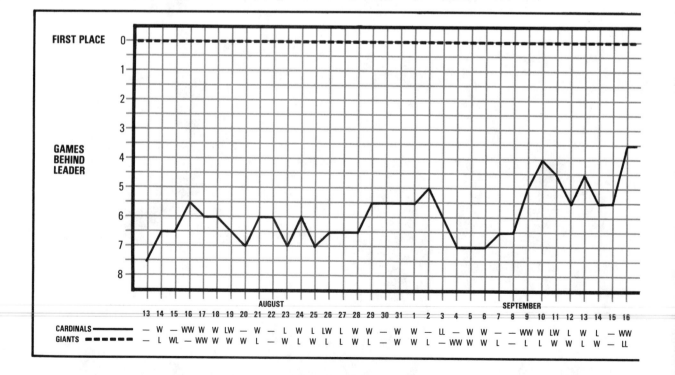

took stock of the situation and then walked toward the plate. "I hate to do this, Bill," he called to the batter, "but I promised some kids in a hospital today that I'd strike you out with the bases loaded."

Three pitches later the deed was done. "Bill thought I was too smart to put that third one through the middle," chortled Dean, who retired Mel Ott on a pop foul to end the game. "He stood there and took it."

In itself, the incident was nothing more than a footnote to a season in which New York won its first National League pennant in nine years while St. Louis finished fifth. But though neither Dean nor Terry knew it yet, the incident was a microcosm of the type of year that 1934 would be for the principals—surpassing victory for one, abject defeat for the other.

In January 1934, three months after the Giants beat the Washington Senators in the World Series, Terry visited New York to consult with club officials. While there, he submitted to a press conference in which he was asked his views on the upcoming N.L. pennant race. Memphis Bill predicted that the Giants' most formidable opposition would be supplied by the Cardinals, Chicago Cubs, Pittsburgh Pirates and Boston Braves.

"What about Brooklyn?" a newsman asked.

"Brooklyn?" Terry repeated. "Is Brooklyn still in the league?"

Terry's wisecrack was published in every daily journal in New York, and nowhere was it resented more deeply than in Brooklyn. Bob Quinn, the Dodgers' general manager, spearheaded the anti-Terry crusade.

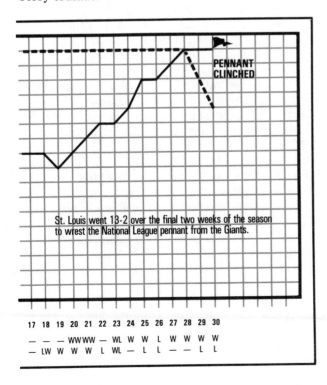

St. Louis went 13-2 over the final two weeks of the season to wrest the National League pennant from the Giants.

17 18 19 20 21 22 23 24 25 26 27 28 29 30

—   —   — W W W W — W L W W W L W W W W
— L W W W W L W L — L L — — L L

After ascertaining that Bill had been quoted correctly, Quinn "broadcast to all and sundry what he thought of Mr. Terry," according to Tommy Holmes, the Brooklyn correspondent for The Sporting News. "He pointed out that it ill became the manager of the Giants to knock a rival club; that there were some empty seats at the Polo Grounds last year, even though the Giants were winning the pennant; that such cracks would serve to discourage Brooklyn fans about their own ball club, kill interest, subtract from the attendance when the Giants play at Ebbets Field or when the Dodgers play at the Polo Grounds; that the Giants won the pennant last year although the experts picked them to finish sixth and there might be another miracle in 1934, etc. etc."

The correspondent then thanked Terry for providing baseball news in the dead of winter and added: "Personally, I think it would be a good idea for Mr. Terry to insult the Dodgers at regular intervals hereafter and especially just before the Giants and Dodgers were due to meet in a series. If I know my Brooklyn fan, he would go to the ball game if he had to hammer down the gate. He might throw a pop bottle or two, but by that time his admission tariff would be in the box office."

A couple of weeks later, Terry again gave the local journalists some lively quotes. At the annual dinner of the New York Baseball Writers' Association, Terry taunted Dodgers Manager Max Carey about his club and provoked an argument. By the time the final pointed words were exchanged (and reported), Bill's unpopularity in Brooklyn was even greater.

Shortly thereafter, in an unrelated move, Carey was dismissed as skipper. He was succeeded by Casey Stengel, one of his coaches.

In his inaugural address, Stengel announced: "The first thing I want to say is that the Dodgers are still in the league. Tell that to Terry. I think I'll let our Mr. Van Mungo (pitcher) do a lot of arguing for me against the Giants this summer. When he starts heaving that fastball, I'm quite sure that he won't be easy to contradict."

Actually, Terry had ample reason to take the Dodgers lightly. In 1933, Brooklyn won only 65 games and finished 26½ lengths behind the Giants.

Moreover, the New York roster was essentially the same. The Big Four of the pitching staff—left-hander Carl Hubbell and righthanders Hal Schumacher, Freddie Fitzsimmons and Leroy (Bud) Parmelee—was intact, with Dolf Luque and others in the bullpen.

Among the regulars returning in the lineup were Terry at first base, Critz at second, Johnny Vergez at third, Ott in right field, Joe Moore in left and Gus Mancuso at catcher. Blondy Ryan, an inspirational rookie and the starting shortstop in '33, was avail-

Key members of St. Louis' 1934 Gas House Gang were (left to right) Dizzy Dean, Leo Durocher, Ernie Orsatti, Bill DeLancey, Rip Collins, Joe Medwick, Frankie Frisch, Jack Rothrock and Pepper Martin.

able at second, third and short. The Giants also had 30-year-old Travis Jackson, who would rebound from two forgettable years to reclaim his shortstop job. The only notable newcomer was center fielder George Watkins, who was obtained from the Cardinals in a winter trade for George (Kiddo) Davis.

At the opposite end of the baseball map were the Cardinals, who were accorded some respect by Terry as a contender in '34 despite their second-division finish the previous year. St. Louis was managed by Frankie Frisch, the club's dynamic second baseman and a former teammate of Terry's in New York. Other infielders included James (Rip) Collins at first base, Leo (Lippy) Durocher at shortstop, Pepper Martin at third and Burgess Whitehead in a utility role.

Joe (Ducky) Medwick, Ernie Orsatti and Jack Rothrock patrolled the outfield, while Virgil (Spud) Davis, an off-season acquisition from the Philadelphia Phillies, and rookie Bill DeLancey were the catchers.

The St. Louis pitching staff was headed by a pair of righthanded brothers: 23-year-old Dizzy Dean, the N.L. strikeout champion in his first two major league seasons, and 20-year-old Paul, fresh from Columbus of the American Association. Righthander Tex Carleton, lefty Bill Walker and such old campaigners as Bill Hallahan, Jesse Haines and Jim Mooney filled out the staff.

In the Associated Press' preseason poll of 97 baseball writers, 40 selected the Giants to finish first, while 34 picked the Cubs. The Pirates, Cards and Braves were picked to land in the next three spots, respectively. The scribes acknowledged that Brooklyn still was in the league by assigning the Dodgers a sixth-place finish. The Philadelphia Phillies and Cincinnati Reds brought up the rear. A similar poll conducted by The Sporting News rendered virtually the same results.

The 1934 season opened April 17. At the Polo Grounds, a large crowd stood for a moment of silence and a bugler sounded taps in memory of John J. McGraw, the longtime manager of the Giants who had died the previous February. Then Hubbell, Terry's "Meal Ticket," defeated the Phillies, 6-1. The victory was the first of five that the New York team amassed before tasting defeat.

On the same afternoon, Stengel made his major league managerial debut at Ebbets Field and quickly learned the truth of a current saying that "Everything happens in Brooklyn." The Dodgers beat the Braves, 8-7, but Casey lost the services of three outfielders in the process. Left fielder Hack Wilson, who socked a home run in the third inning, wrenched his ankle while running out a single in the fifth and had to be replaced by Buzz Boyle. Center fielder Danny Taylor also clouted a home run and later collided in the outfield with Boyle, who suffered a bruised leg while Taylor was spiked in the calf.

In the meantime, the Cardinals lost seven of their first nine games and were lodged in last place, tied with the Phillies. After that depressing start, however, the Redbirds won 23 of their next 29 games as the Dean brothers, soon to be celebrated as "Me 'n' Paul," started to win consistently. The Cardinals were in first place by the end of May, having surpassed the Cubs, who had held the top spot for most of the first few weeks, and the Giants.

The animosity that Terry engendered in Brooklyn with his attempt at humor the previous January helped create a record Ebbets Field crowd of more than 41,000 when the Giants appeared for a Memorial Day doubleheader May 30. But those who came to deride Memphis Bill went home keenly disappointed as the Giants swept a pair, 5-2 and 8-6, to raise their season record against the Dodgers to 6-0.

A week later, the Giants moved into first place, a position they would not vacate for quite some time. New York enjoyed a three-game lead over the second-place Cubs and a four-game lead over the Cardinals when the race passed the Fourth of July milestone.

For St. Louisans, the Cards' proximity to the lead was not the most engrossing story of the summer. Rather, it was Dizzy Dean and the legend he was creating as a folk hero. Ol' Diz, an Arkansas native, was the game's most spectacular pitcher and effervescent character.

When the Cards were in New York one time, Dean stopped by the Giants' clubhouse to visit with his buddy, Terry. Greetings were exchanged and then Terry ushered Dizzy toward the door, explaining that the Giants were about to discuss the right and wrong ways to pitch to St. Louis batters.

"That's all right," Ol' Diz replied. "Go right ahead. You can't learn me nothin' about them. I know all their weaknesses."

On September 21, before the Cardinals left their hotel to engage the Dodgers in a doubleheader at Ebbets Field, Ol' Diz confided to a reporter, "(Tom) Zachary and (Ray) Benge will be pitching against one-hit Dean and no-hit Dean today."

Outlandish predictions were not uncommon for Dizzy Dean, who usually made good on such exaggerations. On this date he missed, but not by much.

Before the first game, Frisch called his pitchers into session to discuss the proper methods to handle Brooklyn batters. "Keep the ball high and outside on Sam Leslie," the skipper advised the elder Dean, who was due to pitch the opener.

"That ain't how I pitch him," Dizzy countered. "I don't give that guy nothin' but low inside stuff, and he ain't got a hit off me yet."

Frisch tried again, passing on to Tony Cuccinello. "Nothing but curves," Frankie suggested.

New York Giants Manager Bill Terry made some degrading comments about the Brooklyn Dodgers before the 1934 season and eventually had to eat his words.

Once more Dean differed. "That's mighty peculiar," he said. "I never have bothered to dish him up a curve yet, and he's still tryin' for his first loud foul."

And so it went through the remainder of the batting order, Frisch quoting from the managerial manual and Dean offering contradictory counsel.

Dean pitched his way, as Frisch knew he would, and for 7⅓ innings he held the Dodgers hitless. He wound up with a three-hit, 13-0 victory, missing his prediction by just two hits.

The second half of the prediction panned out with amazing accuracy. Paul Dean held the Dodgers

hitless in posting a 3-0 victory. A walk to center fielder Len Koenecke in the first inning prevented Paul from hurling a perfect game.

Paul's achievement evoked one of Dizzy's most memorable pronouncements. "Paul didn't tell me he was gonna throw a no-hitter," he said. "If I'da known that, I'da throwed one, too."

Laughs flowed freely in Dean's presence in the summer of 1934. But there also were groans and scowls aplenty as the Cardinals rode an emotional roller coaster.

Dizzy was flying high in the popularity polls. One victory followed closely on another. The amount of newspaper ink designated for Ol' Diz was far greater than that left for his teammates, although Paul Dean earned his share of acclaim. In many ways, Dizzy overshadowed the ball club. He felt responsible to only one authority—himself.

On August 12, the brothers Dean pitched and lost a doubleheader against Chicago. Immediately thereafter, the team entrained for Detroit, where it was booked to play an exhibition against the Tigers the next day. But the Deans were conspicuously absent. They had remained in St. Louis because, Dizzy explained to curious newsmen, he was suffering from a sore arm and Paul was nursing a sprained ankle. Management took a dim view of the defection. Dizzy, a former dollar-a-day cotton picker, was fined $100, Paul $50.

Back in St. Louis for an August 14 game with Philadelphia, the Cardinals were engaged in pregame warmups when Frisch wandered into the clubhouse and found the Deans only partly dressed. He ordered them onto the field without further delay.

"Nothin' doin'," replied Diz, the spokesman. "We've decided the fines against us are unjust. We're not a-goin' to do it. We're quittin'."

Frisch had had enough. He informed the brothers that they were suspended as of that moment and ordered them to remove their uniforms. Dizzy went a step farther—he ripped his uniform to shreds. He and Paul then went into a rage and disrupted the clubhouse.

After sitting out a couple of days, Paul Dean accepted his penalty. He paid his fine and was restored to good standing August 17. Dizzy balked. He went to Chicago, where he laid his grievance before Judge Kenesaw M. Landis. The commissioner, in turn, visited St. Louis, where he took testimony from all parties involved in l'affaire Dean. Ultimately, Dizzy abandoned his protest, paid the fine and apologized —to his teammates as well as the fans.

The apology to the club was especially important.

The fiery Leo Durocher, never at a loss for words, anchored the Cardinal defense from his shortstop position.

The Cardinals were annoyed that the Deans would betray them at a crucial point in the season.

"It isn't the proper thing for two players to think they are bigger than a ball club," Durocher said before the pitchers returned. "And you watch our smoke from now on. We'll show those two guys a thing or two."

The Cards showed Dizzy a thing or two by winning six of seven games during his absence. He returned to the mound August 24, the day after Joe Moore's three-run homer in the ninth inning gave the Giants a 5-3 victory over Paul Dean.

Ol' Diz demonstrated convincingly that his layoff had subtracted nothing from his effectiveness. He scattered five New York hits in a 5-0 victory and contributed two singles and a stolen base to the St. Louis cause. It was his 22nd victory of the season and his second shutout of the Giants. The triumph elevated the Cardinals to second place, six games behind New York and half a game in front of Chicago, which had been the Giants' most dogged pursuer since late June.

In the deciding game of the series, the Cards built a 5-0 lead for Bill Walker. But the Giants made it 5-3 after six innings and put two men on base in the seventh to send Walker to the showers. Dizzy was rushed into the breach, but this time he was no puzzle. He gave up five hits and a walk in three innings to be charged with the 7-6 loss, which dropped the Cards back into third, seven lengths off the pace.

At that point, the odds against St. Louis harvesting anything more than a second-place finish seemed substantial. The St. Louis fans had all but given up on the Cardinals, and the local media were talking about the team's chances to finish second, not first. But the players—and their manager—refused to quit. Frisch kept driving, scolding, whipping, cajoling and encouraging the players, who came to be known as the Gas House Gang. The moniker was not actually applied to the club until 1935, but it served well to describe the '34 team, a brash, rough-and-tumble band of players who scraped and clawed for every advantage they could get.

A four-game winning streak lifted St. Louis into second place, but the Cards still trailed the Giants by five games when they went to Pittsburgh for a September 3 twin bill. When darkness fell over Forbes Field, they were six games back, the result of Paul Dean losing the opener, 12-2, and Dizzy Dean, pitching in relief, failing to hold a 5-3 lead and suffering a 6-5 setback. The next day, Ray Gillespie of the St. Louis Star-Times reported that the Cardinals

Another Gas House Gang member with a penchant for making things happen was third baseman Pepper Martin.

"would be willing to give themselves up if properly encouraged. . . . The two defeats virtually eliminated St. Louis from the 1934 pennant scramble."

Frisch would have none of that. "No team of mine will give up," the skipper vowed. "We're in this race until we're out of it, and believe me, we'll fight to the last ditch."

New York's lead increased to seven games September 4, when the Giants swept a doubleheader from the Phillies. The Cards, who played an exhibition game against one of their farm clubs that day, were tied for second with the Cubs.

"I guess we couldn't ask for much more," Terry said in reference to the Giants' cushion. Added Garry Schumacher, a reporter for the New York Evening Journal: "The Giants can be overtaken, but it's a million-to-one shot."

The Cardinals won six of seven games over the next week to inch within 4½ games of the Giants, who had gone 3-3 in the same span. But on September 12, St. Louis dropped a 3-1 decision in Philadelphia. The loss to the seventh-place Phils was particularly embarrassing for the Cards in that the only St. Louis run was produced by a home run off the bat of 43-year-old pitcher Dazzy Vance. And when Dazzy got into trouble in the eighth, the inning in which the Phils scored all their runs, Dizzy Dean was unable to stem the tide for the aging veteran. With the Cards now 5½ games in arrears, Cy Peterman of the Philadelphia Evening Bulletin was prompted to write: "This game shows how futile is this bid of the Cards. They can't go far when nobody makes a run but the pitcher. They didn't deserve to win. They are not to be taken seriously for the pennant."

While St. Louis was losing to Philadelphia, Hubbell was pitching New York to a 3-2 triumph over Pittsburgh to notch his 20th victory of the year. In describing the game for the New York Times, John Drebinger commented that the Giants "put the finishing touches to reinforcing their position until it was generally accepted as practically impregnable."

If such was the case, the Giants had an immediate chance to prove it. On September 13, Terry's club welcomed the Cardinals to the Polo Grounds for the first of four games. It was the last series of the year between the top two clubs in the league.

In the opener, Paul Dean blanked the Giants, 2-0, in 12 innings on a six-hitter. Fitzsimmons held the Cards scoreless for 11 frames, but in the top of the 12th, Medwick scored from third on DeLancey's fly ball and Durocher knocked in a run with a single.

The Giants won the next day, 4-1, to restore their 5½-game lead. Schumacher outdueled Walker and helped his own cause with a solo homer. Dan Daniel announced in the next day's New York World-Telegram that "Bill Terry began to groom Hal Schumacher for the opening game of the World Series."

Rain the next afternoon created a Sunday doubleheader September 16. Despite playing in front of 62,573 fans, the largest crowd ever at the Polo Grounds, the Cardinals won both games. Dizzy Dean received credit for the 5-3 victory over Schumacher, who pitched in relief, in the opener, and brother Paul won the second game, 3-1. Paul and Hubbell battled evenly for 10 innings, each pitcher allowing just one run, but the Cards tallied twice in the 11th on Pepper Martin's leadoff homer and Medwick's run-scoring single.

Despite the St. Louisans' success in winning three of four from the Giants and cutting the leaders' advantage to 3½ games, the media gave them little hope to win the N.L. flag. Daniel wrote that "Frankie Frisch bade a sad adieu, not only to Harlem, but to the 1934 World Series as well."

The Cardinal caravan rumbled on to Boston. While the Giants were winning three of four games against Cincinnati, rain and threatening weather kept the Cards idle until September 20, when Tex Carleton and Walker vanquished the Braves twice. Though St. Louis still was only 3½ games back, readers of the New York World-Telegram were informed that Terry "announced a change in his plans for the World Series after watching Carl Hubbell hang up his 21st victory against the Reds yesterday (September 20). Terry shifted from Hal Schumacher to Hubbell as his pitching choice for the opening game of the classic in Detroit on October 3."

The next afternoon in Brooklyn, "three-hit and no-hit Dean" blanked the Dodgers twice while New York beat Boston, 8-1. The Cardinals gained another half a game September 22 simply by watching rain splash against their hotel windows in Cincinnati. The Giants lost to the Braves, 3-2, in 11 innings. The Cubs, meanwhile, lost a doubleheader to the Pirates to drop to 81-63. They no longer figured in the pennant picture.

Both remaining contenders split doubleheaders September 23, the Cardinals in Cincinnati and the Giants at Boston. With one week of the schedule remaining, the Giants led by 2½ lengths with four games to play. The Cardinals had seven contests remaining.

For Terry and the Giants, the final week of the season was grim. There were no more reports of World Series pitching plans or of the Cardinals being a million-to-one shot as, bit by bit, New York's first-place lead crumbled. After defeating Chicago, 3-1, to complete a 3½-week trip in which they went 17-6, the Cardinals returned home and split a pair with Pittsburgh. Meanwhile, the Phillies toppled the Giants twice, reducing New York's lead to one game.

The next two days of the race were tough for the

Giants to endure. Terry's club was idle while the Cards hosted the first two of four season-ending games with the Reds. As improbable as it had seemed just a few days before, the Cards were poised to claim a share of first place, and there was nothing the Giants could do to stop them.

Nor could the Reds. Walker earned an 8-5 victory in the series opener and Dizzy Dean, pitching on just two days' rest, hurled a 4-0 shutout September 28 to raise the Cardinals' record to 93-58—exactly the same as New York's. After leading the pack continuously from June 6, the Giants were in danger of blowing the pennant.

To make matters worse, the Giants had to complete their schedule with two games at home against the sixth-place Dodgers—the same team their manager had maligned the previous winter. Is Brooklyn still in the league? Terry was about to find out.

Rain fell until just before game time September 29, limiting the turnout to about 15,000. Most of those in attendance, however, came across the bridge from Brooklyn, well fortified with banners, whistles, bells, horns and fully developed voices that they exercised at the slightest provocation. The Giants found themselves in the anomalous position of contending for the pennant in their home park before a largely hostile crowd.

The Dodgers didn't need a pep talk before the game, but Stengel gave them one anyway. "We'll knock those Giants right out from under the pennant!" he proclaimed. "We'll show Terry whether Brooklyn is in the league!"

Before sending the Dodgers onto the field, the skipper offered a final bit of advice. "Mungo's our pitcher," he said. "Parmelee's gonna pitch for them. You know he can be wild. Wait him out. Make him give you your pitch."

Brooklyn batters followed orders flawlessly. They tagged Parmelee for 10 hits and collected three bases on balls en route to a 5-1 victory.

Mungo was exceptional at bat and on the mound. He singled twice, scored once and drove in a run. The big righthander scattered five hits and fanned seven, including three in the ninth when the Giants threatened to pull a victory out of the ashes. A single by Terry and a walk to Ott opened the inning before Mungo closed out the contest with a spectacular display of power pitching, fanning Jackson, Watkins (who had homered for the losers' only run) and pinch-hitter Lefty O'Doul.

Meanwhile, in St. Louis, Paul Dean took the mound after just two days' rest, just as his brother had done the day before. Backed by a 12-hit attack that included a run-scoring triple and two-run homer by Medwick, Dean posted a 6-1 victory, his 19th of the season. The righthander scattered 11 hits, including a home run by Jim Bottomley, to put St. Louis a full game in front of New York.

For Memphis Bill Terry, his question of eight months before had been answered in part. The remainder was delivered September 30, when New York closed out the campaign against Brooklyn. With rain no longer in the forecast, more than 44,000 fans paraded into the Polo Grounds. Once again, the most vocal part of the crowd came from Flatbush. The taunts of the Dodger fans often drowned out the cheers of those who came to support the fading Giants.

The Giants' last forlorn hope rested in their de-

Giants Manager Bill Terry evoked a few smiles with his preseason comments about the Dodgers, but Brooklyn Manager Casey Stengel (above) enjoyed the last laugh.

feating the Dodgers and the last-place Reds, some way and somehow, beating Dizzy Dean in St. Louis. Such a series of events would give both clubs records of 94-59, requiring a three-game playoff for the pennant. So, fans in New York frequently glanced at the scoreboard to follow the progress of the game at Sportsman's Park, where Ol' Diz was gunning for his 30th triumph.

Fitzsimmons, an 18-game winner, was Terry's choice to pitch for the home club. Ray Benge, who had 14 victories to his credit, was Stengel's pick to start for the Dodgers.

Benge proved no mystery to the Giants. The righthander survived two-thirds of an inning. Moore led off with a double and moved to third when Critz laid down a bunt that went for a single. Terry's infield hit drove home Moore with the first run of the game. Benge appeared to resume control when he got Ott to force Terry and struck out Jackson, but he walked Watkins to fill the bases and then passed Mancuso as well, forcing home another run. Blondy Ryan's two-run single made it 4-0 and knocked out Benge.

His successor was Emil (Dutch) Leonard, a 25-year-old knuckleball specialist who had won 14 games. Leonard halted the first-inning rally and, except for a home run by Fitzsimmons in the fourth and two other hits, he muffled the New York bats for the next 6⅔ innings.

The Dodgers, meanwhile, gnawed away at the New York lead. They posted single tallies in the second, fourth and sixth innings and then chased Fitzsimmons when Len Koenecke's run-scoring double made it 5-4. As Schumacher warmed up in relief of Fitzsimmons, a thunderous roar engulfed the Polo Grounds. The Brooklyn fans in attendance had spotted a "3" on the scoreboard, revealing that the Cardinals had increased their lead over the Reds to 5-0 in the fourth inning.

Schumacher eventually allowed the Dodgers to tie the score on a wild pitch that rolled to the edge of the Brooklyn dugout. He then contained the Dodgers until the 10th inning, when Sam Leslie and Tony Cuccinello opened with hits. At that point, Terry summoned Hubbell in a frantic bid to avert disaster.

It was a futile move. After fanning rookie pitcher Johnny Babich, King Carl walked third baseman Joe Stripp to load the bases. Catcher Al Lopez followed with a hot grounder to short that Ryan fumbled, allowing the Dodgers to score the go-ahead run. Two more Brooklyn runners crossed the plate before Hubbell could retire the side.

Babich put down the Giants in order in the bottom of the 10th to seal the Dodgers' 8-5 triumph. The setback was the fifth in a row for the Giants, representing their longest losing streak of the year. Unfortunately for New York, it came at the most inopportune time.

As the New York players trooped wearily to the clubhouse, ecstatic Dodger fans, having witnessed living proof that Brooklyn indeed was still in the league, celebrated wildly. They showered the bulk of their affection on Lopez, carrying him halfway to the clubhouse despite the fact that he had made no hits and scored no runs in the triumphal climax to an otherwise mediocre season.

If there was any consolation in the Giants' camp, it was the knowledge that victory that day would have made no difference in the final standings because Dizzy Dean was toying with the opposition in St. Louis. Thanks to a 14-hit attack that included homers by DeLancey and Collins, Dean strutted before 37,402 happy spectators.

After eight innings he led, 9-0. His 30th win was assured. The Cards were N.L. champions for the fifth time in nine years. Yet, almost by design it seemed, the crowd was in for one more pulsating moment at the hands of Ol' Diz.

With none out in the last frame, the Reds loaded the bases. It was the sort of situation that appealed to Dean, always the showman.

"Grinning in that cocksure way of his," wrote a reporter for the Associated Press, "Dizzy arose to the heights." He struck out the next two batters.

Sparky Adams was the only hurdle between Diz and his seventh shutout of the year. Dean threw a fastball that the second baseman popped into foul territory. As it plodded into DeLancey's mitt, Dean ran over to his catcher, grabbed the ball as a souvenir and shouted, "Bill, we play in the World Series."

The win was the Cardinals' 20th in their last 25 games. That surge lifted them past the Giants, who had lost 13 of their final 21 games after September 6, when they led St. Louis by seven lengths.

As the Cardinals reveled in their sudden success, New York players individually attempted to shoulder the blame for the team's failure. In the midst of the self-recriminations, the commanding voice of Bill Terry sounded.

"Listen you fellows, listen to me a minute," the skipper ordered. "If we had won the pennant, I would have received a lot of credit. Well, we didn't win it, and I'll take the blame. You've all played great ball, better than most people expected you to play. None of you lost the pennant. We just didn't win it. That's all."

Stengel also had some thoughts on New York's demise. "The Giants thought we gave 'em a beating Saturday and yesterday," Casey said after the Dodgers sealed the Giants' fate. "Well, they were right. But I'm sorry for them when I think of the beating they still have to take. Wait until their wives realize they're not going to get those new fur coats. I've been through it, and I know."

Hartnett's Homer Makes Cubs Roar

Pitcher Charley Root (left), Manager Charley Grimm (center) and catcher Gabby Hartnett were among the senior members of the 1938 Chicago Cubs.

Late in the 1921 season, a young catcher with the Worcester Boosters of the Eastern League approached his manager with a familiar request in an era of straitened baseball incomes. He was broke and hungry, he explained, and needed a couple of dollars to tide him over to payday.

"Here's a five spot," replied his boss, "and don't worry about paying it back immediately."

Somewhat startled by his easy success, the player stood there, properly puzzled.

"You can mail it back to me next spring from the Cubs' training camp," the manager explained, for a deal just had been closed with Chicago scout Jack Doyle.

The next year, the young New Englander arrived at the Wrigley family's spring paradise at Catalina Island. Joining in the rugged training regimen prescribed by Manager Bill Killefer, he huffed and puffed up and down mountainsides, perspiring freely with every step as he toughened his huge frame for his first National League season. While others muttered imprecations under their breath, the exuberant native of Woonsocket, R.I., found humor in the punishing workouts. "I hope they've got the infields banked on National League diamonds," he blurted. "My one leg is shorter than the other trying to navigate these damned hills."

The 6-foot-1 catcher was master of the spoken word and practiced his skills endlessly until a Chicago sportswriter asked, "Who's that gabby kid I can hear no matter where I go on the island?"

Ever after, Charles Leo Hartnett was known as, and answered to, "Gabby."

The grinding catcher's enthusiasm and hustle earned him the honors of catching Grover Cleveland Alexander on opening day of the 1922 season. Gabby was used primarily as a backup to Bob O'Farrell during his rookie year, but within two seasons he started catching 100 games regularly. He did so 12 of the next 14 years to set a record.

One notable exception to his workhorse role occurred in 1929, when he appeared in only 25 games and batted 22 times.

The abbreviated program was caused by a sore arm lamed by a foolhardy stunt as spring training opened. Gabby was extremely proud of the rifle-like shots he fired to the infielders. In an expansive mood, the catcher was cutting the ball loose as if he were trying to knock someone over. Finally, he succeeded—at the expense of a useless right arm. Strength was restored only after Gabby spent the year as a pinch-hitter.

Hartnett came back in 1930 to enjoy perhaps the best year of his career as he recorded a .339 average, 37 home runs and 122 runs batted in. For the next nine seasons, he averaged .305, including a .344 mark in 1935, when he led the Cubs to the World Series and was named the National League's Most Valuable Player, and a .354 average in 1937.

The smiling Irishman—kindly referred to as "Old Tomato Face" in later years—was 37 years old and performing in his customary manner when, on July 20, 1938, Charley Grimm was dismissed as manager. Owner Philip K. Wrigley appointed Hartnett as the successor.

Wrigley, who had hinted the week before that a change could be forthcoming, gave no specific reason for the switch. "Well, we're changing managers," he said simply in his announcement. "Starting tomorrow, Hartnett will be in charge.

"The decision to change was not a sudden one," he continued. "I have been thinking about it for quite some time. In fact, I've thought about it so much that I've lost sleep over it and also much of my appetite.

"Grimm did a swell job, but I think that the change is the best for the baseball organization. Charley gave everything he had, but the club was not doing as well as we felt it should. . . ."

After starting the season at 24-15, the Cubs suffered through an 11-14 June. Though they had won seven in a row just before Grimm's firing, they had lost six straight prior to that.

"There certainly is an extra spark needed somewhere and I'm going to find it if it's the last thing I do," Gabby pronounced upon his appointment.

But the command change did not evoke immediate huzzahs from the Chicago faithful. Grimm had led the Bruins to pennants in 1932 and 1935, and the patrons believed he would do it again if only the chewing gum magnate would show a modicum of patience. A headline in The Sporting News following the managerial switch announced: "Chi Still Asks Why Grimm Was Canned/More Interest Shown in Deposed Pilot Than in Successor."

The Cubs occupied third place when Hartnett took charge, 5½ games behind the league-leading Pittsburgh Pirates and four behind the second-place New York Giants. The team was fielding well and hitting decently, with third baseman Stan Hack and

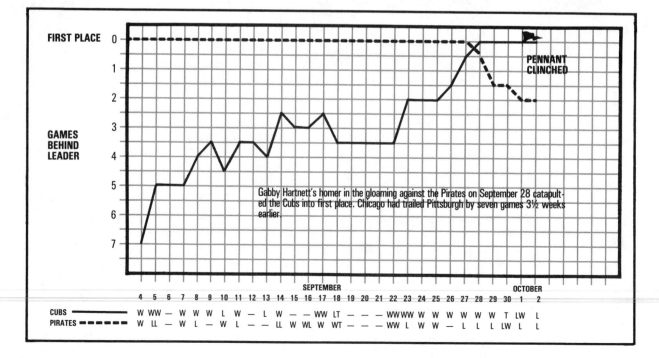

Gabby Hartnett's homer in the gloaming against the Pirates on September 28 catapulted the Cubs into first place. Chicago had trailed Pittsburgh by seven games 3½ weeks earlier.

	4	5	6	7	8	9	10	11	12	13	14	15	16	17	18	19	20	21	22	23	24	25	26	27	28	29	30	1	2
CUBS	W	WW	—	W	W	W	L	W	—	L	W	—	—	WW	LT	—	—	—	WWWW	W	W	W	W	W	W	T	LW	L	
PIRATES	W	LL	—	W	L	—	W	L	—	—	LL	W	WL	W	WT	—	—	—	WW	L	W	W	—	L	L	L	LW	L	L

outfielder Carl Reynolds among the league leaders. But the pitching, with the exception of Bill Lee and Clay Bryant, lacked consistency. In addition, player morale was low.

Prospects of the Cubs overtaking either New York or Pittsburgh were exceedingly grim. The Giants, who had won two consecutive flags under Manager Bill Terry, were still strong. New York took over first place in late April after winning 11 straight and continued riding high with a 25-9 record through May 29. Atop the league for all but four days through July 12, the Giants' offense was led by .300-hitters Harry Danning, Mel Ott and Joe Moore. On the mound, the club was just as sound with Cliff Melton, Carl Hubbell, Harry Gumbert and Hal Schumacher, who had combined for 34 of the 47 Giant wins through July 12.

The Pirates were even more powerful. The Buccos won 40 of 54 games in June and July and moved into first place July 12 on the wings of a 13-game winning streak. The club, managed by Pie Traynor, boasted a potent offense, spearheaded by Paul and Lloyd Waner, Gus Suhr and Arky Vaughan. Critics considered the pitching unspectacular. The team's foremost hurler was reliever Mace Brown, 12-3 through mid-July, but Bob Klinger (7-1), Cy Blanton (5-1) and Jim Tobin (7-3) muzzled the pundits during the rise to first.

Pirates management was confident the World Series would be played partially in Forbes Field. The club constructed an enlarged press box on the grandstand roof, put in more bleachers and made preliminary arrangements to install telegraphic equipment for the host of newspapermen who would descend on the city. Moreover, club President Bill Benswanger authorized the production of 1,000 press pins, which were described as "neat, gold-filled affairs with the face of a forbidding buccaneer."

Pirates coach Jewel Ens liked being in the driver's seat, but was keeping a wary eye on the traffic just behind, especially the Giants. "You can't laugh off Hubbell, Melton, Schumacher, Gumbert and (Slick) Castleman, not to mention a bird named Ott, who has beaten the Pirates so many times it is a bit sickening to think about it." Traynor was thinking hard, too, about the Cubs' strong-armed pitching staff and how it would carry them into the stretch. And he wasn't discounting Cincinnati, either, which came alive after winning 11 of 14 in early June to move briefly into second place.

Within two weeks of donning his managerial toga, Hartnett conducted his first locked-door meeting with his players. In the wake of an 8-3 loss August 3 in New York, it was reported that "gentle swinging with the bases full on more than one occasion had Hartnett sizzling." The primary targets of Gabby's wrath were first baseman Rip Collins, the

Hot-hitting Stan Hack (right) handled third-base duties for the 1938 Cubs with Phil Cavarretta across the diamond at first.

former Gas Houser from St. Louis, and Frank Demaree, a 28-year-old outfielder in his sixth year with the team.

The Cubs did not respond immediately to Gabby's lecture. Actually, they lost ground. A month after Hartnett took over, they bowed to the Pirates in Chicago, their 15th loss against 14 wins under his leadership. Pittsburgh was a distant nine games ahead in first.

Adding to Hartnett's woes was his own physical misery. The catcher-manager was incapacitated for almost a month when a foul tip off the bat of the Cardinals' Joe Medwick fractured his right thumb August 15.

One of the impediments in the Cubs' attempt to catch the pacesetters was their inability to consistently beat second-division clubs. Top-level opponents proved no problem. In Hartnett's first month, Chicago took two series from the Giants, 3-0 and 2-1, and one from Pittsburgh. But against the bottom four teams—Boston, St. Louis, Brooklyn and Philadelphia—the Cubs stumbled to a 5-9 performance.

The frustrating condition, according to Ed Burns,

the Chicago correspondent of The Sporting News, was due to "snootiness." He wrote:

"Failure against pushovers goes back to a certain snootiness that the Cubs apparently can't shake off, no matter how frequently the lowly knock off their high hats. Cub teams usually are overrated, and the members go along with the idea that they are pretty good and don't have to bear down except when they are playing the good teams. The attitude always riles the boys who aren't going any place and they sneak up on the Cubs. There is a flurry, a panic, and the Cubs have lost another ball game they already had counted on the winning side.

"On the other hand . . . the Cubs love a good fight from a classy opponent. The Cubs who folded before the Phillies bore no point of similarity to the Cubs who faced the Pirates two weeks later except in the matter of uniforms."

After committing six errors in their loss to the Pirates on August 20, the Cubs, in the words of Burns, "began to compute the chances of the Boston Bees and the Brooklyn Dodgers to move them into the second division for the first time since 1925."

Any negative notions were quickly dispelled, for overnight, the Cubs made a 180-degree turn. On Sunday, August 21, they upended the Pirates twice before 40,402 screaming patrons at Wrigley Field to reduce the gap behind Pittsburgh to seven games. While the Cubs faced a formidable climb, the lead was not insurmountable.

As the Cubs looked ahead to a challenge, the New York Giants continued to fade from the race, having never recovered from their 4-11 swoon in late July. Beset by injuries to key players such as Hubbell and shortstop Dick Bartell, the Giants shuffled positions with the Cubs. An 8-1 streak by Cincinnati, including a doubleheader sweep of the Cubs, pushed the Reds back into second briefly and the Giants into fourth as September began.

On Labor Day, the Cubs won a doubleheader in Pittsburgh as speculation brewed about Hartnett's future as manager. A headline in the next issue of The Sporting News proclaimed: "Cubs' Rocky Ride Jolts Hartnett Job / Gabby on Outside So Far in '39 Plans / Wrigley Believed Holding Out To See What Happens."

In his weekly report, Burns noted, "The fact that Hartnett has not been entrusted with the announcement or direction of any rebuilding program is looked upon in some quarters as significant, if not ominous."

The correspondent added: "Those who have watched the Cubs play daily have found few flaws in their managerial strategy since Gabby took charge. He has been morose, but not jittery, when some of his high-priced stalwarts showed minor league skill. And he has carried on the added worry

of not knowing where he stands."

Gabby's record at that juncture was 26-22.

Before the Pirates began their final eastern swing of the year, they played exemplary baseball. There was little reason to suspect trouble in visits to New York, Boston, Philadelphia and Brooklyn. But then, too, nobody expected the hurricane that swept the East Coast and wreaked havoc with the schedule.

Initially, it looked as if the Pirates would float into the pennant aboard an ark. With rains drenching the seaboard daily, the Bucs won and tied the Phillies in a Sunday, September 18 twin bill. Brooklyn did the same against the closing Cubs, and doubleheaders were scheduled for the next day to resolve the ties. But the downpour continued Monday, washing away for good Pittsburgh's games with Philadelphia. Chicago, however, still had a chance to play the Dodgers two on an open date Friday.

At first, Hartnett was eager to schedule the games, considering he could make up ground on Pittsburgh's 3½-game lead. But when he learned of the Pirates' fate, he hesitated.

"Shucks," Gabby said, "the Pirates are no better off than we are. We've got to be in Chicago Saturday to start a series with the Cards, and if I play you fellows twice Friday, I'll be using up two good pitchers on the chance of winning both games—and that's quite a chance."

Gabby admitted that Traynor and his team probably would admit "a quality of mercy" in all this "gentle rain from heaven."

Games that couldn't be played, couldn't be lost. At 81-57, the Bucs were four games up in the loss column, and if games disappeared in the floodwaters, tough luck for the pursuers making up lost ground. Which is why Traynor and club President Benswanger roared to National League President Ford Frick when they learned of the Cubs' option to reschedule their games with the Dodgers.

Frick sat back bemoaning the situation. "This is terrible," he said. "From the artistic point of view, of course. Here we have a swell pennant race and the contending teams can't do anything about it."

Gabby, meanwhile, nixed the Friday games, but not because of the Pirates' protests. "If we're going to beat the Pirates," he told Frick, "we'll have to do it in the three games we play them and also by beating the Cardinals while (the Pirates are) playing the Reds. There's no sense in piling up three straight doubleheaders for my club before hopping back to Chicago to begin those important games against Pittsburgh."

If Pittsburgh won only half of its remaining 14 games, the Cubs still would need to win 10 of their last 13 to tie. But Chicago was hot, having won 17 of its previous 24 games.

Veterans Billy Jurges (left) at shortstop and Billy Herman at second base centered the Cubs' strong middle defense.

The Cubs ended up playing Friday anyway—much to their benefit. Rain canceled doubleheaders pitting Pittsburgh against Brooklyn and Chicago against Philadelphia on both Tuesday and Wednesday. The Pirates swept the Dodgers Thursday in a makeup and then traveled to Cincinnati. But the Cubs, after sweeping the Phillies Thursday, made up the lost twin bill Friday and got two big wins.

Thus, the Pirates' rain factor in the schedule was washed out to sea as they missed playing two games each against Brooklyn and Philadelphia. When Pittsburgh lost to the Reds September 23, the Cubs were just two games behind. And after a three-game sweep of the Cardinals, the Bruins welcomed the Buccos to Wrigley Field on September 27 just 1½ games from the top.

The showdown for first opened with 42,238 noisy fans packed into the park. Jim Tobin, a knuckleball artist, drew the starting assignment for the Pirates.

Hartnett's selection required some deliberation.

His aces, Lee, 21-9, and Bryant, 19-11, were weary from extra work, which turned his thoughts to his second-line pitchers.

Eventually, he settled on Dizzy Dean. The Cubs had obtained the garrulous righthander from the Cardinals just three days before the season began for $185,000 and three players. An injured arm in 1937 slowed his once-fearsome fastball, forcing Dean to get by on guile and his "nothingball." Through an abbreviated season, Ol' Diz, bad arm and all, had won six games, lost only one and had a

1.80 earned-run average. And since Dean always rose to an occasion, particularly the critical ones, Gabby gave him the ball.

Diz had not started since August 20, but it made little difference. His "nothingball" was more than the Pirates could handle. While the Cubs nicked Tobin for single runs in the third and sixth innings, Jay Hanna Dean blanked the Bucs on six hits through the first eight innings.

In the ninth, however, with Woody Jensen on base and two out, Lee Handley rapped a double, advancing Jensen to third. Hartnett pondered his options. The next batter, catcher Al Todd, already had two hits. In 1931, when both were in the Texas League, Todd had taken exception to a beanball, walked to the mound and flattened Diz with a right to the mandible. That episode, of course, had no bearing on Gabby's decision. Although Lee had pitched a complete game to beat the Cardinals the day before, Hartnett summoned the righthander to nail down the victory.

Lee's first pitch to Todd gave Gabby cause for a second-guess. It was a wild heave that allowed Jensen to score and Handley to take third. The runner advanced no farther, however, as Todd struck out. The Cubs, by virtue of their 2-1 victory, were within one half game of the top.

Diz, thinking over another great feat in his pitching career, revealed he had relief help of a higher order to earn the victory. "It was the Lord," he said solemnly and with great sincerity. "He had his arms

Commissioner Ford Frick (right) raised eyebrows when he let Gabby Hartnett (left) decide whether his team would make up a couple of key games.

around me all the time, yes sir. Lik'd to choke me, he held me so tight. Whenever I was gonna go wild, he just patted me on the head and the next guy popped up. It was a grand feeling."

The triumph, however, did cost the Cubs a player. In the second inning, left fielder Augie Galan wrenched a troublesome knee and had to be carried from the field. He missed the rest of the series.

In the lineup shuffle that followed, Phil Cavarretta was shifted to the outfield and Collins, whose "gentle swinging" earlier had earned him a seat on the bench, took over at first base. Collins tripled and scored the Cubs first run in the third.

Wednesday, September 28, was heavily overcast. Only 34,465 fans were in the stands when Umpire George Barr took his stance behind the catcher. Bryant, starting his third game in seven days, opened for the Cubs. The 26-year-old righthander got into an immediate jam by walking the first three batters. He settled down, though, forcing Paul Waner to hit into a home-to-first double play and Suhr to fly out.

Traynor selected Klinger, a 20-year-old righthander with a 12-5 record, to halt the Cubs' streak toward first. Chicago scored once on the rookie in the second inning due to sloppy play by the Pirates. Third baseman Lee Handley threw the ball into the stands after fielding Bryant's grounder, and catcher Todd dropped a third strike on what should have been the third out.

Bryant stymied the Pirates for five innings on one hit, a double by Lloyd Waner. In the sixth, however, rookie outfielder Johnny Rizzo hit his 21st home run to tie the score with two out.

Vaughan's single, walks to Suhr and Pep Young,

and Handley's two-run single put the Pirates ahead and finished Bryant. Hartnett summoned Jack Russell, who had provided three key relief stints over the last week, to kill the rally.

The Cubs bounced right back. Doubles by Hartnett and Collins netted one run, and a bunt single by Billy Jurges and an infield out scored Rip with the tying run.

Vance Page, a 33-year-old rookie righthander purchased from Indianapolis at midseason, was on the hill when the Pirates threatened in the seventh inning. Rizzo stepped to the plate with runners on first and third and one out. After Page missed with two balls, something happened that infuriated the Pirates. The Pittsburgh correspondent for The Sporting News explained the controversy:

"Page was facing the batter when he made a noticeable move toward the plate and then held up. Coach Jewel Ens sprang forward to call the umpires' attention to the illegal movement, and the Pirate bench warmers, who were close to first base where (Dolly) Stark was operating, insist that the arbiter rushed forward. Rizzo . . . apparently was so intent on smacking what he thought would be a fat pitch he swung at the ball, hitting to Hack, who went through the motions of starting a double play."

The Buccos protested vehemently, but the double play was allowed to stand.

The Pirates did break through against Page in the eighth. Vaughan, a .329 hitter, drew a walk to open the inning and Suhr followed with a single. When Heinie Manush, a lefthanded batter, was announced as a pinch-hitter for Young, southpaw Larry French replaced Page. The strategy misfired when Manush singled off the former Pirate to drive in Vaughan. Hartnett brought in the weary Lee, making his third appearance in as many days. The big right-hander yielded a single to Handley, and the Pirates led, 5-3.

But with a chance for an even more productive inning, Traynor allowed Klinger to bat. The decision provoked an instant debate, which escalated into controversy when the rookie, who had 10 hits all season, hit into an inning-ending double play. Traynor then yanked the pitcher when Collins singled to lead off the bottom of the eighth.

Reliever Bill Swift proved ineffective. He started by walking Jurges, which brought player-coach Tony Lazzeri up as a pinch-hitter for Lee.

Ordered to sacrifice, the former Yankee jabbed at Swift's first pitch and missed as Collins swiped third. No longer needing to bunt, Lazzeri swung away and ripped a double to left, scoring Collins and advancing Jurges to third. An intentional walk to Hack, the Cubs' top hitter at .315, loaded the bases. Billy Herman continued his timely hitting down the stretch by singling home Jurges with the tying run. But Joe Marty, running for Lazzeri, also tried to score and was cut down on a strong throw from right fielder Paul Waner.

With only one out, Traynor went to his bullpen again. He summoned Brown, his remarkable reliever. The 28-year-old righthander was the premier fireman in the National League. In the seventh inning of that year's All-Star Game in Cincinnati, the Iowan had fanned Detroit slugger Rudy York with the bases loaded and two out to star in the senior circuit's 4-1 victory.

The 15-game winner was strictly a reliever, a role he earned through his failures as a starter. In May, Brown had started against the Giants and faced only five batters. He walked one and surrendered two hits before Johnnie McCarthy homered into the upper deck at Forbes Field.

The first batter to face Brown in the perilous eighth inning September 28 was Demaree, hitless in four at-bats. Brown frustrated the outfielder again as Demaree grounded into a double play.

Charley Root, the sixth Chicago pitcher of the day, relieved for the ninth inning. In the fast-falling darkness, the 39-year-old righthander shut out the Pirates while allowing one hit.

As the teams changed sides for the last half of the ninth inning, the umpires conferred to discuss the dusk that was hanging a gloomy shroud on an already-dark day. If the Cubs failed to score, the game could be called, creating a doubleheader the next day. Chicago, with its weakened pitching staff, could ill afford such strain. The Pittsburgh staff, however, was refreshed and better able to handle the burden.

Brown breezed through the first two batters, get-

When Cubs Manager Gabby Hartnett needed a rested arm for a key late-season game against Pittsburgh, he turned to veteran Dizzy Dean (above).

ting Cavarretta to fly out and Carl Reynolds on an infield roller. Hartnett was the last hurdle between the Buccos and the desirable tie game.

Brown's first pitch was a crackling curve that Gabby watched for a called strike. Hartnett swung on the next pitch, another curve, and missed. Brown had the batter set up. He could waste a pitch or two, and maybe Gabby would chase one.

Brown fired once more. Again, a curve. Over the plate. Charles Leo Hartnett had seen it twice before.

Ace Pittsburgh reliever Mace Brown became the unwitting goat in Chicago's drive to the 1938 National League pennant.

He timed it. Perfectly.

Everyone in Wrigley Field heard the crack of the bat against the ball, but in the murky dusk, few could predict the ball's destination.

Brown had no doubts. At the moment of impact, he brushed his hand over his eyes and strolled from the mound.

For a second, the spectators sat in silence, unsure of the half-veiled drama unfolding before them. Then, like a detonation, they erupted into a thunderous roar as the baseball streaked through the gloaming into the left-field bleachers.

A Chicago Tribune reporter described the scene:

". . . The mob started to gather around Gabby before he reached first base. By the time he reached second base, he couldn't have been recognized in the mass of Cub players, frenzied fans and excited ushers except for the red face that shone out even in the gray shadows.

"After the skipper had finally struggled to the plate, things became worse. The ushers, who had fanned out to form the protective barrier around the field, forgot their constantly rehearsed maneuver and rushed to save Hartnett's life. They tugged and they shoved and finally they started swinging their fists before the players could carry their boss to safety.

"There was further hysteria when Gabby reached the catwalk leading to the clubhouse. But by this time, the gendarmes were organized. Gabby got to the bathhouse without being stripped by souvenir maniacs."

The dramatic victory, the Cubs' ninth in a row and 19th in 22 games, lifted them into first place by two percentage points. The Pirates never recovered from the crushing defeat. They bowed to Lee, 10-1, the next day and were mathematically eliminated from the pennant race on the next-to-last day of the season, when the Cubs beat the Cardinals in the second game of a doubleheader.

Chicago ended the season with an 89-63 record. Because of the hurricane in the East a few weeks earlier, the Pirates played only 150 games and finished 86-64.

The unplayed games against last-place Philadelphia and seventh-place Brooklyn decided the race, maintained Benswanger, who had fainted in his private box when Gabby homered.

"The pennant was lost before the Cub series," he said. "The hurricane . . . prevented us from winning. We went east on the final trip, good and hot. Everybody knows that when a club is hot, it can make wrong plays and win; when it is cold, nothing turns out right. Well, we were winning game after game, close ones and easy ones. For example, in Boston (on September 17) we defeated Milt Shoffner, the lefthander who always had been a nemesis to us. And how did we do it?

"Hits by Gus Suhr and Lloyd Waner, both lefthanders, against a southpaw, which gave us a 2-1 victory in the ninth. That's the way things were going when the hurricane struck.

"We were unable to play in Brooklyn and Philadelphia just when we needed every game, even with the odds all in our favor. I wanted to play. Ford Frick and newspapermen told me not to worry, as we had the pennant sewed up. To my way of thinking, pennants are won only by winning ball games, and ball games can be won only if you play them. To lose by losing ball games is one thing, to lose by idleness is another.

"If we played all those games in the East we would have gone to Chicago with such a lead that we could have lost all three games and still have won the flag. But as we sat around hotel lobbies . . . a hot team cooled off and never regained its winning momentum. The Hartnett home run was an anticlimax, not the cause of our defeat."

Hartnett managed the Cubs through 1940 and was succeeded by Jimmy Wilson. After serving as a player-coach for the New York Giants in '41, Gabby managed three years in the minors. He was elected to the Hall of Fame in 1955. Ten years later, he came out of retirement to coach the Kansas City A's. He died at Park Ridge, Ill., on December 20, 1972.

Brown, the other principal in the "homer in the gloaming" drama, pitched in the majors through 1946. A member of the pennant-winning Red Sox that year, he was 3-1 in 18 games. Brown pitched one inning in the World Series against the Cardinals and gave up three runs, four hits and one walk.

Revitalized Dodgers Dethrone Braves

Wally Moon arrived in Los Angeles in 1959 and soon began pumping his 'Moonshots' over the Coliseum's short left-field screen.

The 1958 National League season was an unrelieved disaster for the Los Angeles Dodgers. After winning the pennant in 1956 and finishing third in '57, their last season in Brooklyn, the Dodgers tumbled to seventh in '58. At 71-83, they finished 21 games behind the first-place Milwaukee Braves. Not since the war year of 1944 had a Dodger club finished below .500.

Still, more than 1.8 million customers poured through the turnstiles in the club's first season in Southern California. The welcome was most heartening, but it was commonly agreed that such enthusiasm would not long endure unless the team regained its role as a pennant contender.

Nobody was more conscious of this imminent danger than Emil J. (Buzzie) Bavasi, the Dodgers' energetic vice president and general manager. Bavasi had been schooled in the Dodger organization and was accustomed to success on the field and at the ticket window. If those salutary conditions were to be preserved, it was imperative that the rebuilding begin as soon as the 1958 horror show was laid to rest. And what better place to begin than at the World Series. Every major league club would be represented in an atmosphere conducive to trade negotiations.

Bavasi booked a flight to Milwaukee, where the Braves were about to engage the New York Yankees.

As he slipped into his seat at County Stadium on October 1, Buzzie discovered Bing Devine, the first-year general manager of the St. Louis Cardinals, in the next pew. The conversation flowed easily as they watched Warren Spahn defeat the American League champions, 4-3, in 10 innings.

Talk about the game led to discussion of the deficiencies on their rosters. Devine mentioned he was in the market for a righthanded-hitting outfielder for the Redbird lineup. Bavasi countered that he was on the prowl for a lefthanded-hitting flyhawk who might add balance to the Dodgers' bench.

Devine threw out a name. Would the Dodgers be interested in Wally Moon, the N.L. Rookie of the Year in 1954? After batting .304 his first season, Moon hit .295, .298 and .295 before skidding to .238 in 1958.

Bavasi thought the 28-year-old Arkansan might solve his problem. In return, he suggested Gino Cimoli, also 28. A native of San Francisco, the righthanded batter had slipped to .246 in '58 after hitting .293 the previous year.

The proposal appealed to Devine but Bavasi was still hesitant, wanting to give the deal serious thought. By mutual agreement, the discussion stopped there. Each would present the proposed trade to other front-office colleagues and resume negotiations after the Cardinals returned from a six-week tour of Japan.

When they met again at the winter baseball meetings in Washington, D.C., Bavasi inquired, "How about tossing a pitcher into the deal?"

"Will you take Phil Paine?" asked Devine, referring to a minor league pitcher.

Buzzie agreed. He offered several thousand dollars along with Cimoli, and on December 4, the trade was announced.

By any comparison, the trade was no blockbuster. It created scarcely a ripple. But in the months ahead it proved to be one of the most important deals ever engineered by Bavasi.

When Moon was informed of the trade, he blurted, "The Dodgers made a helluva deal, a lot better than the Cardinals."

Los Angeles officials were inclined to agree. "I've always liked Moon's aggressiveness, ever since he was at Rochester and I was managing Montreal," said Walter Alston, about to start his sixth year as the Dodgers' skipper.

Fresco Thompson, the team's director of minor league operations, was smitten by Moon's attitude. "He's the kind of player who can go home happy if he goes 0-for-4, as long as his team wins. You could ask Cimoli who won and he'd say, 'I don't know, but I got two hits.' "

The Dodgers knew 0-for-4 performances weren't Moon samples.

"Good hitters don't collapse suddenly all at once," Bavasi said, alluding to Wally's three seasons in the .290s before his tailspin in 1958.

Buzzie was right, of course. Moon's batting decline could be traced largely to an injury. While chasing a long fly at Busch Stadium in St. Louis, Wally collided with Joe Cunningham. His left arm was pinned against the wall, straining muscles and ligaments in his elbow which hindered him the rest of the campaign.

By the time he joined the Dodgers, Moon's strength was fully restored, helped by his generous use of weights and pulleys and exercise with a weighted bat.

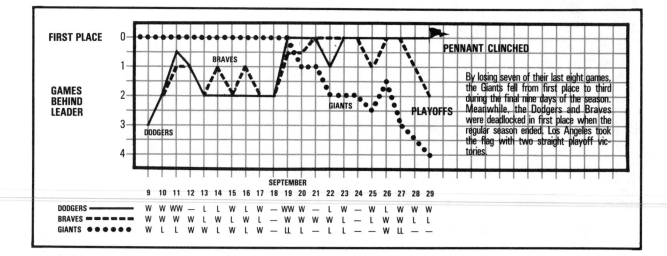

PENNANT CLINCHED

By losing seven of their last eight games, the Giants fell from first place to third during the final nine days of the season. Meanwhile, the Dodgers and Braves were deadlocked in first place when the regular season ended. Los Angeles took the flag with two straight playoff victories.

		9	10	11	12	13	14	15	16	17	18	19	20	21	22	23	24	25	26	27	28	29
DODGERS	—	W	W	WW	—	L	L	W	L	W	—	WW	W	—	L	W	—	W	L	W	W	W
BRAVES	= = =	W	W	W	W	L	W	L	W	L	—	W	W	W	W	L	—	L	W	W	L	L
GIANTS	● ● ● ● ●	W	L	L	W	W	L	W	L	W	—	LL	L	—	L	L	—	—	W	LL	—	—

Wallace Wade Moon, named for Wallace Wade, the outstanding Alabama and Duke football coach, was born at Bay, Ark., on April 3, 1920. He not only brought his hitting ability to Los Angeles, but also had intelligence as well. Moon, a graduate of Texas A&M, had a master's degree in education. In the winter months he taught mathematics, including algebra, and was qualified to teach psychology and history.

Playing for the Cardinals, Moon was a pull hitter, taking aim at the rather close pavilion in right field, a chummy 310 feet away. In Los Angeles, however, he was forced to alter his style. The right-field foul line at Memorial Coliseum measured 333 feet from home plate, and the center-field wall was 420 feet away. But in left field the barrier was a cozy 251 feet away, topped by a 42-foot-high screen stretching 140 feet from the foul line to left-center field.

Moon sized up the situation early and harkened to a bit of advice offered by Stan Musial. "If you can't beat a park," advised The Man, "join it." Wally became an instant joiner. He resurrected the "inside-out" swing that he had learned from Harry Walker, his manager at Rochester in 1953. In the unorthodox swing, the wrists and bat are held close to the body, and the head of the bat trails the hands as the batter takes his cut. The result is a "slice" to the opposite field, or in the case of a lefthanded batter like Moon, to left field. Moon's drives would either crash against the inviting barrier or sail over it. He succeeded so handsomely with the unconventional swing that 12 of his 19 home runs cleared the wire monster.

A new expression also was added to baseball's vocabulary that season. In September, the Russians announced they had struck the moon with a rocket. Wally was on a tear then as he created some "Moonshots" of his own, belting six homers in a six-game stretch. His arcing drives that cleared the "Bamboo Curtain" in left became the "Moonshots" the fans delighted in most.

But Moon did not represent the only significant change on the Los Angeles roster. Three major changes occurred when the season was under way.

Less than two months into the schedule, it became apparent that help was needed at shortstop. A call went out to the Spokane farm club. It was answered June 6 with the arrival of Maury Wills, who had been batting .313 and had stolen 25 bases in 29 attempts.

A native of Washington, D.C., the 160-pound Wills was an outstanding baseball and basketball player in high school. He attended a tryout camp conducted by the Giants, then based in New York, and excelled in a three-inning, nine-strikeout pitching performance. Despite recording another string of strikeouts in a second start, the Giants were unimpressed. His size, they maintained, argued against

Maury Wills took over at shortstop and stabilized the Dodgers' middle infield while providing a much-needed offensive boost.

his becoming a major league hurler.

The Dodgers, however, were less conscious of a prospect's size. He was signed in 1951 to a contract with Hornell of the Pony League and had one no-decision outing in the Class-D circuit. But more importantly, he shifted to second base and shortstop and began a long climb through the Dodger chain. Wills was in his 10th season as a farmhand when he was rescued.

In 83 games with the Dodgers, the rookie batted .260, but he hit .429 in the last 17 games when each day brought a new crisis.

Another acquisition who weighed heavily on Dodger fortunes in 1959 was Roger Lee Craig. The 6-foot-4 righthander had compiled a 23-23 record on the Dodger pitching staff from 1955-57, before he was waived to the St. Paul farm club in 1958 with a 2-1 record and a sore arm.

Pitcher Roger Craig blossomed in 1959 in Los Angeles after several mediocre seasons under Manager Walter Alston (left) in Brooklyn.

Craig spent a disheartening season in the American Association, losing 17 games while winning only five. He was on the brink of quitting when his wife persuaded him to give the game one more chance.

Craig opened the '59 campaign with Spokane, where a newly perfected slider and sinker restored his confidence. Early in June, he told a reporter, "If Bavasi takes me back up, I'll win the pennant for him."

The Dodgers called. They had dropped to fifth place by June 16, 4½ games behind the league-leading Milwaukee Braves. Three days later, Craig gave up only five hits in his first start to beat the Cincinnati Reds, 6-2.

The North Carolinian won 11 games, lost only five and missed winning the league earned-run championship by only 1⅓ innings with a mark of 2.06. Roger started 17 games and hurled four shutouts, good for a share of the league lead.

But Craig's most impressive stretch of scoreless pitching did not appear in any pitching leaders' statistics. On July 9, he relieved Danny McDevitt at the

start of the third and hurled 11 shutout innings to gain credit for a 4-3 victory over the Braves. The victory knocked Milwaukee from first to third place.

Other gilt-edged performances included a 1-0 win over the San Francisco Giants, July 21; a 2-0 decision over the Pittsburgh Pirates, July 29; a three-hit, 5-0 verdict over the Philadelphia Phillies, September 10, and a five-hit, 3-0 conquest of the Cardinals, September 23.

The third vitally important addition to the club during the 1959 campaign was another righthanded pitcher—23-year-old Larry Sherry, who had labored six years in the Dodger farm system and compiled a lackluster 47-65 record. In 1958, he was 6-14 for Spokane.

But at spring training the next year at Vero Beach, Fla., a batting practice incident caught the eye of club officials, Bavasi told the Saturday Evening Post in 1960. After Larry's brother Norm, an aspiring catcher, rifled a couple of drives to the outfield, Larry fired the next pitch at the batter's skull. "Nobody's diggin' in against me, even if he is my brother," Larry seethed.

Sherry started his first game for the Dodgers on July 4 and lost to the Chicago Cubs, 2-1. In his second start, July 12, he again pitched impressively but bowed to the Reds, 4-3.

But he would lose no more that season. Sherry won his next seven decisions and finished with a 2.20 ERA. In his final 23⅔ innings, Sherry allowed only three runs for a 1.14 ERA.

The youngster possessed an overabundance of confidence, and he did not hesitate to differ with his manager on the correct way to pitch to a batter. One instance was related to the Post.

Pitching in a critical extra-inning game at Chicago on September 25, he faced pinch-hitter Dale Long, a home run threat, with the tying run on second base.

Alston called time and strolled to the mound. "You can get him out with fastballs up," counseled the skipper.

"I'd rather throw fastballs down," answered the cocky kid.

"Do it your way," conceded Alston, and was glad he did.

Sherry struck out Long to end the game and earn the win.

The slider was Sherry's most effective pitch. "Any guy who is a pull hitter is dead if he tries to pull my slider," asserted Sherry, who attributed his failures while a minor leaguer to "a tired arm, and I didn't know how to cope with it."

The Dodgers started the season sluggishly. A 10-5 getaway pushed them briefly into first place in late April, but they hovered around fourth from May through mid-June. May was their worst month, when they won 14 and lost 17. After dropping to 23-23 on May 29, they cleared the .500 level for good the next day.

Along with Moon, third baseman Junior Gilliam helped lead the Dodgers' offense early as he batted .349 through midseason. Gil Hodges, Charlie Neal and Norm Larker also were hitting over .300. Pitchers Johnny Podres, Don Drysdale and Danny McDevitt kept Los Angeles from dropping too far back before the club's midseason additions.

Milwaukee, the heavy favorite to win a third straight N.L. pennant, sat atop the league for most of three months. Righthander Bob Buhl, out from May to September in '58 with shoulder problems, re-emerged as a starter and joined Lew Burdette and Spahn to give the Braves a solid "Big Three" up front. Burdette was 11-8, Spahn 10-8 and Buhl 6-5 at the All-Star break. Hank Aaron was leading the league in hitting with a .370 average, 22 home runs and 72 runs batted in. Shortstop Johnny Logan, helping to carry the load with second baseman Red Schoendienst out for all but the last few days of the year, bolted to a .332 start to complement the power of Joe Adcock and Eddie Mathews.

But everything did not go smoothly for the Braves. They encountered some uncomfortable turbulence in June, when they won 14 and lost 13. The Dodgers made a big move during a June 15-30 home stand. Los Angeles went 12-5 and suddenly was just 1½ games out of first place.

The Giants, led by the pitching of Johnny Antonelli (11-4 at midseason), Stu Miller and new arrivals Sam Jones (from St. Louis) and Jack Sanford (from Philadelphia), moved into second in late May. But while the Braves played close to .500 in June, so did the Giants.

At the All-Star break, first place had become a hotly contested three-team battle. The Braves, who would regain first only one other day before the last week of the season, led the Giants by percentage points, while the Dodgers trailed by just half a game.

As the schedule resumed, the Giants took over first, a spot they would occupy for all but two days over the next 10 weeks. If June was uncomfortable for Milwaukee, mid-July was sickening. Beginning July 14, the Braves were really knocked about, losing seven straight and dropping briefly into fourth place. But just as quickly, they regained control and won 11 of 13 games from July 24 to August 2, with Spahn and Burdette winning three starts each.

As August began, the Giants took off on the bat of a gangling rookie arriving from Phoenix—Willie McCovey. The first baseman clubbed seven home runs and drove in 16 through August 20, and the Giants won 13 of their first 20 games. The Dodgers continued hanging close, despite the pitching collapse of Drysdale, who won seven straight from

First baseman Gil Hodges (left) and pitcher Larry Sherry were two important cogs in the Dodgers' 1959 pennant drive.

June 30 to August 8, only to lose his next six decisions.

The situation remained the same for the up-and-down Braves.

Injuries, inconsistency and disappointing play plagued Milwaukee on its roller-coaster ride. Missing Schoendienst, Logan, Buhl and Wes Covington at one time or another, the Braves couldn't match their late-season surge of the year before.

After compiling a 15-16 record in August, the Braves had been left for dead September 5, when they fell 4½ games behind the Giants.

"We'll get going," Manager Fred Haney said. "All we need is a winning streak."

The Braves promptly won their next seven games.

On September 14, the Giants still led the pack with a two-game edge over both the Braves and Dodgers. The race was unchanged two days later after the Braves divided a pair of games in Los Angeles and the Giants split with the Reds. On September 16, the Braves traveled to San Francisco for a crucial series. Burdette cut the lead in half when he outdueled Sam Jones, 2-0, to win his 21st game. A victory behind Spahn the next day would lift the Braves into a first-place tie. The veteran lefthander failed to survive the first inning, however, and the Giants prevailed, 13-6, behind Sanford's 15th win to lead the race by two lengths with eight games to play.

The Dodgers shared second with the Braves, but their outlook appeared particularly grim with the rest of their games on the road.

Suddenly, however, the picture brightened for Los Angeles. A rainout at San Francisco on September 18 forced a day-night doubleheader the next day. A capacity crowd of more than 22,000 jammed Seals Stadium for the twin attraction and all departed gloomily when the Dodgers captured both games. Craig beat Antonelli, making a third try for his 20th win, 4-1, in the afternoon, and Drysdale received credit for win No. 17 in a 5-3 victory over Mike McCormick that night. The Giants, held to six hits in each game, dropped into a first-place deadlock with the victors, while the Braves were third, one game back.

The final week of the season showed these fluctuations:

Monday, September 21: Spahn beats the Pirates to win his 20th and push the Braves into a first-place tie with the idle Dodgers. The Giants are one game back.

Tuesday, September 22: The Braves win and move into first place, one game ahead of the Dodgers, two ahead of the third-place Giants.

Wednesday, September 23: Craig blanks the Cardinals and pushes the Dodgers into a tie with the Braves. The Giants fall two games back after losing their fifth straight.

Thursday, September 24: Open date.

Friday, September 25: The Dodgers gain undisputed possession of the lead, beating the Cubs, 5-4, on Gil Hodges' 11th-inning homer while the Braves and Burdette bow to the Phillies, 6-3. Rain idles the Giants in St. Louis.

Saturday, September 26: With only the fifth-place Cubs obstructing their path to the pennant, the Dodgers lose in Wrigley Field, 12-2, as Dave Hillman scatters seven hits. Spahn delights 23,763 fans at County Stadium by hurling a five-hit, 3-2 victory over Robin Roberts and the Phils. At St. Louis, Sam Jones hurls the Giants to a 4-0, no-hit win shortened to eight innings by rain, which washes out the balance of a scheduled twin bill. An unprecedented triple tie is now possible if the Dodgers and Braves lose their finales and the Giants win a doubleheader on closing day.

Sunday, September 27: Craig dashes San Francisco's hopes. Backed by home runs from Charlie Neal and John Roseboro, Roger handcuffs the Cubs, 7-1, to raise his record to 11-5. The Dodger victory is on Milwaukee's scoreboard as the Braves battle the

Phils. A record crowd of 48,642 squirms uneasily as the teams enter the last of the seventh inning with the score tied, 1-1. But the Braves score three unearned runs and pull out a 5-2 win. With nothing at stake, the Giants lose twice to the Cards, 2-1 and 14-8.

The Dodgers again would play in a three-game playoff for the N.L. pennant after losing tie-breakers, while in Brooklyn, to the Cardinals in 1946 and to the New York Giants in 1951.

The playoff opened Monday at County Stadium in Milwaukee, where a pregame shower delayed the start for 47 minutes and held attendance down to 18,297. Alston chose lefthander McDevitt to start while Haney countered with a surprise choice, Carlton Willey. Neither pitcher had enjoyed an exceptional season in 1959. McDevitt, who finished at 10-8, had split two decisions with the Braves. Willey, a righthander, had been named Rookie Pitcher of the Year in the National League for 1958 after leading the league with four shutouts and winning nine games. But Willey had slipped to 5-8 in 1959 and had pitched only three innings since his last start August 30.

The Dodgers took a 1-0 first-inning lead when Neal singled, moved to second on Moon's infield out and scored on Larker's single.

McDevitt didn't last two innings. A walk to Logan and singles by Del Crandall and Bill Bruton scored the tying run. When his first two pitches to Willey missed the strike zone, Alston signaled for Sherry.

Wills then bobbled Willey's grounder to load the bases and an infield out sent Crandall home with a 2-1 Braves lead.

Willey survived six innings. He yielded the tying run in the third on singles by Neal, Larker and Hodges and surrendered the winning run to open the sixth, when Roseboro hit his 10th home run of the year.

The 3-2 Los Angeles victory was credited to Sherry, who allowed only four hits in 7⅔ innings and did not permit a runner past first base.

As the teams flew west for the second game on Tuesday, the pitching rotation appeared to favor the Braves. Burdette, who had victimized the Dodgers twice in his 21-win season, was scheduled to oppose Drysdale, 3-3 against the Braves, in the second encounter, with Buhl, 5-1 against Los Angeles, ready for the third game. Spahn, beaten five times by the Dodgers without a victory, did not figure in Haney's blueprint.

Drysdale, carrying a 5.43 ERA in his last 13 appearances, was cuffed for two runs in the first inning when Mathews walked on a 3-2 pitch, Aaron doubled off the Coliseum screen and Frank Torre singled.

The Dodgers answered back immediately as Burdette gave up a one-out, first-inning triple to Neal and a single to Moon. But the Braves escaped with their lead when Wally was cut down stealing and Duke Snider struck out.

Milwaukee regained its two-run margin in the second on singles by Logan and Burdette and a throwing error by Snider that allowed Logan to score.

Neal, a .286 hitter, drew the Dodgers to within one run again in the fourth, when he cracked a leadoff homer, his 19th of the year.

Once more, the Braves widened their advantage to two runs. Leading off the fifth, Mathews smashed his 46th home run, giving him the N.L. home run title over Ernie Banks of Chicago.

Crandall's triple off the screen and Felix Mantilla's sacrifice fly gave Milwaukee a 5-2 lead in the eighth. Even the staunchest diehards among the 36,583 customers were ready to admit that a third contest would be necessary.

Through the first eight innings, Burdette parceled out seven hits. His 22nd victory seemed a certainty. The only negative element for Milwaukee was an injury to Logan. The shortstop was bowled over by Larker while turning a double play in the seventh inning and was carried off the field with a severely bruised side. Mantilla shifted from second base to replace Logan, and Schoendienst, back after battling tuberculosis almost all season, took over at the keystone.

Burdette, who had retired six consecutive batters after Larker's leadoff single in the seventh, ran into a buzz saw in the ninth. After singles by Moon, Snider and Hodges loaded the bases with none out, Burdette took a seat in the dugout. He was succeeded by Don McMahon, making his 60th appearance of the season.

The ace fireman made only three pitches. With a 1-1 count, Larker drilled

Young slugger Hank Aaron was the driving force behind Milwaukee's bid to hold off the Dodgers and win its third straight National League pennant.

Milwaukee Manager Fred Haney (center) possessed a potent 1-2 pitching punch in lefthander Warren Spahn (left) and righthander Lew Burdette.

a two-run single off the screen that moved Hodges to third.

Haney summoned Spahn to face the lefthanded-hitting Roseboro, but Alston sent up Carl Furillo, a righthander, as a pinch-hitter. Furillo's fly to right field drove in Hodges with the tying run. After Wills singled, Joey Jay relieved and the Braves escaped the inning when Aaron speared Gilliam's drive as he banged into the right-field fence.

Snider had an inkling of what was to come before the inning, and called the shots to Moon.

"I told Wally we were going to get five straight hits," Snider said. "I almost called it perfectly because we got four hits in a row and then a sacrifice fly, which doesn't count as a time at bat, and then another hit.

"You can't predict anything much better than that. Wish I could pick the horses that way."

Stan Williams, a 23-year-old second-year right-hander, became the sixth Los Angeles hurler. Though he walked the bases full in the 11th inning, Williams held the Braves scoreless for three frames.

Bob Rush became the fifth Milwaukee pitcher and 22nd Brave tossed into the fray by Haney when the Dodgers came to bat in the 12th. The righthand-er retired Moon and Dick Williams to open the inning before walking Hodges. Joe Pignatano fol-lowed with a single and Furillo, who had remained in the game, bounced a ball through the infield that Mantilla fielded behind second base. Hodges stopped at third but then saw the off-balance Man-tilla make a needless throw to first. The ball bounced wildly past Torre and Hodges trotted home with the winning run, climaxing the Dodgers' exciting rise from seventh place in '58 to their first pennant in Los Angeles.

In his first season as a Dodger, Moon batted .302 with 19 home runs and 74 RBIs. He finished fourth in the Most Valuable Player voting but was named on every ballot. In the Dodgers' six-game triumph over the Chicago White Sox in the World Series, Wally batted .261 (6-for-23) and clouted one home run. Alston called him "the most consistent force on the team" that season.

Sherry was incomparable in the Series. He was credited with two victories, saved two others and had a 0.71 ERA in 12⅔ innings. Wills batted .250 and stole a base while Craig started two games, one of which he lost, as the Dodgers won their second world championship in 10 appearances.

Cubs Streak To 1935 Pennant

When Philip K. Wrigley (right) purchased the Cubs, he made it clear to Manager Charley Grimm and the rest of the team that he expected to win.

A headline in The Sporting News early in 1935 announced: "Flag, Nothing Less, to satisfy Wrigley/P.K. Wants Pennant to Mark First Year of Administration."

The story that followed warned that "Owner Phil K. Wrigley probably will become very testy if the Cubs finish as low as third again now that he has taken the helm."

After winning the National League pennant in 1932, Chicago slipped to third the next two years, six games behind the champion New York Giants in 1933 and eight lengths behind the St. Louis Cardinals in 1934. Wrigley, the new president of the organization for 1935, wasted little time in sweeping away lingering memories of the Cubs' slide. He and Charley Grimm, the club's vice president and manager, disposed of 10 players from November '34 to January '35, including hefty Babe Phelps, a part-time catcher, and first baseman Don Hurst, a former Phillies star who had flopped with Chicago. Outfielder Babe Herman and righthanded starters Guy Bush and Jim Weaver also departed, to Pittsburgh, in exchange for pitcher Larry French and third baseman-outfielder Freddy Lindstrom.

The deal with the Pirates failed to stir gales of enthusiasm among Chicago's North Side partisans. Swapping two pitchers for one, the Cubs surrendered 29 combined wins in 1934 for 12. Bush had won 15 games or more for seven straight seasons in Chicago, but a reputed feud with Grimm was believed to have been his ticket out of town. With French, the Cubs gained youth—he was 26—and a lefthander for a starting rotation that had right-handers Lon Warneke, Bill Lee and Charley Root.

Before Grimm herded the Cubs to spring training on Catalina Island, Wrigley devised a bonus incentive plan that, he hoped, would entice extra effort from the players. Instead of delaying their rewards

until they signed their contracts the following year, the chewing gum magnate promised on-the-spot payments for extraordinary contributions. Grimm would be the sole judge of those deserving extra compensation.

The team that evoked Wrigley's high optimism was composed of catcher Gabby Hartnett, an infield of Lindstrom at third base, Billy Jurges at shortstop, Billy Herman at second base and Grimm at first, and an outfield of Augie Galan in left, and Kiki Cuyler, Frank Demaree and Chuck Klein rotating in center and right.

The lineup represented a fine blend of experience and youth, with Grimm the senior at 36 years old, followed by Cuyler, 35, and Hartnett, 34. The others were under 30, with Galan the youngest at 22.

Most observers, however, liked the makeup of the world champion Cardinals, who upset the Detroit Tigers in the '34 World Series.

The 1935 Cardinals were virtually unchanged from '34. Virgil Davis and Bill DeLancey were the catchers. The infield consisted of Ripper Collins at first base, Manager Frankie Frisch at second, Pepper Martin at third and Leo Durocher at shortstop. In the outfield, Joe Medwick was in left and Jack Rothrock in right. Rookie Terry Moore was being worked into center with Ernie Orsatti. The Cardinals' pitching was strong with Dizzy and Paul Dean, Bill Hallahan, Bill Walker and veteran Jesse Haines. Gone, however, was Tex Carleton, a 16-game winner traded to the Cubs over the winter for pitchers Bud Tinning and Dick Ward.

Grimm, regarded as somewhat of a prophet in St. Louis, his hometown, couldn't join in the singing of praise for the Redbirds. At a dinner given by the Mound City Chamber of Commerce just before the season opened, the manager listened to speaker after speaker predict another Cardinal pennant.

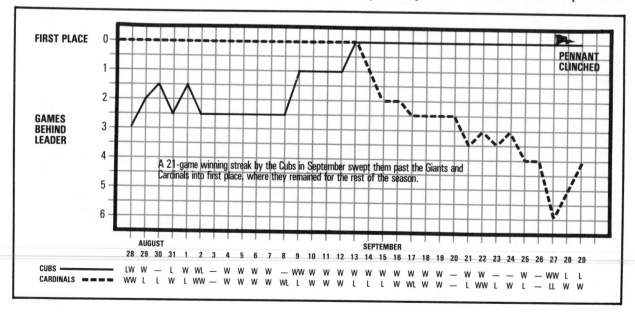

When Grimm was summoned for a speech, he said: "I'm glad I'm here, but I can't agree with all you people that the Cardinals will repeat. They are a fine ball club, but the best I can see ahead of them is a second-place finish, with the Cubs first."

Grimm's and Wrigley's enthusiasm over the Cubs' prospects did not immediately rub off on the ticket-buying public. Opening day drew only 15,500 spectators despite a tailor-made attraction that matched Dizzy Dean, the Cardinals' 30-game winner and N.L. Most Valuable Player in '34, against Cubs ace Warneke, who had won 22.

The Cubs knocked Dean out of the game—literally—in the first inning. With runners on first and third, Lindstrom smashed a line drive off Dean's shin for a single. Ol' Diz crumpled onto the mound as a covey of teammates rushed to his side. The fallen warrior was in excruciating pain, but it must have grown infinitely worse when the band struck up "Happy Days Are Here Again."

An examination showed that Dean suffered only a bruise. The injury that the musicians inflicted on his pride never was calculated.

The Cubs won the opener, 4-3, pinning the loss on Ray Harrell. French made his debut as a Cub two days later. Though he allowed only five hits, he lost, 1-0, on a home run by Medwick.

A 2-3 showing for the opening week did not please the owner or the manager. One of the skipper's major concerns was that old gaffer playing first base—Charles John Grimm. Hitless in 43 consecutive at-bats, including preseason games, Jolly Cholly decided that advancing years had taken their inevitable toll. He turned over the first-base job to Phil Cavarretta, an 18-year-old product of the Chicago sandlots.

"All I have said this spring about Phil's youth (and impressive play) goes with emphasis," Grimm said in announcing his voluntary retirement in May. "The youngster looks better to me at first and at bat every day. The Cubs won't suffer a bit by his continued presence in the lineup."

Grimm also was perplexed over Klein, the N.L.'s Most Valuable Player in 1932 and Triple Crown winner in 1933 when he was with the Philadelphia Phillies. Acquired by the Cubs before the 1934 season, Klein's average had declined from .368 in '33 to .301 with Chicago. His totals in hits, doubles, homers and runs batted in, which had topped the league in '33, also dipped sharply. In 1935, Chuck started sluggishly, provoking Grimm to bench him occasionally in favor of second-year outfielder Tuck Stainback. When Lindstrom cooled briefly in May after a hot start, Grimm inserted Stan Hack at third

The bat of young left fielder Augie Galan was a major factor in the Cubs' incredible stretch drive.

base. Hack, a former bank clerk in Sacramento, Calif., had hit .289 the year before while coming back from a broken arm. Stan responded to Grimm's call in '35 by hitting .333 his first month. Hartnett, at .307 for the year, was the only other regular to hit with consistency.

As the offense loped along into June, Grimm reached the boiling point and gave his troops a rare tongue-lashing. There would be some hitting, or else, he warned, and no more all-night card games. Poker was strictly off-limits at all times.

The Cubs snapped to attention on a trip East, with Herman finally getting over .250 and Galan hitting three homers, three doubles and four singles in a series against Philadelphia. Even Klein shook off the batting bug by hitting four homers against the Phils.

An elated Wrigley began a "fellowship dinner" plan for the team, offering to dine each player individually to bring a closer bond between the dugout and front office. Such efforts, he reasoned, would help make the Cubs a big, happy family.

But until the All-Star break, the Cubs had little to smile about. For three months they had lost almost as often as they had won. In third with a 40-32 record, they trailed the first-place Giants by 9½ games and the Cardinals by 2½.

The runaway Giants took over first place in late April. The pitching problem of 1934 had become a pitching paradise in '35 as the rest of the league tried to combat a five-man starting rotation. Slick Castleman, called up for a brief stint in 1934, became the fifth hurler and compiled an 8-2 record by midseason. He augmented an already-strong lineup of Hal Schumacher (12-2), Roy Parmelee (9-2), Carl Hubbell (10-5) and Fred Fitzsimmons (4-4). That crew usually was staked to a substantial lead by the batting attack of Manager Bill Terry (.341), Hank Leiber (.333), Mel Ott (.319, 18 home runs), Joe Moore (.314) and Mark Koenig (.301).

If the Giants' fans were assuring one another of a World Series matchup against the New York Yankees, a dispatch from Daniel M. Daniel, the New York correspondent of The Sporting News, surely heightened the pennant hysteria.

"The runaway which the Giants are making has the National League by the ears," he reported. "As you know, the old circuit has prided itself on its keen, open races. But along come the Giants, and the ancient organization is in a state of indignation and panic. Baseball historians are busy thumbing their tomes for the counterpart of this mad dash of the Giants, and they find they must go all the way back to 1909 and Fred Clarke's Pirates, who ran off with 110 victories and played .724 ball."

Cardinals Manager Frisch reasoned that anyone expecting to keep up with New York would also need a fifth starter. His staff slowly came around

going into the break and appeared ready for the second-half challenge. Haines joined the two Deans and Walker on the front line after Hallahan faltered early. Phil Collins, picked up from the Phillies, was expected to help out until "Wild Bill" returned to form.

When the season resumed, the Cubs began an extended home stand against the four eastern clubs and Cincinnati. With 23 games scheduled for Wrigley Field, the Cubs had a golden opportunity to start fulfilling the hopes of P.K. Wrigley—or dash them beyond repair.

As matters unfolded, it was the former. A coordinated batting attack and effective pitching produced 20 victories in 23 games. By the end of July, the Cubs trailed the faltering Giants by only two games.

During the remarkable resurgence, the Cubs lost only to the Phillies, twice, and the Dodgers, 14-13, in 11 innings. They beat Boston and Brooklyn five times each, New York and Cincinnati four times each, and Philadelphia twice.

At the end of the home stand, six regulars were batting over .300, led by Hartnett's .340. Galan was hitting .320 and in the headlines almost daily with his glittering performances. The former laundry delivery boy from Berkeley, Calif., never left center stage against Cincinnati as he reached base 13 times and scored nine runs in four games.

The Cubs' pitchers also shared in the glory. Root won six games without a loss; Warneke posted a 5-0 record; Carleton was 3-0; French had a 3-1 mark, and Lee went 2-1.

After completing the triumphant home stand, the Cubs traveled to Pittsburgh, where they defeated the Pirates, 9-6, on July 30. French was shelled by his former team in a four-run first inning. Lee relieved and allowed only four hits the rest of the game to earn the victory.

The next day's newspapers detailed the win, of course, but they also entertained their readers by recounting a brawl between Jurges and third-string catcher Wally Stephenson.

The fracas, staged in full view of the spectators, was ignited by, of all things, the Civil War. Jurges, a Brooklyn, N.Y., native, taunted his North Carolina teammate about the conduct of his forebears in the war between the states. Jurges bragged that Billy Yank, armed with nothing more than a cornstalk, had chased Johnny Reb across an unidentified battlefield. Intersectional strife erupted anew in the form of fisticuffs.

Grimm, who cared little, if anything, about who did what to whom in the 1860s, took instant disciplinary action. That night he sent Stephenson packing back to Chicago with explicit instructions to remain there until arrangements were made to send the catcher to "Strawberry Bend or someplace like that."

"Until yesterday, we were a 100 percent harmonious ball club in the thick of a pennant fight," Grimm declared the next day. "That little flare-up of Stephenson's jarred all of us for awhile, but you can quote me as saying there's no dissension on the team now." Hours later, Grimm would be sending an SOS to the patriotic Southerner.

While Wally was relaxing in the Windy City, the Cubs engaged the Pirates in a doubleheader. In the second game, Hartnett fractured a bone in his ankle while sliding into second. The casualty reduced the Chicago catching corps to only Ken O'Dea. Instead of awaiting assignment to the fictional Strawberry Bend, Wally was ordered to rejoin the team in Cincinnati.

A contrite Tarheel arrived Friday in the Queen City and was in the dugout for the game. If a smile flickered across his face when Jurges dropped a pop fly that contributed to the Chicago defeat, it was perfectly understandable.

Losing pitcher Lee, a Louisianian nicknamed "The General," did not accept Jurges' error in silence. The opportunity to fan the flames of acrimony was too strong to resist. With unconcealed bitterness, he suggested to Jurges that the shortstop wear one of his grandpappy's war helmets because, "It might keep you from getting killed by a pop fly."

The team mood softened briefly thereafter—for a day, at least—until the first game of the Sunday twin bill at Crosley Field. Warneke, the "Arkansas Hummingbird," was leading 1-0 in the last of the eighth. A bobble by Jurges, however, opened the way for a five-run uprising and a Cincinnati victory.

"As the downcast Cubs left the arena for the intermission," wrote Ed Burns, a Chicago correspondent for The Sporting News, "Lee escorted Warneke with a flourish of brotherly feeling and Southern chivalry."

In the nightcap, Stephenson made his first start above Class D. Besides calling a heady game, he collected three hits and scored the deciding run in a 4-3 victory.

Returning home for a brief stay, the Cubs ran

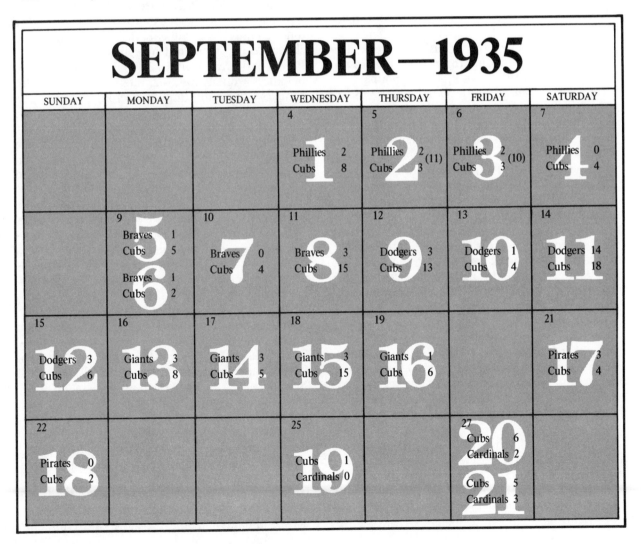

afoul of their old tormentors, the Cardinals, who had beaten them 10 times in 14 games. More humiliation was reaped upon them when Dizzy and Paul Dean won the first two games before Root salvaged the finale.

In mid-August, the Cubs embarked on their final trip East without having aroused much optimism over a pennant. Even Burns, normally a buoyant spirit, noted glumly, "The Cubs, if recent performances mean anything, must have been kidding when they staged the spurt that got them talked about as pennant contenders."

Brooklyn was the first port of call, a stop the Cubs welcomed. Casey Stengel's Dodgers had bowed meekly to the Cubs in 11 of 13 contests. This time, however, the Flatbush Flock rose up in all its righteous wrath and slapped the Cubs with a doubleheader loss to open the series. The Bruins regrouped quickly and posted 11 wins in their 19-game junket.

While that performance narrowed the lead of the faltering second-place Giants, it was overshadowed by the Cardinals' 14-7 showing over the same period.

The Giants had been knocked out of first place for good August 25, when the Cubs won their third game in a four-game series against New York. The Cubs frustrated the Giants throughout the season, beating them 10 of 18 games up to that point.

Terry, ever mindful of the awful collapse in '34, told his players to "win or out you go" in a clubhouse meeting after they fell from the lead.

Even with St. Louis gaining momentum, Burns found encouragement in the N.L. schedule. In the September 5 issue of TSN, Burns reported:

"The Cubs . . . still have their big chance ahead of them. They now are under way in their final home stand, in which 20 games are involved. These 20 will be followed by five at St. Louis, and the five will mark the season's conclusion as well as the end for the Cards of 30 consecutive games on their own lot. So if the Cubs can get through the next 20 and come up on even terms with the Cardinals, they still will have five tough games with the latter before reaching the finish."

The same issue reported that Wrigley was satisfied with the team's performance. The Cubs' play met his expectations, he said, and Grimm would manage the club again in 1936, whatever the season's outcome. The headline proclaimed: "Wrigley Will Stick to Grimm Even If Cubs Gum Up Pennant."

The home stand that Burns based his hopes upon began on a blue note. After Warneke defeated the seventh-place Reds, 3-1, in the first game of a Labor Day doubleheader, Gene Schott of Cincinnati outpitched Lee and three relievers in the nightcap.

The Cardinals enjoyed a holiday sweep of Pitts-

burgh and increased their lead to two games over the rained-out Giants and 2½ games over the Cubs.

After the Reds departed Wrigley, the Phillies arrived—the same, sometimes-futile Phils who won two games when the Cubs last visited Philadelphia. The sixth-place club again played the Cubs tough and twice battled them into extra innings. The net result: four Chicago victories.

The series provided another starring role for Galan, the left-field sensation who had struggled badly the year before as an erratic part-time infielder. In the first game of the series, Galan clouted two home runs, one a grand slam. In the third game, Joe Bowman had checked the Cubs on three hits for seven innings. Augie tripled to lead off the eighth and scored the tying run. Leading off the 10th inning, Galan cracked a home run to win the contest, 3-2.

In the series windup, the Californian rapped a pair of singles and drove in two runs to help Lee to a 4-0 decision and his 16th victory.

With the win, the Cubs snatched second place from the Giants and kept pace with the Cards, who beat the Braves for their sixth straight triumph.

When rain washed out Chicago's game with Boston on Sunday, September 8, the Redbirds muffed a chance to pad their lead by splitting two with the Phils. Dizzy Dean won his 25th game in the opener, but the Cardinals lost, 4-2, after they stranded 16 runners while outhitting Philadelphia, 13 to 4.

The Chicago battlewagon cruised onward. On September 9 the Cubs increased their winning streak to six as Carleton and French defeated the Braves in a twin bill. In St. Louis, the Cards encountered more misery. They lost to Curt Davis and the Phils and saw their lead shrink to one game.

Root, 36 but still crafty, blanked the Braves, 4-0, on September 10, and Lee completed the series sweep with a 15-3 blowout. Momentum was shoving the Cubs forward, but each time they shot a curious glance at the scoreboard, the Cardinals were winning again and protecting their slim advantage.

On Thursday, September 12, the energized Chicago hitting attack erupted for 15 hits, including two singles, a double and homer—good for five RBIs—from Galan. The 13-3 conquest of Brooklyn kept Chicago one game behind the Cardinals, who beat New York, 5-2, as Dizzy Dean posted win No. 26.

By now, the Cubs believed in themselves—but not without owing a bit to the unexplained.

Superstitious teammates believed that 15-year-old Paul Dominick was the good-luck charm in the team's winning streak. The day the streak began, the Cubs spied the chubby youngster outside the ball park and joked that he looked like a miniature Gabby Hartnett. They brought the youngster inside, decked him out in a uniform and sneaked him onto the end of the bench.

He was there the next day, too, for another victory and the following day for a third. That was all it took for the superstitious lot to demand his presence on the bench each game. The boy refused to attend school for fear that his absence would jinx the club, but Grimm arranged for an automobile to shuttle the boy to and from the park. "We've got to have you here with us, but you must go to school, too," Grimm told the youth.

Jolly Cholly also carried on a daily ritual, something more akin to a cobbler's line of work. Before each game, Grimm pegged a tack into his right shoe. He did it for no particular reason the first game of the streak, but with each tack he hammered, the Cubs added a victory.

The Cardinals also came upon a bit of luck, though it turned out to be bad.

Friday, September 13, brought to the Cards all

A midseason fight between Chicago teammates Wally Stephenson (left) and Billy Jurges prompted Manager Charley Grimm to take prompt disciplinary action and publicly dispel rumors of team turmoil.

Superstitious Cubs players believed that 15-year-old Paul Dominick was a
good-luck charm during their 21-game winning streak.

the dire consequences predicted by hex cultists.
Trailing 10-6 in the last of the ninth, the Redbirds
tied the game and turned the pitching chores over
to Dizzy Dean. Just as he did in 1934, the Great One
welcomed the opportunity to pitch in or out of
turn. Pride was a powerful motivator for Dean, but
on this afternoon, willingness succumbed to weariness. Diz yielded three runs in the 10th and the
Cards lost, 13-10.

The scoreboard in Sportsman's Park displayed
additional disturbing news: French and Chicago
had whipped the Dodgers, 4-1. With an 87-50 record, the Cards led the 89-52 Cubs by a mere four

percentage points. What's more, the Cardinals were
overworking the Dean brothers as it became evident that their pitching rotation lacked the depth
and consistency needed down the stretch. The opposite was true for the Cubs. French was the 10th
pitcher in the Cubs' 10 straight wins to finish a
game without relief. In addition, no Cub hurler had
allowed more than three runs.

Relentlessly, Chicago bulled ahead. The last ob-
struction to sole occupancy of first place was removed September 14, when Brooklyn became the
Cubs' 11th straight victim by bowing, 18-14. The
Cardinals, meanwhile, struggled grimly against the

Giants. New York pitcher Slick Castleman whacked a two-out, 11th-inning double and rode home on Joe Moore's single to give the Giants a 5-4 win.

Throughout the country, sportswriters were calling the Cubs the "Grimm Reapers." When Chicago beat the Dodgers, 6-3, on September 15, the winning streak mounted to 12 games, all at the expense of second-division teams. But the Giants were heading to Chicago, the revitalized Giants who had won three of four games in St. Louis and were 3½ games out of first.

No rivalry in the National League was waged more bitterly than the Cub-Giants showdown. It dated back to the days of Frank Chance and John McGraw and had lost none of its heat in the intervening years. The arrival of the Giants at Wrigley Field affected attendance the way an electric switch affects a light bulb. Chicago fans were turned on instantly, and the Wrigley Field gate count, which had been near 8,000, shot up dramatically. The four contests attracted crowds of 29,740, 30,239, 32,885 and 30,237.

Even a few more newsmen were brought out by the commotion. Grimm recalled in his autobiography, "Jolly Cholly's Story," a post-game interview during the streak. "Trainer Andy Lotshaw walked over to my locker while I was enjoying a beer," he said.

" 'There's a guy outside who wants to interview you,' said Andy.

"I dusted off a chair for my visitor, feeling in an expansive mood.

" 'How's the club been doing?' was his first question.

" 'Throw this guy out, Andy, he's an impostor,' I yelled. He was substituting that day for one of the radio station regulars and hadn't been reading the papers lately."

Having worked his pitching staff to a frazzle in St. Louis, Terry was forced to start Harry Gumbert in the series opener. The young righthander, who had only 2⅓ innings of major league experience, was sadly miscast. Galan rapped his first pitch for a double and Lindstrom, continuing a torrid September pace, singled him home. The Cubs won, 8-3.

Hal Schumacher and French hooked up the next day, and the Giants took an early 2-1 lead on a

Righthander Lon Warneke was the ace of the 1935 Chicago Cubs' surprisingly deep and efficient pitching staff.

prodigious home run by Terry. In the fifth, however, Schumacher gripped his shoulder and staggered toward the dugout after a ball four pitch to Jurges. Halfway there he stopped, returned to the mound and retired the side. He came out for the sixth inning but issued a leadoff walk to Galan. Terry immediately lifted Prince Hal for Allyn Stout, who was charged with the 5-3 defeat. Afterward, Schumacher reported that a sharp pain shot through his shoulder on the last pitch to Jurges.

Castleman was next in the New York rotation, but he wasn't the solution to Terry's pitching problem, either. The 22-year-old righthander was pummeled early as the Cubs piled up 20 hits, four by Herman, and coasted in, 15-3. The Cubs completed the sweep by beating Carl Hubbell, 6-1, for win No. 16 in their resolute march.

After the game, Grimm entered the clubhouse and gestured for silence. The manager's message was brief: "Boys, there ain't gonna be any Gas House Gang in the World Series."

Grimm's prediction was contrary to the opinion of a baseball writer for the New York Herald Tribune. After witnessing the dismemberment of the Giants at Wrigley Field, he wrote, "One cannot help thinking that if the Cards are still close to the Cubs when they play the five-game series in St. Louis at the close of the season, the Cardinals will win."

Two victories over the Pirates in Chicago pushed the Cubs' streak to 18. As Ed Burns had speculated weeks before, the championship of the National League would hinge on the St. Louis series, commencing September 25.

When they entrained for the showdown at Sportsman's Park, the Cubs enjoyed a three-game lead. If they captured just one of the five games, they were assured of a first-place tie. Two victories would bring the flag to Chicago.

The first game matched Warneke against Paul Dean, who already had won 19 games to equal the total of his 1934 rookie season.

Dean began by striking out four of the first five batters he faced. Cavarretta was the next to step in. The Lane Technical High School product had started his first major league game exactly one year ago against Cincinnati. In his first at-bat, he had poled a home run off Whitey Wistert to give the Cubs a 1-0 victory.

Dean's first pitch was a curve, waist high. The kid whom Grimm called "Philibuck" swung with unrestrained fury and drove the ball over the roof of the right-field pavilion. That was all the support Warneke needed to register his 20th win. Lon allowed only two hits, a single by rookie Lynn King, who was doubled off first on Frisch's outfield fly, and Rip Collins' eighth-inning double. Collins got as far as third, but he was stranded when Galan raced to the left-field wall to corral Durocher's bid for an extra-base hit.

With the chance to clinch the pennant at hand, Grimm decided to go with a St. Louis outcast on the mound. Big Bill Lee, who already had racked up 19 wins, had been sold right off the Cardinals' Columbus farm club in 1933. He opposed Dizzy Dean in the first game of a doubleheader on September 27.

The Cardinals provided their 28-game winner with a 2-0 lead in the first inning, but Diz was unable to contain the explosive power in the Chicago bats. Lindstrom tagged him for four hits, Galan and Hack had three apiece and the Cubs rolled to a 6-2 win that clinched the 14th pennant in club history. Chicago also won the nightcap, 5-3, for their 21st win in a row. The string was snapped the next day, but Chicago went on to finish the season at 100-54, four games ahead of the Cardinals.

The winning streak was the longest in the major leagues since the 1916 New York Giants reeled off 26 with one tie. But Chicago tied the record for most consecutive games won in a season without a tie, matching the mark the club set in 1880.

During the spectacular dash to the pennant, Herman led all the regulars with a .400 batting average (38 for 95); Galan posted a .384 mark (33 for 86); Lindstrom hit .354 (28 for 79); Demaree, .341 (28 for 82); Hack, .343 (24 for 70); Hartnett, .351 (21 for 59); Cavarretta .260 (21 for 82), and Jurges, .209 (14 for 67). Klein, who had another disappointing year, was benched for most of the streak and went 0 for 13.

Of the 21 victories, five each were credited to Lee and French, four apiece to Warneke and Root, two to Roy Henshaw and one to Carleton. Warneke and Lee won 20 games for the year, while French finished with 17, Root 15, Henshaw 13 and Carleton 11.

Hartnett hit .344 and won the MVP award, Herman hit .341, Demaree .325, Galan .314 and Hack .311.

Years later, Grimm fondly recalled the magical year. "The Cubs we put together in 1935 . . . were the best group I ever managed. . . .

"In all my 50 years in baseball, I never experienced a season to come close to 1935. . . ."

Wrigley was so stirred by the championship season, despite the loss to Detroit in the World Series, that he sent out early Christmas greetings announcing a club profit after $600,000 in losses the previous three years.

"The holiday season has again rolled around and while red is generally considered a Christmas color, we must be frank and say that the fact our business is not in the red this year, but in the black, helps considerably in our outlook on life. And while we reached only half of our objective this year, we feel that our boys put up a good fight and one pennant alone is better than none."

Yankees Overcome Adversity, Red Sox

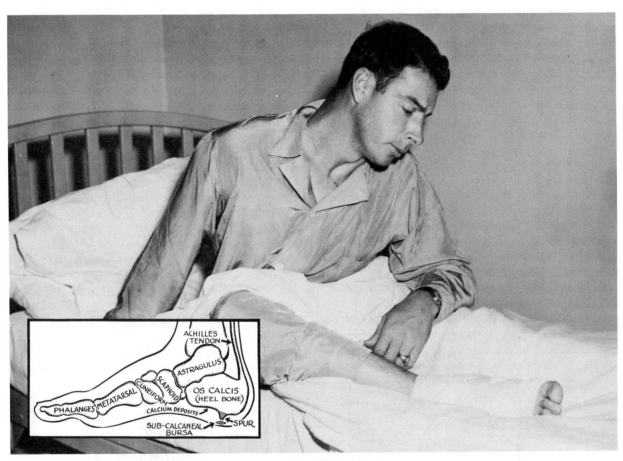

As the 1949 season approached, Yankee slugger Joe DiMaggio was
undergoing tests and trying to fight off another heel injury. The inset shows
the positioning of the bone spur that chronically plagued the Yankee Clipper.

One night during the 1935 World Series, a number of baseball writers were socializing at press headquarters. A curious New York representative turned to San Franciscan Tom Laird and inquired, "Just how good is this kid DiMaggio?"

The columnist and sports editor was well qualified to answer queries about the young outfielder whom the Yankees had recently acquired. For three seasons Laird had watched the son of a Bay Area fisherman display his incredible talent for the San Francisco Seals of the Pacific Coast League. He had marveled at the youngster's grace and style, his powerful arm and the batting stroke that produced hits in 61 straight games in 1933. Laird was delight-

ed to present an intimate evaluation of the phenom.

"Well, I'll tell you," he began, "I won't say that he's a second Babe Ruth, see?"

The listeners were willing to accept that.

"And I won't say that he's a second Ty Cobb, see?" Laird continued.

That, too, seemed perfectly reasonable.

"Nor will I say that he's a second Tris Speaker, see?" Laird went on.

For the third time, heads nodded in agreement.

"I will say this, however," he concluded, deftly leading his listeners on, "he's better than all three put together."

Polite laughter followed. Quite clearly, this was a

flagrant case of West Coast chauvinism. No wide-eyed dreamer could expect a 21-year-old prospect to hit like the Bambino, run the bases like the Georgia Peach or field in the elegant manner of the Gray Eagle.

When the congenial party disbanded, the non-Californians still were chuckling over a native son's exaggerated appraisal of Joseph Paul DiMaggio.

Years passed and the remarkable athlete, wearing the distinguished pinstripes of the New York Yankees, established himself among the game's elite. One season he hit safely in 56 consecutive games. Three times he was voted the American League's Most Valuable Player. Twice he won batting championships. He was the model of the quintessential major league player and an inspiration to anyone inclined to give less than 100 percent in his chosen profession.

Maybe Tom Laird wasn't too far off the mark after all.

New York broadcasters christened DiMaggio the "Yankee Clipper" because of the superior way he cruised the outfield, reminding admirers of the majestic sailing ships of an earlier era. To others, he was "Joltin' Joe," a nickname that inspired a popular tune by the Les Brown Orchestra, "Joltin' Joe DiMaggio." In all respects, he was "Mr. Baseball," this reticent athlete with unsurpassed skills.

If DiMaggio had a weakness, it was his susceptibility to injury. In his first 11 years as a Yankee—excluding his three years of military service in World War II—Joe missed the season opener six

times. Only once, in 1942, could he play the full 154-game schedule. From his thighs to the bottom of his heels, DiMaggio's legs suffered more damage than a barroom chair's.

Though the Yankees finished third in 1948, 2½ games behind the Cleveland Indians, Joe D enjoyed a good season. He batted .320 and led the league with 39 home runs and 155 runs batted in. But it also was a season of growing discomfort. A sore right heel made running painful, sometimes unbearably so. After the close of the campaign, DiMaggio underwent surgery for the removal of a bone spur. The operation, however, was nothing new. In January 1947, Joe had had a three-inch spur removed from his left heel.

Dr. George Bennett, who performed the surgery on the right heel at Johns Hopkins University hospital, assured DiMaggio and the Yankees that the source of the trouble had been removed. With a proper recovery, DiMaggio would be able to test the heel by spring training.

For the next several months, the worries and fears subsided. Of more importance, it seemed, was the team's new manager, Charles Dillon (Casey) Stengel. The man better known for his waggish style than managerial wisdom succeeded Bucky Harris, whose relaxed discipline, many contended, contributed to the Yanks' third-place showing.

Bucky readily conceded that he had permitted the players to spend their evenings at the dog tracks. "At least I know where they are," he explained.

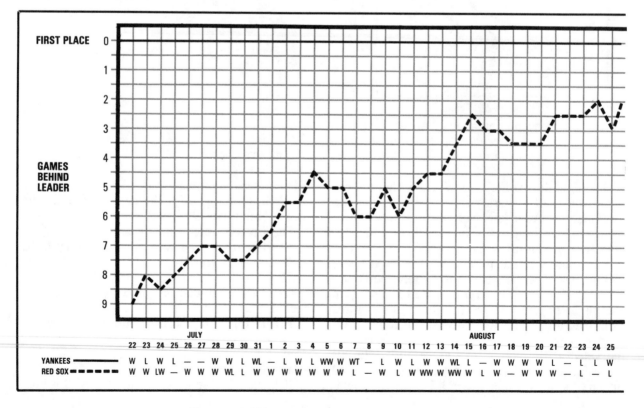

Those days and nights were over, Stengel informed the team in his first lecture at St. Petersburg, Fla. The players would be permitted only one weekly visit to the tracks and Stengel would choose the night. Moreover, two workouts would be conducted daily, instead of one, and a new midnight curfew would be strictly enforced.

While veteran players were still muttering darkly under their breath, more bad news raced through the ranks: DiMaggio's heel was flaring up again. It pained Joe to put his full weight on the foot. Running was out of the question. DiMag had only one option—fly to Baltimore and consult Bennett.

At Johns Hopkins, the surgeon's examination indicated that tissue had been aggravated in his right ankle. But, Joe was told, don't be unduly alarmed. Time would provide a cure. He returned to Florida with instruction to treat the aching heel with daily whirlpool baths. In addition, sponge protective pads were designated for his shoes to lessen the shock of running.

When the Grapefruit League season began, DiMaggio still was in pain and limping about the field. He played a few innings in some games and pinch-hit in others. The Yankees were touring through Texas and Joe was batting .229 (7 for 31) when the pain again became intolerable. Once more, the doctors were summoned.

Bennett and Dr. P. M. Girard of Dallas said the heel now was suffering from a "hot condition." They recommended Novocain injections and X-ray treatments and put Joltin' Joe back on a plane for Baltimore.

At Johns Hopkins, doctors issued a bulletin. DiMaggio had "immature calcium deposits" in the tissue next to his heel bone, and his recovery would be determined by the results of the treatment. Although the doctors were optimistic the problem would clear up quickly, Joe was deeply concerned.

The physical irritation was compounded by persistent questioning from the press. Everyday he heard the same questions. "How's the heel?" "What are the chances for recovery?" When he was discharged from the hospital after one day, the questions came again. By then, Joe had heard enough.

"Don't you think you've gone far enough?" he snapped. "You guys are driving me batty. Can't you leave me alone? This affects me mentally, too, you know."

And always the question that bothered him most: "Do you plan to quit baseball?" DiMag later apologized for the outburst in an article for Life magazine, but, still that question had hung over him like a black cloud.

"It was a sensible question, and I don't blame them for asking, but I hated it," he explained. "I was worrying almost every waking hour about the same thing. Was I going to have to quit the game I love? Was I through before my time?"

Little was expected of the Bombers in 1949. In a preseason poll conducted by The Sporting News among 206 Baseball Writers of America, the Yanks drew only six votes for first place. They were badly outdistanced by the Boston Red Sox, who received

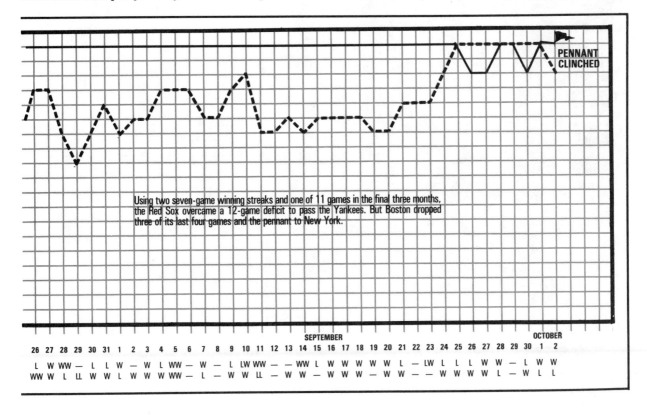

Using two seven-game winning streaks and one of 11 games in the final three months, the Red Sox overcame a 12-game deficit to pass the Yankees. But Boston dropped three of its last four games and the pennant to New York.

PENNANT CLINCHED

														SEPTEMBER																				OCTOBER	
26	27	28	29	30	31	1	2	3	4	5	6	7	8	9	10	11	12	13	14	15	16	17	18	19	20	21	22	23	24	25	26	27	28	29	30	1	2
L	W	WW	—	L	L	W	—	W	L	WW	—	W	—	L	LW	WW	—	—	WW	L	W	W	W	W	L	—	LW	L	L	L	W	W	—	L	W	W
WW	W	L	LL	W	W	L	W	W	W	WW	—	L	—	W	W	LL	—	W	W	—	W	W	W	—	W	W	—	—	W	W	W	W	L	—	W	L	L

Despite the absence of offensive weapon Joe DiMaggio (left), Yankee Manager Casey Stengel kept his team in the 1949 pennant chase.

When Joe DiMaggio returned to the Yankee lineup near the end of June, he scored a first-inning run (above) after singling and later hit a home run.

118 votes, and the Indians, who collected 79.

The club Stengel led into Yankee Stadium for the April 19 inaugural boasted such veterans as Tommy Henrich, Phil Rizzuto, Charlie Keller, Johnny Lindell and Snuffy Stirnweiss. The emerging superstar was Yogi Berra, and there was an assortment of rookies. The highly rated pitching staff was dominated by Vic Raschi, Allie Reynolds, Ed Lopat, Tommy Byrne and Joe Page, the bullpen master of 1947 whose earned-run average had ballooned to 4.25 in 1948. But Raschi had won 19 games in '48, his first full season in New York, Reynolds was 16-7 and Lopat had won 17 after being acquired from the Chicago White Sox.

Gene Woodling, the leading hitter (.385) in the Pacific Coast League in 1948, patrolled DiMaggio's center-field territory on opening day against Washington. The lefthanded batter's single led to New York's first run in the third, and he added another

hit before the teams entered the ninth tied, 2-2. With two out for the Yankees, Henrich came to bat.

Until then, Old Reliable had suffered through a dismal day. Three times he had made the final out with two runners on base, quite uncharacteristic of the right fielder-first baseman. This time, however, he made amends and drove a pitch from Sid Hudson into the right-field seats for a 3-2 Yankee victory.

Tommy repeated his heroics the next day. His second home run of the year was the deciding tally in Raschi's three-hit, 3-0 shutout of the Senators.

Lefthander Byrne beat the Nats in the third game, and Reynolds opened the first Red Sox series with his first victory. To the surprise of the cognoscenti, the Yankees were 4-0 and in first place, where they would remain for weeks to come. If the Yankees are this strong without Joltin' Joe, people asked, how much more devastating will they be when he re-

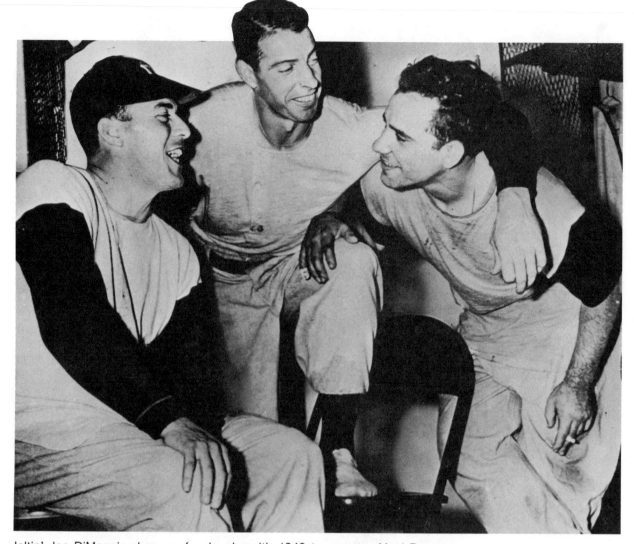

Joltin' Joe DiMaggio shares a few laughs with 1949 teammates Yogi Berra (right) and pitcher Vic Raschi (left).

turns?

Stengel also wondered. Until DiMaggio recovered, Henrich was counted on to shoulder most of the offensive burden. To guard against any misfortune to his key player, Casey offered Tommy this advice: "Don't slip and fall in the shower. And under no circumstances are you to eat fish because those bones could be murder. Drive carefully and stay in the slow lane, and sit quietly in the clubhouse until the game begins. I can't let anything happen to you."

Henrich did as requested and retained his health. Other Yankees were less fortunate. Three days before the season, promising young righthander Bob Porterfield injured his arm. On opening day, outfielder Keller tore a muscle in his side during batting practice, and Stirnweiss, the second baseman, damaged a nerve in his hand. Outfielders Hank Bauer and Lindell were hobbled by ankle injuries and Bauer was tatooed with bruises by foul tips, pitched balls and enemy spikes.

If a rash of injuries had occurred when Stengel

had been managing the Brooklyn Dodgers or Boston Braves, Casey probably would have muttered one of his patented wisecracks to shatter the gloom. But those teams were second-division clubs. They were expected to lose and Casey was expected to clown. These were the Yankees, a club accustomed to winning. Injuries would not be accepted as an excuse for failure.

And so day after day, Casey confounded his critics and exercised his managerial acumen. He used his reserves—often. If a player failed to produce, others were poised to take over. He employed the platoon system as it had never been employed before. In the face of widespread criticism, the Old Perfessor inserted and withdrew players to counteract lefthanded or righthanded pitchers.

One game illustrates Casey's platoon wizardry. In a midseason contest at Washington, the Yankees trailed, 4-1, after eight innings. Senators lefthander Mickey Harris walked the bases full to start the ninth, setting Stengel's bench maneuvering into motion.

Woodling, a lefthanded batter, pinch-hit for Bauer, a righthander, and singled in one run. That finished Harris. Washington righthander Dick Welteroth relieved and Stengel retaliated with Berra, a lefthander, for Charlie Silvera, a righthanded batter. Berra singled in another run, cutting the lead to one. With the pitcher due to bat next, Ol' Case pinch-hit Keller, who tripled to give New York the lead. In the last of the ninth, Stengel beckoned for Page. The big southpaw recorded two strikeouts as he finished off the Senators.

Similarly, Stengel reaped maximum production from his daily lineup. At third base, Bobby Brown started against righthanders while Billy Johnson was used against lefthanders. First basemen Dick Kryhoski and Jack Phillips shared duties early, with Phillips facing southpaws. During DiMaggio's prolonged absence from the outfield, Woodling and Cliff Mapes worked against righthanders while Lindell and Bauer played against lefties. Henrich was in right field daily, except when he filled in at first base.

Stengel had two capable second basemen, thanks to a little competition. When Stirnweiss was injured, Casey gave the job to Jerry Coleman. The rookie came through so handsomely that Snuffy became his backup.

The Yankees kept winning and tooled along ahead of the pack in the early weeks of the race. Still, one question remained unanswered. When would DiMaggio, now living in his New York hotel apartment, return to the lineup?

To all interrogators, Casey gave the same reply. "Mr. DiMaggio will let me know when he's ready to play," he rasped.

One morning in early June, Joe got out of bed and noticed something different in his heel. It no longer was hot, but cool, and felt good for the first time in months. When the Yankees arrived home from a trip west, DiMaggio met them at the park and donned his uniform for practice. He started back slowly, taking a few minutes of batting practice, fielding a few grounders and shagging some flies. Each day, he tested himself a little more, hoping trouble would stay away.

On June 27, DiMaggio arrived at the clubhouse with a message for Stengel: He was ready to play. The Yanks took on the Giants that night in the Mayor's Trophy Game, an exhibition for charity. When DiMaggio was announced in the starting lineup, Yankee fans cheered like they hadn't done in months.

In four at-bats he failed to hit the ball out of the infield, and he gasped for breath after long sprints in the outfield. But more importantly, his heel withstood the stresses of the game.

At that point, the Yankees had played 65 games, more than one-third of the schedule, without their

This 1949 cartoon bluntly made the point that without Joe DiMaggio, the Yankees were in deep trouble.

biggest weapon. Their 41-24 record placed them 4½ games ahead of the Philadelphia Athletics and five in front of the Red Sox.

The Yankees resumed their regular schedule June 28 in Boston, where the Sox had won 10 of their last 11 games.

While planning his comeback, DiMaggio had reasoned that the three-game series would be ideal. "We figured to have a tough series against them," he wrote in *Life,* "and I thought that if I got lucky I might help a little—especially because they've got a nice, friendly fence up there, just 315 feet from home plate. I pull my hits to left, and I might be lucky enough to hit a nice, long pop fly right out of the park. Of all the places to try, Boston was the best."

The largest night turnout in club history, 36,228 fans, packed Fenway Park for the first game. They were there to howl for Joe McCarthy's Red Sox and hoot the Yankees, whom Marse Joe had managed for 15 years. But they also were there to see the Yankee Clipper.

Maury McDermott, a hard-throwing 20-year-old lefthander recently recalled from Louisville, pitched a complete game for Boston. Among the eight hits he surrendered, two were especially noteworthy. DiMaggio, in his first time at bat, singled and scored on a three-run homer by Bauer. In his second time at bat, DiMaggio blasted a pitch high above the left-field wall with Rizzuto aboard to give New York a 5-0 lead. The final: Yankees 5, Red Sox 4.

Seven-game winner Ellis Kinder was selected to

stop the Yankees in the second game. For four innings the righthander was in command, holding the Bombers to one run while the Red Sox piled up seven. In the fifth, however, Kinder walked Rizzuto and Henrich with two outs. DiMaggio then stepped up and belted a drive into the net in left-center field. Suddenly, Boston's substantial lead was cut in half.

Reliever Tex Hughson got Kinder out of trouble in the sixth, but his wildness created a major embarrassment in the seventh. He walked the bases full before Woodling doubled to tie the score, 7-7.

Earl Johnson, a sore-armed lefthander, succeeded Hughson and retired the first two batters in the eighth to bring up DiMaggio. Joe showed no more respect for the reliever than he had for the starter. His third home run in two days cleared the net in left field and bounced onto the street beyond as 29,563 fans cheered in admiration. The blow was the decisive run in the Yankees' 9-7 victory, which was credited to Page for three scoreless innings of relief.

The Boston reporters swarmed the Yankees' clubhouse after the game, hoping to learn of some untold strength within the dominating DiMaggio. "You say you had only eight workouts, then you rip our boys to pieces," one newsman said to Joe. "How do you do it?"

"Just go up and swing, and manage to hit the ball," DiMaggio replied. "There is, of course, no skill involved."

Mel Parnell, trying for his 11th win, was McCarthy's choice to start the series finale. In the third inning, the lefthander allowed the Yanks to tie the game, 1-1, on two walks, a single and a wild pitch. An inning later he surrendered two runs, but the Red Sox narrowed the lead to 3-2 with a tally in the sixth.

Stirnweiss and Henrich started a New York rally in the seventh with back-to-back singles. Up stepped DiMaggio, who had been hit by a pitch, grounded into a double play and walked. Joltin' Joe worked the count to 3 and 2, then teed off again. The drive was his most savage of the series. The ball crashed into the left-field light tower and rebounded onto the field for a three-run homer. Once again, his homer won the game for the Yankees, who prevailed, 6-3, for Raschi's 12th victory.

Unquestionably, DiMaggio was back, as superlative as ever. Even without sufficient training and complete strength, he cracked four home runs and a single, drove in nine runs and handled 13 fielding chances flawlessly in the series.

Everyone wondered how far in front the Yankees would have been if Joe had begun his heroics on opening day. "Well, what interests me is this—how are the other contenders going to take Joe's return?" Stengel mused. "They won't like it too much, will they?

"Babe Ruth alone could match Joe's flair for drama, for putting on a show and responding to an occasion. And not even Ruth would have put on the kind of demonstration DiMaggio staged here. Eight workouts, and then, socko, four homers. . . . The man is a pro."

The teams renewed their rivalry in a Fourth of July doubleheader at Yankee Stadium. The Red Sox now trailed by 10 games, and the Yankees quickly made it 12 by sweeping the twin bill. The Red Sox might have fared better except for a freak development that cost them one run and mystified the spectators and, for an instant, umpire Joe Paparella.

With the Yanks leading, 3-2, in the ninth inning, Boston loaded the bases with one out. Al Zarilla was at bat when, without warning, dark clouds swept across the sky and obscured the sun. A strong wind then swirled through the stadium, whipping up a dust storm that almost hid DiMaggio in center field.

Raschi fired a pitch homeward and Zarilla stroked a hit into right field. At third base, Johnny Pesky peered through the dust cloud, trying to determine whether Mapes caught the ball. Without a sign from his coaches, Pesky tagged up and broke for home. Mapes' throw beat him easily and Berra touched the plate for a forceout.

But Paparella thought the tying run had scored ahead of Pesky, and called Johnny safe with the go-ahead run. When he checked the bases, however, he discovered they still were loaded and reversed his call. Bobby Doerr flied out to end the game.

In the press box, Tommy Connolly, the chief of the A.L. umpiring staff, said he never had seen such a play in more than 50 years of umpiring and watching baseball.

The Yankees' comfortable lead began to shrivel after the All-Star Game. In one stretch the Red Sox won 19 of 23 games, and they compiled a 24-8 record in August. By Labor Day, Boston trailed New York by only 1½ games.

"Weakness" was not a word in Boston's vocabulary. When the A.L. leaders' statistics were published in the newspapers, Red Sox were at the top of the lists. As September began, four-time batting champion Ted Williams led the league with 170 hits and a .355 batting average. Center fielder Dom DiMaggio, who had a 34-game hitting streak halted by Raschi on August 9, was fourth in hits, 162, and average, .321. In the RBI category, shortstop Vern Stephens led the league with 140 while Williams followed with 138. In home runs, the Splendid Splinter led Stephens, 36 to 35.

Boston's pitching was just as strong. Parnell already had 20 victories, and Kinder's 17-5 record topped the league in winning percentage. Joe Dobson and Chuck Stobbs gave Boston another two solid starters with 22 victories between them. Dur-

The 1949 Yankees were in a festive, singing mood after beating the Boston
Red Sox on the final day and capturing the A.L. pennant.

ing the August surge, the staff pitched 22 complete games.

At the same time, the Yankees encountered another rash of injuries.

The most damaging blows occurred in an August 28 doubleheader in Chicago. Henrich, playing right field, fractured two lumbar vertebrae when he crashed into the wall while chasing a fly ball in the first game. He was out for three weeks.

In the second game, newly acquired slugger Johnny Mize dislocated his shoulder in a play at first base. Big Jawn, obtained from the Giants to play first base, was sidelined for the rest of the season, except for seven pinch-hit appearances.

Just before those injuries, Berra suffered a broken thumb when he was hit by a pitch, putting him out for a month. In Philadelphia, Bauer slipped in the outfield and wrenched his back, good for a one-week stint on the sideline. DiMaggio also was lost briefly when he sprained his left shoulder. At the same time, pitcher Porterfield's comeback was halted when he suffered his third arm injury of the year.

Fortunately for New York, its other pitchers

stayed healthy. Reynolds recorded 10 straight victories on his way to a 16-4 record, and Byrne won five straight to recover from midseason troubles. Lopat won seven in a row through July and August, and Raschi continued on course toward his 20th win. Most impressive was Page. The league's top relief specialist earned his 11th victory on August 13 and showed the same coolness under pressure that had paced the Yankees to their title in 1947. "There are two things that make Page a great relief pitcher," Stengel said. "First, he's got a great arm. Second, he's got a great heart."

As Henrich recovered in the hospital, he speculated that the hustle in the Yankees' lineup had some bearing on the length of the injury list. "I suppose it has been written a hundred times that the 1949 Yankees have been hit harder by injuries and illnesses than any other club in the history of the American League," Henrich said. "However, why all these injuries? You say the tension of the race and the ages of some of our men are the major factors.

"That is not the complete diagnosis. Though I will say that after having been picked quite generally to finish no better than third, we felt ourselves challenged. I never saw a lot of players give out to the limit and hustle the way our men have played out their opportunities to the utmost."

Many observers, however, believed opportunity had knocked for the last time. And September 18, when DiMaggio was stricken with a form of pneumonia, they were convinced it had.

The last vestige of the Yanks' once-commanding lead disappeared September 25, when they bowed to Parnell, 4-1, at Boston.

The teams met the next day in New York before 66,156 fans. Again the Yankees went into battle with one shoe off, for DiMaggio still was ill. The Bombers lost, 7-6, when Boston rallied for four runs in the eighth inning. Doerr's squeeze bunt drove in Pesky with the deciding run, sparking a violent Yankee protest led by Stengel and catcher Ralph Houk. They insisted Pesky was tagged out and continued the dispute with umpire Bill Grieve after the game. Stengel's and Houk's remarks grew so offensive that A.L. President Will Harridge fined them $100 apiece. He slapped a $200 penalty on Mapes for reportedly asking Grieve, "So how much did you have on the game?"

The defeat dropped the Yankees out of the lead for the first time in the 161-day-old season.

The Red Sox held on to first as the race dwindled down to the final weekend of the season. With a two-game series set for Yankee Stadium, Boston, at 96-56, needed only one victory to win the pennant. The 95-57 Yanks, however, faced the necessity of sweeping the pair.

The first game, played Saturday, October 1, at-

tracted nearly 70,000 fans. They were there as much for "Joe DiMaggio Day" as they were for the critical nature of the game itself. Though still drained by his illness, Joe knew he was needed back in the Yankee lineup.

For an hour before the game, the Yankee Clipper was extolled by admirers bestowing gifts ranging from 300 quarts of ice cream to a speedboat. Joe even received a plaque containing the autographs of all the Boston players. When he finally stepped to the microphone, Joe told the crowd in simple eloquence:

"When I was in San Francisco, Lefty O'Doul (his manager) told me, 'Joe, don't let the big city scare you. New York is the friendliest town in the world.' This day proves it. I want to thank the fans, my friends, my manager, Casey Stengel, and my teammates, the gamest, fightingest bunch that ever lived. And I want to thank the good Lord for making me a Yankee."

From the emotional high of the DiMaggio ceremonies, the mood plummeted drastically when the Red Sox took a 4-0 lead behind Parnell, their 25-game winner.

After scoring once in the first inning, the Sox knocked out Reynolds when he gave up a single, three walks and another run in the third.

Ordinarily, Stengel would have disdained the use of Page so early in a game. But this was no ordinary contest. If the game was lost, the flag was lost. Tomorrow would be too late. The Old Perfessor waved to the bullpen and the redoubtable reliever started the long hike to the pitching mound, his jacket draped characteristically over his shoulder. It was his 60th appearance of the season.

Page was not the immediate solution. Still tight after a short warmup, he walked the first two batters to force in two more runs. But once he found his groove, he was virtually untouchable. He allowed only one hit, an eighth-inning single by Doerr, and twice retired Williams on pop flies to the infield.

The Yankees solved Parnell for two runs in the fourth inning on DiMaggio's ground-rule double, singles by Bauer and Lindell, and a sacrifice fly from Coleman. Four singles, including one by DiMaggio, and a double play netted two runs in the fifth inning off Parnell and Dobson to tie the score, 4-4.

The righthanded Dobson settled down for two innings and had two out in the eighth when Lindell strolled to the plate. The big Californian had not enjoyed a vintage season. He was batting .240 and had not hit a home run since July 31. In the past, Stengel often lifted Johnny because of his bad luck against righthanders, but this time, for some reason, the Old Perfessor let him bat. It was one of Casey's most sagacious decisions. Lindell ripped a fastball

The Boston Red Sox, led by Birdie Tebbetts (left) and Dom DiMaggio, make
the long trek to the locker room after losing the pennant-clinching season
finale to the Yankees.

One of the most controversial plays of the 1949 pennant race occurred on
September 26 when Boston's Johnny Pesky was called safe at the plate on
Bobby Doerr's squeeze bunt. The Yankee catcher was Ralph Houk.

into the left-field stands for his sixth home run of
the year to top the incredible comeback. After
being four runs down with six innings to play, the
Yankees had endured, 5-4.

The elated Yankees mobbed the two heroes in the
clubhouse. "I was long overdue," crowed Lindell.
Stengel lavished more praise on his prized reliever
Page. "He was wonderful," Casey said. "Before I
sent him in, I asked Joe, 'How far can you go?' and
he answered, 'A long way,' so I told him to get
going and he did."

The season was now compressed into a single day.

The managers chose their most proficient righthanders for the showdown. McCarthy nominated
Kinder, who had won his last 14 decisions for a 23-5
record. Stengel countered with Raschi, who, in his
last start, won his 20th game for the first time in his
career.

Kinder was thrown into a first-inning predicament through no fault of his own. Rizzuto's leadoff
fly to left field fell untouched when Williams was
blinded by the sun. By the time Ted retrieved the
ball, the Scooter was on third base. He scored on
Henrich's slow hopper to second.

Thereafter, Kinder was superb. But so was Raschi
and the Yankees still led, 1-0, when Kinder was lifted for a pinch-hitter in the eighth. Parnell, making
his second appearance in as many days, relieved as
Henrich led off for the Yankees. Tommy pulled
Parnell's second pitch into the right-field seats and
68,055 New York diehards breathed more easily.
When Berra singled, McCarthy quickly summoned
the righthanded Hughson to pitch to DiMaggio. Tex
forced the Jolter to ground into a double play, but
he then yielded singles to Lindell and Billy Johnson.
A walk to Mapes loaded the bases and brought up
Coleman, a pesky hitter batting .275 in his rookie

season. The second baseman, a Marine bomber
pilot in World War II, already had 122 hits to his
credit, but none was as crucial as the one he was
about to deliver. He poked a tantalizing flare over
the head of second baseman Doerr for a bases-clearing double.

Coleman's wrong-field blooper assumed heroic
proportions when the Red Sox struck back in the
ninth. A one-out walk to Williams, a single by Stephens and Doerr's triple over DiMaggio's head netted two runs as Yankee fans squirmed in fear that
Raschi would squander the big lead.

As Al Zarilla walked toward the plate, DiMaggio,
still weak and shaky from his illness, strolled in
from center field. Later he explained: "I should
have removed myself on Stephens' single. And
when I didn't catch Doerr's triple, which was catch-
able, I didn't hesitate any longer. . . . I didn't want
to hurt the club by falling on my face if another fly
had been hit to me." Woodling was sent to left, with
Mapes shifting to center and Bauer to right.

With Doerr on third base and still only one out,
Raschi retired Zarilla on an outfield fly. But a single
by Billy Goodman drove in Doerr, making the
score 5-3, and Birdie Tebbetts stepped up representing the tying run. The best effort from the No. 8
batter was a pop foul that plopped into Henrich's
mitt behind first base. The Yankees were A.L.
champions for the 16th time.

The sight of Henrich squeezing the final out produced an unusual, if typically painful, reaction on
the Yankee bench. Coach Bill Dickey, a veteran of
eight World Series, leaped jubilantly from his seat
and struck his head against the dugout roof. The
former catcher was knocked unconscious. After
more than 70 incapacitating injuries that year,
Dickey's somehow seemed like a fitting conclusion.

Astros Hold Off
Late Dodger Rush

The Houston Astros had just whipped the St. Louis Cardinals behind a 14-hit attack that included three singles by Jose Cruz and a grand slam by Cesar Cedeno. The players were jabbering gleefully in the clubhouse when the reporters started pouring through the door.

The journalists headed straight for Cruz—then right past him. Cedeno was the Astro they wanted.

The player whose only hit had accounted for four runs made for better copy than the one who had the most hits, they believed.

As Cruz surveyed the knot of writers around his teammate, his expression mirrored the rejection he felt. It was not a new sensation for the 33-year-old Puerto Rican. Regardless of his achievements, others drew public attention, others gave the interviews.

The condition had existed almost from the day he earned his badge as a Houston regular. One eastern writer, more perceptive than his colleagues, labeled Jose the "Invisible Superstar" in recognition of his transparent image and remarkable accomplishments.

Outside of Texas, Jose's totals were written on unturned pages. Over five years in Houston, Cruz had quietly averaged .296, 70 runs batted in a season and 30 annual stolen bases. Others, with inferior statistics, were receiving greater acclaim, primarily because they labored in the media mainstream of the nation.

Year by year, Cruz was passed over as the National League All-Star squad was selected. That oversight was rectified in 1980, but even then it was a hollow distinction. Jose was permitted to savor the N.L.'s 4-2 victory from the privacy of the Dodger Stadium dugout.

Despite Cruz's glittering performances in the late 1970s, the Astros fell short of similar attainments. No symbols of excellence adorned their trophy case, no championship banners graced the Astrodome. Since they were born as the Colt .45s in 1962, they had finished above .500 only three times. Twice they had forged into second place in the N.L. West Division, most recently in 1979, when they finished 1½ games behind the Cincinnati Reds. The Astros were in first from May 30 to August 27 before battling the Reds down the stretch.

In the weeks following the near-miss, the Astros

After a career of anonymity, baseball's vast spotlight finally focused on Jose Cruz and the Houston Astros in 1980.

made two significant additions. They acquired pitcher Nolan Ryan and second baseman Joe Morgan, two native sons who were well-established among the game's elite.

Ryan, from nearby Alvin, Tex., had fired a baseball that was clocked at more than 100 mph, and his string of strikeout records testified to his blinding speed. The 33-year-old righthander became baseball's highest-paid pitcher by signing a four-year, $4 million contract after gaining his free agency from the California Angels.

Morgan was a native of Bonham, Tex., but grew up in Oakland, Calif. The little second baseman had played with Houston from 1964 to 1971, when he was traded to Cincinnati. With the Reds, Joe blossomed into superstardom. He won the Most Valuable Player award in 1975 and 1976 as he led the team to two world championships. Now he was back, and the Astros were hopeful that Joe could work his inspirational magic on the club that Bill Virdon would lead into the 1980 race.

Virdon, entering his fifth full season as the Astros' skipper, relished the notion of Ryan fogging his fastball past batters one day, Joe Niekro frustrating them the next with his tantalizing knuckleball, J.R. Richard, another fireballer, blowing them away the third day and Ken Forsch baffling opponents the fourth day with his varied arsenal. If the starters needed relief, Virdon had Joe Sambito, one of the game's most effective firemen.

When a fifth starter was required, Virdon could call on veteran righthander Vern Ruhle or two-time N.L. All-Star Joaquin Andujar. After undergoing back surgery in May 1979, Ruhle had returned to pitch at the end of the season before leading his winter team to the league championship in Puerto Rico. Andujar had demanded to be traded in the final days of the '79 season after he was pulled from the rotation. Still, the spirited Dominican won 12 games.

"We made great strides during the 1979 season, and the pennant race provided some experience for us," Virdon announced during spring training at Cocoa, Fla. "That should make us a better club in 1980. . . . If we get good offensive production and pitching, we'll be legitimate contenders."

The manager was unconcerned about Ryan's shabby exhibition showing because he knew there was substance in the pitcher's often-repeated remark: "If I ever had to make a club on the basis of my spring training performances, I'd never succeed."

Ryan had won 16 games with the Angels in 1979 and had captured his seventh A.L. strikeout crown. For the Astros, Niekro had won 21, Richard 18 while leading the league in strikeouts, and Forsch 11, despite a month on the disabled list. Sambito finished fourth in the league with 22 saves.

J.R. Richard was at his fireballing best midway through the 1980 season when he raised his arm in triumph after blanking the Chicago Cubs.

Morgan enhanced a regular lineup that included Art Howe, Denny Walling and Dave Bergman at first base, Craig Reynolds at shortstop, Enos Cabell at third base, Cruz, Cedeno, Terry Puhl and Jeff Leonard in the outfield, and Alan Ashby and Luis Pujols behind the plate.

The Astros' game conditioning suffered a setback —along with every other team's—when a general player strike wiped out the final week of the exhibition season. While the interruption was lamented widely, it proved little more than an inconvenience to Houston's hurlers.

The dominating pitching that Virdon had anticipated surfaced as soon as the 162-game schedule got underway. Richard and Forsch won their first four decisions, and Niekro won four of his first five. The 6-foot-8 Richard, who had hurled 19 complete games the previous campaign, was especially brilliant against the Dodgers. In the season opener, he pitched seven perfect innings before yielding his first hit. In his second appearance against Los Angeles, James Rodney allowed only one hit, an infield single by Reggie Smith.

The superlative performances extended Richard's

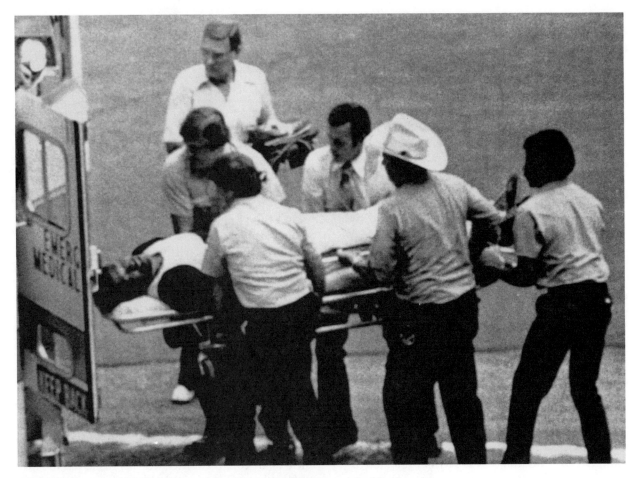

Misfortune struck J.R. Richard and the Houston Astros on July 30 when the big righthander was rushed to the hospital after suffering a major stroke.

winning streak over the Dodgers to 13 games and lowered his career earned-run average against them to 1.94.

In his first three outings, J.R. pitched 22 innings, allowed seven hits and struck out 32 batters. Richard wasn't surprised by his overpowering start. "My rhythm has never been this good early in the season," he explained. "I wore out two or three mirrors just practicing my delivery during the winter."

Richard was flying, and so were the Astros after J.R. outpitched Tom Seaver of the Reds and hoisted the Texans into first place on April 30. Nobody expected the pitcher's dizzying pace to continue—and it didn't. At Montreal on May 5, Richard lasted only one-third of an inning. Five hits and a walk produced four runs and handed J.R. the first of three straight losses. Thereafter, the 30-year-old star regained his stride and won six of his next seven decisions.

J.R.'s rebound was particularly timely because the Astros were struggling at the plate. While losing 12 of 17 games during Richard's slump, Houston's team batting average plunged 20 points. Virdon employed 29 different lineups in the first 40 games

while trying to discover a combination that would produce runs. Fortunately for the Astros, the pitching staff's ERA remained below 3.00. And when they did reach base, the runners often advanced on their own. Cedeno, Morgan, Puhl, Cruz, Cabell, Leonard, Reynolds and supersub Rafael Landestoy had a green light to steal on their own. Through July, the Astros swiped 84 bases while being caught 34 times.

Richard's 10-4 record and 1.89 ERA in early July kindled predictions of a truly memorable season. Twenty-five to 30 wins were a distinct possibility, a Cy Young Award a definite reality.

"He's the best righthander in the league, easy," said his good friend Cabell. "And J.R. gets better when the weather gets hot. If he's this good now, what's he gonna do when it gets hot?"

At the peak of Richard-mania, however, warning signals sounded in the Astrodome. In years past, the rugged fellow had seldom missed a start or left a game because of physical ailments. Now he complained of an arm that was stiff, weak or tired, and back pains when he threw his slider. Richard had been forced to leave a June 17 game against the Cubs because of a "dead arm" after five innings. He didn't pitch for 11 days, but when he returned, against the Reds, he exited after 3⅓ innings. "The arm's fine. I anticipate no more problems," Richard insisted. But in 16 starts, J.R. had left early three times with a sore back, three with a stiff shoulder and three with a weak forearm.

As the All-Star Game approached, J.R. told reporters there was "no way" he could pitch in the midseason classic. Not only did he pitch, he started the game and hurled two shutout innings as the National League won, 4-2, for its ninth consecutive triumph.

"I felt great, my arm felt great, I would have liked to have pitched longer," said the enigmatic right-hander, who was limited to the short term at Virdon's request.

While in Los Angeles, J.R. consulted the Dodgers physician, Dr. Frank Jobe. The famed orthopedic surgeon found nothing clinically wrong with Richard's arm. But when J.R. returned to Houston he announced: "Dr. Jobe told me not to pitch for 30 days. I'm going fishing."

The Astros hadn't heard a word from Jobe. When they finally reached him, they learned he had said no such thing. "That's just something I told y'all," Richard explained.

With the contradiction resolved, Richard started against the Atlanta Braves on July 14 and showed flashes of his old form. In the second inning, he fanned Gary Matthews, Bob Horner and Jeff Burroughs in succession.

Still, revealed one observer, something was wrong. While his fastball still blistered, Richard's movements were sluggish. He had difficulty seeing the catcher's signs.

When his teammates took the field at the start of the fourth inning, the pitcher remained seated in the dugout. He returned to the mound only when Virdon prodded him into action.

Richard retired the first Atlanta batter. When he covered first on the next play, he was through. He walked off the hill because, a club spokesman said, he had a stomach ache.

Later, the hurler said he felt nauseated and asked to be removed. He offered the explanation while munching fried chicken, meat balls and rice smothered with gravy.

The next afternoon, J.R. met with General Manager Tal Smith for an hour. The two had "a positive general discussion," Smith said. The pitcher also conferred with Virdon for 30 minutes. This session, reported the manager, was "congenial."

The next evening, Richard tossed lightly on the sideline and was placed on the 21-day disabled list.

Richard's problem was as puzzling to club officials as it was to the pitcher. "People have to understand this is new to J.R.," said Smith. "It's the first arm trouble he's ever had."

Virdon attributed Richard's contradictory remarks to "something physically wrong and it's bothering him."

The source of Richard's trouble was discovered during a three-day examination at a Houston hospital. A circulatory problem was restricting the flow of blood to the pitcher's right arm, sapping it of strength.

Physicians recommended that Richard's workouts be closely supervised by Jim Ewell, former trainer of the Astros. On July 30, J.R. ran one lap around the field at the Astrodome, pitched for about 12 minutes, then went to the outfield to test his arm with long throws. After about 10 such heaves, he collapsed. Richard was rushed to the hospital, where a blood clot in his neck was removed in emergency surgery. He was a victim, doctors agreed, of "a major stroke."

The loss of Richard for the rest of the season placed an additional burden on Ryan and Forsch at a time they could ill afford the extra weight. After Forsch's 8-5 start and Ryan's 5-5 beginning, neither won a game for more than 40 days. Forsch even tried a variety of home cures to reverse the trend.

"I changed my breakfast food and I changed what I ate for lunch," he said. "I changed what I wore. Nothing worked. I finally took it out on my wife—I made her go to New York on a trip."

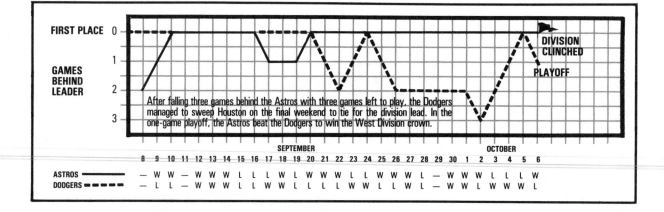

After falling three games behind the Astros with three games left to play, the Dodgers managed to sweep Houston on the final weekend to tie for the division lead. In the one-game playoff, the Astros beat the Dodgers to win the West Division crown.

The dry spell was broken when Ryan beat the San Francisco Giants in his first start in August to raise his record to 6-8. Two days later, Forsch defeated the same team to square his record at 9-9.

When Richard went down, the Astros held a fingertip grip on first place with a 56-44 record. Over the next two weeks, they briefly slipped to second behind the Dodgers for one day, and then occupied third behind the Dodgers and Reds before snapping back.

Los Angeles already had been in first for three weeks when the Astros slipped in late May. After leading the division around the All-Star break, the Dodgers never fell more than 3½ games behind.

When the season opened, few observers had given the Dodgers a chance with six rookies on their roster. But first-year pitcher Steve Howe emerged as Manager Tom Lasorda's bullpen stopper while starters Jerry Reuss (11-4), Burt Hooton (10-3) and Bob Welch (9-6) rivaled Houston's lauded front line going into August. Anchoring the L.A. offense was right fielder Reggie Smith, who was on a tear with 15 home runs, 55 RBIs and a .322 average, and left fielder Dusty Baker, who had 19 homers and 63 RBIs.

The defending-champion Reds were not counted out, despite the loss of key members of their pitching rotation. Seaver was placed on the disabled list for the first time in his career and missed all of July. At the same time, 10-game winner Frank Pastore was disabled with tendinitis in the middle finger of his pitching hand, and Bill Bonham was plagued by shoulder trouble. But like the Dodgers, the Reds were always close, falling no more than 5½ games behind.

Though the Astros had lost only Richard to injury, the pitching staff was badly frayed as the second half of the season unfolded. Cedeno, .301 and 42 RBIs; Cruz, .308 and 57 RBIs; Puhl, .275 and 10 home runs, and Walling, .310, were leading the offense. Clutch hits and solid defense were returning after a midseason drought. The bullpen of Sambito, 6-1, 2.17 ERA and 10 saves; Frank LaCorte, 7-3, 2.08 ERA, nine saves; Dave Smith, 1.86 ERA, five saves, and Bert Roberge was outstanding. But the relievers were dead tired. In five weeks, they pitched in all but three games. Between July 1 and August 17, the starters completed only six games.

On August 24, Virdon decided that a policy change was mandatory. "I'm giving Nolan Ryan the ball tonight," the skipper announced, "and unless he gets hurt, he's going nine innings."

When Ryan arrived at the Astrodome that evening, he found a sign tacked over his locker. It read: "Go Nine," and was signed, "The Bullpen."

Ryan did as ordered. He not only went the route, but he held the Chicago Cubs to two hits and posted the Astros' 10th straight victory, tying a club rec-

Joe Morgan, a veteran of Cincinnati's Big Red Machine pennant winners of the mid-1970s, helped the Astros discover how to win.

ord.

"I read what Bill said," commented Ryan. "I saw the sign. I figured they meant it."

Ryan's nine-inning performance provided a welcome respite for the weary firemen. During the streak, the relievers had shut out the opposition in 37⅔ innings and wrapped up overtime victories of 20, 17 and 12 innings.

When Ryan suffered back spasms and Forsch struggled at the end of the month, Virdon brought Andujar and Ruhle into the rotation. Both responded magnificently. Andujar pitched 19 consecutive scoreless innings and Ruhle improved his record to 8-3 with a shutout over the Cubs on August 30.

Andujar, who had threatened to go to Yugoslavia earlier in the season, remained disillusioned by the situation in Houston. "I just wish Bill Virdon would give me the ball and let me pitch every fourth or fifth day," Joaquin groused. "It seems I only get to pitch when someone is hurt. I've been in Bill Virdon's doghouse all year...."

"He can't be in my doghouse because I don't have a doghouse," Virdon countered. "Performance dictates whether someone pitches or plays."

The Astro whose playing defined performance was Cruz. Jose's first career grand slam clinched a doubleheader sweep of St. Louis on September 6.

Four nights later, he crashed a 12th-inning homer to beat the Dodgers. The veteran outfielder was among the league's top five in batting and led the Astros in hits, game-winning hits, RBIs and runs scored.

"Maybe in the past I've been booed sometimes, but the fans have been good to me this year," Jose said.

And for good reason. "Jose has been our most consistent player, both offensively and defensively," Virdon said.

With 18 games remaining on the schedule, the Astros and Dodgers shared first place with 82-62 records. On September 17, Virdon's club embarked on its most grueling trip of the year, nine consecutive games at Cincinnati, San Francisco, San Diego and Atlanta. At the same time, the Dodgers played the same four clubs at home.

The unfavorable schedule did not dismay Morgan. Before the first game, which the Astros lost,

7-0, to Mario Soto and the Reds, the perpetual optimist declared: "I think we're going to win it because . . . we're the best team. Our club has a lot of character. We've overcome adversity all year. We lost our lead a couple of times, and the toughest thing to do is to get back in first place after you've been knocked out. But we did it. That took character. We lost not only our best pitcher, but the best pitcher in baseball (Richard), and we could have quit, but we didn't. That's character."

Morgan's spirit infected his teammates. When they returned home, they could look back on five victories and only four defeats.

The Dodgers, meanwhile, were trying to stay close. After winning 17 of 20 games in late August

The Astros drew first blood in the 1980 playoff when Terry Puhl jarred the ball loose from Dodger catcher Joe Ferguson while scoring a first-inning run.

to storm back into the lead, Los Angeles was hit with a series of injuries. Outfielders Smith, Rick Monday and rookie Pedro Guerrero were out. Shortstop Bill Russell was gone for the year after a wild pitch fractured a finger on his right hand. Third baseman Ron Cey also was struck on the hand and sidelined.

One day, after misfortune had done its worst, Davey Lopes checked the batting order with its numerous rookies and commented, "You look at this lineup and you'd say, 'No way that team can win the pennant.' Well, you know, we might anyway."

Considering their crippled condition, the Dodgers did well to win four of nine games on their home stand. With nine games to go, they trailed by only one length.

But now it was the Dodgers' turn to hit the road to San Diego and San Francisco while the Astros entertained Cincinnati and Atlanta at home. In many instances, a split of the six road games would have satisfied Lasorda's club. Not this time, however, because the Astros won five of six to take a three-game lead before traveling to Los Angeles for the final three games of the season. One victory would clinch the first title in the history of the Houston organization.

The Dodgers needed to sweep the series to force a one-game playoff for the division championship. Los Angeles had won four of six meetings at home against Houston, but the season series was tied at seven games apiece. "At least we have a say in our destiny," reasoned first baseman Steve Garvey.

At least two factors gave the Dodgers a wisp of hope. Except for Russell and Smith, the regulars were in reasonably good health. And in the bullpen a reinforcement had recently arrived—a 19-year-old Mexican lefthander named Fernando Valenzuela. A brilliant future was predicted for the pudgy screwball artist.

Neither contender lacked confidence when the first act began October 3. A sign on the Los Angeles clubhouse door warned, "Anyone who doesn't think we can win four in a row, don't bother getting dressed."

The crowd of 49,642 was on its feet roaring before the first pitch. Usually noted for their laid-back attitude, the Dodgers' fans left little doubt that they were going to be a factor in the game.

After seven innings, the teams were deadlocked, 1-1, as veteran Don Sutton battled Forsch for the advantage. The Astros gained that edge in the eighth when Cedeno walked with one out, took third on Howe's single and scored on a sacrifice fly by Ashby, who had doubled and scored the first Houston run in the second inning.

The Astros were within two outs of the title when Monday tagged Forsch for a single, his third hit of the game. Baker then rapped a grounder to the

right side that might have produced the second out if Morgan had been playing second base. But Joe was on the bench with a sprained knee and Landestoy booted the ball for an error. The tying run scored moments later when Cey bounced a single up the middle.

Leading off the bottom of the 10th, catcher Joe Ferguson hit Forsch's first pitch for his ninth homer of the year and a 3-2 Dodger triumph. The rookie Valenzuela earned his second victory for two scoreless innings of relief.

"It's the biggest home run of my career," Ferguson crowed afterward, "but it's only the first leg of what we have to do." Reuss was given the chore of completing the second step. The Dodger hitters would have to do their part against the fireballing Ryan.

As in the series opener, the Astros outhit Los Angeles. But once again, they failed to clinch the division, chiefly because of Garvey's productive bat. Singles by Garvey, Guerrero and Derrel Thomas gave Reuss a 1-0 lead in the second inning, but the Astros tied the game in the fourth on a single by Cruz, a stolen base and Howe's single.

Garvey's 26th home run in the bottom of the inning completed the scoring, giving Reuss his 18th win and Ryan his 10th loss against 11 victories.

The Houston lead was shaved to one game. "We haven't lost our confidence," Virdon said. "Even if we lost all four (counting the playoff), our confidence wouldn't be affected."

"This team has a lot of character," Niekro said. "We'll battle to the end."

An Astro with abundant character was selected to start the crucial season finale. Just one year after back surgery, Ruhle had come back to win 12 games.

The righthander drew the assignment despite being the victim of a freak accident. A few days before, Ruhle snagged his right index finger on a nail while reaching for a towel in the dugout. Two stitches were required to close the gash.

The Dodgers gave the ball to Hooton, the University of Texas product who had won 14 games in his ninth full major league season.

Neither starter was long for the mound. Hooton was chased before he could retire a batter in the second inning. He was charged with two runs before he gave way to Bobby Castillo, who surrendered another run in the fourth.

Ruhle departed with none out in the third when his injured finger began to bleed. Andujar relieved and checked the Dodgers until the fifth, when three singles produced their first tally. They scored again off Sambito in the seventh, and entered the bottom of the eighth against LaCorte trailing, 3-2.

LaCorte, in his first season with the Astros, was making his 55th relief appearance of the year. He

One of the few bright spots for the Dodgers in the 1980 N.L. playoff game was Rick Monday's diving catch in the third inning.

already had won eight games, had yielded only three homers in 81 innings and owned a 2.77 ERA.

LaCorte opened the eighth by forcing Garvey to hit a hard grounder toward third. Cabell blocked it, but couldn't pick it up and the Dodger first baseman was aboard on an error.

Cey then stepped in with instructions to advance Garvey with a sacrifice. The third baseman had sacrificed only four times all year. He failed twice, fouling off two pitches, but ran the count to 3 and 2. Then he slammed a home run to give the Dodgers a 4-3 lead and create pandemonium among the 52,339 spectators.

The Astros threatened to tie the game in the ninth by placing runners on first and third with two out. Exit Steve Howe. Lasorda wigwagged for Sutton, the 21st Dodger thrown into the struggle. Making his first relief appearance after 31 starts, the righthander forced pinch-hitter Walling to ground into a game-ending out.

The Dodgers had swept the series. What had appeared a rank impossibility three days before had become a pulsating reality.

That elusive championship was fast slipping away from a frustrated Astro club. "It's been emotionally draining," Puhl said. "I knew it wasn't going to be easy. But I didn't think it was going to be this tough. . . ."

Sambito concurred. "You can't let them prey on your mind. But this has been tough."

One more game, awarded by a coin toss to Dodger Stadium, would affirm or refute Morgan's prophecy that "there's no way they can win four games . . . from us."

The Astros' hope to shatter the Dodgers' dream was Niekro, who had won his 19th game four days earlier against the Atlanta Braves. The 35-year-old knuckleball specialist had lost, 4-2, in his only other 1980 start against the Dodgers.

Lasorda's starter was Dave Goltz, a 31-year-old righthander who was completing his first season in

Dodger blue. Goltz, 7-10 for Los Angeles, had signed a six-year, $3 million contract after obtaining his free agency from Minnesota.

Goltz couldn't be blamed for a rocky start in the biggest game of his career. Puhl's leadoff grounder was fumbled by Lopes at second base. Puhl then scored the first run when Ferguson bobbled the throw on a close play at the plate. A second run scored on Cedeno's infield out.

Goltz shut out the Astros in the second inning and retired the first two batters in the third before Cedeno stroked a single. The next batter was Howe, the first baseman who would finish this game at third base.

The season had started dismally for the University of Wyoming graduate when Achilles tendon injuries in both legs hampered his spring training program. But the Pittsburgh native had bounced back and was batting in the .280s with nine home runs and 42 RBIs for the year.

One swing of Howe's bat increased all three figures and gave the Astros a 4-0 lead.

After Goltz was removed for a pinch-hitter in the third, relievers Rick Sutcliffe and Joe Beckwith surrendered three more in the fourth, including two that scored on Howe's single.

Considering Howe's three hits and four RBIs, the Astros might have harkened back to an early-season headline in The Sporting News and hummed a few bars of "How Great Howe Art."

The plush, seven-run lead was more than Niekro needed. He lost his shutout in the fourth when singles by Baker and Monday and an error by Cabell produced the lone Los Angeles tally. But he finished with a tidy six-hitter for his 20th win, the only National Leaguer besides Steve Carlton of the Philadelphia Phillies to gain that plateau.

By the slimmest of margins, the Western Division champions failed to win the National League pennant. They won two of the first three games against the Phillies in the League Championship Series,

Astros ace Joe Niekro proclaimed his team No. 1 after recording his 20th victory with a 7 - 1 playoff decision over the Dodgers.

both in extra innings. But the 11-inning, 1-0 victory in Game 3 proved costly when Cedeno, trying to beat a double-play relay, stepped awkwardly on first base and dislocated his right ankle.

Without their center fielder, the Astros led the next two games after seven innings, only to lose both in the 10th.

Cruz finally earned some long-overdue recognition by finishing third in the Most Valuable Player voting. Jose finished the season with a career-high 91 RBIs, 11 home runs, 185 hits, a .302 batting aver-

age and 36 stolen bases. Houston's pitching staff led the league with a 3.10 ERA, which set a team record, along with the club's 93 wins.

"We didn't get to the end of the rainbow," Sambito said. "But we proved a lot to ourselves.

"We've got much to be thankful for, much to be proud of. I'm not going to let the fact that we lost the playoffs get in the way of the success we had. We had a great year. We didn't achieve our goal. But every year, 25 or 26 teams in the major leagues don't achieve their goal. We got further than most."

Indians Capture First-Ever Pennant

Tris Speaker hit with authority, covered center field like a blanket and managed the Cleveland Indians to award-winning heights in 1920.

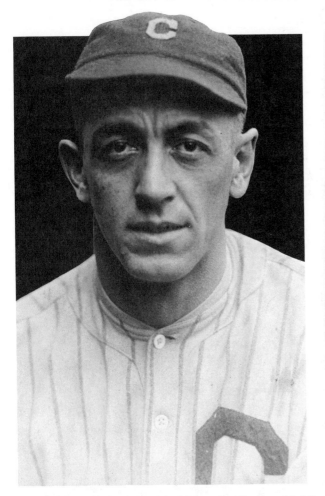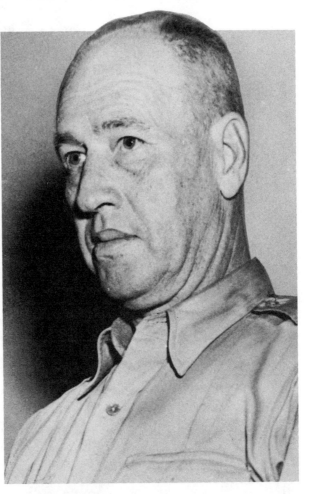

Ray Caldwell (left) joined holdover Jim Bagby (right) on a powerful Indians staff that also included Stan Coveleski.

Raymond Benjamin Caldwell was a slender right-hander known as much for his achievements with amber fluids as for his accomplishments on the pitching mound. After one classic bout with the bottle in 1916, "Slim" disappeared from the New York Yankees for weeks. He was discovered in Panama, playing in a small league under an assumed name.

No one questioned Caldwell's ability to pitch a baseball. He threw hard, had a devastating curve, good control and a graceful delivery. Moreover, Caldwell hit with authority. As a Yankee in 1915, he homered in three consecutive games, twice while pinch-hitting. He won 19 games that year, topping his previous career high of 17, set in 1914.

But the big fellow's after-hours capers drove managers to distraction. From New York, he moved on to Boston and then to unemployment. While his cash reserve rapidly dwindled in the summer of 1919, Slim sat home in Corydon, Pa., plotting his next move. Perhaps he would return to his job as a telegrapher, a career he abandoned when he entered professional baseball.

As he pondered his future, Slim received a letter from Tris Speaker, the newly appointed manager of the Cleveland Indians, inviting him to Cleveland to discuss a job.

The meeting between the player-manager and the 31-year-old hurler was richly productive. After Caldwell convincingly proved that his arm was fit, Speaker produced a prepared contract.

While economics surely convinced the pitcher to sign, Slim's confidants maintained that something even more powerful than money motivated him to close the deal. Longtime Cleveland sports editor Franklin (Whitey) Lewis recounted the bizarre anecdote in his 1949 book, "The Cleveland Indians."

"Read it carefully," Speaker counseled, handing him the contract.

Slim glanced at the salary. It matched what he had demanded for years and never received. He reached for a pen.

Speaker lifted a restraining hand. "Read all the terms of the contract," he advised.

Obediently, Caldwell read: "After each game he pitches, Ray Caldwell must get drunk. He is not to report to the clubhouse the next day. The second day he is to report to Manager Speaker and run around the ball park as many times as Manager Speaker stipulates. The third day he is to pitch bat-

The 1920 Indians expected a strong challenge from the Yankees, who featured diminutive Manager Miller Huggins and slugger Babe Ruth.

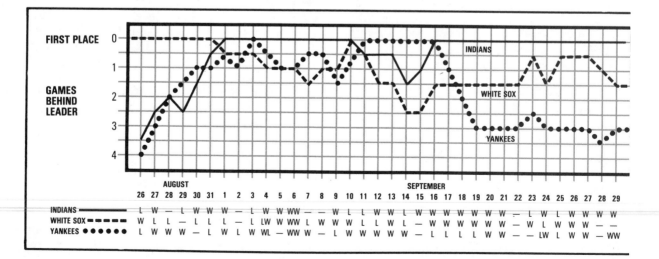

ting practice and the fourth day he is to pitch in a championship game."

Slim glanced up from the table. "You left out one word," he said. "Where it says I've got to get drunk after every game, the word 'not' has been left out. It should read that I'm 'not' to get drunk."

Speaker assured Slim that the stenographer had not erred. "It says you *are* to get drunk," Tris replied.

The terms were tailor-made for a pitcher with a powerful arm and a thirst to match. No agreement ever was signed more speedily. Slim's adherence to the unusual terms was not recorded. But in his first appearance with the Indians, something more potent than booze almost knocked Caldwell out of action—permanently.

On August 24, 1919, Caldwell started against the Philadelphia Athletics at Cleveland's League Park. Leading, 2-1, with two out in the ninth, Slim had a one-strike count on Jumping Joe Dugan.

As Caldwell prepared to deliver his next pitch, near tragedy struck. Henry P. Edwards, the Cleveland correspondent for The Sporting News, described the scene:

"The game was almost over when a thunderstorm blew up. Before players or spectators could scurry to cover, there came a series of lightning flashes and terrific sky cannonading. The bolts flashed here and there, causing much excitement. There was a blinding flash that seemed to set the diamond on fire, and Caldwell was knocked flat. His teammates rushed to him, fearing he might have been killed. But he struggled to his feet, and after frisking himself to see if he was all there, pitched what was left of the game before the rain became a downpour."

The redoubtable Slim won five of six decisions the rest of the year, including a 3-0 no-hitter against the Yankees at the Polo Grounds on September 10. One newsman reported that after being hit by the

bolt from above, Slim drank nothing stronger than iced tea.

Caldwell provided a hefty boost to the Indians' 1919 pitching staff, which included Stan Coveleski, 24-12, and Jim Bagby, 17-11. But the Tribe couldn't close the gap between them and the Chicago White Sox and finished as the runner-up for the second year in a row.

Fresh optimism permeated the club and its fans in the spring of 1920, particularly because of two factors—Speaker, everybody's favorite player, would be managing the entire season, and Caldwell, contented and clever, would be pitching from start to finish. Few observers disputed the popular notion that the Indians were going to win their first championship.

The strong mound corps would be working to Steve O'Neill, one of the league's top catchers and a big favorite with the fans. O'Neill, like Coveleski, came out of the Pennsylvania coal region. The scrapping catcher had three brothers who played in the major leagues.

Speaker also would rely on backups Les Nunamaker and Chet Thomas. Sizing up his catching staff, Tris bragged, "There are no second-string catchers—they're all first stringers."

Wheeler (Doc) Johnston, a .305 hitter in 1919, was the Tribe's regular first baseman until midseason, when George Burns was acquired from Philadelphia to ease the workload. A holdout by hard-hitting Joe Harris was met with indifference. Harris, who had won the first-base job midway through the previous year, was insulted by Cleveland's $5,000 contract offer after hitting .375. He spent the next two years in the Franklin-Oil City League.

Rounding out Cleveland's infield were Bill Wambsganss, a fixture at second base; Ray Chapman, an eight-year veteran who had hit .300 with 84 walks in 1919, at shortstop, and Larry Gardner, another .300 hitter, at third base.

Speaker, the majors' only player-manager, covered center field as it had never been covered before. He had batted above .300 in 10 of his 12 years in the majors—including .383 in 1912 and .386 in 1916—and set an A.L. outfielders record with 35 assists in 1909 and 1912. Speaker was flanked, as circumstances dictated, by Elmer Smith, Jack Graney, Charley Jamieson, Joey Evans or Smoky Joe Wood, who won 34 games for the Red Sox in 1912 before a dead arm forced a shift to the outfield.

The White Sox, managed by Kid Gleason, were expected to furnish the most formidable opposition. Chicago had the foremost pitching staff in the majors with Lefty (Claude) Williams, Dickie Kerr, Eddie Cicotte and Urban (Red) Faber. Few expected them to duplicate their performances of the past season, but each would win 20 or more games in

PENNANT CLINCHED

Although both the Indians and White Sox enjoyed seven-game winning streaks in September, Cleveland was able to profit from a subsequent seven-game losing streak by Chicago. The Yankees also were able to take the lead for a week and a half in September, thanks to a period in which they went 10-2, but it took only four straight losses to move New York back into third place.

OCTOBER
30 1   2   3
— LW W   L
— L   W   L

Yankee righthander Carl Mays threw the fateful pitch that temporarily dulled the 1920 pennant chase.

1920. The Sox boasted a potent hitting attack built around Eddie Collins, Shoeless Joe Jackson and Buck Weaver.

A vigorous challenge also was expected from the New York Yankees, in search of their first pennant ever. Third-year Manager Miller Huggins had three sterling pitchers in Carl Mays and Bob Shawkey, 20-game winners two times each, and Jack Quinn, a 15-game winner the year before. But a former pitcher named George Herman Ruth had captured the public fancy in 1919 by smacking a record 29 home runs. The 1920 Spalding Official Base Ball Record applauded the feat but noted, "Perhaps, and very likely, Ruth will not be so successful in 1920." The Babe had hammered 54 by year's end.

Throughout the league, players and executives alike picked the Indians as the pennant favorite. Connie Mack, winner of six championships at Philadelphia and regarded as a prophet by his contemporaries, announced his prediction with becoming modesty: "I'm picking the Indians and I generally pick the winner."

The Tall Tactician's forecast was affirmed by Duffy Lewis, Speaker's former teammate with the Boston Red Sox. Now an outfielder with the Yankees, Lewis visited the Tribe's training camp in New Orleans and assured his old friend, "The team that beats you out will win it."

Speaker shrank from the notion. "There you go, making it tough on me by saying we'll win," he responded in mock horror.

When Indians Owner Jim Dunn also succumbed to the wave of optimism and gave an exaggerated prediction to New Orleans reporters, Speaker took him aside. Speak carefully and with caution, Tris advised, lest the months ahead show the club—the boss included—in a bad light.

But Speaker was powerless to quell the enthusiasm of the Indians' fans. Despite bitter cold and pockets of ice and snow in the shade at League Park, 20,000 fans turned out on opening day, April 14. Coveleski pitched a five-hit, 5-0 shutout over the St. Louis Browns, struck out seven and contributed a single and double to the Tribe's 13-hit attack. Cleveland won six of its first seven games and occupied third place at the end of the month. When Coveleski beat the White Sox on May 9 for his seventh straight win, the Indians moved into first place for a long stay.

Except for two days in May, when they surrendered the lead to the fast-starting Boston Red Sox, and four days in July, when they yielded to the streaking Yankees, the Indians remained in first place into August.

Cleveland persevered in May and June when Coveleski left the team for two weeks upon his wife's unexpected death, and O'Neill took leave when his wife became ill after giving birth to twin daughters.

But "Covey" resumed his brilliant hurling when he returned and had a 17-7 record through July. That performance was topped by only one other A.L. pitcher—Jim Bagby, who had won 21 games and lost only five. Caldwell's comeback of 1919 carried over into '20 as Ray won 11 games in the first three months. Caldwell attributed his success to his regular spot in the rotation and Speaker's confidence in his game.

Spoke had compiled some impressive numbers of his own. The Gray Eagle led the major leagues with a .414 batting average and 153 hits in 370 at-bats. His 11 consecutive hits July 8-10 also established an A.L. record. Speaker set the pace for the rest of the Indians, who had combined for a .313 team average. Seven other regulars were hitting .300 or better: outfielders Jamieson, .343, Evans, .330, and Smith, .305; first baseman Johnston, .325; shortstop Chapman, .323; third baseman Gardner, .300, and catcher O'Neill, .317. The dominating offense helped the Indians thwart repeated threats by the Yankees and White Sox.

After starting the season in fourth place at 15-15, the Yankees had won 10 straight and 20 of their next 25 games to roar back into the pennant race. The Yanks' ascension was sparked by a slugging hitting attack and the anticipated top-notch pitching of Mays, 15-7, Shawkey, 12-6, and Collins, 9-4. The Babe had already swatted 37 home runs to break his record. Third baseman-outfielder Bob Meusel had 10 homers, 7 triples and 34 doubles; center fielder Ping Bodie had seven home runs and 10 triples, and shortstop Roger Peckinpaugh had eight home runs.

After losing a June series against Cleveland three games to one, the Yankees took seven of the next eight games against the Indians, including a four-game sweep August 9-13 at League Park.

That beating came just a month after Speaker had dismissed the Yankees as a flash in the pan.

"The Indians are the best club in the league, and I can't see how the White Sox or Yanks will beat them out of the pennant," Tris boasted. "You'll notice I mention Chicago first and New York second. Well, that's just the way I have doped them all along. I figured if the Sox had the harmony, they would be harder to beat than the Yanks.

". . . I don't want anyone to think I am overconfident, but I honestly believe we will be out in front by seven or eight games on the first of September. Then, well, they will have their work cut out for them to catch us."

The White Sox were cruising on a 43-21 clip since May, and they pulled even with the Yankees entering August. Chicago's hurlers were approaching 20-win seasons, and Shoeless Joe Jackson was hitting .392, with Eddie Collins at .354.

When the Indians left on their final eastern trip of the year, their 70-40 record placed them ahead of New York and Chicago, both at 72-42, by percentage points.

The Tribe arrived at the Polo Grounds in New York on Monday afternoon, August 16. Clouds hung low over the Harlem horseshoe at game time, and a light drizzle was spreading discomfort when Chapman led off the fifth inning. Chappie was enjoying a good year both on and off the field. Ray had married his wife, Kate, during the off-season

Cleveland shortstop Ray Chapman couldn't get out of the way of a Carl Mays pitch and became baseball's first on-field casualty.

and the couple were expecting their first child. Besides hitting over .300, Ray had played in his 1000th game as an Indian, tops on the team, and was considering retiring after the season.

Mays, a 26-year-old righthander on his way to a 26-11 record, was on the mound for the Yankees. The Kentuckian's submarine delivery struck fear in many batters. Mays released the ball near his shoetops, propelling it on an upward course toward the plate. Some said the deliveries that whistled close to a batter's head were not always accidental.

As was his custom, the righthanded Chapman, an adept bunter, assumed a crouched stance at the plate, his head hanging into the strike zone. If the pitch was high and tight, Chappie was ready to pull back at the last instant.

With a count of one ball and one strike, Mays took his sign from catcher Muddy Ruel and fired. The pitch, a fastball, sailed in toward the batter's head. Surely, Chappie would jerk back. But there was no hint of such a move. Chapman seemed to lean into the pitch, as if bunting, but then froze. A sickening thud sounded through the park as the ball crashed into his left temple. The ball bounded in front of the plate, where Mays, believing the pitch had struck the bat, fielded the ball and threw it to first.

Others knew differently. They saw Chappie take a few steps toward first, then collapse with blood spurting from both ears.

The Indians rushed to his aid and a doctor was summoned from the stands. After first-aid treatment, Chapman tried to walk to the dugout with the help of two teammates. He collapsed again and was rushed to St. Lawrence Hospital. Surgeons performed surgery immediately after discovering a skull fracture extending to the base of the brain. Speaker and a few others maintained an all-night vigil.

Shortly before 5 a.m. Tuesday, long after the Indians had beaten the Yankees, 4-3, a nurse informed them, "He's gone."

Out of respect for the memory of the popular shortstop, the Yankees postponed the August 17 game. The following day, Wally Pipp's two-run homer in the ninth inning gave New York a 4-3 victory, but Caldwell won the rubber game of the series, 3-2.

Mays was exonerated of all blame in the tragedy. The pitcher expressed shock and sorrow over the first fatality in baseball history.

"If I were not absolutely sure in my heart that it was an accident, pure and simple, I do not think I could stand it," he said. "I always have had a horror of hitting a player ever since the accident to Chick Fewster." That spring, Fewster, a Yankee infielder, was seriously injured when a pitch from the Brooklyn Superbas' Jeff Pfeffer fractured his skull.

"This fear affected my work," Mays continued. "In the early part of the season, I could not do my best. I kept (the pitches) on the outside because whenever I felt that the ball was going close to a batter's head, I saw a picture of poor Fewster lying beside the plate. I had to fight that down. I had to play the game.

"Poor Chapman was one of the hardest batters I know of to pitch to. He had a peculiar crouch. He bent low and his head was close to where a curve might break. Babe Ruth's batting position was like this.

"I have often dreaded pitching to Ray Chapman for that reason. As I remember it, the ball that I pitched was a straight one on the inside. While I was holding the ball, I felt a roughened place on it. This may have turned it into a 'sailer,' though it was not my intention to pitch it.

"I confidently expected that Chapman would be able to gauge the ball. Even when he dropped I thought that he had ducked, as Babe Ruth often ducked from a ball that takes this kind of a twist. I had my mind on the game and when the ball rolled out to me, I automatically fielded it, thinking that it had struck his bat. But when I turned to throw to first base, I had a horrible sensation that something was wrong."

Speaker, a good friend of Chapman's, said the Indians were not blaming Mays for their teammate's death. "I consider it a pure accident," he said. "Any attempt to create animosities or bitterness out of this would be unfair to the game of baseball. Also, it would be unfair to the memory of the dead boy, my friend, who was a square player, a square man and a true sportsman."

With the cooperation of the Red Sox, the game in Boston on August 20 was postponed to permit the Indians to attend Chapman's funeral in Cleveland. One day later, they returned to the East Coast for a doubleheader at Fenway Park. Harry Lunte, a second-year utility infielder, took over at shortstop for the Indians. While Lunte was solid defensively, he had hit only .195 a year ago and lacked the leadership spark of his predecessor.

During the off-season, some writers had speculated that the Indians would acquire shortstop Everett Scott. Had the club done so, Speaker would have had one of the majors' top fielders and a .270 hitter to plug into the regular lineup. Scott had announced his desire to leave the Red Sox for the Indians and join former Boston teammates Speaker, Wood, Gardner, Nunamaker and Pinch Thomas. But with Chapman, a better hitter, electing to play another year, Cleveland wasn't eager to trade for a part-time player.

Looking back at the story in the October 30, 1919, issue of The Sporting News, the sadness of Chapman's death assumed an eerie, ominous quality. The report was headlined, "Scott Would Like to be with Old Pals/But With Chapman Alive, There's No Place for Him."

Appearing listless and ill at ease, the mentally burdened Indians bowed meekly to Waite Hoyt and Herb Pennock in the twin bill at Boston. They failed to score a run and collected only three hits in each game.

"It would have been strange had it happened otherwise," a Cleveland sportswriter reported.

The doubleheader loss dropped the Indians into

second place behind Chicago, which had won 10 of its last 12 games with overpowering pitching. In the 10 victories, the Chicago staff surrendered only 23 runs while the offense produced 53.

After the Indians lost two of three more games in Boston, they entrained for Philadelphia, ordinarily an oasis for visiting teams. This time, however, the last-place Athletics scored two one-run victories before Cleveland exploded in a 15-3 rout.

The tourists moved on to Washington for the final four games of the trip. Cleveland split the first two games and fell to third place behind the Sox and Yankees. Caldwell then won his 17th game, however, and the Indians were back in second, just one-half game behind Chicago, which had lost four in a row.

Speaker examined his overworked starting staff and decided to call on a newcomer for the trip finale. Just days ago, team President Jim Dunn gave up pitchers Tony Faeth and Dick Niehaus for a tall lefthander who had won 18 games for Sacramento of the Pacific Coast League.

He was John Walter Mails, a former shipyard worker and Army machine gunner in World War I. Mails was no stranger to the major leagues. In 1915-16 he had labored for Wilbert Robinson's band of madcaps in Brooklyn. Though John Walter worked only 22 innings over both seasons, he acquired a nickname that would remain with him the rest of his days. He was christened "Duster" because of his penchant for knocking batters into the dirt with his high, inside pitches.

Tales of John Walter's irregular behavior swirled about him. He liked to refer to himself as "The Great Mails," a legend he attached to his car's license plate. At times he would halt the game at a critical juncture and tell the hushed crowd precisely what he would do to the next batter. Occasionally,

When the Indians needed late-season help to nail down the 1920 American League pennant, shortstop Joe Sewell (left) and pitcher Walter Mails (below) came to the rescue.

he made good on his boast.

Duster's A.L. debut did nothing to enhance his self-proclaimed greatness. He was gone in less than two innings. After yielding three runs, three hits and two walks, he gave way to Guy Morton with nobody out in the second. Morton, again showing signs of the form that produced 14 wins in 1918, allowed only five hits the rest of the game as Cleveland won, 9-5. Combined with Chicago's 6-2 loss to Boston, the Indians were back in first place.

Mails' lackluster bow, reported the Cleveland correspondent of The Sporting News, "probably didn't mean a lot as the best of them are hammered now and then. If Mails is anything like the pitcher he is touted to be, he will yet prove of value."

Mails was given another chance and, indeed, proved his value. He pitched the morning game of a Labor Day doubleheader and hurled the Indians to a 7-2 win over the St. Louis Browns.

The victory was blighted, however, when Lunte injured his leg, forcing Speaker to move Evans from the outfield to shortstop. It was apparent that Evans was only a stopgap, not the solution to a problem that could spoil a successful bid for the pennant.

Speaker remembered a stocky kid he had seen with the New Orleans Pelicans during spring training. Spoke was unimpressed with the University of Alabama graduate at that time. But the youngster now was batting .289 in the Southern Association and he was, after all, a shortstop, which was more than Speaker had available.

Although the Indians had options on all New Orleans players, the Pelicans were reluctant to release the shortstop. Only when the Indians agreed to pay $6,000 and grant New Orleans first recall rights on other players next spring was Joe Sewell ordered to join the A.L. club.

Sewell made his major league debut September 10. Replacing Evans in a 6-1 loss to the Yankees — the first of two in a three-game series — Sewell committed an error and went hitless in two at-bats. It was the type of debut that inspired a Cleveland writer to type, "We can only pray that Harry Lunte will recover rapidly."

Lunte recovered but never regained his job. Sewell rapped 10 hits in his next 22 at-bats to win over the doubting critics. Joe started his first game at shortstop on September 12 and smacked a single and triple against Philadelphia to help Mails register a 5-2 victory, one of seven for the unbeaten left-hander that season. Sewell collected 23 hits en route to a .329 batting average in his abbreviated rookie campaign.

The reinforcements arrived none too soon for Speaker. The Yankees had won 12 of their last 16 games, including the two victories over the Indians, and trailed by only percentage points, .6194 to

.6187. When the Yanks won their next two games against the Detroit Tigers, they moved into first place by half a game with an 88-53 record. Their situation, however, was precarious.

In an exhibition game the week before against the Pittsburgh Pirates, New York lost two regulars to injury when Ruel split a finger and Bodie sprained an ankle. Those injuries culminated a season that had left the Yankees, at various times, without Shawkey, Quinn, Ruth, Peckinpaugh, Collins, Fewster, outfielder Duffy Lewis and catcher Truck Hannah. The latest injuries prompted Joe Vila, The Sporting News' New York correspondent, to write, "Yankee boosters still are hopeful, but they will not be surprised if either the Clevelands or the White Sox land the prize."

One week later, Vila filed this dispatch: (The Yankees') collapse not only ended their stay in first place, but also ended the hopes of all except those who are so hard-boiled in their optimism that their sympathies blind their reason." Between the reports, the Yankees were swept by Chicago and lost once to St. Louis to fall three games behind the Indians.

Now the White Sox were challenging again.

Fresh from their sweep of New York, the Sox invaded Cleveland on September 23, trailing by only 1½ games. That margin shrank instantly when Dickie Kerr denied Bagby his 30th victory by winning the opener of the three-game set, 10-3. Mails squared the series with a three-hit, 2-0 triumph the next afternoon. But Chicago again closed to within half a game by winning the finale, 5-1, behind an attack that included three hits from Jackson.

The White Sox outfielder was enjoying one of his more remarkable seasons in 1920. Jackson was batting over .380 and had driven in more than 100 runs. The name "Shoeless Joe" was known nationwide. He was idolized by legions of youngsters and admired by teammates and opponents as perhaps the best natural hitter in baseball.

But his name also was being bandied about in another less respectable context. Allegations were growing and gaining credence that several members of the White Sox, Jackson included, had conspired with gamblers to throw the 1919 World Series to the Cincinnati Reds.

With five days remaining in the season and the White Sox trailing the Indians by 1½ games, baseball was rocked by the "Black Sox" scandal. Tuesday morning, September 28, the Cook County grand jury in Illinois returned indictments against eight players who confessed their guilt or were implicated in the scandal.

Immediately afterward, Charles A. (Old Roman) Comiskey, owner of the White Sox, sent telegrams to the accused athletes. The wire to Jackson, Cicotte,

Williams, first baseman Chick Gandil, shortstop Swede Risberg, third baseman Weaver, center fielder Happy Felsch and utility player Fred McMullin read:

"You and each of you are hereby notified of your indefinite suspension as a member of the Chicago American League Baseball Club.

"Your suspension is brought about by information which has just come to me directly involving you and each of you in the baseball scandal now being investigated by the present grand jury of Cook County resulting from the World Series of 1919.

"If you are innocent of any wrongdoing, you and each of you will be reinstated; if you are guilty, you will be retired from organized baseball for the rest of your lives, if I can accomplish it.

"Until there is a finality to this investigation, it is due to the public that I take this action even though it costs Chicago the pennant."

The White Sox were not scheduled to play for the next two afternoons. But with the team dismantled, they dropped two of their last three games in St. Louis. The makeshift lineups' one win was enough to ensure a second-place finish.

The Indians, meanwhile, had defeated the Browns twice before traveling to Detroit to wind up the season. On October 1, Bagby, pitching in relief, lost the 10-inning opener of a doubleheader, 5-4, to Howard Ehmke before Caldwell coasted to his 20th victory in the nightcap. The 10-3 victory clinched a tie for the pennant.

Bagby, the tireless Georgian, returned to the mound October 2. Though touched for 11 hits, Old Sarge was tight in the pinch and won his 31st game of the year, 10-1, to lock up Cleveland's first championship ever.

Speaker had three singles in the title-winning game and finished the season with a .388 batting average, second in the league to the Browns' George Sisler, who hit .407. Tris, Gardner and Smith had 100-RBI seasons as the team compiled a .303 average and 98-56 record.

In the World Series, the Indians were sparked by Coveleski's three wins (he won 24 for the year) and an unassisted triple play by Wambsganss in the fifth game as they defeated Brooklyn, five games to two, in a scheduled nine-game series.

The White Sox's pennant hopes sank quickly when Shoeless Joe Jackson (right) and seven other players were suspended from baseball with five days remaining in the season.

Greenberg Makes A Timely Return

At 6:30 on the morning of May 7, 1941, a tall and trim figure with the easy grace of an athlete walked into a converted corset factory in downtown Detroit. There, in the company of 300 others, he raised his right hand and, in a clear and earnest baritone, he repeated after a uniformed officer, "I, Henry Greenberg, solemnly swear. . . ."

The brief ceremony interrupted the major league baseball career of Hank Greenberg. No longer the slugging outfielder of the Detroit Tigers, he was now Pvt. Henry Benjamin Greenberg, Army of the United States.

That afternoon, the Tigers raised the 1940 American League pennant toward which Greenberg had contributed 41 home runs and 150 runs batted in, both league-leading totals. The new draftee was offered time off to return to Briggs Stadium and participate in a ceremony that would include Commissioner Kenesaw M. Landis, A.L. President Will Harridge and club officials. Hank declined the offer with thanks. Baseball was behind him. He was now a member of the rapidly expanding military force that Uncle Sam was assembling in preparation for World War II.

Greenberg, the son of Romanian immigrants, grew up in New York within hailing distance of Yankee Stadium. As a schoolboy athlete, he was wooed by the Yankees. Hank might have been interested except that he played first base, and the seemingly indestructible Lou Gehrig was holding down that position for the Yanks. Young Hank saw little future waiting for the Iron Horse to retire.

Signed by Detroit as a 19-year-old, Greenberg spent three years in the minor leagues before winning a regular job with the Tigers in 1933 and gaining instant acclaim for his powerful bat and compulsive work ethic.

From '33 through 1940, Greenberg never failed to bat .300. Three times he led the league or shared the A.L. top spot in home runs, once hitting 58 homers (just two shy of the existing major league record). Three times he paced the circuit in runs batted in, once totaling 183 (only one short of the A.L. stan-

The Hall of Fame career of Detroit slugger Hank Greenberg was interrupted by a 1941 call from Uncle Sam.

dard). Twice, in Detroit's pennant-winning years of 1935 and 1940, he was named the league's Most Valuable Player.

The 6-foot-3½, 215-pound Greenberg was firmly established as the league's premier first baseman when he was asked to become an outfielder in 1940. As it was explained to Hank, and as he undoubtedly already had concluded, a spot had to be found in the lineup for Rudy York.

York, a muscular Alabamian, had proved a liability in the outfield, at third base and behind the plate in his first three full seasons with the Tigers. If York's productive bat were to stay in the lineup, Rudy would have to play a position presenting minimal "risk" defensively. And that was judged to be first base.

Hank agreed to make the switch and was turned over to coach Bing Miller for a crash course in the fine art of outfield play. With fiendish glee, Miller bounced wicked grounders at Hank. He cracked caroms off the outfield wall and made Greenberg run until he could go no further.

At the finish of the program, Hank knew his way around the outfield. Moreover, Greenberg's batting stroke was still intact and the explosive York was in the daily lineup.

After his exceptional campaign in 1940, Hank got away slowly the next spring. In the first 18 regular-season games of 1941, Greenberg was homer-less in 62 at-bats. Fittingly, he broke the spell on May 6 by cracking two round-trippers against the Yankees in a farewell salute to baseball (he would not return for four years).

While Greenberg was away, the Tigers fell from first place to a fourth-place tie in 1941 and then to fifth the next two seasons before climbing to second in 1944. Meanwhile, as his old team was going down, Hank was going up. He earned his sergeant's stripes and attended Officer Candidate School, where he earned a commission in the Army Air Force. In 1944, he was a captain in the China-Burma-India theater and participated in the first land-based bombing of Japan.

When he was placed on inactive duty in 1945,

Hank was 34 years old. Unlike the situations involving many other major leaguers, there had been no opportunity for Greenberg to play baseball in the service. Serious doubts were expressed that a player of his age could help a major league team after such a prolonged absence.

Jack Zeller did not share those doubts. "Hank will help if he never gets the bat off his shoulder," predicted the Tigers' general manager. "Just having him around will pay off in inspiration to the rest of the fellows. We need somebody with his type of personality."

Greenberg returned to Briggs Stadium on June 21, 1945. He confessed to being five or six pounds over his playing weight, but reported with a touch of pride that "I've got on a suit that I wore in 1941 and it fits perfectly."

In the days that followed, Hank renewed acquaintances with old teammates and was introduced to new players. He knew his outfield mates, Roger (Doc) Cramer and Roy Cullenbine. Cramer had been a teammate on the American League All-Star team in the prewar years and the two had opposed each other frequently when Cramer was with the Philadelphia Athletics and the Boston Red Sox. Cullenbine had been a Tiger in the late 1930s, but was with the St. Louis Browns when Hank went into service.

York was an old friend, of course, but second baseman Eddie Mayo, outfielder-third baseman Jimmy Outlaw and infielder Bob Maier had been in the minors at the time of Hank's induction. Shortstop Jimmy (Skeeter) Webb, son-in-law of Manager Steve O'Neill, was with the White Sox in 1941.

Greenberg had a nodding acquaintance with the catchers, Bob Swift, who had been with the Browns four years earlier, and Paul Richards, once a league rival while with Philadelphia, but playing manager for Atlanta of the Southern Association when Hank went to war.

Among the leading pitchers, Hal Newhouser, Dizzy Trout and Al Benton were old friends. Frank (Stubby) Overmire had joined the club in 1943, the same year that O'Neill became the Tigers' manager.

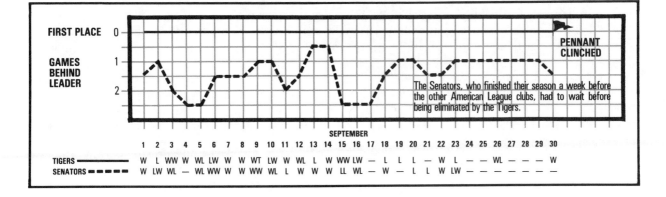

Righthander Dizzy Trout settled into Detroit's rotation in 1945 after battling personality problems in his early years.

Al Benton, a 34-year-old righthander, was the Tigers' most effective hurler through the early weeks of the 1945 season.

In 1941, Newhouser was a 20-year-old lefthander with a blazing fastball and a sizzling temper. Once, after being knocked out of the box in Washington, he stalked to the clubhouse and vented his wrath by firing a case of pop bottles, bottle by bottle, against the wall.

After the 1943 season, Detroit native Newhouser asked to be traded. Zeller arranged to swap the disgruntled pitcher to Cleveland for righthander Jim Bagby. The deal needed only the approval of Tigers Owner Walter O. Briggs, but the industrialist turned it down flat. It proved to be a classic example of a good trade being one that isn't made. While Bagby won four games for the Indians in 1944, Newhouser won 29 for Detroit and was selected the American League's Most Valuable Player.

In his early years, Trout was every bit as combustible as Newhouser. The uninhibited righthander from Sandcut, Ind., was a constant source of irritation to teammates with his incessant chatter and bizarre conduct.

In an early-career spring exhibition game against the Cardinals, Trout was deluged with catcalls from the St. Louis bench. In the mistaken notion that the heckling came from the spectators, he charged to the stands and challenged the fans to a fight. When there were no takers, he stomped to the dugout and kicked over the bat rack and water cooler.

Another time, Diz failed to field an easy ground ball. He flew into a blind rage and grooved pitches for the next several batters—and blew a substantial lead in the process.

On a third occasion, an umpire's decision kindled Trout's short fuse and, the story goes, he deliberately walked the next six batters.

By the next day, all traces of temper had disappeared. When he arrived at the ball park, Trout was ready for a new adventure. Spotting a policeman's motorcycle at rest, Diz jumped aboard and raced around the field.

Hal Newhouser, a young lefthander with a blazing fastball and a sizzling temper, was the ace of Detroit's 1945 staff.

As he approached Manager Mickey Cochrane, he shouted, "How'd you like my motorcycle?"

"Great," replied Black Mike, "and don't stop. Keep right on going till you're 3,000 miles away."

Cochrane's mileage estimate may have been erroneous, but there was truth in his message. The next day, Trout was given a train ticket from Florida to Ohio (where he pitched for the Toledo club of the American Association in 1937 and 1938).

Advancing years had brought maturity to Trout and in 1944, he won 27 games with an earned-run average of 2.12 (compared with 2.22 for Newhouser).

Like Greenberg, Al Benton was 34 years old in 1945. The Oklahoma righthander had wandered the baseball trail before sticking with Detroit after his August call-up from Toledo in 1938. Originally, he had only a fastball, and not a very good one at that. But when he returned to the majors after two years in the Navy, Benton threw a curve and slider as

well.

In his first five starts of 1945, Al allowed only 22 hits and two runs. He went nine innings in each contest and won all five games, three by shutouts. Clearly, Benton was the most effective Detroit pitcher until late May when he was struck by a line drive and suffered a broken ankle.

The Tigers were hanging precariously onto first place when Greenberg rejoined the club. For 10 days, he worked out feverishly and then announced he was ready to face the Philadelphia A's in the first game of a doubleheader at Briggs Stadium on July 1. More than 47,000 fans were on hand to greet their old idol and Hank did not let them down. He signaled his return the same way he had bade goodbye, with a home run, connecting for a bases-empty shot off Charley Gassaway that climaxed a 9-5 victory.

Most emphatically, Greenberg was back. Without benefit of a full spring training period, though, the transition would not be easy. Hank developed a charley horse. His hands, unaccustomed to gripping a bat, broke out in blisters. A sore arm followed, and then a sprained ankle. Through all the adversity, High Henry, or Hankus-Pankus as some writers called him, fulfilled Zeller's prediction. He was an inspiration to his teammates.

Injuries also struck Cramer and Mayo in the heat of the pennant race. The 39-year-old center fielder was hampered by a sore side; the 32-year-old second baseman saw limited duty over a two-week period because of an ailing arm resulting from an unorthodox throw.

By early September, the walking wounded were fully recovered and O'Neill could heave a sigh of relief that a crisis had been survived with his team still ahead of the hard-pressing Washington Senators. "I don't know what we'd have done without Greenberg's hitting and Newhouser's pitching," observed Stout Steve.

Newhouser became the majors' first 20-game winner of the year when he defeated Philadelphia, 4-0, on August 20. Prince Hal received batting support from Cramer and Cullenbine, who clouted home runs, but none from Greenberg, who was stopped after hitting safely in 15 straight games.

The Tigers were holding stubbornly to their lead when a major scare raced through the ranks on September 1. Newhouser was engaged in a pitching battle with Cleveland's Bob Feller when he was forced to retire with a wrenched back. While the club departed on its last eastern swing of the year, Newhouser remained behind to undergo an examination.

The Tigers were in New York for a seven-game series when the lefthander rejoined the team on

September 7 and announced that X-rays had revealed no pathology and that he was ready to pitch. O'Neill agreed to start him, but promised that a reliever would be available—as early as the first inning, if needed.

Hal did not require any help in the first, nor in any subsequent inning. He scattered four singles and beat the Bombers, 5-0, for his 22nd victory of the year.

From New York, where they won five games, the Tigers moved on to Boston and then to Philadelphia. When they arrived in Washington on September 15 for the start of a five-game series, their lead over the second-place Senators stood at one-half game.

Manager Ossie Bluege's Senators were well primed for the crucial series. One day previously, a three-run rally in the ninth inning had enabled Washington to edge the Indians and more pulsating drama was promised in the get-together with the Tigers.

Bluege's four knuckleball pitchers, Dutch Leonard, Roger Wolff, Mickey Haefner and Johnny Niggeling, were rested and ready, as was Walter Masterson, who on September 13 had blanked the Indians on two hits in his first start after being discharged from the Navy.

Slugger Hank Greenberg marked his return to baseball in 1945 by homering in a 9-5 Detroit victory over the Philadelphia A's.

Bluege, the third baseman on Washington's only three pennant-winning teams, presided over an aggregation that had made headlines recently because of intramural strife.

Ossie himself was involved in one of the incidents. His adversary was Fred Vaughn, an infielder who took exception to the pilot's harsh censure after he mishandled a routine play. Vaughn challenged his boss to fisticuffs and even threatened to forsake the club. Later, he had a change of heart. If he had quit the team, he would have forfeited World Series or second-place money. Vaughn stayed and paid a $100 fine.

The second fracas revolved around a bat and was between pitchers Alejandro Carrasquel, a 6-foot-1 Venezuelan, and Marino Pieretti, a native of Italy who stood 5-7. Pieretti recently had collected three hits in a victory over St. Louis.

Carrasquel, a poor hitter and a man with an underdeveloped sense of humor, taunted his smaller teammate by grabbing his cherished bat and refusing to surrender it upon demand. A scuffle ensued and Carrasquel broke the bat. Pieretti answered with a solid poke to the miscreant's mandible and in turn, was struck on the arm by the shattered bat in the hand of the wildly swinging Alejandro. Teammates separated the combatants and a handshake restored a degree of amity before the Tigers came to town.

The crucial series opened with a Saturday doubleheader, featuring Newhouser versus Leonard in the opener and Trout against Haefner in the nightcap.

The expected pitching duel in the first game failed to materialize. An attack of rheumatism sidelined Newhouser after the first inning. An attack of Detroit bats and back problems kayoed Leonard in the Tigers' two-run second inning. A four-run rally in the sixth against Overmire enabled the Senators to tie the score, 4-4, but a three-run outburst in the seventh, highlighted by Cramer's triple, gave the Tigers a 7-4 triumph. The victory was credited to George Jasper Caster, who had been acquired from the Browns in August. Carrasquel took the loss. Trout outpitched Haefner in the second game, 7-3, for his fifth victory on the Eastern junket.

Newhouser returned to the mound the next day, but the lefthander, who had beaten the Senators 10 straight times, was no match for Wolff. The knuckleballer allowed only five hits in winning the opener of another doubleheader, 3-2. If the Senators could win the second contest, they again could climb within one-half game of the leaders, with a chance to go ahead in the series finale.

After seven innings of the nightcap, the Senators trailed, 5-0, but two Washington runs in the eighth and another pair in the ninth narrowed the gap to one run with the potential tying run on third base and two out. At that critical juncture, O'Neill signaled for Trout and the ever-willing righthander responded by retiring the last batter and preserving the 5-4 victory.

Overwork caught up with Diz in the series finale. Pitching for the sixth time in 10 days, he was shelled in the Nats' four-run first inning. Though the Bengals later tied the score, the Senators won easily, 12-5. When the Tigers entrained for home, they led their challengers by 1½ games.

That the Senators should be in the thick of the pennant race was a complete surprise to many, even a shock to some. After finishing in eighth place, 25 games off the pace, in 1944, little improvement was envisioned for the club in 1945. Accordingly Owner Clark Griffith made a highly irregular move (but this was wartime baseball): He leased Griffith Stadium, his club's home park, to the Washington Redskins for the final week of the 1945 American League season. By creating doubleheaders, he concluded the team's season on September 23, a week earlier than six of the Senator's league rivals were scheduled to complete their seasons.

A seventh-place team on June 12, Washington

Washington's George (Bingo) Binks forgot to wear his sunglasses in a game against Philadelphia and the mistake proved costly.

found itself in second place—4½ games behind Detroit—a month later. And the Senators stayed in the thick of the battle.

Causes for the rise to prominence were numerous. For one, Wolff, a four-game winner in 1944, was on a 20-victory course. Leonard was headed for 17 victories, Haefner for 16 and Pieretti for 14. And outfielder Buddy Lewis returned from military service in late July and bolstered the attack by batting .333 in 69 games.

The Senators' abbreviated schedule ended with a doubleheader in Philadelphia on September 23. Leonard was handed a 3-0 lead in the first game, but the butterfly specialist weakened in the eighth and the A's tied the score. Masterson replaced Leonard and hurled effectively until the last of the 12th, when the sun and an imprudent outfielder played him false.

An inning before, when the sun broke through the overcast, center fielder Sam Chapman called time and sent to the bench for his sunglasses. Somehow, the brief episode escaped the attention of Sam's Washington counterpart, George (Bingo) Binks, and when the Senators took the field for the bottom of the 12th, Binks left his glasses on the bench.

The omission augured evil for Washington. A soft fly to center by Ernie Kish would have posed no problem for a provident outfielder. But Binks trotted under the ball and then lost it in the sun. Kish loped into second base with a "gift" double and scored moments later when George Kell singled. The Senators won the nightcap, but it was of little solace to the dejected players. There were dark mutterings about depriving Binks of World Series or second-place money, but that was as far as the matter went.

After 154 games, the Senators had a record of 87 victories and 67 losses and were one game behind the Tigers, who had a record of 86-64 and four games remaining (two against Cleveland in Detroit and two in St. Louis). For the Senators to have a chance at the pennant, the Bengals would have to lose three games, thereby falling into a first-place tie and necessitating a one-game playoff for the flag.

Toward that possibility, Griffith sent his three top hurlers, Wolff, Leonard and Haefner, plus Masterson, to Detroit early in the final week. They were there when the Tigers split a Wednesday doubleheader with the Indians and when rain washed out the Saturday game in St. Louis (necessitating a doubleheader Sunday).

As they sat by the radio in their Detroit hotel room on Sunday, September 30, the final day of the season, the Washington refugees heard distressing news from St. Louis: Rain was delaying the start of the first game of the Tigers-Browns doubleheader.

A rainout of even one game of the doubleheader would have killed Washington's pennant hopes, for these were days when late-season rainouts were not made up (regardless of their impact on the standings) unless the makeup games could be fitted within the confines of the regular-season schedule. So, for the 87-67 Senators to have a shot at the flag, the 87-65 Tigers would have to get in both games of their twin bill in St. Louis—and lose both.

Then came welcome tidings for the Senators. Groundskeepers had put the field at Sportsman's Park in a playable condition and the starting pitchers were warming up for the third time.

Manager Luke Sewell's choice to start game one for the Browns was Nelson Potter, a 34-year-old righthander who a week earlier had tossed a two-hit shutout against the Tigers. Potter was seeking his 16th victory.

The Detroit starter was Virgil Oliver (Fire) Trucks. Seven years before, while pitching in the Alabama-Florida League, the righthander had fanned 418 batters in one season and registered a 1.25 earned-run average. In 1943, his second full season with the Tigers, Trucks won 16 games and then entered military service.

Now, just three days after his discharge from the Navy, Virgil was back. He pronounced himself fit and eager to pitch the game that could clinch the pennant. O'Neill took him at his word and scribbled "Trucks" on the lineup card.

From the first pitch, it was clear that Trucks' fastball was as swift as ever. But it also cut the middle of the plate. A double by Don Gutteridge and Lou Finney's single produced a first-inning run for the Browns.

The Tigers struck back with a run in the fifth and a go-ahead marker in the sixth on two bases on balls (one of them intentional) and Paul Richards' single.

Trucks faltered with one out in the sixth when a double by Potter and a walk to Gutteridge brought Newhouser to his rescue. The lefthander made a ticklish situation infinitely worse by walking Finney, loading the bases. Some of the tension dissipated when Mark Christman, a righthanded pinch-hitter, went down swinging. Newhouser still had to deal with lefthanded-hitting George McQuinn, a respected RBI man. For an instant, it appeared that McQuinn had scored a direct hit. His solid smash to right-center field raised hopes of a bases-clearing double, but Cramer pushed his 39-year-old legs to the utmost and snatched the ball at full gallop. The side had been retired.

Newhouser was less fortunate in the seventh inning. Gene Moore's double and Vern Stephens' single enabled the Browns to tie the score, and the home team went ahead in the eighth when Pete

A happy group of Tigers celebrate the clinching of the 1945 pennant on Hank Greenberg's final-day grand slam.

Gray, the one-armed phenom, raced from first base to home on McQuinn's double.

Intermittent drizzle and enveloping darkness were now working in the Bengals' favor. Even if they lost the game, there seemed virtually no chance that the Tigers could play the nightcap to a decision. In that case, they would finish the season with an 87-66 record and win the flag by one-half game over Washington.

In a bid to win the championship on the field and preclude the designation of his team as the "Umbrella Champion," O'Neill lifted Newhouser for pinch-hitter Hub Walker to open the final frame. A reserve outfielder, Walker had two hits in 22 at-bats; by contrast, Newhouser had 28 hits and was outhitting Walker by more than 150 points.

Walker, however, singled, and Skeeter Webb followed with a bunt. In the opinion of many observers, including the Browns, the throw to second base appeared to beat the runner. Umpire Joe Rue disagreed. After the howl subsided, Red Borom ran for Walker and Mayo followed with another bunt. With runners now stationed at second and third, Cramer was walked intentionally to load the bases.

Then it was Greenberg's turn. Since returning from the service, High Henry had clouted 12 home runs, with 56 RBIs, in 269 trips to the plate. No other Tiger could match Hank's .309 batting average.

Greenberg swung lustily on a Potter offering and from the crack of the bat the 5,582 spectators knew the ball was headed for the left-field bleachers. There was only one question—would it remain fair.

It did, but barely. Three runners crossed the plate ahead of Hank, who was pummeled, slapped, hugged and kissed in the parade to the dugout. A few minutes later, Al Benton retired the Browns in the bottom of the ninth and Detroit was a 6-3 victor —and the A.L. champion.

In a Detroit hotel room, a radio was turned off and four disappointed Senators pitchers started for the railroad depot. In Washington, their teammates gazed wistfully at packed bags and scattered for their homes.

The Tigers celebrated the championship in comparative calm before taking the field for the nightcap, which was rained out in the first inning. Greenberg was the least emotional of all the Tigers, whose .575 winning percentage was the lowest of any major league pennant-winner to that time.

Asked what type of pitch he had socked for the homer that lifted Detroit to its seventh pennant, Hank deadpanned: "It was just a baseball. I kinda liked it."

Wallbangers Give
A Power Display

As a successful American League executive, Harry Dalton developed a keen appreciation of cause and effect, a sharp awareness of how a congenial atmosphere influences a professional baseball club.

In the spring of 1982, Dalton surmised that a negative spirit was gnawing at the Milwaukee Brewers. The team he had assembled in just over four years as general manager was too talented to have played so pitifully. The Brewers lost six of their first nine games, then 14 of 20 a month later as they floundered far behind the leaders in the East Division.

Dalton's suspicions were confirmed when he accompanied the Brewers on a trip to the West Coast in late May. His manager had created a sterile environment. His practice of pacing the dugout and uttering inflammatory remarks had generated dissent among many players. No team that was tense and inhibited could ever reach its potential, Dalton concluded. A change was imperative.

A 2-1 victory at Seattle on June 1 failed to shake Harry's conviction. Thoughtfully, he let Manager Robert (Buck) Rodgers enjoy a good night's rest before firing him the next morning.

The dismissal was extremely painful, Dalton confessed.

"It's always difficult to fire anybody, especially when he's your manager, and especially when he's your friend," Dalton said. "I wanted to give Buck every opportunity to right the ship."

Rodgers, who had replaced George Bamberger during the 1980 campaign, had led the Brewers to the division title in the second half of the strike-shortened 1981 season. Still, he was not surprised he was ousted. The club's consistent losing had imparted a sense of impending doom. Rodgers maintained, however, that the team was discontented because of two "cancers." He would not identify the malignancies, but insiders agreed they were Ted Simmons, a disgruntled catcher batting near .200, and Mike Caldwell, a pitcher who had quarreled with Rodgers aboard a plane.

Dalton's first choice to replace Rodgers was Sal Bando, a former third baseman with the Oakland Athletics and the Brewers. Bando, serving as a special assistant to Dalton, declined.

The second preference was Harvey Kuenn, the Brewers' hitting coach for the previous 11 years and a favorite with the players. Kuenn had broken into the majors full-time as a shortstop with the Detroit Tigers in 1953 and earned Rookie of the Year honors after batting .308. He was the A.L. batting champion in 1959 and compiled a career average of .303 before retiring in 1966.

Kuenn accepted the job, even though Dalton announced that it was only temporary. Harvey was made an interim manager out of consideration for his health, Dalton said. Years before, Kuenn had undergone stomach surgery and then a heart bypass. In 1980, after four unsuccessful operations to remove blood clots, the lower part of his right leg was amputated.

The new 51-year-old skipper dismissed concerns that he would be unable to endure through a stressful season. "I hope it's to the end of the season and beyond that. I don't even know what the word interim means."

His wife also had reservations until she "saw him on television, sitting in the dugout, seeing that ear-to-ear grin and his eyes sparkling."

Harvey Edward Kuenn, a native of West Allis, Wis., was an uncomplicated personality. He believed that baseball should be played for the pleasure it afforded, unencumbered by ponderous theories. His inaugural address in the visitors' clubhouse at Seattle accentuated the theme: "Have fun, have a laugh and enjoy yourself."

He also had a special message for the relief pitchers. "Don't worry about not having enough time to warm up," he told them. Then, alluding to his artificial leg, he quipped, "By the time I get to the mound, there's no way you won't be ready."

The wisecrack sent a roar through the ranks. This was their type of manager, a man with an unfettered approach to the game, a friend who refused to change simply because he had become field commander.

The improvement in the atmosphere was nothing short of remarkable, Gorman Thomas reported. "It was like after an all-night poker game when the room fills with smoke," the outfielder said. "Somebody opens the door and the stale air goes out, the fresh air comes in."

Harvey's simplistic view of how baseball should be played paid quick dividends.

In the first four games under Kuenn, all victories, the Brewers batted .346, clouted nine homers and scored 33 runs. At Oakland on June 5, their long-dormant offense exploded in full fury. In the seventh inning, Robin Yount, Cecil Cooper and Ben Oglivie smashed consecutive home runs. Two innings later, a happier Simmons and Thomas clouted back-to-back homers.

In the press box at Oakland-Alameda County Coliseum, an excited Dalton informed the writers that such an explosive team deserved a nickname. "How about 'Harvey's Ballbangers?' " he asked.

The name had a fine ring to it, Cooper agreed in the clubhouse, but it needed a dash of flavor. It should be, the first baseman said, "just like a drink, Harvey's Wallbangers, because we bang 'em off the wall."

And Wallbangers they remained. By the end of the season, they had smacked 216 drives over A.L. walls and countless others against them. The Brewers tied a major league record by hitting 200 or more home runs in two seasons and tied an A.L. record with three players finishing with 30 or more home runs— Thomas, a league-leading 39, Oglivie, 34, and Cooper, 32.

Dalton could take credit as the chief architect of the club that Kuenn inherited. Shortly after leaving the Angels to join the Brewers in November 1977, Dalton obtained Oglivie, an outfielder, from the Detroit Tigers. He also reacquired the slugging Thomas from the Texas Rangers. Thomas had been let go in October as the player to be named later in a deal for Ed Kirkpatrick.

But the general manager's biggest coup was scored on December 12, 1980, in a deal with the St. Louis Cardinals. The Brewers acquired Simmons, pitcher Pete Vuckovich and star relief specialist Rollie Fingers for pitchers Lary Sorenson and Dave LaPoint and outfielders Sixto Lezcano and David Green.

Jim Baumer, Dalton's predecessor, had obtained Cooper, the first baseman, from the Boston Red Sox in 1976, Caldwell from the San Francisco Giants in 1977, and pitcher Bob McClure from the Kansas City Royals in 1977. Veteran infielder-outfielder Don Money was acquired from the Philadelphia Phillies in 1972.

Yount, the shortstop, had joined the Brewers as an 18-year-old phenom out of California in 1974, five years after the Seattle Pilots franchise was transferred to Milwaukee. Now, at 26, he was ac-

Harvey Kuenn took control of a power-packed Milwaukee Brewers team that literally pounded its way to the American League pennant while earning the nickname 'Harvey's Wallbangers.'

Rollie Fingers spelled instant relief for Milwaukee when Harry Dalton acquired him in December 1980 from St. Louis.

knowledged as the dominant shortstop in the league.

Paul Molitor, a former All-America at the University of Minnesota, was the third baseman. Selected in the free-agent draft as a shortstop, Molitor also had played second base and the outfield. But after missing most of 1981 with an ankle injury, the Brewers decided to return the four-year veteran to the infield in 1982.

Jim Gantner was in his second season as the full-time second baseman. Following knee surgery over the winter, Gantner suffered a shoulder injury two weeks after Kuenn took charge and was sidelined for a month. But when he returned, Gantner rapped 14 hits in 19 at-bats and was acclaimed A.L. Player of the Week.

Charlie Moore, a member of the Brewers since 1973, teamed with Oglivie and Thomas in the outfield. The Alabamian had mainly been a part-time catcher with occasional stints at third base or the outfield. After playing only 48 games in 1981, however, Moore asked to be traded, a request he withdrew when he was promised an opportunity to become the regular right fielder. By the middle of the season, Charlie was recognized league wide as one of the best, especially for his outstanding arm.

The Milwaukee pitching staff was far from dominating, but it was effective enough to hold opponents to fewer than four runs per game.

Vuckovich, the most productive hurler, had the best winning percentage in baseball combining his two seasons in Milwaukee. The righthander had compiled a 14-4 record in 1981, and he was averag-

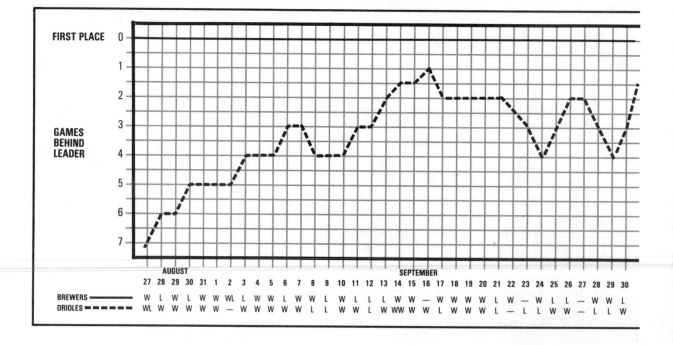

ing three wins in every four decisions on his way to an 18-6 mark in '82 and the Cy Young Award.

The 29-year-old former Cardinal had command of a good fastball, slider, curve and changeup, but he had an extra dimension that shattered a batter's concentration.

While peering toward home plate, Vuckovich wouldn't hesitate to cross his eyes and distort his face into a clownish grimace. The antics could be as devastating to a batter as a screwball on the outside corner.

Pete's contortions, some critics believed, indicated he did not take the game seriously. That, Vuckovich insisted, was a lie.

"I try to have a little fun," the pitcher said, picking up on the Kuenn theme. "The only problem is the onlookers get the wrong impression. They think you're lackadaisical. I know the situation when I'm not there. There's no reason to make my job tougher than it already is by spending too much time thinking what I'm going to do."

"He just knows how to pitch," Kuenn said. "Some guys would take a lifetime to learn what he's learned in just six years in the major leagues. He just flat out knows what he's doing on the mound."

When Vuckovich was referred to as an eccentric, he responded with some heat. "I'm not even left-handed."

The other starters behind Vuckovich were Caldwell, 17 wins for the year; McClure, 12 wins; Moose Haas, 11 wins, and Randy Lerch, eight wins. With little doubt, those totals would have been lower had it not been for Fingers, who sauntered in from the bullpen 50 times to douse enemy fires. The 1981 Most Valuable Player and Cy Young Award winner

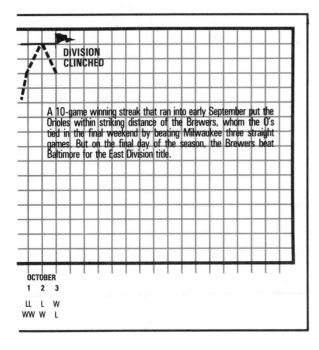

DIVISION CLINCHED

A 10-game winning streak that ran into early September put the Orioles within striking distance of the Brewers, whom the O's tied in the final weekend by beating Milwaukee three straight games. But on the final day of the season, the Brewers beat Baltimore for the East Division title.

OCTOBER
1 2 3

LL L W
WW W L

Also acquired in the deal with the Cardinals was starting pitcher Pete Vuckovich, who became the ace of the Brewers' staff.

registered his 300th career save and 28th of the year when he hurled the last two innings of a 3-2 victory over Seattle on August 21.

Employing the Kuenn "fun" method, the Wallbangers won 20 of 27 games in June, the best showing in both leagues. On June 1 under Rodgers, the Brewers were 23-24 and tied for fifth place with the Baltimore Orioles, seven games behind Detroit. One day and one month later, Milwaukee was tied for first with Boston.

The Brewers batted .294 during June, hit 47 home runs and had a .514 slugging average. "What makes this team so tough to pitch to is the complement of hitting styles," Kuenn explained.

The Wallbangers were winning with a coordinated onslaught. Molitor and Yount were reaching base regularly. If Cooper didn't drive them home with a single or double, he hammered the ball over the fence. Then came more power, more run production and more consistency with Oglivie, Simmons and Thomas.

At the All-Star break, Thomas led the league with 22 home runs. Oglivie and Cooper were tied for fourth with 19, and Yount had 15. Simmons had belted 14 homers, Molitor a career-high 10, and Don Money nine as a part-time designated hitter.

"I thank the Lord that when he made out the rosters, he picked me to be on the Brewers," McClure said.

Kuenn also was enjoying the show. "I've never seen this kind of hitting for this long a time in my entire career in baseball," he said. "There's only one explanation—they're all good hitters."

Especially Cooper and Yount, two of the best in baseball that season.

Cooper, the starting first baseman for the A.L. All-Star team, was seventh in the league in batting with a .321 average, fourth in hits with 103, third in doubles with 23, and second in runs batted in with 68.

Hitting never had been a problem for the 32-year-old Texan. In 1980, Cooper enjoyed his best year since he broke into the majors full-time with Boston in 1974. Cecil led the league in RBIs with 122, hit 25 home runs and had a .352 batting average, second to George Brett's .390.

"I'd like to win a batting title, but I'm not going to lose any sleep over it," Cooper said, reflecting on his start in '82. "More than that, I just want to be a consistent ball player. That's what I want to be remembered as, a guy who went out and did it consistently, day in and day out. There aren't many guys who do that over the years."

Cooper had done it over five with the Brewers by hitting at least .300 each season.

While Cooper was the hottest hitter early, Yount was the omnipotent force in July. Yount's statistics would have been impressive for a cleanup hitter, let

alone the No. 2 batter in the order. Near the end of July, Yount was second in the league in batting at .322, first in hits with 122, and fifth in both RBIs and runs with 67. He led the league with a .616 slugging average and 223 total bases.

"There's the MVP," Thomas proclaimed. "If he's not, there's just no justice. He can cool off the rest of the season and still walk off with it."

(There was no need for Thomas to be concerned. In October, Yount collected 27 of 28 first-place votes to win the honor.)

Personal awards, however, were not what Robin was playing for. "That's not what I'm concerned about," he said. "I'm just doing something I enjoy. This is what I want to do. But what I want to do more than anything is play in a World Series."

With Yount leading the charge, the Wallbangers swatted their way toward that goal. The Brewers won 16 games in July and had a ½-game lead over the Red Sox entering August. In the next month, they won 19 games to open a comfortable 4½-game lead.

While the Brewers had been pounding their way to the top of the division, another team had followed a similar, if slightly less fantastic, course.

The Baltimore Orioles stumbled badly at the beginning of the year by losing nine straight in April. Manager Earl Weaver, who had announced that '82 would be his last season as skipper, was seeking his fifth pennant and seventh division championship in his 14th full year with the club. For two months, however, the timid Orioles bounced between fifth and seventh place. Star righthanded pitcher Jim Palmer won only two games over that stretch.

But a seven-game winning streak in July moved Baltimore into contention. Reliever Tippy Martinez was named Pitcher of the Month for consistently saving the Orioles. The lefthander pitched in 16 games without allowing a run. In 19 innings, he surrendered only six hits, struck out 22, won two games and saved five.

Baltimore followed that streak by losing five straight and then eight of 10 in August to fall 7½ games behind. "It's the same cycle we ran into early in the year," Weaver said. "The same cycle that put us in a nine-game losing streak in April. . . . It got us again. Nobody can explain why these things happen in baseball, but they do."

Baltimore hit a positive cycle at the end of August and won 11 of 12 games. The explanation? A slugging attack that rivaled the Brewers' and the resurgence of Palmer.

First baseman Eddie Murray was batting .312 with 27 homers and 89 RBIs; left fielder John Lowenstein had a .317 average with 22 homers and 53 RBIs in only 268 at-bats; shortstop Cal Ripken was making a bid for Rookie of the Year honors with 23 home runs and 77 RBIs; outfielder Gary

Roenicke had 21 homers and 64 RBIs, and designated hitter Ken Singleton had 13 homers and 69 RBIs.

Palmer had won 10 consecutive decisions beginning June 7 to improve his record to 12-3. Dennis Martinez led the staff with 13 victories, followed by Palmer and Scott McGregor with 12, and Mike Flanagan with 11.

As the Brewers banged their way from park to park, Dalton, the architect, had been reinforcing the mound staff for the crucial final month of the race. Three transactions proved to be strokes of genius when Fingers injured his arm September 2 and was sidelined for the rest of the season.

In July, the Brewers had recalled pitcher Pete Ladd from Vancouver of the Pacific Coast League. Nicknamed "Big Foot" for his size 15 EEE shoes, the 240-pound righthander had only 12 innings of major league experience with the Houston Astros. Ladd made his first appearance for Milwaukee on July 17, his 26th birthday, before 53,000 fans. Summoned in the seventh inning with the Chicago White Sox trying to add to a 2-0 lead, Ladd pitched 1⅔ scoreless innings and the Brewers rallied for a 5-2 win. Ladd was credited with his first A.L. victory.

On August 11, Dalton purchased Doc Medich from the Texas Rangers. The veteran righthander picked up five wins as a starter to take the place of Lerch. The lefthander, plagued by inconsistency, was sold to the Montreal Expos on August 14. Later in the month, Dalton traded pitching prospects Frank DiPino and Mike Madden and outfielder Kevin Bass to Houston for Don Sutton, who had won 13 games for the Astros. In 15 years with the Los Angeles Dodgers, Sutton had pitched under pennant pressure countless times.

The Milwaukee general manager said he had been angling for Sutton while working on the Medich deal. "He was our number one goal," Dalton disclosed. "We were talking with Houston officials for more than a month."

But some observers feared that the Brewers were gambling away too much young talent for immediate help.

"There are always risks in this sort of thing," Dalton said. "I've tried to find inside straights before and never drawn a king. . . . Don Sutton, at 37, is a very successful starting pitcher. And his experience is so important. He's been there before. A pennant race is no new thing to him.

"Our team is in place. Fingers is in his 30s, Oglivie and Cooper are, too. We think we're at the moment that we have to capture. Not only that, this is a franchise that has never won, so it's terribly important for us to win."

Cecil Cooper, acquired from the Boston Red Sox, played steady defense at first base and was a devastating RBI man.

Taking their 4½-game lead over Boston into September, the Brewers won 17 games and lost only 11 for the month. That finished the fading Red Sox, but not the charging Orioles. Baltimore's 19-9 record reduced Milwaukee's lead to three games with four contests to play—in Baltimore against the Brewers.

Baltimore had won 27 of 32 games from August 20 to September 20 and had the best record in the major leagues since the All-Star break, 47-29. But more importantly, they had defeated the Brewers six times in nine games. To win that seventh championship for Weaver, the Orioles needed to sweep the series. The Brewers needed only one victory to bring the first division or league title to Milwaukee since the Braves won the National League pennant in 1958.

Expectations were high along the Chesapeake Bay as 51,583 spectators packed Memorial Stadium for a doubleheader on Friday, October 1. In the opener, Vuckovich, the Brewers' stopper, opposed Dennis Martinez, a 15-game winner who had defeated Milwaukee four games ago on a six-hitter. Martinez hurled 6⅓ innings to earn another win and Baltimore was still alive with an 8-3 victory. Jim Dwyer and Rich Dauer led the winners' 15-hit attack with three safeties apiece. A four-homer salvo off Caldwell by Murray, Ripken, Len Sakata and John Shelby helped Storm Davis win the nightcap, 7-1, on a six-hitter.

With two games remaining, the Brewers still needed to play only .500 ball to win the division.

Weaver selected McGregor, 14-12, to stop the Wallbangers on October 2, but the lefthander couldn't last the fourth inning. Milwaukee scored one run then to tie the game, 3-3, but reliever Dave Stewart allowed only two singles the rest of the way. The Orioles rallied for four runs in both the fourth and eighth innings for an 11-3 win. They rapped Medich, the Brewers' starter, and two relievers for 18 hits, three each by Lowenstein and catcher Rick Dempsey. Stewart earned the decision, his 10th win of the year.

The victory lifted Baltimore into a first-place tie with a 94-67 record. The winner of the 162nd game of the season would travel to Anaheim, Calif., to play the West Division-champion California Angels in the League Championship Series. If the Brewers were to prevent a miracle finish by the Orioles, Sutton would have to outduel Palmer, a career 22-9 pitcher against Milwaukee. The Baltimore righthander 15-4 for the season, had defeated the Brewers twice in 1982 while Sutton, 3-1 in the American League, had defeated Baltimore on September 24, 15-6.

A throng of 51,642 packed the East 33rd Street park for the winner-take-all encounter. They were drawn there not only by the pitching matchup and the one-shot pennant showdown, but also to offer a parting salute to Weaver, the sometimes-controversial skipper.

(While Weaver did step down after the season, he returned to manage the Orioles in 1985 and 1986, when he retired a second time.)

Palmer's bid to heap a fourth straight indignity upon the Brewers failed. Yount, the second batter of the game, rocketed his 28th homer over the left-field wall, and Palmer's wild throw on a pickoff play led to the Brewers' second run the next inning.

Yount, among the league leaders in eight batting categories, tagged Palmer for his second homer in the third inning, increasing the Wallbangers' lead to 3-0. It was the seventh two-homer game of the season for Yount.

The Orioles squandered a scoring chance in the first inning, when Glenn Gulliver ignored a coach's "stop" sign at third base and was nailed at the plate by Moore's throw from right field. Gulliver, a 27-year-old rookie, made amends for his boner by hitting his first major league homer in the third.

Palmer blanked the Brewers in the fourth and fifth innings and faced Cooper leading off the sixth. The Orioles' pitchers had handcuffed the Milwaukee first baseman all season. Though he had 118 RBIs, none had come against Baltimore. This time, however, Coop snapped the bonds with his 32nd home run to give the Brewers a 4-1 lead.

After Yount's triple led to another Milwaukee run in the eighth, the Orioles mounted a threat in the bottom of the inning. Two walks and Terry Crowley's 103rd career pinch-hit cut the lead to 5-2. But the uprising ended when Oglivie raced to the left-field foul line and made a somersaulting catch of pinch-batter Joe Nolan's bid for an extra-base hit.

Initially, Oglivie "couldn't believe" he made the catch. But in his next breath, he explained: "I did my homework. I watch to see how Simmons moves behind the plate. I was moving . . . when the ball was pitched and had the speed to get there."

Simmons, concluding one of his finest seasons in a cordial mood, whacked his 23rd homer to cap a five-run explosion in the ninth inning and end the Orioles' hopes. The Brewers won their first championship, 10-2.

Cooper was especially elated during the postgame celebration. "When they got those four runs in the eighth inning yesterday, I said, 'That's it.' They were slapping us in the face," he said.

"This was like the seventh game of a World Series," Simmons observed. "With that cheerleader (Wild Bill Hagy, a city cab driver) going through his routine on the Orioles' dugout—I can't believe a final game of the Series could produce more noise."

The Baltimore fans stayed long after the final out, bringing Weaver back onto the field twice as they

Robin Yount, shown rounding third on the first of his two final-game home runs, was the nastiest thorn in Baltimore pitcher Jim Palmer's side.

roared their best wishes.

The Brewers barely had time to savor their division championship. The Angels sounded last call for the Wallbangers by winning the first two games of the Championship Series at Anaheim Stadium.

Tommy John, a 39-year-old lefthander with a surgically reconstructed pitching arm, beat the Brewers in the series opener. The victory was his fifth for California since he was acquired from New York on August 31. Bruce Kison, the Angels' starter in Game Two, had spent most of 1980 and 1981 on the disabled list and had undergone elbow and wrist surgery. But he surrendered only five hits and

struck out eight in a 4-2 win. The game was "nowhere near as close as the final margin would indicate," Money said.

The Brewers faced overwhelming odds when the series resumed in Milwaukee on October 8. Since the playoffs were begun in 1969, no team in either league had rebounded from a 2-0 deficit to win the pennant.

The Brewers, however, weren't about to throw in the towel. "We've had the walls behind our backs before," Kuenn said. "I mean, you'd have to say our backs are behind the walls." Anyway, the Brewers had come back before.

The Western Division's California Angels jumped on the Brewers early in the A.L. Championship Series, thanks in part to the pitching of Tommy John and the lusty hitting of Don Baylor (center).

"Remember the miniseries (divisional playoff) last year with the New York Yankees?" Simmons asked. "We lost the first two games at home, then went to New York, where we won two and nearly took the series. Remember? We were leading in the fifth game. I'm convinced it can be done."

California shortstop Tim Foli even agreed. "By no stretch of the imagination do I feel we have it made," he said. "With that lineup, they are capable of doing anything."

Angels Manager Gene Mauch assumed that starter Geoff Zahn would make sure they didn't. Zahn had won 18 games during the season but had lost to the Brewers twice. He did no better in a championship setting. Mauch pulled the lefthander in the fourth inning with the Brewers on top, 3-0.

In the seventh, Molitor's second two-run homer in as many games gave Milwaukee and Sutton a 5-0 lead.

Those last two tallies proved to be crucial as the Angels gained a new life. Catcher Bob Boone led off the eighth inning and drove a fly to deep left field. Oglivie faded back to the fence and leaped to make the catch, but a fan in the stands reached out to snare the ball away. Umpire Larry Barnett declined to call interference. He ruled the ball had already cleared the fence and awarded Boone a home run.

A single by first baseman Rod Carew and doubles by center fielder Fred Lynn and designated hitter Don Baylor netted two more runs. The next batter, third baseman Doug DeCinces, represented the tying run. DeCinces had two hits in the series after batting .301 with 30 home runs in the regular season. Kuenn had insisted since the series started that Fingers, his bullpen ace, would be able to pitch "to a couple of batters in a key situation, if needed." But when Harvey went to the mound to yank Sutton, he beckoned instead for Ladd, the off-season probation and parole officer from Portland, Me.

In similar situations during the stretch drive, Ladd had surrendered home runs to Detroit's Lance Parrish and New York's Jerry Mumphrey. But now, Big Foot was "in a state of greater concentration . . . more intense." He retired DeCinces on a grounder to third and set down the side in order in the ninth to preserve the 5-3 victory.

"I never figured I'd be pitching with the game on the line," Ladd said. "Heck, a week ago I was just hoping to make the playoff roster." In Game Two, Ladd had struck out Reggie Jackson, Carew and Lynn in succession.

Still teetering on the brink of elimination, the Brewers entrusted the fourth game to Haas. In 27 starts during the season, Moose had only three complete games. He had ample time to think about pitching a fourth when rain delayed the start of the contest an hour and 44 minutes.

Haas was opposed by John, who was far less puzzling than he had been four days earlier. Before making his exit in the fourth inning, the southpaw gave up six runs on four hits and walked five batters.

Mauch was sharply criticized for pitching John on only three days of rest with 13-game winner Ken Forsch available. But John was a finesse pitcher, not a power pitcher, and said the short rest was nothing new for him. "I lost it because my sinker ball was traveling only 60 feet, which is six inches too short."

Haas had a no-hitter for five innings but surrendered a run in the sixth on an RBI double by Lynn.

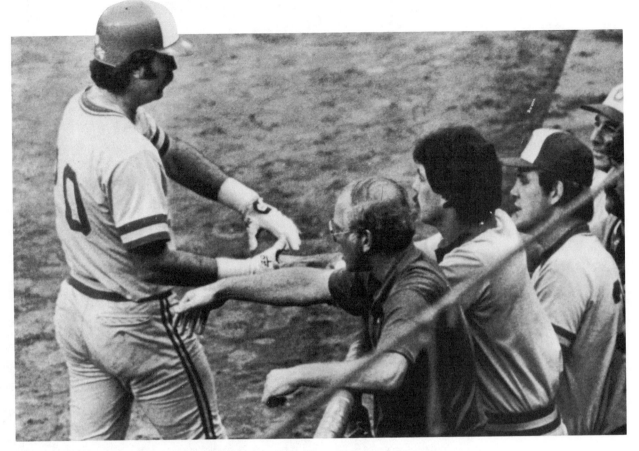

One of the top guns in Milwaukee's offensive arsenal was Gorman Thomas, who received a warm greeting after a home run in the Championship Series.

In the eighth, Baylor hit a grand slam to narrow the lead to 7-5. The home run gave Baylor 10 RBIs in the series to set an A.L. playoff record. Jim Slaton, a 10-game winner as a spot starter and reliever, got the final five outs for the Brewers.

The clutch pitching of Haas and Slaton was overshadowed by the punch provided by an unexpected source. Mark Brouhard, a reserve outfielder formerly in the Angels' organization, had been in the minors until August 30 and had not played since September 11. But Oglivie was sidelined with bruised ribs and "Bro" was thrust into the lineup. He marked the occasion with a single, double and homer, three RBIs and four runs scored in the 9-5 triumph.

For the second time in a week, Harvey and his Wallbangers had compacted their season into a single game. If they won, they would move on to St. Louis for the World Series. The pitching matchup for the October 10 championship showdown pitted Vuckovich, 3-0 versus California, against Kison, pitching with only three days of rest.

The 54,968 fans who packed County Stadium rode an emotional roller coaster in the opening inning. The Angels scored on left fielder Brian Downing's double and Lynn's single, but the Brewers retaliated on Molitor's double, an infield out and Simmons' sacrifice fly.

The Angels regained the lead in the third, when Lynn drove in his second run with a single, and increased their margin to two runs on Boone's RBI single in the fourth. Oglivie's first playoff homer in the bottom of the inning made the score 3-2.

Reckless baserunning in the fifth cost California a potentially big inning. Reggie Jackson, batting only .133 in the series, reached base on a walk. But "Mr. October" tried to advance to third on Lynn's single and was cut down by Moore's superb throw from right field. It was Moore's 14th assist of the year. Jackson's careless scamper was magnified when Baylor followed with another single. But Vuckovich retired the side without any scoring.

After holding the Brewers to three hits in five innings, Kison left the game rather than risk damage to his arm. Mauch brought in Luis Sanchez, a hard-throwing Venezuelan righthander. Sanchez breezed through the sixth but got entangled in a tough-luck, seventh-inning predicament.

With one out, Moore hacked a soft fly over the middle of the infield. Second baseman Bobby Grich raced over and dived to catch the ball. Al Clark, umpiring at first base, ruled the batter out, but home-plate umpire Don Denkinger reversed the decision, calling it a trapped ball. With Moore on first, Gantner singled and Yount walked with two outs to load the bases for Cooper.

On other days, Mauch might have called on southpaw Andy Hassler, a workhorse in 54 regular-season games. But the lefthanded-hitting Cooper had only two hits in 19 at-bats in the playoffs. "If somebody asked where Cecil Cooper had been during the playoffs, it would have been a fair question," Cooper said after the series. The Angels' manager gambled on Sanchez.

On a 1-and-1 pitch, Cooper slapped a soft fly down the left-field line. Running to first, Cooper waved landing signals for fair territory. The ball dropped on target, Moore and Gantner pranced home and the Brewers led, 4-3. "I thought it might carry too far and be the third out," Cooper said. "When it didn't, I had the most satisfying hit of my life."

Trailing for the first time in the game, Mauch signaled for Hassler, who pitched hitless ball the rest of the game.

In the top of the eighth, Kuenn removed center fielder Thomas, who was hobbling on an injured knee. Marshall Edwards, a 30-year-old rookie, took over and immediately demonstrated the wisdom of the move. Baylor, the second batter, lifted a long fly to left-center field that surely would have eluded the gimpy Thomas. But the speedier Edwards raced back and leaped to glove the ball against the fence.

The Angels mounted their final bid for victory in the ninth against McClure. A leadoff pinch single by Ron Jackson brought Kuenn from the dugout. The signal went to the bullpen: Send in Ladd.

As he had done throughout the series, Big Foot spiked the California guns. After retiring Boone on a sacrifice, Ladd forced Downing and Carew to hit infield grounders for routine putouts, saving the game and sending the Brewers into the World Series.

Nobody appreciated Ladd's superlative work more than Kuenn. In three appearances, Ladd retired 10 consecutive batters, allowed no hits and posted a 0.00 earned-run average. Who could have done better when every pitch was critical? Pete, insisted the manager, should be a landslide winner of the series MVP award.

Unfortunately for Big Foot, Harvey had no voice in the voting. The award went to Lynn, whose 11 hits and .611 batting average set a record for a five-game Championship Series.

"Fred Lynn got the MVP?" asked a surprised Kuenn. "Not in my book. It should have gone to Ladd. Why? How can you ask why?"

"Freddie deserved the MVP," Ladd said. "But what we got is a chance to go to the World Series. And we deserved that."

The surprise hero of Milwaukee's drive to the American League pennant was relief pitcher Pete Ladd, alias Big Foot.

Cardinals Survive Disappearing Act

Several months after the 1930 season, Ed Burns, a droll baseball writer for the Chicago Tribune, composed a story about pitcher Flint Rhem. The St. Louis Cardinal had an affinity for the bottle that was as renowned as his pitching talent. Burns wrote:

"Lovers of fair play have not forgotten how foul gangsters seized Flint on the eve of an important Brooklyn game which he was to have pitched. Bundling him to their den, they took demijohns from under their black capes and forced him to quaff again and again until greatly against his will and to his utter consternation, he became so soused that he was unable to perform his scheduled pitching chores."

Rhem's misadventure occurred during the thick of a wildly intoxicating pennant race and inspired titillating headlines nationwide. Those who knew Rhem nodded their heads knowingly with a twinkle in their eyes. When it came to sniffing out red-eye during the "Noble Experiment" known as Prohibition, Flint had few equals.

Charles Flint Rhem of Rhems, S.C., was a lovable lush. He was always willing to submerge his own selfish interests for the common good.

Witness his magnanimous gesture in 1926. Bumming with the great Grover Cleveland Alexander, Flint swilled great quantities of liquor set before Alex to safeguard the veteran's sobriety. No greater sacrifice!

Rhem won 20 games in 1926, tying for the National League lead, as the Cardinals won the World Series over the New York Yankees. He won 10 games the next season and 11 in 1928, but his wayward lifestyle bought him a ticket to the minors in 1929. The Cardinals reinstated Rhem over the winter, hoping the 29-year-old righthander would concentrate on pitching rather than the bright lights of the big city.

The Cardinals' new field boss for 1930 was Charles (Gabby) Street, nicknamed "Old Sarge" for his combat service in World War I. Street, a former batterymate of Walter Johnson with the Washington Senators, was best remembered for catching a baseball dropped from the top of the Washington Monument in 1908.

Encouraged by Cardinals Manager Branch Rickey, Gabby had become a minor league manager in

1920, a job he would hold for nine years.

In 1928, Street was managing the Knoxville Smokies in the Sally League when the Cardinals visited for an exhibition game after spring training. Old Sarge directed his troops to a 9-8 victory and caught the eye of Sam Breadon, president of the Cardinals. The next spring, Breadon and Rickey, now the club's vice president, lured Gabby to St. Louis to become Manager Billy Southworth's battery coach.

Near midseason, Southworth traded jobs with

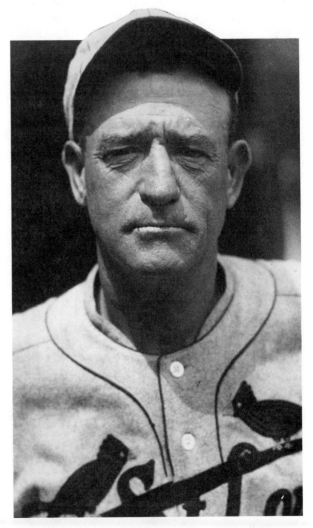

Gabby Street, alias Old Sarge, was asked to guide the 1930 St. Louis Cardinals back to the top of the National League standings.

Bill McKechnie, manager of the Cardinals' Rochester farm club in the International League. As McKechnie's second lieutenant, Gabby's rapport with the players and his baseball instincts again attracted the St. Louis executives' attention.

McKechnie's No. 1 aide was Alfred Earle (Greasy) Neale, a former outfielder with the Cincinnati Reds and Philadelphia Phillies. Neale, however, was making a bigger name for himself as a top college football coach. He had led Washington and Jefferson College to a 0-0 tie in the 1922 Rose Bowl game, but joined the Cardinals at the invitation of Southworth, his old friend. With Billy gone, the lure of football was too great. Neale departed and Street took over as the manager's first assistant.

When McKechnie signed a lucrative contract after the season to manage the Boston Braves, Breadon promptly appointed Street to be the new manager.

The team that Gabby inherited had finished fourth in 1929, 20 games behind the pennant-winning Chicago Cubs. The Redbirds were a distant 9½ games behind the second-place Pittsburgh Pirates and 6½ in back of John McGraw's New York Giants.

As the Cardinals prepared to depart for the annual rigors of spring, Gabby reflected on the team's prospects for 1930.

"I am anxious to make good in my first year as a major league manager, and that is also why I consider myself so fortunate," he said. "Given an initial assignment and handed a group of players like those on the Cardinals is enough to make anyone feel well-fixed.

"After striving for a number of years to reach the goal of a major league leader, almost anyone would be glad to get the opportunity to break in anyplace. But to have a team that is considered a contender is more than a good break, and I appreciate this fact."

The Cardinals boasted one of the strongest, most experienced lineups in the league.

First baseman Sunny Jim Bottomley had enjoyed a great career since joining the Cardinals in 1922. The lefthanded-hitting native of Oglesby, Ill., had batted under .300 only once—.299 in 1926—and was the N.L. Most Valuable Player in 1928, when he led the league with 31 home runs and 136 runs batted in. Always an RBI threat, Sunny Jim had set a major league single-game record when he knocked in 12 runs against the Brooklyn Dodgers on September 16, 1924.

Second baseman Frankie Frisch was one of the best to ever play the keystone. The "Fordham Flash" had joined the Giants in 1919 directly from the campus of Fordham University. He came to the Cardinals after the 1926 season in an unpopular trade for Rogers Hornsby, but Frank had won over the St. Louis fans with his hard-nosed play and .300 batting average each year.

At shortstop, 24-year-old Charley Gelbert was entering his second season after a .262 rookie campaign.

The third-base duties were shared by two graybeards, Andy High, 32, and Sparky Adams, 35, who was purchased from the Pirates before the season. "I can't tell who will play third," Street announced in spring training. "Adams is a new man, and I have not been able to see much of him. High is a great little fellow, and for two or three months at the start, I know he can travel at a fast speed. He may need a short rest after that, but when he gets it he can hop right back in there and go at the same

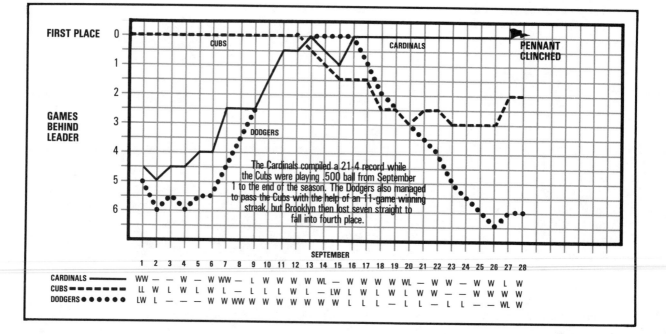

old gait."

In the outfield, "anyone would be glad to have (what) the Cardinals have," Gabby said.

Left fielder Chick Hafey, an early product of the Cards' burgeoning farm system, possessed one of the most powerful arms in the game. Once, in a pregame throwing contest at Cincinnati, he reportedly threw a baseball from home plate over the 18-foot high outfield wall 328 feet away.

No batter had more natural ability than the 26-year-old Californian. Hafey could drive the ball to all fields and had hit .329, .337 and .339 in his previous three seasons. But just when Hafey was enjoying his greatest success, sinus problems began to

Young lefthander Bill Hallahan (below) finally conquered his wildness and veteran Burleigh Grimes (right) brought some much-needed experience and leadership to the 1930 Cardinal pitching staff when acquired from the Boston Braves.

affect his eyesight. A series of operations failed to restore his complete vision, and the outfielder was wearing glasses regularly in 1929.

Fleet-footed Taylor Douthit, 29, was in his fifth season as the club's regular center fielder. Douthit had his best year in the majors in 1929, when he had 206 hits and a .336 average. Ernie Orsatti, who batted .332 as a part-time outfielder-first baseman, and George Watkins, a promising 27-year-old rookie who had hit .337 for Rochester, were expected to compete for the right-field job. On the bench, St. Louis had either Ray Blades or George (Showboat) Fisher as replacements.

"No team in the league has better catching than the Cardinals," Gabby boasted.

Jimmy Wilson, a seven-year veteran, had been acquired by the Cardinals early in the 1928 season from the Philadelphia Phillies. Wilson batted .325 for the Redbirds in 1929. Gus Mancuso, 24, the Cardinals' backup, might have been in the minors had it not been for Commissioner Kenesaw Mountain Landis. St. Louis tried to ship Gus to Rochester for the season, but the Judge ruled that the Cards had exhausted their options on him. Landis ordered them to retain Mancuso or release him. The Birds chose to keep the catcher, luckily, for Gus batted .366 and adeptly handled the pitching staff when Wilson was injured.

In addition to Rhem, the staff was comprised mainly of righthander Jesse Haines, a Cardinal since 1920 but a winner of only 13 games in 1929; lefthander Bill Hallahan, frequently tried and frequently found wanting because of wildness; righthander Sylvester Johnson, a 13-game winner the previous year; lefthander Wee Willie Sherdel, a 12-year veteran who had won 150 games; righthander Fred Frankhouse, a 26-year-old lefthander who was 15-5 over three seasons; lefthander Al Grabowski, who was 3-2 in his rookie year in '29, and righthander Jim Lindsey, who had totaled 46 victories the past two seasons with Houston in the Texas League.

"Our pitching seems to be our only big problem," Street remarked early in the spring. "We have a staff with plenty of pitching talent on it, but the big task, in my mind, is to get the boys in shape in order that they can use the ability which they have."

The fabric of the mound corps underwent a significant change as the trading deadline approached in June. Sherdel and Frankhouse were sent to the Boston Braves for Burleigh Grimes, a veteran spitballer who had starred for Brooklyn in the early 1920s. Old Stubblebeard was a key factor in refining the staff. At 37, Grimes still was agile enough to rack up 13 wins for the Cardinals and calloused enough to low-bridge a batter when the situation required it.

When the season started, the Cardinals quickly fell behind. After losing four straight to the Brooklyn Robins to begin a long May home stand, the Redbirds fell to last place. They were 5½ games out of first with a 6-12 record on May 4. Most of the blame was directed toward the suspect pitching staff. L.H. Addington, reporting on the Cardinals for The Sporting News, wrote:

"Twenty runs in two of the last three games with the Robins plainly indicates that the local team has plenty of punch, but they could not win with such a collection of tallies. It's not the lack of ability to make runs that's hurting the Cardinals—it's the lack of pitching to stop the other fellow from making runs, too.

"There are a good many more games to play at home before the Cards leave for other lands, but the team will have to snap into a different cadence if it is to make the most of its opportunity on home real estate. To be more explicit, the pitching must show a vast improvement. . . . No one knows it any better than the Old Sergeant, who has looked at all kinds of pitching through a mask for nearly 20 seasons."

For the next three weeks, Street looked out of the Sportsman's Park dugout and saw a staff that had refined its ways. The Cardinals won 15 of 16 games and moved into first place with a 21-13 record, half a game ahead of Brooklyn.

In two starts, Grabowski surrendered only three runs in 15 innings for two victories. Haines pitched three complete games, won three times and gave up only six runs. "Wild Bill" Hallahan showed enough control to last at least seven innings in three victories. Johnson pitched a nine-inning shutout over the Reds. Lindsey showed cool savvy for a rookie and won two games in relief.

Addington now reported:

"The spirit of the team was superb as the getaway was made. Heartened by their great record at home, the players have a wholesome confidence that should carry them far.

"The entire play of the team has been outstanding. A marked improvement in pitching, hard and timely hitting, a tight defense and a hustling spirit all have played their parts. Manager Street, in addition, has shown himself to be a leader who is not only able to inspire his men, but to point the way for them in their pennant drive. They have come to idolize the Old Sergeant and will fight on the ball field through literally fire and brimstone for him."

The Cardinals improved their streak to 17 victories in 18 games when they beat Chicago and Pittsburgh to open a long road trip.

But just as suddenly, the Cards reversed their trend. They lost 12 of their next 13 games and fell to fourth place with a 24-25 record on June 8, seven games behind Brooklyn.

The relapse was partly due to an epidemic of injuries. Gelbert, exceeding all expectations by hitting near .350, suffered a charley horse and played only twice during the first two weeks of June. Frisch was disabled for 17 days when he injured a leg in a collision with Farrell. Orsatti was hampered by a sore ankle, Hafey's sinus trouble flared up and Haines was hit by a line drive. In addition, Bottomley, who had missed two weeks in May, was still nagged by a sore thumb.

The Cardinals limped through June with a 10-15 record and remained in fourth entering July. At 33-32, the Redbirds were eight games behind the league-leading Cubs, 6½ behind the second-place Robins and half a game behind the third-place

Giants.

Joe McCarthy's Cubs, the preseason favorites to win their second straight pennant, streaked into first by winning 20 of 27 games in June. Even without second baseman Rogers Hornsby, who was sidelined with a broken ankle, the Cubs' lineup packed plenty of punch. Hack Wilson had hit 23 home runs on his way to 56 for the season, an N.L. record. The center fielder finished with 190 runs batted in, a major league record. Left fielder Riggs Stephenson was sixth in the batting race with a .379 average and catcher Gabby Hartnett had 17 homers.

But the Cardinals, Robins and Giants had their offenses cranked up, too. For the Cards, Watkins was batting .385 and Frisch .362. Mancuso was hitting .439, Fisher .429, Blades .400, and Orsatti .380 in part-time duty. In Brooklyn, right fielder Babe Herman had 18 home runs and a .380 average, first baseman Del Bissonette was batting .357 and second baseman Jake Flowers .356. For the Giants, right fielder Mel Ott had 16 home runs, first baseman Bill Terry had 10 homers and a .389 average, and catcher Bob O'Farrell sported a .369 mark.

The skyrocketing averages were not indigenous to the contenders—baseballs were flying everywhere in all of the major league parks. Nine of the 16 clubs had team averages above .300. Double-digit scores were accepted, production in the 20s shrugged off. Gratified as he was that his Giants could score runs, McGraw spoke for many when he bemoaned the state of the game.

"It's not the pitching," he said. "It's that new jack-rabbit ball. The pitchers have had their stuff. But with that jack-rabbit ball, they haven't a chance. All a batter has to do is meet it, and if the ball is not hit right at somebody, it's a base hit. That ball travels like a bullet, and unless you are in front of it, you haven't a chance to stop it. Just tap it and it lands in the stands. It's making a joke of the game."

Which reminded one reporter of the man who encountered a ball player standing on the edge of a road, far away from the game.

"How's the game going?" the man asked.

"Fine," the player said.

"What's the score?"

"Twenty-two to nothing."

"What?" the man exclaimed. "And you call that fine?"

"Sure," the ball player replied. "We ain't been up yet."

Perhaps it was the lively baseball that kept Street hopeful in the midst of the Cardinals' dismal streak.

While others were dismissing the Cards as viable contenders, Gabby maintained a bold front. A headline in the July 3 issue of The Sporting News announced: "Street Is Not Ready to Count Cards Out." The manager asserted that his team was quite

Veteran pitcher Dazzy Vance was the top dog in Brooklyn's futile drive for the National League pennant.

capable of mounting another drive to the top of the league.

"We are keeping our noses to the wheel," Street said, "and just sawing wood, winning all the games we can and expecting to strike a stride that will advance us in the race. Our morale has held up through all the misfortunes, and if there are any fans who have counted us out of the final reckoning, their opinions are not shared by the Cardinal players.

"I can't ask my men to do any more, for they are giving everything they have. They are hustling for me as I want my team to hustle, and eventually we ought to get some good breaks through the law of averages. Give us just a few of those breaks and I'll bank on the boys to take advantage of them."

Street's optimism, however, failed to attract many converts. The Cardinals lost 13 times on a 21-game road trip and had a 15-17 record for July. Old Sarge's patience wore thin after losing 11 games by one run. Finally, he decided to practice some of the stern discipline he had exercised during World War I.

Sunny Jim Bottomley, a Cardinal since 1922, played first base and wielded a big bat for the 1930 N.L. champions.

"I am tired of having persons tell me we have the best team in the National League and then watch it lose games that should be won," Gabby barked in announcing his get-tough policy. "Most of the boys are hustling and giving all they can, but there are a few who are not taking the game seriously. They are not thinking baseball, and I am tired of continually seeing throws made to the wrong base and rallies snuffed by dumb plays on the sacks."

The first players to feel Gabby's sting were Rhem and reliever Harold Haid. Rhem was fined $100 and Haid $50, for derelictions during a game.

Street's no-nonsense program translated into quick success. The club that languished in fourth place, 12 games behind Brooklyn on August 9, closed the month with 17 victories in 23 games. Entering September, the Cards still were in fourth, with a 71-58 record. But they were only half a game behind the Robins, now in third, 1½ games behind the third-place Giants and 4½ behind the front-running Cubs.

The Cardinals moved into a second-place tie on September 4, when they mauled the Reds, 13-2, as the Giants lost in Boston, 7-1. The idle Redbirds took over sole possession of second the next day, when the Giants lost their third straight game in Boston.

After sweeping a September 7 doubleheader from the Reds before more than 36,000 excited fans at Sportsman's Park, the Cardinals departed for New York, trailing first-place Chicago by 2½ games. At the same time, the Cubs traveled to Brooklyn for a crucial series after having won only three of their last nine games.

The Cubs' visit to Ebbets Field was a total disaster. The team with a .311 batting average scored only one run in three games. Chicago lost to Ray Phelps, 3-0, to Dolf Luque, 6-0, and to Dazzy Vance, 2-1.

The Cardinals, meanwhile, won three of the four games at the Polo Grounds. After losing the opener, 2-1, to former Redbird Clarence Mitchell, the Redbirds triumphed 5-3 behind Johnson's 11th win, 5-4 behind Hallahan's 14th victory, and 5-2 behind Rhem's 10th win.

Each St. Louis victory was clinched in the late innings: Bottomley's three-run homer capped a four-run eighth inning to win the first game; High's infield single scored Hafey in the eighth inning of the second contest, and four singles and a throwing error by Terry produced three runs in the ninth of the final victory.

The Robins' four victories over Cincinnati extended their winning streak to 11 games and boosted them to first place, one game ahead of the Cardinals, who had lost one of three games in Boston. The two red-hot teams finally crossed paths in Brooklyn to play the most important three-game series of the year.

When the series opened September 16, more than 30,000 fans jammed Ebbets Field to watch a duel between the teams' top hurlers, Vance and Hallahan.

At 39, Vance no longer possessed the blinding speed that had won him 28 games in 1924. But he still was crafty enough to have won 16 games and would finish as the N.L. leader in earned-run average with a 2.61 mark.

Hallahan had made commendable progress under the counsel of Street and the knowledgeable Grimes. After a 4-4 season in 1929, the lefthander had become the club's leading winner with a 14-8 record, although he still had spells of wildness.

Many Eastern writers gave the Cardinals only a slim chance to capture the flag. Considering the Cards' 82-60 record and Brooklyn's 84-60 mark, one New York scribe pointed out: "The Robins have played two more games than the Cardinals and won both of them. That also makes the work of the St. Louisans a little harder. For they have no written guarantee that they will win those two games in bringing their schedule up to date."

The drama that unfolded in the first game was pure artistry. Hallahan was magnificent and retired the first 20 batters in order. Herman, who had hit in the .390s most of the year, became Brooklyn's first baserunner when Hallahan fumbled his dribbler with two outs in the seventh. Left fielder Harvey Hendrick's single into left field spoiled the no-hitter with one out in the eighth.

Although the Cards recorded an occasional hit, they couldn't score either. They threatened to in the sixth inning, when Adams, on third with two out, tried to steal home as Vance was taking his exaggerated windup. Sparky would have succeeded except that Dazzy quickly fired a pitch that hit Hafey. The dead ball forced Adams back to third, where he was stranded.

A Brooklyn threat in the ninth was nipped by the type of baserunning that earned the Robins the nickname of "Daffiness Boys." After the first two batters reached base, center fielder Eddie Moore tried to bunt but popped weakly to Mancuso. The alert catcher quickly threw to second and caught the unwary runner off base.

High, who broke into the majors with Brooklyn in 1922, led off the 10th inning for the Redbirds. The 5-foot-6 infielder came off the bench after Gelbert was shaken up in a collision at second in the eighth inning.

After batting .295 and leading the league in fielding at third the year before, Andy had been used

mostly as a backup to Adams, a .309 hitter, in 1930. But when High got his chances, he made the most of them. He blasted a pitch from Vance to right-center field for a double and scored moments later on Douthit's looping single to right field, the seventh hit off Vance.

Hallahan narrowly escaped with the victory after the Robins rallied in the bottom of the inning. Shortstop Glenn Wright led off with a double. A walk to Bissonette, a sacrifice and an intentional pass to pinch-hitter Jake Flowers loaded the bases with one out. The next batter was Al Lopez, a 22-year-old catcher in the first year of a distinguished career that would lead to the Hall of Fame.

The Senor rapped a vicious grounder which shortstop Adams knocked down between third and short. Just when it appeared that the tying run would score, Adams pounced on the ball and flipped it to Frisch, who relayed to first for a lightning-quick double play. The twin-killing was executed so rapidly, one writer insisted, few spectators realized the game was over.

Sinus problems and failing eyesight had become major problems for the talented Chick Hafey by the 1930 season.

Brooklyn Manager Wilbert Robinson was reluctant to applaud the St. Louis wizardry. "It took Al exactly 15 minutes to get down to first base," Uncle Robbie grumbled.

By any standard, the game ranked as a classic. Covering the contest for the New York Herald Tribune, Murray Tynan gushed:

"There may have been other ball games played through the years that had more great plays and more dramatic moments than this one, but you would have a job on your hands trying to convince any of the 30,000 fans of that. The pitching . . . was gorgeous, the defense of both clubs was closely woven and almost impossible to penetrate. No one could ask any more of any group of athletes, and there is small doubt but that hundreds of fans would have been willing to pay their way going out as well as in."

The 1-0 victory pushed the Cardinals into first place by one percentage point. Rhem, winner of six consecutive decisions, was scheduled to pitch the second game of the series.

But where was Rhem? Flint had not been seen for more than 24 hours. Could he have met with foul play? Perhaps even been kidnapped? Maybe something worse? Street was stumped and, for once, the erudite Rickey was at a loss for words.

As club officials prepared to summon police for a full-scale investigation, the mystery was solved. Bleary-eyed and disheveled, Rhem reappeared at the team's hotel on the morning of September 17. As related in The Sporting News, Street "took one glance at his star pitcher . . . summoned bellhops to prepare Rhem's bed (and) listened patiently to his tale of woe."

News accounts of Flint's disappearance smacked of underworld intrigue.

The pitcher said he was standing on the sidewalk outside the hotel, drinking in the evening air, when an automobile braked to a stop and a voice called to him. Unable to hear the indistinct remark, Rhem approached the vehicle. Suddenly, a door opened and he was muscled inside.

He was taken, he said, to a hoodlum hangout in New Jersey, where he was forced to guzzle vast quantities of liquor. When Rhem's captors were convinced he was sufficiently inebriated and incapable of taking his turn on the mound, he was returned to the hotel. As he was dumped out, the gunmen issued a somber warning: If Flint enjoyed life, he was not to pitch against the Robins. Or so the newspapers reported.

Those familiar with Flint's drinking habits appreciated his fertile imagination. Roy Stockton, a St. Louis baseball writer, let his own lively sense of humor rule his judgment. "Flint said he was kidnapped," Stockton observed. "Who am I to spoil his good story?"

Street took a charitable view of Rhem's transgression. "That's the first time this year Flint has leaped over the traces," the skipper said. "He has been a good boy and helped us to our present position. We are more interested in winning the pennant now than in meting out punishment. . . ."

Rickey labeled Flint's tale of horror "pure fabrication" but took no disciplinary action.

With Rhem unfit to start the game, Street called on Johnson, an 11-game winner to oppose Luque, who had won 14. The Robins took an early two-run lead, but Hafey's 26th homer, with Bottomley aboard, tied the score in the fourth inning. Left fielder Ike Boone's round-tripper in the bottom of the inning gave Luque his second lead, which the Cuban protected until the eighth, when a walk, Adams' double and a sacrifice fly tied the game again.

After Grabowski relieved and set down the Robins in order in the bottom of the eighth inning, Luque retired the first two Cardinals in the ninth before walking Mancuso. Gelbert's infield single brought up High to pinch-hit for Grabowski. Once again Andy delivered the big blow in the clutch. He slammed another double, this time off the right-field wall, and two runners scampered home for a 5-3 victory, which gave the Cards a one-game lead over the Robins.

The little fellow's success shocked some observers, but "Merry Andrew" had a simple explanation. "I'd been away for five years," he reminded folks, "but Robinson never thought it necessary to change the signs. His whole strategy was like an open book."

Grimes, another former member of the Brooklyn cast, concluded the series on September 18 with his 15th win, a 4-3 decision over Phelps. The Redbirds collected only five hits, but one was an RBI triple by Frisch, who then scored on Bottomley's homer. Another triple, by Douthit to start the sixth, led to the winning run.

The Robins never recovered from the critical losses. The team that had won 11 games in a row before the Cardinals arrived dropped four more after the Redbirds departed and finished in fourth place.

The Cards, meanwhile, moved on to Philadelphia, where they took three of four games. They won one game, 15-7, and another, 19-16, after staking Rhem to an 11-0 cushion. That lead quickly disintegrated and Rhem was lifted in the fifth inning. But under the scoring rules of the era, Flint received credit for his 12th victory, even though he failed to complete the required five innings.

While Brooklyn was effectually eliminated, Chicago and New York continued to pressure the Cardinals. The outcome remained unsettled as the Redbirds returned home for the final four games of the season. To heighten the suspense, the Birds' opponents were the Pirates, who already had defeated the Cards 12 times in 18 games.

This time, however, the script was changed. Grimes shut out the Buccos, 9-0, on September 25 for his 16th victory, and Haines won his 13th game, 10-5, to clinch the pennant the next afternoon. Watkins led the attack in the clincher with two singles, his 17th home run and three RBIs to cap a .373 rookie season.

With the pennant wrapped up, Street unveiled a 19-year-old pitcher in the season finale September 28. The gangling righthander, a loquacious chap with supreme confidence, had won 17 games for St. Joseph of the Western Association and eight more after being promoted to Houston.

Unintimidated by the major league environment, the former cotton picker from Oklahoma allowed only three hits and fanned five to pitch the Cards to a 3-1 win. It was the first of 150 big-league victories for Dizzy Dean and the Cards' 39th win in their last 49 games.

After their dramatic surge, the Cardinals lost the World Series to the Philadelphia Athletics in six games. The Redbirds repeated as pennant winners in 1931, aided by 11 victories from Rhem, and avenged their earlier Series defeat by beating the A's in seven games.

As the years passed, Rhem and his 1930 escapade faded from memory. After stops in Philadelphia, St. Louis, again, and Boston, Flint finished his career with the Cardinals in 1936 and returned to his native South Carolina to farm.

In 1961, Bob Talbert, a sportswriter for the Columbia State, interviewed the 60-year-old Rhem. On the veranda of his rambling country home, Flint reminisced about his years as a major league pitcher. Eventually, the conversation shifted to the caper for which he was most famous. Rhem remembered he and Hallahan had been roommates on the road and then narrated this different version of the incident:

"Wild Bill and I were a lot alike. We liked to roam about at the amusement parks, roller coaster rides, and take a drink or two and live a little bit.

"The night before the series (in Brooklyn), we went out. Now it wasn't a big party or anything like that. Just something to eat and maybe—I don't remember exactly—a couple of drinks.

"Well, the next morning when I woke up I was sicker than I had ever been in my life. It was terrible. It must have been some bad piece of meat I'd eaten the night before.

"Oh, I was sick all over. Stomach, head, even the bottom of my feet. Hallahan just looked at me and shook his head.

"'What should I tell Sarge?' he asked me. 'Tell him any damn thing you want to,' I answered back

One of the big stories of 1930 was the mysterious disappearance of Cardinal pitcher Flint Rhem on the eve of an important starting assignment.

and rolled over in the bed. 'I ain't going to no ball park as bad as I feel. I couldn't do nothing anyway.'

"The next day, Mr. Rickey came by our hotel room and knocked on the door. I was still sicker than a mule. Mr. Rickey came in the room and sort of left the door cracked a little bit, about two feet. Outside in the hall I could see some sportswriters standing around trying to listen.

"'Shad,' Mr. Rickey asks me by the name he gave me because of all the fish stories I used to tell him, 'what's the matter with you? I guess somebody kidnapped you.'

"I was still pretty green around the gills when I looked at him. 'You can call it what you want,' I said. 'All I know is I'm sicker than can be.' Now that's all I said, so help me.

"Well, those writers outside the door took that little conversation and built up this story—I don't know if Mr. Rickey helped 'em or not—that I had been kidnapped and taken to New Jersey, where the kidnappers fed me whiskey to get me so drunk I couldn't pitch in the Brooklyn series.

"All the while I was supposed to be sick, I was in my own hotel room. So help me that's what happened."

Rhem died on July 30, 1969, leaving the world to ponder, and probably chuckle over, his bizarre experience 39 years before.

Injured Dodgers Find The Winning Formula

The 1964 season had been disappointing for Tommy Davis. The two-time National League batting champion had slipped to .275, a 51-point plunge from the year before. And as Tommy skidded, so did the Los Angeles Dodgers, all the way from the world championship to a sixth-place tie.

Not noted for his power, Davis had hit 14 home runs that dismal campaign, second only to Frank Howard among the Dodgers. When Howard was traded to the Washington Senators after the season, Davis was left as the team's major power threat.

But that was history. As Tommy stood on first base the evening of May 1, 1965, both he and the team appeared to have recovered their dominant touch of 1963, when the Dodgers won the pennant by six games over the St. Louis Cardinals and Davis led N.L. hitters with a .326 average.

On this Saturday night, the Dodgers were in first place, and Davis, with his single leading off the fourth inning, had six hits in his last nine at-bats.

The crowd of 49,758 relished moments such as these in Chavez Ravine—the Dodgers were facing their bitter rivals, the San Francisco Giants, the game was tied, 1-1, and Gaylord Perry was pitching to Ron Fairly. Whose blood would not run warm at a time like this?

Davis glanced over his shoulder at first baseman Orlando Cepeda as Perry delivered. Fairly swung and rapped a grounder to the right side. With Davis streaking toward second in full stride, Cepeda tossed to Perry for a routine putout at first base.

At second base, the action was far from ordinary. Undecided on whether to hit the dirt or stay up, Davis fell into an awkward slide. His spike caught on the rock-hard basepath, and he flipped forward onto his face. He lay motionless as Perry raced down the base line and tagged him out, all too vigorously in the opinion of the concerned spectators.

Racing onto the field, Dodgers trainer Wayne Anderson took one look at Davis' twisted right ankle and knew it was fractured. The injury, doctors disclosed soberly, would sideline the Brooklyn native probably for the rest of the season.

Dodger officials frantically searched for a new left fielder. Al (The Bull) Ferrara was on the roster, but he was an untried rookie better known for having once played the piano at Carnegie Hall.

The quest turned toward the farm system. In Spokane, a righthanded-hitting outfielder was ripping Pacific Coast League pitching for a .311 average. The year before, he had hit .328 to finish second in that Triple-A circuit.

But the fellow was 31 years old. He was a baseball vagabond who had played for 18 teams in 13 years since leaving his hometown of Lexington, Ky. He also had a reputation as a "bad guy," a chip-on-the-shoulder type who spawned turmoil wherever he went. He had brief trials with three major league clubs, and a fourth, the Detroit Tigers, left him in the minors before swapping him to the Dodgers for pitcher Larry Sherry.

Nevertheless, Los Angeles was in dire need of a left fielder. On May 4, while the Dodgers were in Cincinnati, Louis Brown Johnson walked into the visitors' clubhouse. Within days, he became "LBJ," baseball's equivalent of the occupant of the White House, Lyndon Baines Johnson.

About the same time, Buzzie Bavasi made one of his rare clubhouse appearances. The executive vice president and general manager had a message for the lugubrious players.

"Frankly, the reason I came here is because I am concerned about the morale of the club after Tommy's injury," Bavasi said.

"I want you players to know that just because Tommy is out for a time, our season is not over. It won't be easy, of course, taking up the slack . . . but we must, and will do it."

Manager Walter Alston concurred. "We can't replace Tommy, I know that," he said. "But we still can do the job. This is a tough team."

The first thing that Johnson's teammates noticed about him was his personality. Lou was the exact opposite of what they had expected—he was lighthearted, cheerful, congenial. Johnson had an explanation. "There was a guy in the minors with (a similar) name," he said, "and he was a bad guy. Knife fights, all that. They got me mixed up with him."

Even in a profession where characters abound, Johnson was a remarkable creature. Signed initially by the New York Yankees' farm system, he joined Olean of the Pony League in 1953. He remained there only long enough to get nailed in the head by a pitch. He returned to his native Bluegrass Country until the next season, when he played in the Mountain State and West Texas-New Mexico leagues. In

With the Davis boys, Tommy (left) and Willie, patrolling two-thirds of their outfield, the Dodgers were confident heading into the 1965 season.

1955, a Pittsburgh scout persuaded Lou to join the Pirates' St. Jean farm club in Canada, the beginning of a jagged course to such towns as Clinton, Ponca City, Burlington, Paris and Lancaster.

With Ponca City in 1956, Johnson was purported to have been part of an attempt at medical history.

Lou and several teammates were driving to Muskogee, Okla., for a Sooner State League game when a tire blew out in their station wagon. The car flipped into a ditch, throwing Lou through a window—without part of his right ear. Johnson and his ear were wheeled off to the hospital, where surgeons were waiting.

Don Biebel, the Ponca manager, was quoted as saying that doctors sliced open Johnson's abdomen, "stored" the ear there and then removed it when it was time to sew it in place.

"The doctors decided that the cells of the severed part of the ear might be revived if the ear was inserted in Lou's stomach," Biebel said. "It was my job to tell him, and when I did he said, 'No, no, Skip. They're not cutting open my stomach. I'm going home to Mama.'"

Johnson survived, but the experiment failed.

That was not all that set Johnson apart. His experience with the bean ball at Olean was only the first of a long series of such incidents. Wherever he played, speeding baseballs found their way to his body.

When he was with the Cubs, LBJ was struck on the wrist by a pitch from the Dodgers' Stan Williams in a spring exhibition game. He retired to the dugout and was relaxing there when a foul ball was smashed into the dugout. Of all the potential targets, the ball singled out Johnson. Lou was conked on the head and hospitalized for a week.

Johnson readily accepted the pain inflicted by whizzing baseballs. The discomfort he suffered from frustration in his static career was another matter. By 1965, Lou and his wife, Doris, had en-

dured enough. They decided to abandon their nomadic lifestyle at the end of the '65 season and settle in San Diego, where Doris would teach school and Lou would work as a salesman.

The call from the Dodgers interrupted those plans, but not Lou's penchant for stopping baseballs with his anatomy. On May 13, eight days after his first appearance in Dodger blue, Johnson was beaned in the middle of the forehead by Houston, righthander Bob Bruce. Johnson's batting helmet received a ghastly puncture and Lou missed two games.

On June 12, an inside pitch from New York Mets lefthander Alvin Jackson fractured Lou's thumb and knocked him out of the starting lineup for 12 days.

"I'm beginning to think I'll never leave this game alive," said Lou, who refused to back off from the plate. "I guess I have to figure that the book on me is to pitch me inside with fastballs."

But when LBJ was healthy, he supplied precisely what the Dodgers needed—timely hitting, good speed, an adequate glove and unwavering spirit.

Johnson fit the mold for this hustling bunch of Dodgers perfectly. A week after Davis went down, shortstop Maury Wills told The Sporting News: "Our spirit since Tommy was hurt is not as good as before—it's better. In fact, it's amazing.

"Fairly came to me after (the injury) and said, 'Maury, with Tommy out, you and I plus Willie (Davis) and Rosie (John Roseboro) can take up the slack. We can keep on going.'

"We have more enthusiasm on this club than ever before."

The Dodgers' regular lineup featured Roseboro, the catcher, who had hit a career-high .287 in 1964; an all-switch-hitting infield of Wes Parker, entering his second year at first base, rookie Jim Lefebvre at second, the speedster Wills at short, and 12-year veteran Jim Gilliam at third; and an outfield of John-

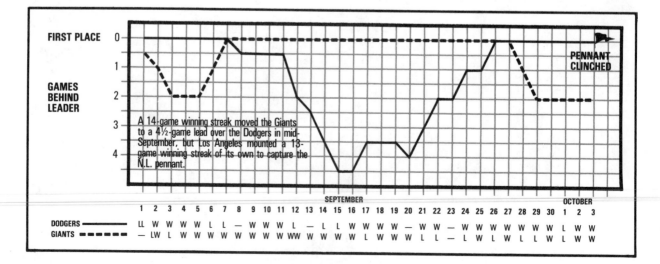

A 14-game winning streak moved the Giants to a 4½-game lead over the Dodgers in mid-September, but Los Angeles mounted a 13-game winning streak of its own to capture the N.L. pennant.

When hard-hitting Tommy Davis suffered a broken ankle, the Dodgers turned
to 31-year-old Lou Johnson (above), who filled in admirably.

son in left, swift Willie Davis in center and Fairly in right.

The Los Angeles pitching staff overshadowed all others. Lefthander Sandy Koufax, the premier pitcher in baseball, was the rotation stopper. The 1963 Cy Young Award winner finished 19-5 in 1964, and his 1.74 earned-run average topped the league for the third straight year. Sandy would be the major leagues' workhorse in 1965 by pitching 336 innings. Don Drysdale, his righthanded counterpart, would hurl 308 innings as the runner-up after pitching 314, 315 and 321 innings the previous three years. The 1962 Cy Young Award winner had managed 18 victories in 1964 and a 2.19 ERA. Johnny Podres, the dean of the staff, was returning after elbow surgery in '64 and Claude Osteen, acquired in the Howard trade after winning 15 for the Senators, completed the rotation.

"We want to get into a regular rotation of Drysdale and then three lefthanders—Koufax, Podres and Osteen, in sequence," Alston said in spring training.

"That Osteen is a serious fellow and a real pitcher," the manager said. "He'll be a good addition to this outfit in more ways than one."

In the bullpen, the Dodgers had lefthanders Jim Brewer, Ron Perranoski and Mike Kekich, and righthanders Bob Miller, Howie Reed and John Purdin.

After their collapse of 1964, little was expected of the Dodgers in 1965. The Sporting News' preseason poll of the Baseball Writers Association of America established the Philadelphia Phillies as favorites. The Phils, who had blown a 6½-game lead and the 1964 pennant in the last two weeks of the season, were followed in the balloting by the Cardinals, the Cincinnati Reds, the Dodgers and the Giants.

As the season opened, it was apparent the experts had misread their tea leaves. These Dodgers were a different breed. After bouncing in and out of the lead before Davis' injury, the Dodgers moved into a first-place tie with the Reds on May 4, when they beat Cincinnati, 8-6, in the first game of the three-game series. The Dodgers won 10 out of their next 14 games and remained in first place for two months as Johnson stepped in to lead the offense.

Lou clubbed his first home run May 13—four innings before he was beaned by Bruce—as Koufax beat the Astros, 3-0. Johnson smacked a pair of round-trippers May 29 to help Drysdale defeat the Milwaukee Braves, 5-3. Willie Davis was the only other Dodger to hit two homers in one game in 1965.

Johnson's fourth homer, on June 6, helped Drysdale beat Milwaukee, 4-0, in the first game of a doubleheader, and his fifth blast, the next day, backed Koufax in a 14-3 victory over the Phillies.

When the Dodgers suffered from a power short-

age—which they frequently did—they introduced a new style of baseball. Their strategy featured the "Dodger Double," the "Dodger Triple" and the "Dodger Sacrifice." In the first stratagem, Wills would beat out an infield hopper and steal second base. In the second maneuver, Wills would outleg an infield roller and steal two bases. The Dodger Sacrifice involved a forceout at second base but a theft of the bag by one of the team's greyhounds. When Wills stole his 49th base, against the Astros on July 3, he jumped 20 games ahead of his base-stealing pace of 1962, when he swiped a record 104 bases.

By the All-Star break, the unconventional Dodgers had acquired a reputation as the Banjo Boppers of the league. Besides Fairly, who had a .311 average and 53 runs batted in, Drysdale (.317) was the only other .300 hitter on a team with a .246 average. In the starting lineup, Johnson was batting .280, Wills and Gilliam, .275, Willie Davis, .253, Parker, .246, Roseboro, .232, and Lefebvre, .226.

In the three games just before the All-Star contest and the two following it, Drysdale, Koufax and Osteen combined for a .438 average.

"If I were a manager, I'd have my pitchers take batting practice every day," Drysdale told The Sporting News. "I really believe the reason a lot of pitchers don't hit is simply because they don't practice."

Milwaukee Manager Bobby Bragan explained a popular strategy devised against Los Angeles. "If it were possible, I would like to arrange my pitching so I could use a lefthander against the Dodgers every time we play them," Bragan said. "And so would the other managers in the league.

"Here's what lefthanders do to the Dodgers. They turn those four infielders around at the plate and make them hit righthanded, which is one step removed from first base."

In their first 42 decisions against lefties, the Dodgers were 21-21. Over the same period, they were 37-12 against righthanders.

The only things incapacitated more often than Los Angeles' hitting attack were the players themselves. As Bob Hunter, Los Angeles correspondent for The Sporting News, pointed out: "They're calling Alston the push-button manager. He dials M for Miracle and the Dodgers keep on rolling along Pennant Boulevard."

Except for the starting pitchers, the only Dodgers who didn't miss a game in the first three months were Fairly and Lefebvre. Ferrara broke his finger four days after Tommy Davis was injured. Parker missed 10 days with a shoulder separation in early June; a few days later, Brewer was placed on the disabled list with a bad elbow; Johnson broke his thumb and Willie Davis suffered damaged rib cartilage in a collision.

Johnson and Willie Davis were rushed into action at the end of June to avert an outfield catastrophe. Los Angeles had its worst spell of the season and lost seven times during a 13-game home stand. The club then lost nine more games on a 16-game trip leading up to the All-Star break. The Dodgers dropped into second place with a 51-38 record, three percentage points behind the 49-36 Reds.

The Giants, led by Willie Mays' bat and Juan Marichal's arm, were in third place with a 45-38 record, three games from the top. Mays was leading the league in hitting, .339, and in home runs, 23. Marichal led the circuit in ERA, 1.55, complete games, 15, and shutouts, seven. His 14 victories were second to Koufax's 15.

The Phillies, 3½ games back, Braves, 5½ back, and Pirates, six games behind, were bunched together behind San Francisco.

The Dodgers regained first place when the season resumed by winning six straight games. They held the lead until August 18, when the red-hot Braves briefly took over. Bragan's crew won 10 straight on their way to 28 victories in 37 games. The Braves were led by a slugging attack that would set an N.L. record with six players hitting 20 or more home runs for the season. Hank Aaron and Eddie Mathews led the team with 32 apiece, Mack Jones hit 31, Joe Torre, 27, Felipe Alou, 23, and Gene Oliver, 21.

Trailing by half a game on August 19, Los Angeles invaded Candlestick Park for four games with the third-place Giants. The California rivals split the series, lifting the Dodgers back into first place as the Braves dropped three of four games.

The big news in the Bay Area, however, was not the outcome of the series. Rather it was an incident in the third inning of the final game, when the tensions between the teams had reached a boiling point.

The Dodgers and Koufax, 21-4, had a 2-1 lead over the Giants and Marichal, the volatile Dominican who was seeking his 20th victory. Brushbacks abounded in the opening innings. In the first, Wills

The 1965 Dodgers fielded an all-switch-hitting infield featuring (left to right) Maury Wills, Jim Lefebvre, Jim Gilliam and Wes Parker.

One of the bizarre incidents of baseball history occurred in 1965 when Giants pitcher Juan Marichal attacked Dodger catcher John Roseboro with a bat.

bunted his way on and scored the first Los Angeles run, which prompted Marichal to knock Maury down in the second inning. After Koufax sailed a pitch over Mays' head in the bottom of the second, Marichal decked Fairly in the top of the third. The San Francisco righthander then stepped to the plate for the first time in the Giants' half of the inning.

After Koufax's third pitch, Marichal suddenly clubbed Roseboro on the head with his bat to ignite a full-scale brawl for the next 14 minutes. Players poured off both benches, fists flew, spikes flashed. Players frantically tugged at one another as they tried to halt a fight or start a new one. The fracas apparently unsettled Koufax. When play resumed, he issued two walks before Mays clubbed his 14th homer of the month to give San Francisco a 4-3 win.

Marichal was ejected from the game by umpire Shag Crawford, and Roseboro was forced to leave because of a gash on his head. The next day, Mari-

chal was suspended for eight playing days by N.L. President Warren Giles and slapped with a league-record fine of $1,750.

Roseboro, asked what he thought would be a just penalty for the pitcher, replied, "Just put him and me in a room together for 10 minutes."

The Los Angeles catcher reported this version of his encounter with Marichal:

"Sandy Koufax's pitch to Marichal in the third inning was low and a little inside. I picked it up and threw it back to the mound.

"'You better not hit me with that ball,' Marichal said to me."

Roseboro said he then took a step toward Marichal and was hit over the head.

"I may have come close," Roseboro said, "but the ball didn't hit him. It if had, he would have been lying there.

"No, I won't continue the fight the next time I see him," he continued. "But when you get your head

With Roseboro trying to fend off the bat-wielding Marichal, Dodger pitcher
Sandy Koufax arrived to help his battered teammate.

split open, you don't forget. Marichal and I haven't actually had any trouble, but I'm no fan of his. We're not friendly, put it that way."

In the second inning of the August 20 game, Marichal and first-year Giants Manager Herman Franks had been yelling at Roseboro from the dugout. "But I had practically forgotten about that . . ." the catcher said.

Alston, like everyone else on the Dodgers, was fuming.

"You couldn't print my opinion of that gutless . . ." he said of Marichal. "If Marichal comes up with an excuse, it's a lie."

The assault, the pitcher insisted, was provoked by Roseboro.

"I think Roseboro deliberately dropped the ball on the third pitch so he could get behind me," Marichal said. "Then he threw the ball back to Koufax real hard, and it ticked my ear.

"I turned around and I say, 'Why do you do

that?' Roseboro do not say anything, but he took off his mask and I was afraid he was going to hit me with it, so I hit him with my bat.

"If he had only said something, I would not have swung my bat, but I hit him once with it and I'm sorry. I think the anger started two nights before (September 20). Maury Wills was awarded first base for catcher's interference.

"Our players thought Wills deliberately stepped back, forcing Tom Haller to tip Wills' bat with his glove. So when Matty Alou came to bat the next inning, he did the same thing, but the plate umpire (Doug Harvey) did not award him first.

"Then Roseboro yelled over at our dugout, 'If this stuff doesn't stop, we're going to get one of you guys good—right in the ear,' and later, Roseboro repeated this threat to Orlando Cepeda."

The Dodgers moved on and maintained a slim advantage in first as the race thundered into September. Bunched behind Los Angeles, which had a

Players and umpires converged to try and stop the fight, though Giants shortstop Tito Fuentes (26) seemed to have other ideas.

75-57 record, were San Francisco, 72-57, Cincinnati and Milwaukee, 72-58, and Pittsburgh, 71-62.

On September 1, the Dodgers faced the Pirates in a doubleheader at Pittsburgh. Though Koufax, 21-6, and Drysdale, 18-11, were on the mound, the Dodgers came away empty-handed. They lost the opener, 3-2, in 11 innings and the nightcap, 2-1. The Reds, meanwhile, won a pair from the Braves and took over first place as the Giants were rained out in Philadelphia. The Buccos, in fifth place, pulled to within 2½ games of first with their sweep.

That, however, was the closest the Pirates got. After Osteen beat 14-game winner Bob Veale the next night for his 12th victory, the Braves heaped two more losses on the Pirates and they faded from serious contention.

But before expiring, the Pirates dealt a crippling blow to the Reds. Pittsburgh swept a Labor Day doubleheader at Crosley Field and won two games of a three-game series that opened four days later.

The Dodgers had returned home on Labor Day in first place to open a two-game set with the Giants, now in second. San Francisco and Los Angeles both had 59 losses, but the Dodgers had 79 victories, four more than their rivals.

More than 55,000 fans cheered on the Dodgers in the opener as Los Angeles took a 4-0 lead against Warren Spahn, who had signed with the Giants in July after he was released by the New York Mets. By the fifth inning, however, the Giants were teeing off on Drysdale. They cuffed Big D for two runs in that stanza and tied the game, 5-5, in the eighth. The Dodgers took another one-run lead in their half of the inning, but Haller homered on Drysdale's first pitch in the ninth to send the game into extra innings.

The Giants won the game in the 12th, when third base sub Jim Davenport singled off reliever Howie Reed to score Matty Alou. The 7-6 defeat tarnished the hitting accomplishments of Johnson, Wills and

When peace finally was restored, Marichal, his uniform top ripped open, was led from the field by sympathetic teammates.

Roseboro, who rapped three safeties apiece.

Johnson had three more hits the next night, but once more, Los Angeles couldn't capitalize. The Dodgers collected only three other safeties off Bob Shaw and Masanori Murakami, a 21-year-old left-handed reliever from Japan, and bowed, 3-1. Left fielder Jim Ray Hart drove home the first run with a first-inning single and the final two with a home run, his second in as many games, in the fifth. The victory pushed San Francisco into the lead for the first time in 1965.

The two victories, coming right after a pair in Chicago, propelled the Giants on to a 14-game winning streak, the longest in the major leagues in 14 years. The skein included two victories over the Houston Astros in San Francisco, four more over Chicago at home and four more against the Astros in Houston. In the first game at the Astrodome, Mays hit his 500th career home run to pace Marichal to his 22nd win.

The streak was snapped September 17 when Marichal bowed to Phil Niekro of Milwaukee, 9-1.

But the Giants bounced back with two victories over the Braves and a 4-0 whitewashing of the Reds by Bob Bolin and Murakami for 17 wins in 18 games. Their lead had grown to four games over the Dodgers and 5½ over the Reds.

But the Dodgers were not dead, not even comatose.

When the Giants dumped Los Angeles out of first with the two-game sweep, Alston had calmly prevailed over the struggling club.

"It's way too early to size up the outcome of this thing," he said quietly. "I'll settle right now for being half a game behind on the last Thursday, and I'll be glad to take any chances.

"We've got Koufax going against the Cubs tomorrow night, and I can't think of a better man to straighten us out again."

All Koufax did was pitch a perfect game Septem-

The Big Two of the 1965 Dodger pitching staff were lefthander Sandy Koufax
(left) and righthander Don Drysdale.

ber 9 to become the first pitcher to hurl four no-
hitters. The 29-year-old bachelor struck out 14 Cubs
as the Dodgers won, 1-0, on one hit. Bob Hendley, a
26-year-old lefthander recalled from the minors,
surrendered only a seventh-inning, two-out double
to Johnson as he lost the only major league game
ever played with only one hit.

The Dodgers scored in the fifth, when Johnson
walked, was sacrificed to second, stole third and
continued home on catcher Chris Krug's high
throw.

"In the seventh, I thought the no-hitter was in
reach," Sandy said. "And believe me, I really wanted it. I didn't think too much about the perfect
game."

Asked what he threw in the final inning, Koufax
replied, "Everything I had."

A week later, on September 16, Osteen launched
a Los Angeles winning streak when he won his 14th
game, a 2-0 decision over the Cubs. The Dodgers

then flew to St. Louis and swept three games. Drysdale won his 20th game in the opener, 3-2, Koufax
won the second, 1-0, on a four-hitter, and Osteen
won his third straight, 5-0, with the help of home
runs by Lefebvre and Parker.

The Dodgers moved on to Milwaukee, where Lefebvre cracked another homer to help Drysdale
beat the Braves, 3-1. The next day, the rookie second baseman hit yet another homer, and Perranoski hurled six innings in relief to gain credit for an
11-inning, 7-6 win. The game was the last the Braves
would ever play in Milwaukee. The Giants, meanwhile, lost two of three games to Cincinnati and
watched their lead dwindle to two games.

The two front-runners returned home September
24 for the final 10 games of the season. More grief
befell the Giants in Northern California as the
Braves' Tony Cloninger threw a four-hitter to beat
Ron Herbel, 8-2. Down the coast, Perranoski won
again in relief, 4-3, over the Cardinals, and the San

The incomparable Willie Mays, the Giants' top gun, combined with teammate
Willie McCovey (44) for 91 home runs in 1965.

By the end of the 1965 season, Dodgers ace Sandy Koufax was at the top of the pitching world and much decorated for his achievements.

Francisco lead was shaved to a single game.

Mays' 50th homer of the year helped Bolin defeat Milwaukee, 7-5, September 25, but the Dodgers kept pace when Koufax shut out the Cards, 2-0, on five hits. Sandy's 12 strikeouts gave him 356 for the season, which topped Bob Feller's previous major league record of 348.

The Giants gave the ball to Marichal the next day to protect their slender advantage. Wonderful Juan and two relievers allowed only seven hits and Willie McCovey rapped his 39th homer, but the Braves still won, 3-2. In Los Angeles, Drysdale matched Koufax's five-hit effort to beat the Cards, 1-0. Drysdale set an N.L. record by striking out 200 or more batters for a sixth season.

After being four games apart only six days before, the Giants and Dodgers were deadlocked with 91-64 records and seven games to play.

The Reds visited Dodger Stadium on September 27 with luck no better than the Cardinals'. Podres hurled five innings to earn his seventh victory and Perranoski sparkled again in relief as Willie Davis' two homers led the Dodgers to a 6-1 triumph. In Candlestick, Haller also clouted two home runs and reliever Frank Linzy earned credit for an 8-4 victory over Tracy Stallard and the Cardinals.

Johnson's 12th-inning homer, the Dodgers' 78th and last of the campaign, edged the Reds, 2-1, September 28, while Bill White, a former Giant, belted a homer, two doubles and a single to lead the Cardinals to a 9-1 win. After three weeks at the head of the pack, the Giants fell to second place.

September 29—The Dodgers and Koufax rolled relentlessly on. The lefthander blanked the Reds, 5-0, on a two-hitter as Wills furnished a bases-loaded triple. In San Francisco, the Giants scored six runs in the ninth inning, only to bow, 8-6, to Bob Gibson, who accounted for half of the Cards' runs with his first career grand slam. The Dodgers took a two-game lead.

September 30—Drysdale scattered three hits and shut out the Braves, 4-0, for his 23rd victory. Hart and Cepeda hit homers in San Francisco to help the Giants defeat the Reds, 5-3.

October 1—Denny Lemaster halted the Los Angeles winning streak at 13 games as he pitched the Braves to a 2-0 victory, but the Giants fumbled an opportunity to advance when they got bombed by the Reds, 17-2.

October 2—The Giants recovered from their humiliation, albeit too late. Their 3-2 victory was meaningless because Koufax pushed his record to 26-8 with a 3-1 decision over the Braves to clinch the Dodgers' third pennant in Los Angeles.

Appropriately, Johnson caught a fly for the final putout. He danced to the clubhouse shouting, "Hey sweetie," to the ball as he pounded it into his glove. "Oh, you sweetie!" Teammates agreed unanimously with Koufax when the pitcher announced: "Johnson's the guy. If it hadn't been for the job he did, we might not be here today." In 131 games, LBJ belted 12 home runs to tie Lefebvre—the N.L. Rookie of the Year—for the club lead, rapped 24 doubles and drove in 58 runs.

"My mom always told me just to have faith and things would turn out OK," Johnson reflected.

Koufax stood alone as baseball's dominant performer. The lefthander tied a major league record by leading the league in ERA for the fourth straight year (2.04); set major league records for strikeouts in a season (382) and most games in a career with 10 or more strikeouts (82); set an N.L. record for most consecutive years leading the league in both winning percentage and ERA (two); set an N.L. record for wins by a lefthander (26), and tied a league record for most consecutive years with 200 or more strikeouts (five). Sandy was named the N.L. Cy Young Award winner and The Sporting News' Player of the Year.

Wills led the Dodgers in hitting with a .286 mark and topped the league in stolen bases for a record sixth consecutive year. He swiped 94 sacks and probably would have broken his record of 104, but a knee injury hobbled the shortstop for more than a month.

The team finished seventh in batting with a .245 average, the lowest by a pennant winner in N.L. history. The Dodgers could have cared less.

"Maybe we weren't the best on paper," utility infielder Dick Tracewski reasoned, "but we play this game on the field."